This is a remarkable book on a scarcely researched topic. Focusing on Turkey and Egypt, *Caring for the Poor* offers a comparative study of Islamic and Christian charitable ethics and the non-market economies arising therefrom. At a time of cultural reductionism and Islamophobia, *Caring for the Poor* is a particularly timely book and must be read by all those interested in countering the ideology of the clash of civilizations, which, in recent times, has been flaunting a renewed viciousness.
Boaventura de Sousa Santos, Distinguished Legal Scholar of the University of Wisconsin, Madison and author of Epistemologies of the South: Justice against Epistemicide

This scholarly study of the ethical transformations of charity from early times to today is an attempt to analyze the emergence of what Cihan Tuğal calls 'neo-liberal subjectivity' – first in Euro-America, and subsequently in the Middle East. The book contains a rich account of the development of Islamist charity organizations in modern Egypt and Turkey based on the author's own fieldwork. Most thought provokingly, this work demonstrates how central the history of an apparently marginal social practice can be for understanding major problems of our world. *Caring for the Poor* is a welcome contribution to an important question and deserves to be widely read.
Talal Asad, Distinguished Professor of Anthropology Emeritus, Graduate Center, City University of New York

CARING FOR THE POOR

Based on several years of fieldwork in Egypt and Turkey, *Caring for the Poor* tells the stories of charity providers and volunteers, placing them within the overall development of Islamic ethics. Muslim charity, Tuğal argues, has interacted with Christian and secular Western ethics over the centuries, which themselves have a conflict-ridden and still-evolving history. The overall arch that connects all of these distinct elements is (a combined and uneven) liberalization, which tends to transform care into a cold, calculating, and individualizing set of practices. *Caring for the Poor* meticulously documents this insidious process in Egypt and Turkey, while also drawing attention to its limits and contradictions (by using the American case to highlight the contested nature of liberalization even in its world leader). However, as historians have shown, charitable actors have often intervened in decisive ways in the rise and demise of social formations. Tuğal raises the possibility, especially through his study of two controversial Turkish organizations, that Islamic charity might appropriate elements of liberalism to shift the world in a post-liberal direction.

Cihan Tuğal is Associate Professor of Sociology at UC Berkeley. He works on mobilization, socioeconomic change, and religion. Tuğal's first book, *Passive Revolution* (2009), studied pro-capitalist Islam and its popularization among the poor. In his second book, *The Fall of the Turkish Model* (2016), Tuğal analyzed Islamic movements and regimes in Turkey, Egypt, Tunisia, and Iran.

CARING FOR THE POOR

Islamic and Christian Benevolence in a Liberal World

Cihan Tuğal

NEW YORK AND LONDON

First published 2017
by Routledge
711 Third Avenue, New York, NY 10017

and by Routledge
2 Park Square, Milton Park, Abingdon, Oxon OX14 4RN

Routledge is an imprint of the Taylor & Francis Group, an informa business

© 2017 Taylor & Francis

The right of Cihan Tuğal to be identified as author of this work has been asserted by him/her in accordance with sections 77 and 78 of the Copyright, Designs and Patents Act 1988.

All rights reserved. No part of this book may be reprinted or reproduced or utilised in any form or by any electronic, mechanical, or other means, now known or hereafter invented, including photocopying and recording, or in any information storage or retrieval system, without permission in writing from the publishers.

Trademark notice: Product or corporate names may be trademarks or registered trademarks, and are used only for identification and explanation without intent to infringe.

Library of Congress Cataloging in Publication Data
Names: Tugal, Cihan, author.
Title: Caring for the poor : Islamic and Christian benevolence in a liberal world / Cihan Tugal.
Description: New York, NY ; Abingdon, Oxon : Routledge, 2017. | Includes bibliographical references and index.
Identifiers: LCCN 2016056792 (print) | LCCN 2017008355 (ebook) | ISBN 9781138041035 (hardback) | ISBN 9781138041042 (pbk.) | ISBN 9781315173498 (Ebook)
Subjects: LCSH: Charity. | Christian ethics. | Islamic ethics. | Benevolence.
Classification: LCC BV4639 .T84 2017 (print) | LCC BV4639 (ebook) | DDC 205/.677--dc23
LC record available at https://lccn.loc.gov/2016056792

ISBN: 978-1-138-04103-5 (hbk)
ISBN: 978-1-138-04104-2 (pbk)
ISBN: 978-1-315-17349-8 (ebk)

Typeset in Bembo
by Taylor & Francis Books

To Aynur

CONTENTS

List of Tables   *x*
Acknowledgements   *xi*

    Introduction: Varieties of Care   1

1   Generosity as an Alternative: Is Giving a Challenge to the Market Logic?   15

2   The Genealogy of Islamic and Christian Ethics: From Renunciation and Redistribution to Interdependence   34

3   The World Historical Revolution in Ethics: The Dismantling of Interdependence and the Rise of the Liberal Subject   57

4   Comprehensive Religion: Communitarian Associations in Egypt   96

5   Mobilizing Volunteers on Rocky Terrain: Neoliberal Benevolence in Egypt   126

6   Walking the Tightrope between Professionalism and *Tebliğ*: Turkey's Neoliberal Associations   154

7   Punching above Their Weight: Turkey's Communitarian and Redistributive Associations   184

    Conclusion: Combined and Uneven Liberalization   217

References   *228*
Index   *241*

LIST OF TABLES

5.1	Contrasting Dispositions of Egyptian Charitable Actors	149
5.2	Egyptian Organizational Structures and Logics	151
5.3	Egyptian Benevolent Actors' Backgrounds and Perspectives	152
7.1	Contrasting Dispositions of Turkish Charitable Actors	213
7.2	Turkish Organizational Structures and Logics	214
7.3	Turkish Benevolent Actors' Backgrounds and Perspectives	215

ACKNOWLEDGEMENTS

This text, like all others, is a joint product. My ideas are the outcome of many conversations and debates. While I am thankful to all who indulged my obsession with charity, they certainly are not complicit in what I am about to present. Michael Burawoy remained a passionate reader and critic in every step along the way. He provided extensive comments on articles, chapters, and drafts of ideas from the very beginning of this project circa 2007. He also read and commented on the entire manuscript. I still have not figured out how he finds the time, energy, and patience to be so generous. Peter Evans also remained an inspiration throughout these years. He was crucial in framing the initial comparison. Peter was also my primary guide in comparing the welfare regimes. Ann Swidler read and commented on a few of the articles and drafts that led to the final product. My ongoing debates with her were constant reminders of the breadth and depth of aid, and the restrictions of my project. Raka Ray's interventions sharpened the field analyses and discussions of methodology.

Ayşe Buğra, Çağlar Keyder, and Ayşe Öncü offered many comments on my presentations and drafts. They were especially helpful in thinking about how welfare regimes interact with charity on the ground. Nadir Özbek provided extensive feedback on the Introduction and the historical chapters. Julia Adams, Ayşe Akalın, Ayfer Bartu, Sinan Birdal, Alpkan Birelma, Robert Brenner, Rogers Brubaker, Elisabeth Clemens, Marion Fourcade, Alperen Gençosmanoğlu, Serap Kayatekin, Biray Kolluoğlu, Bülent Küçük, Ching Kwan Lee, Saba Mahmood, Ann Orloff, Ceren Özselçuk, Osman Savaşkan, Baki Tezcan, Zafer Yenal, and Zafer Yılmaz were thoughtful interlocutors. The extensive reports of two anonymous Routledge reviewers were essential to my revisions of the manuscript.

Comments and criticisms of the audiences at several presentations supported my attempts first in developing and then refining the project. Presentations at the

Middle East Studies Association's Annual Meetings (San Diego, 2010), the Institute for the Study of Societal Issues (UC Berkeley, 2013), and the Political Sociology Global South Working Group (UCLA, 2015) encouraged me to think further about my analysis of Egypt and my framework's conceptual gaps. I got rich feedback on Turkish welfare and charity, as well as on my theoretical framework, during and after talks at Sabancı University (Cultural Studies Seminar, 2015) and Boğaziçi University (Atatürk Institute, 2015).

The one year I spent at Koç University allowed me to condense about ten years of work into a coherent argument. Conversations with Çetin Çelik, Rossen Djagalov, Harun Ercan, Emrah Göker, Ekin Kocabaş, Osman Şahin, Bilge Yağmurlu, Erdem Yörük, Deniz Yükseker, and Murat Yüksel were quite informative (and the lunch and tea breaks unforgettable). Murat played a special role as my host.

My research in Egypt was funded by the Hellman Family Faculty Fund (UC Berkeley). The Mellon Project Grant Program (of the Andrew W. Mellon Foundation) and Tübitak (The Scientific and Technological Research Council of Turkey) supported the Turkish portion of the research.

I would not have been able to sustain my research in Egypt if it were not for Momen El-Husseiny's reliable assistance. Momen's family also made me feel welcome in Egypt. They were almost a second family while away from home. Momen provided such insightful guidance on the intricacies of Egyptian dynamics that I feel this book falls short of what it could have been, had I learned to see Egypt more fully through his eyes.

I also thank the hundreds of charity practitioners and beneficiaries I have talked to over seven years. This book would not see the light of day without their warmth and openness.

Eren, Deniz, and Aynur taught me how to care, even though I must admit to being still a novice in this realm. Aynur made me realize the roots of my social scientific interests in the peculiarity of my upbringing. If this book has any meaningful insights on matters of the heart and their relation to charity, I owe them to Aynur, who opened my eyes to the centrality of emotions in broader social structures.

INTRODUCTION
Varieties of Care

"Service" is a quite common word pious Muslims use when they speak of benevolent activities. Throughout my fieldwork in Egypt, I heard it so many times that it ultimately seeped into my vocabulary. I was therefore taken aback when (an otherwise patient and kind) manager of the Piety Association[1] (one of Egypt's largest benevolent organizations) impatiently interrupted me after I referred to their work as service. He insisted that what they provided to the community was not service; receiving this provision was rather the "community's right." A few days later, the theologically trained, national director of the organization gave me a longer lecture on "God's rights" in each Muslim's property. He emphasized that Muslims should abundantly give away their wealth to prevent the community from disintegrating. This identification between God's and the community's rights on property-holders led the organization to distance itself from what was perhaps the most common-sense word among Egyptian charitable actors.

Some Islamists in nearby Turkey had other issues with the widespread understanding of benevolence. Learning from, but differentiating themselves from, secular as well as Christian aid organizations worldwide, Islamist leaders of the Humanitarian Relief Foundation (henceforth IHH) argued that charitable activity had to have a political and social movement dimension, for the root causes of misfortune were political. Delivering aid therefore involved political confrontation. The IHH helped organize a humanitarian convoy to the Gaza Strip that sought to bypass regular Israeli control. The convoy's most crowded ship (the Islamist-controlled *Mavi Marmara*) was attacked, resulting in several deaths.

A prominent Turkish cleric who lived in Pennsylvania gave an interview to the *Washington Post* and declared the IHH's action un-Islamic. Challenging authority holders, Fethullah Gülen pointed out, is a grave sin in Islam. While much public discussion focused on international balances and this specific cleric's position in them, neglected was the huge charitable organization under his control, which competed with the IHH for benevolent money (*zakat* and *sadaqa*). His organization had a distinct understanding of charitable activity, at odds with both the Piety Association *and* the IHH. Its goal was creating responsible individuals, able to stand on their own feet. Gülen's followers distinguished themselves from not only the confrontational IHH, but also the allegedly "more traditional" organizations, which distributed aid without strict control of whether the beneficiaries used them for appropriate personal development. Interestingly, Gülen's followers had recently started to call themselves the "Service Movement": they attempted to appropriate and monopolize the word service[2] that the "more traditional" organizations also employed to characterize their benevolent activities.

These three approaches exemplify the main tendencies that characterize Islamic benevolence today. The third, individualizing understanding (which for convenience sake I will call "neoliberal" benevolence), was the fastest growing charitable orientation in the 1990s and 2000s. It was so widespread that the other major Islamic organizations in Turkey, not only Gülen's, had thoroughly integrated it; this was the case for many Egyptian organizations too. *Caring for the Poor* explores whether there is a worldwide, cross-cultural tendency for charitable work to become neoliberal.

The first tendency, exemplified by the Piety Association, seeks to maintain balance within the community of Muslims, and return God's due where it belongs. For lack of a better word, I will call this "communitarian" charity (see Chapters 1–3 for further clarification). The second—and the weakest—tendency seeks to politicize generosity; it is built on the assumption that property should be redistributed worldwide through active struggle (as well as via willing donations). This I call "redistributive" generosity. *Caring for the Poor* seeks to understand why any of these tendencies becomes predominant in certain contexts, and how each shapes world history.

I analyze both Islamic and Western charitable ethics as not only components, but also makers of the medieval and modern world orders. Today, the "American model" of individualizing charity diffuses throughout the world, but is *adapted selectively*. The prevailing "liberal" charitable transformation can be captured in a single clause: progression from an ethics of interdependence to one of self-reliance. Rather than taking the American model as the beginning point, however, the book studies *the combined and uneven development of charitable ethics*. Christians and Muslims make (big or small) contributions to this "global ethical formation," which is a culmination of a millennia-long evolution. Their contributions are determined neither by inevitable rationalization nor cultural uniqueness, but by their relations to other charitable actors (that is, by "field" structures), to states, and to their challengers.

Scholars capture the partial "Americanization" of Islam by statements such as "Muslim charity is redefining itself based on the framework of ... Western thought."[3] However, such statements ignore the "combined" making of ethics and reify both Islamic and Western charity, the ethics of which are hotly contested in both contexts. Actually, remarks regarding the "Western"ization of "Islamic" charity are based on an unquestioned assumption: Islamic aid embodies "a fundamentally different culture than that of [Western] development aid" (Petersen 2011, p. 73; also see p. 83). Yet, the (initial) essentialness of this contrast has to be brought into question as much as the thoroughness of contemporary convergence.[4] To the extent that American compassion does indeed become a model that pious Muslims follow (Haenni 2005, p. 12), the relation is one of *selective adaptivity shaped by fields*, rather than imitation.

Caring for the Poor ends by showing how new trends in Turkish generosity might potentially re-shape society and even lead to a new world order. Charity has the power to overturn centuries of liberalization and redefine society.

Giving and World History

Marcel Mauss (1990, p. 52) once hypothesized that the Greeks and Romans passed from the gift economy to the interest-based economy—a process that he captured with the ambitious and perhaps ironic phrase "venerable revolution." The gift economy ritualized and personalized exchange, while the new, "fair exchange"-based one creates no bonds or obligations between giver and receiver. However, the venerable revolution was shaken by the rise of Christianity and its ritualizations of giving, and then vigorously resuscitated by the demise of the medieval order and the rise of capitalism. Jesus's injunction to give one's wealth to the poor put a stick in the wheel of the venerable revolution. The Christian emphasis on "good works" (with its complex and contested expectations) became a major guiding principle that shaped ethical conduct. A benevolence-centered re-reading of *The Gift* (1990) in the post-welfare age requires not so much "standing Mauss on his head" as spinning this great thinker around himself. Taking a cue from Mauss, I argue that a pious generosity (cultivated as a set of deeply internalized dispositions) still remains the "believer's gift" (and her gift *to* this world). The gift economy, arguably, survives in religious practice.

Gauging to what degree such a non-market economy survives is all the more important in our current era of "high commodification." Scholars have noted that, in the last decades, Muslim associations have shifted from emphasizing the community-generating aspects of benevolence[5] to an individualizing "empowerment" logic that seeks to transform the poor into entrepreneurs. We will call this neoliberal or marketized giving, with some major caveats (see below). What is less explored is how communitarian dispositions persist and vie with neoliberal dispositions. A different kind of disposition, based on a redistributive ethic, is not even discussed in the literature on Muslim charity and philanthropy[6] (although it is relatively well-documented in the study of Christian charity in the West). Why, when, and where do neoliberal dispositions gain prominence? Can communitarian and redistributive dispositions survive or gain the upper hand?

I will explore these questions by studying Egyptian and Turkish charities (within the context of a comparative study of Islam and Christianity). *Caring for the Poor* points out that there is a fragile balance between neoliberal and communitarian giving in Egypt (despite the global predominance of the "American" model of giving), whereas in Turkey the former has marginalized the latter. However, Turkey is also home to quite visible redistributive dispositions, which is not the case in Egypt.[7]

Historical context and politics thoroughly shape the reasons why people give. This study highlights the variation by bringing in three cases: a developed capitalist nation, indeed the leader of world capitalism, where we would expect giving to be neoliberal; a rising capitalist power, where giving would be on its way to marketization; and finally, a case where capitalism is less developed, where we would expect to see less neoliberal forms of giving. However, since the rationalities of giving are situated within a *combined, challenged, and uneven development of liberalism and capitalism*, the story is more complicated. The logic(s) of giving in all three cases are shaped not only by the overall levels of marketization, but by histories of religious mobilization and state-society links. We see consent for the most aggressively individualized motivations (if not the most developed techniques) in the rising capitalist power (Turkey). The consent experienced in some Turkish circles goes even deeper than that observed in the United States. Moreover, even though non-neoliberal forms of giving are more sustained in Egypt (as we would expect), the challenges against neoliberal ways of giving are more public in the United States and Turkey.

The book's theoretical goal is to provide Mauss's totalizing generalizations about non-market conduct and marketization with comparative-historical specificity. It studies forms of giving in a comparative light, rather than tracing one logic of the gift through civilizations and then contrasting it to market logic. I also problematize assumptions about the radical alterity of traditions of giving. Convergences and divergences between Islam and Christianity will be discussed to evaluate how much of the variation can be attributed to "purely" cultural factors. Articulations of factors, rather than purely religious differences, shed more light on the variations. *Caring for the Poor* situates the liberalization of Islamic generosity in the *combined and uneven development of ethics* worldwide, rather than explain it based on Islam's uniqueness (or explain it away as the outcome of "modernization").

Uneven Neoliberalizations of Egyptian and Turkish Charity

The ethnographic parts of this book (Chapters 4–7) are embedded in this broader history (Chapters 1–3). The case studies demonstrate that the Turkish-Islamic mainstream has thoroughly neoliberalized giving. Turkish associations seek to create work-, market-, and success-oriented beneficiaries who will no longer need charity. The organization of charity itself is based on the business model, even though the recruitment of personnel depends on religious ideology and networks as much as CVs. Egypt is also home to ambitious, young, neoliberalizing charities,[8] but they share the Islamic generosity field with larger, communitarian organizations. Personnel recruitment is more professionalized in Egypt (i.e. less dependent on non-market criteria), even though the rest of the charity operation is less so.

Much of this story could be reduced to modernization: if there is more neoliberalization of ethics in Turkey, it is because Turkey is more integrated to "world society" than Egypt. Modernization implies rationalization: the replacement of calculated (and formal) for random (and informal) giving. As the American model of generosity diffuses throughout the world, charitable organizations cannot but become more individualized (in their dealings with the beneficiaries) and more professionalized in their management. The ethnographic chapters are indeed full of examples of "isomorphism"'s with American charitable models (which are well captured by "new institutionalist" scholarship). Yet, does this diffusion exhaust the story?

The complexity of charitable recruitment already problematizes such simplification. The presence of communitarian, even magical, spirits and practices in the bosom of neoliberal organizations raises many questions (which Chapters 4–7 grapple with). However, Chapter 7 further underlines the ambiguity and unpredictability of the whole process. Neoliberalism survives and thrives by injecting high doses of communitarianism into even the most market-oriented organizations. But more importantly, the overall emphasis on independence creates the possibility that communitarian actors will appropriate rational procedures and language to politicize and collectivize generosity. This could deal serious blows to the depoliticized and individualized world of modern charity. Such appropriation can even throw off track the overall integration of a country in world markets, as the IHH-orchestrated *Mavi Marmara* affair indicates. Changes in charitable ethics are not simply *outcomes* of "world society" integration. Benevolent interventions can potentially become *makers* or unmakers of that integration.

Contrasting histories of Islamic mobilization account for some of the differences studied in the ethnographic chapters. Whereas in Turkey a tightly disciplined and united religious movement has controlled the Islamic charity field, the Islamic movement in Egypt has not exhibited the same level of unity. At the same time, the Egyptian Islamic movement(s) has entrenched networks and visions of charity; the link between political mobilization and charity is relatively new in Turkey, which allows new turns in politics to shape the charitable field more freely. Moreover, the recent neoliberal turn of Turkey's Islamic movement has also reinforced the near-merger of benevolent organizations with the state. The state-benevolence merger is more restricted in Egypt. Finally, communitarian modes of distinction and techniques of giving have been more thoroughly overhauled in Turkey, though that transformation has also led to a public questioning of market-oriented giving.

These differences are scrutinized through a "Gramscianized" version of Bourdieu's field theory (outlined in Chapter 1 and deployed in the following chapters). The Conclusion returns to broader Gramscian themes to argue that the study of charity sheds new light on *modernity as hegemonic ethical reform*. The integrated study of Christian and Islamic benevolence allows us to picture a single, global, contested, and contingent modernity, an alternative to the more entrenched studies of modernity as convergence (as in new institutionalist accounts) and the poststructuralist emphases on alternative or multiple modernities.

"Good Works" as Alternative Ethics?

Are acts of religiously-inspired kindness alternatives to profit maximization, market exchange, and commodification? Or are they more likely to be absorbed into capitalist ethics (which seeks morality in "fair exchange" rather than in social bonds, communities, and subjection to God)? In a previous book (*Passive Revolution* 2009), I had asked similar questions, but there the empirics focused on whether Islamists built alternative urban spaces, everyday life patterns, and daily economic orientations. Here, by contrast, the focus is solidly on ethics and more specifically charitable ethics.

The Islamist movement has been refashioning pious Muslims' economic conduct. In broad strokes, mainstream Islamism had shifted from calling for a solidaristic adaptation to the modern economy (from the end of the nineteenth century up until the mid-twentieth century) to a rejection of modern economic logic (around the 1960s and 1970s). This was not a smooth transformation, since what the "modern economy" entailed was itself a matter of debate. Whereas the term clearly implied market capitalism around the turn of the twentieth century, Islamists put faith in state socialism around the middle of that century. Even though Shariati's, Qutb's, and others' wholesale attack on (both capitalist and socialist) economistic thought had increasing impact up until the 1980s, the trend was reversed thereafter. Islamists were caught up in the global flame of neoliberalization (Tripp 2006; Tuğal 2009). Chapters 2 and 3 will further delineate the contours of this long twentieth (Islamist) century.

This book traces the spread of neoliberal *ethics* among *charitable* actors. Why focus on ethics? Why focus on charity? Ethical conduct has significance beyond the issues of ethics and morality. I follow Max Weber in emphasizing ethical conduct over textual doctrine. My analyses are also inspired by Michel Foucault's (1977, 1990, 1992) attention to "ethical conduct" as a set of *techniques* that not only control subjects but *make* them (whether oneself, as in the second and third volumes of the *History of Sexuality*, or others, as in *Discipline and Punish*).[9] Vying political projects re-construct the self's outward behaviors, more than the way she "thinks" (Mahmood 2005, pp. 32–33, 120).[10] Nevertheless, active thinking is frequently a route to enacting systematic behavioral change: the "subject" (or the ethical self) is formed through a self-reflexive subjugation to certain discourses, emotions, norms, and practices. *Caring for the Poor* therefore focuses on how practitioners of charity reflect on their conduct and organizations.

Weber has argued that one specific ethical conduct has laid the roots of capitalism (a thesis attacked from many angles). I am less interested in the historical veracity of this claim than the potential questions it raises for today. Even if Calvinist ethics have *not* paved the way for capitalism, certain spirits and ethics *have* been part and parcel of this system (although their centrality to its production has waxed and waned). Today too neoliberalism and alternatives to it pervade society through the routinization of certain ethical conducts. These ethics might not always be explicitly religious. Nevertheless, studying the history and present of Christian and Muslim charity is adamant because of the way they have shaped apparently "secular" aid, which still has strong theological underpinnings (Barnett and Stein 2012, pp. 16–18, 22–28; Fassin 2012, pp. 248–251).

We are confronted with the following questions: is the Muslim world facing an ethical upheaval in the scale of that experienced in Europe of the sixteenth through the eighteenth centuries? How do Muslims negotiate the new ethics as neoliberalization hits painful limits (ecological destruction, financial busts, etc.)? Do pious Muslims simply revise their new ethical conduct, revert to old ethical patterns, or rather develop insurgent conducts?

Even though this focus on ethical conduct is Weber- and Foucault-influenced, the book's approach to the question of change is Gramscian. In his analysis of hegemony, Gramsci pointed out that one core component of procuring consent was moral reform. Civil society and the state had to rebuild people's moral practices to integrate them into capitalist society. I therefore handle the history of ethics as *one level of reality*. Ethical transformations are always entangled with economic and sociopolitical realities, which are under-studied in Foucault and under-theorized in Weber. Bourdieu will work as the bridge between the political economic-Gramscian and Weberian-Foucaultian (as well as new institutionalist) traditions. Especially when it comes to "disinterested" acts such as charity, Bourdieu is the prime theorist of the "double truth." Power-ridden relations frequently survive through a shared and sincere belief in their class-blind beneficence (a belief that is not merely illusory). Bourdieu calls the relations of domination "objective truth" and the benign feelings and experiences that sustain them "subjective truth." But as Chapter 1 will show, Bourdieu's "double truth" approach suffers from insufficient historicization. Only a neo-Gramscian approach to charitable change, which re-theorizes it as *hegemonic ethical reform*, can properly situate acts of benevolence in world history.

The reader might ask: Why not explore capitalist ethical reform through a focus on work or on the shop floor (or yet other venues)? First of all, this book does not claim to provide a comprehensive answer to these vast questions. It rather fills in some gaps in mostly uncharted territory. A broader scholarship (on business associations, factories, municipal reform, etc.) indeed explores roughly the same questions. Second, this study is a call to recognize the centrality of charity to the making of the world, despite the relevance of the mentioned scholarship in answering our broader questions. In medieval Christian and middle Islamic times, charity was core to the construction of what poverty is and who the poor are. The answers to these questions also reinforced the dignity of society's other members. Charity was a class-maker and world-maker. The re-imagination of charity later became the linchpin of the negation of medieval Christianity and middle-era Islam. As the poor were put into their new places in the modern world through charitable debates and practices, so were the respectable classes. Since we are today possibly on the brink of the destruction of the modern world, we have to recontextualize Mauss's question of whether reciprocity is a potential alternative to market exchange (and re-evaluate his charge that charity is a distortion of reciprocity). Before answering this question, however, we need a proper understanding of the neoliberal revolution.

The *Long Durée* of the Liberal Revolution

The neoliberal sea change in charitable conduct is a symptom of the great bouleversement in religion, the last conquest of the liberal revolution. Stretching back to the twelfth century, the world has been undergoing a long revolution: the toppling of interdependence by the rise of the independent individual (which reinforces Mauss's millennia-long "venerable revolution"). As Chapters 2 and 3 will demonstrate, waves of marketization, the Reformation, liberal philosophy, political economy, and ultimately industrial capitalism have converged in an attack against people's dependence on each other. As the mature Bourdieu has pointed out, religion, family, and art had been relatively immune from the venerable revolution.

Religion, especially, seemed to be a last bastion against what I call "liberalization"—the centering of the individual, his/her property, happiness, and freedom. Even the Protestant faith (one of the primary makers of this long revolution) harbored many anti-individualistic, paternalistic, and communitarian elements. However, the last four decades have witnessed an aggressive liberalization of religious values themselves, a process Bourdieu left untheorized. This has been a deeply contradictory process. On the one hand, rigorous piety (long assumed to be at odds with individual freedom) was summoned to protect families and communities in a world of crumbling welfare states. On the other hand, many faith traditions (their comprehensive capacities weakened by centuries of modernization) have come back onto the scene in individualist garb. Should we read this process as the liberal conquest of a territory that used to be gift-based? Or does religion rather infuse our times with unexpected doses of communitarianism, which might eventually destabilize the overall individualizing push?

Our era has been called "neo"liberal. Indeed, many parts of the world have undergone "neoliberalization" ever since the 1970s: privatization, retrenchment, or individualist structuring of the welfare state, and financialization. Yet, continuities with the classical liberal period (1830s–1920s) are too many (see Chapters 2 and 3), even if both the intensity and the contradictions of liberalism are experienced more fully today. Although the following chapters draw further attention to this continuity, I stick to the label neoliberal to remain intelligible. I take "liberalism" as a centuries-long revolution that "made" the self-interested individual through contradiction-ridden processes (e.g. in politics, the summoning of the state to render the individual free of the state; in philosophy and ethics, the splitting of the subject into a self-interested half and a caring half). Despite claims to the contrary, neoliberalism does not terminate those contradictions but further complicates them (see Chapter 1 for Deleuzian criticisms of Brown, Feher, and Ong). In that sense, it is a new chapter of the long revolution rather than a totally new stage in human history. Nevertheless, neoliberalism's deepening contradictions perhaps portend the approaching end of the revolution.

What distinguishes the current crisis of neoliberalism is the liberalizers' intense and desperate turn to community. Even though the overall project remains the creation of the independent individual, state and society cannot but foster more interdependence, new meaningful bonds, and paternalisms as they face the destruction wrought by the individual's isolation. Charity, seen from this angle, is a form of care targeted at the donors and volunteers as much as the beneficiaries. If the liberal revolution survives, it is only thanks to the new spirit of caring interdependency.

Yet, this religious medicine has too many unpredictable side effects. Putting into question sociological standardization and rationalization accounts, the material presented here points out that the new spirit of giving has the potential to overturn the long liberal revolution. Liberalism's last conquest, then, has come at an awful price.

Caring for the Poor documents how the liberal revolution has run against limits in the United States (the global leader of liberalization), Egypt (a follower), and Turkey. However, it is specifically in Turkey, a regional leader of neoliberalization, that we see the most surprising turning of the tables against liberal ethics. It is here that the *event* might disturb the *long durée*.

Methodology

The arguments of this book are based on fieldwork and comparative historical analysis. A total of 87 interviews were conducted for the first phase of this research. For the Egyptian part of the project, I interviewed 52 people (during 2009 and 2010) and carried out research on 17 organizations. These associations were located in Cairo and two other major Egyptian cities. I visited the headquarters, branches, and premises of some and observed their activities on-site. I conducted 35 interviews in Istanbul for the Turkish part of the research (during 2011 and 2012) and studied 12 Turkish organizations. The interviewees were contacted through snowballing. I aimed to interview people of various ages and backgrounds, though high and middle socioeconomic status interviewees constitute the majority of the sample due to the nature of benevolent work (as well as my entry points). Most interviews were conducted in the native tongue of the respondents.[11]

In 2014–2015, I conducted a follow-up study in Turkey. This consisted of interviews with additional people; structured conversations with previous interviewees; and direct observation of changes in charitable activities and architecture. For this portion of the study, I carried out 33 interviews, bringing the total number of interviewees to 120. The goal of the interviews in 2014–2015 was to gauge how charitable actors responded to the changing political climate. The structure of the political field studied in Chapter 3 was undergoing significant change and I wanted to see whether this had an impact on charity, as my arguments based on the 2011–2012 phase of the research would predict. Nevertheless, this was an ongoing metamorphosis; since the transformation of ethics takes a longer time than quick political shifts, I did not expect immense changes. (Therefore, my conclusions about this potentially new phase of Islamic charity are tentative.) Another goal of this final visit was the filling of gaps in the data, especially regarding the beneficiaries.[12]

In both countries, I tried to contact all of the nationally prominent or visible (Islamic-inspired) benevolent organizations. Due to the repressiveness of the Mubarak regime's final two years, I was not able to access the charity networks of two major Islamist political organizations. All other organizations that have become household names were contacted and studied. The smaller, more local organizations were included in the study to get a broader sense of the variation. This was seen as necessary, since depending on interviewee assessments as well as publicly available numbers, smaller organizations mobilized considerable resources and reached big numbers of people. However, since these organizations were contacted through snowballing, no claims about representativeness can be made. Representativeness is impossible to achieve also since, unlike in some Western countries, there is no official category that groups together religiously inspired benevolent organizations (such as "Religiously Motivated Associations" or RMAs): "the universe of the organizations is not known" (Göçmen 2010, pp. 137–138).

The snowballing technique also introduces the risk of collecting homogenous views. Specific points of entry lead to specific networks and a researcher with different networks could end up with a different story (Dezalay and Garth 2002, pp. 10–12). In my case, this was a more serious problem in Egypt, where I entered the field primarily as a foreign academic (even if still with several points of entry), whereas in Turkey I have multiple identities and therefore quite diverse networks (academic, former teacher of a poor district, activist, etc.). In order to deal with these problems, I resorted to insiders and outsiders of the Islamist movement, academics and activists, locals and non-locals, etc. as points of entry to diversify interviewees' points of view *and* field positions.

The main goal of data collection was to understand how the organizations differed with respect to their dispositions to benevolence, religion, and the state.

Along these lines, I explored organizational structures, recruitment strategies, the weight of each benevolent activity in the overall budget, the criteria with which the beneficiaries are selected, expectations from beneficiaries, and cooperation with ministries. I also asked all interviewees (donors, managers, staff, volunteers, and beneficiaries)[13] about their own personal history of involvement in benevolent activities, their understanding of the reasons behind poverty, and the changes in their perceptions of the poor throughout the years. Questions about the interviewees' religious lives, their religious upbringing and involvement, and the religious motivations behind their benevolent work were asked too. Most interviews were recorded and lasted between half an hour and one hour and a half. In addition, I had structured conversations with journalists, academics, and government representatives, who ranged from being sympathizers to opponents of pious charitable organizations.

The ethnographic analysis is divided into three foci: an analysis of dispositions; of organizational structures; and of perspectives and backgrounds. The tables in Chapters 5 and 7 present condensed summaries of the ethnographic findings. While interviews gave indispensable insights into the respondents' practical beliefs, direct observation was crucial to get a better sense of especially organizational structures and hierarchies, recruitment patterns, and political relations (with the state, the municipalities, movements, and parties). Interviews too were analyzed ethnographically: rather than only re-presenting the way organizations wanted to picture themselves, I followed several techniques to catch what a participant observer would seek. For instance, I studied tensions between self-presentation and life histories, which revealed Sufi-based recruitment in organizations that claimed exclusive professionalism. Likewise, I explored the tensions between managers', staff's, and beneficiaries' reconstructions of aid delivery, which led me to discover gaps between "empowerment" aims and survival ends.

Since national contexts have deeply shaped benevolent orientations, the book also presents a comparative analysis of charitable histories. This analysis does not simply provide a background. Rather, I point out that contrasting paths of Islamic mobilization (in the context of changing welfare regimes) are among the factors that account for different field structures in the two nations. While most of the historical scrutiny is based on secondary documents, an analysis of primary texts is also integrated into Chapter 3. This study of Islamic theology (and jurisprudence on economics and charity) further contextualizes the ethnographic analysis within an evolving history of thought.

My discussion of the preceding centuries (Chapter 2 and parts of 3), I must admit, provides less than a full explanatory history. Still, this discussion was necessary to point out the unrealized potentials in sadaqa, Christian charity, and zakat. In that sense, the historical account resembles a Foucaultian genealogy (which uncovers lost voices and marginalized practices), even though the book's overall methodological approach is one of (explanatory) field analysis.[14] A full field analysis of the centuries covered would require several more books. I hope other authors will take up the theoretical framework and methodology developed here to fill in the gaps. In other words, much of Chapters 2 and 3 consists of provocative invitations more than finalized analyses. Readers more interested in the contemporary scene can jump to p. 78 (where the field analysis of Turkish and Egyptian Islamism begins) after finishing Chapter 1. Certainly, no single book can exhaust the comparison of the world's two most widespread religions, even on a single issue. A partial comparison of the kind I am embarking on here has been conducted by Talal Asad (1993, 2003) and Armando Salvatore (2016) on the topics of discipline, knowledge, civility, reason, and pain in Christianity and Islam. Much comparative analysis remains to be done for understanding either of the traditions better—by using its "other" as a lens onto itself.

★★★

The world has undergone a revolution that replaced the ethics of individual independence for communal interdependence. Has that transformation also created the conditions for the development of an ethics of *collective* independence (in conjunction with egalitarian forms of interdependence)? So far, the latter has structured world history mostly to the extent that the working class has adapted it. Today, that class does not have the prominence it once had in the nineteenth and twentieth centuries (Hobsbawm 1978; Therborn 2012). Do we see the flowering of an ethics of collective independence in other realms, such as the quite unlikely world of charity (unlikely, since it is so much associated with pity and dependency)? Has neoliberalism cultivated the right breeding ground for a charitable ethics of collective responsibility, just like the classical liberal emphasis on independence had (unintentionally) laid the groundwork for proletarian self-pride and self-discipline (Polanyi 2001)? Weber had sought the escape route from the iron cage in the gift of charisma. This book asks whether we can build a less disastrous route through the gift of benevolence.

Notes

1 The organization and individual names used in this book are pseudonyms, except for the Egyptian Muslim Brotherhood and the Turkish IHH, the two names that had to be disclosed due to their political centrality and visibility in the refashioning of benevolence. The charitable actors in these organizations were notified that the name of the organization would be used in the book and scholarly articles, even though the names and identifying characteristics of the individuals are still removed.
2 The word *hizmet* is a Turkified version of the Arabic original, *khidma*. Even though *hizmet* and *khidma* are daily terms in Turkey and Egypt, pious Muslims (and more broadly, conservatives) use them in a more emphatic way and with rich connotations.
3 Haenni 2005, p. 9, translation mine. The author makes similar arguments regarding Muslim adaptation of "the Protestant Ethic" (p. 10), importation of "Western culture" (p. 18)—categories and concepts that will be problematized throughout this book (also see pp. 21–22).

4 Even though Petersen and Haenni both analyze how the two cultures "meet" today, I seek to show (especially in the historical chapters) how their development had been entangled from the beginning.
5 While "giving," "benevolence," and "good works" are certainly very broad concepts, this book focuses on a field of associations that (overtly or covertly) compete over the legitimate monopoly of the Qur'anic term *khayr* in the Turkish and Egyptian contexts (and a parallel competition to monopolize the resources associated with khayr: *zakat* and *sadaqa*). The closest biblical equivalent of khayr is good works; the multiple similarities and differences between these two terms are yet to be discussed by scholars.
6 I use these terms interchangeably throughout the book, even though their differentiation is the object of an ongoing war, worthy of a sustained examination. Historically speaking, Christian charity ("caritas")—a poor-focused practice—emerged as an alternative to ancient Roman philanthropy (a gift exchange concentrated within rich circles, see Chapter 2). In our era, some Muslim organizations seek to differentiate their development-oriented "philanthropy" from what they perceive as "traditional" charity, though centuries of Islamic practice belie such neat binaries (see Chapters 2 and 3; see also Tuğal 2013 on this contemporary terminology).
7 James Ferguson's (2015) conceptualization of distribution as an alternative both to the market and the gift presents some parallels to my discussion of redistributive giving (as distinct from neoliberal and communitarian generosity). However, I point out that the logic of the gift cuts through these three forms of aid. See Chapter 1 for further discussion.
8 Some scholarship on neoliberal Islam in Egypt and Turkey has emphasized the similarity of religious transformations in the two countries (Haenni 2005, p. 17), while I point out the structured unevenness, despite a general trend of neoliberalization in both contexts. For more discussion of the macro-determinants of this differentiation, see Tuğal (2016a).
9 I leave out, however, Foucault's tight distinction between morality (and his Nietzschean distaste for it) and ethics. Foucault's (not only anti-Christian, but also anti-"herd") baggage leads to a dichotomy that is formative of his work: (in the words of a sympathizer) a "contrast between a morality the self *merely receives* or applies and an ethics it invents by forming its self by some ideals" (Marchetti 2011, p. 130, emphasis mine). This binary is based on the forgetting of how those ideals and "inventions" are handed down through generations during the long course of the liberal revolution. The binary gives away how Foucault, frequently interpreted to be a critic of neoliberalism, himself is a maker of the long liberal revolution (and its fantasy of individual choice). For a different (non-liberal) take on the Foucaultian binary between ethics and morality, see Mahmood (2005, pp. 28–29). Also note, at the other end of the spectrum, *a self-consciously* Foucaultian-neoliberal position (Feher 2009).
10 As Saba Mahmood (2005, pp. 25–29) points out, this focus breaks with a long tradition of Western thought that takes outward behavior as an index of inner thoughts.
11 For a discussion of the exceptions, where English was also used, see Chapter 5, fn. 4. Due to my imperfect Arabic, a translator was present during some of the interviews conducted in Egypt.
12 I tried out a similar follow-up study in Egypt in 2012, given that Islamic politics there too was undergoing significant change. However, my efforts to conduct a systematic study on charitable organizations in post-Mubarak Egypt's chaotic atmosphere proved unproductive. The interviews I conducted revolved around phrases such as "we cannot do much" as long as they focused on charity; interviewees wanted to talk rather about the ongoing political changes (with only tenuous links to their activities).
13 While I interviewed many beneficiaries, I cannot provide reliable information on them. I rather develop testable hypotheses based on this more restricted dimension of my research. First of all, my entry point was the associations. The poor may, in such

situations, deploy public scripts acceptable to the association of which they are beneficiaries (i.e. speak neoliberal language if the association is neoliberal, etc.). While we should not assume that the poor always harbor hidden, anti-domination scripts, this is a *possibility*. My bottom-up ethnography (Tuğal 2009)—where I formed relations with the poor through coffeehouses—revealed hidden scripts and resistance here and there, but not everywhere (in contrast to Scott 1990; but see Kidd 2002 for a pro-Scottian argument concerning beneficiaries). Second, the number of beneficiaries I talked to was significantly less than the charitable actors. Some studies have jumped to quick conclusions about beneficiary responsiveness without a thorough penetration of their world. Yet, only multi-year ethnographic studies that specifically focus on beneficiaries would be able to ascertain whether the poor are buying into an ethical project.

14 I see this as a marriage of convenience—a logically untenable, but practically necessary partnership—between post-structuralist genealogy and what the late Bourdieu (2014, pp. 86–93) has called "genetic structuralism."

1

GENEROSITY AS AN ALTERNATIVE

Is Giving a Challenge to the Market Logic?

Charity associations seem to spring up from everywhere in our contemporary world. Does this resurgence inevitably reinforce the major socioeconomic trends of our era (the neoliberal restructuring of the welfare state and the spread of business mentality to all institutions)? Or does charity breed practices and moralities that go beyond the free market? Indeed, what could be more remote from the marketplace than the sincere act of giving away a part of one's wealth or time?

This chapter begins by handling these questions through a discussion of theories of giving. Even though seemingly removed from the immediacy of our questions, almost all the major theories of generosity have been formulated against the background of commodification. Nevertheless, the insights of these theories become helpful only when grounded in comparative-historical inquiry, since the benevolent acts under scrutiny are situated in particular societies. This specificity is best captured through a review of the (mostly new institutionalist) voluntary sector literature, studies of neoliberal subjectivity, and political economy.

The Prevalent Accounts of Giving: Community-Generation vs. Domination

What kinds of discourses, institutions, and individuals do acts of giving and caring create? Who really benefits from generosity? These questions dovetail the problem of motivation. Is the core drive behind giving an innate desire to please, to share, to communicate, to connect, and to form community? Or, alternatively, do people resort to generosity as a way of building up their reputation, or even as a method of legitimizing domination? These questions are impossible to resolve, due to the unobservable nature of drives. However, no critical discussion of giving can avoid addressing them, even if obliquely. This introduces insurmountable problems of measurement. When assessed through surveys and interviews, there are only restricted methodological means to ascertain whether the respondents are giving honest answers (they might not even be honest with themselves). Although participant observation has an edge, even the direct observer has to speculate on the actual drives (e.g. when s/he catches glimpses of contradictions between stated aims and actual behaviors).

While some discussion of motivations is unavoidable, my analyses will draw attention to actual processes and products (including discursive ones). We might have little opportunity to know whether the donor/volunteer is motivated by an "innate" desire to share and connect or by a sly logic of reputation management. However, we can know whether the end result of caring is more connection and communication throughout society or, by contrast, more division between the poor and the wealthy, and the perpetuation of the latter's domination.

I will call the two major approaches I am drawing on "communitarian"[1] and "domination" accounts of giving.[2] This book will first historicize and then ultimately dissolve the theoretical opposition between communitarian and "interested," domination-oriented giving. The opposition is historically made. This was recognized by scholars as early as Marcel Mauss (who pointed out that interested and disinterested acts, as well as market exchange and gift giving, were not institutionally separated until modernity, the only era where people developed the idea of a disinterested gift). Several theorists of giving and caring have expanded on Mauss's insights; some have also pointed out that his historicization was inadequate (James and Allen 1998). But scholars have neglected the weight of *political interventions* in these historical processes. Caring for the poor integrates elements of both community-generation and domination-sustenance; but historical and political conditions determine the specific combination and relative weight of each dimension. More importantly, caring for the poor has the potential of going beyond both, though this potential is heavily circumscribed.

Giving as Community-Generation

According to the communitarian approach, giving to others has its basis in (mostly positive) aspects of social psychology. Associations, faiths, and communities instill in people dispositions to give, which generate further communities. We can call this the "virtuous cycle of giving." Good works have biographical roots, which allow people to internalize generosity. Parents and schools teach children how to engage in volunteer work, a model of behavior they repeat later in life (Flanagan et al. 1998, p. 471; Sundeen and Raskoff 1994, p. 392; Wuthnow 1995).[3] More generally, the senses of reciprocity, justice, and responsibility children get from parents form the basis of generous motivations in their adult years (Flanagan et al. 1998, p. 469; Fogelman 1997, p. 150).

Moreover, the doctrines of the major religions support giving and helpfulness (Bellah 1991; Ellison 1992, p. 413). People learn how to be selfless from the dictates of these religions. Religion not only motivates giving at the individual level, but creates altruistic communities and attachments (Wuthnow 1991). These emphases are in line with statistical findings: church membership and attendance increase volunteering (Sundeen and Raskoff 1994, p. 393).[4] In sum, altruism is not an accidental choice, but an entrenched inclination ingrained in individuals through family, church, and school. Yet, is the positive relationship between churchgoing and volunteer activity due to the doctrines of religion, or its other characteristics? This question brings us to the more Durkheimian face of the communitarian approach.

The (mostly belief-based) "proto-Weberian"[5] arguments above can be synthesized with Durkheimian[6] arguments to come up with a fuller communitarian theorization. Basically, frequent interaction within networks increases volunteering. People who attend religious service meet others who are civically involved and thereby become more likely to volunteer. Networks built in religious institutions lead to "reserves of trust and reciprocity" (Wood 1997, p. 601). Social ties reduce the work, uncertainty, and risk involved in volunteering, thereby encouraging people to donate time and resources. Commitment to and congruence with an organization's goals also motivate people to give beyond what is required (Murnighan et al. 1993, pp. 535–536; Wilson 2000).

Since these dynamics are observable in secular institutions too, why emphasize religion? Religious institutions, argue these scholars, have a special role in our era, since other institutions that build such ties (e.g. unions, crowded workplaces, families, etc.) have considerably weakened (Wood 1997). Religion even has a "spillover effect," as religious citizens volunteer more for *even* secular organizations. Furthermore, nonreligious people who have religious friends are encouraged to participate in civic activities (Ruiter and De Graaf 2006; but see Van der Meer et al. 2010).[7] The dense networks that result from religious participation render acts of caring almost natural (due to intensified flow of information, motivation, and recruitment efforts). They also increase the costs of not volunteering.

Classical sociology's concern with community is today supplemented by an intense focus on civil society and social capital. What community did for classical sociology, civil society and social capital do for contemporary sociology. Due to his centrality in developing and popularizing the civil society and social capital paradigms, Robert Putnam's increasing emphasis on religious networks is worth discussing. In *American Grace* (2010), Putnam and Campbell support the Durkheimian approach based on three broad surveys. Religiosity interacts with social capital to bolster trust, they argue, which in turn leads to giving and volunteering. Regular churchgoers help the poor, the elderly and the young more than less religious people (Putnam and Campbell 2010, p. 444–446). People who attend religious service frequently are more equipped with the skills of giving and caring (pp. 466–468). The factor that Putnam and Campbell (p. 472) single out to account for this impact of religiosity is "religious social networks (number of close friends in your congregation, participation in small groups in your congregation, and frequency of talking about religion with family and friends)." This is an important spin on Putnam's (2000) earlier work, as the findings indicate that church attendance is much more important than any other kind of civic engagement (say, in bowling leagues, Putnam and Campbell 2010, p. 475).

In the Durkheimian literature, the emphasis is on social ties at the expense of ideas, symbols, and religious language. Yet, some authors thoroughly integrate the arguments summarized above with an analysis of religious meanings that encourage giving (Wilson and Musick 1997; Wood 1997, p. 603). The Weberian and Durkheimian trends come together vigorously in Wuthnow's (1991, 1995) work, which can be taken as the most cogent synthesis of these two major sociological schools in the contemporary sociology of religion.

The anthropological theories of the gift provide a complementary angle to communitarian sociology and political science. Drawing on Mauss's essay on the gift (itself a partially Durkheimian work), anthropologists argue that giving creates reciprocal bonds and expectations, which foster and bolster communal ties. Gift exchange is therefore strictly separate from commodity exchange, the goal of which is not the creation of bonds but the accumulation of things (Gregory 1980). That donors and beneficiaries do not know each other in many cases of charity does not obviate the usefulness of these insights (also see Titmuss 1997): the ties in question might be built not only between the giver and the receiver, but among givers themselves too (which, as shall be seen in my case studies, is a central part of the process).

But what if the lines between the accumulation of relations and the accumulation of things are sometimes blurry, as Bourdieu argues in his discussion of the convertibility of social capital to economic capital? What if the social ties formed through generosity have the implicit purpose of excluding some people and relegating yet others to subordinate positions?

Giving as Domination

Pushing such doubts to their logical conclusion, some scholars emphasize the benefits of generosity to especially dominant groups (Baylouny 2010, pp. 141–142). Both historians (Kidd 2002) and sociologists (Zelizer 1997) draw attention to how charity has tangible returns, such as expanded political patronage and "even the acquisition of public office." Yet, wouldn't communitarian scholars object that generosity *really* benefits the poor regardless of such perks to the rich? Domination accounts throw a doubt on this dimension of charity too. Starting with early modernity, charitable work has allowed disciplinary mechanisms to spread out from enclosed institutions (such as factories, schools, and prisons) and enter the homes and bedrooms of the poor to further regulate them (Foucault 1977, p. 212). Viviana Zelizer (1997, pp. 142, 168–169 and *passim*) points that whereas earlier American charity maintained status distinctions and sustained obedience, twentieth century versions were even more insidious: they attempted to control the very psyche of poor people (in order to turn them into thrifty, calculating, and productive workers and consumers).

While the communitarian literature emphasizes the solidaristic results of volunteering, critics warn that there are serious reasons to doubt this too. Communitarian scholars argue that giving produces generalized trust (Stolle 1998), as well as feelings of social responsibility toward the public in general (Flanagan et al. 1998), and the needy in particular. However, domination accounts underline that philanthropy can produce the reverse effect: the "responsibilization" of the poor (the naturalization of the assumption that poor people's characteristics are the real cause of poverty). This assumption leads to the conclusion that the poor should become individually responsible to correct their deficiencies (Atia 2013; Roy 2010). Giving thus undermines trust (in the poor), community (among the poor), and the public (as an imagined space where the rich and poor can come together). It instead re-channels society's resources to produce "individualized" subjects.

Pierre Bourdieu is one of the few to attempt a thorough integration of communitarian insights into an overall domination framework. Bourdieu (1990, pp. 98–99) points out that objectivist social science (in the person of Lévi-Strauss) has rightly accused Mauss of remaining trapped within the "phenomenology" of giving. Yet, objectivist accounts of giving fall into another trap: they completely ignore the seemingly "disinterested" aspects of the gift (which are core to its sustainability as an "interested" exchange). By overemphasizing the scientifically determinable rules of exchange (which people are unaware of), objectivism kills *the charm*, anticipation, and unpredictability of giving. As Silber (1998) also points out, uncertainty remains a core part of generosity, despite its ongoing bureaucratization (in the welfare state, NGOs, etc.). Whereas predictability and explicit calculation are at the heart of the cash economy, "ambiguity" is the core characteristic of the gift economy.

In objectivist accounts,[8] giving in general and gift-giving in particular become indistinguishable from market exchange. Yet, the gift/counter-gift is different from a loan/loan payment, which is (presumably) predictable and calculable: the counter-gift needs to come later, at an unpredictable time, and in an unpredictable shape. While Bourdieu too ultimately reduces gift-giving to a form of exchange, just like other domination (and rational choice) theorists, unlike them he insists that *misrecognition* of the gift's objective truth is a necessary ingredient of gift exchange (Bourdieu 1990, pp. 105–106).[9] This subjective dimension of generosity is not simply false consciousness; it is rather a different kind of truth without which the cycle of generosity would collapse. For that very reason, Bourdieu speaks of a "double truth" of practices, of which generosity is a paradigmatic case (Silber 2009).

Giving, argues Bourdieu, is *capital accumulation*, but of a special sort. In societies where the logic of capital accumulation is denied (in Bourdieu's case, tribal regions of Algeria), only roundabout methods can enable wealth concentration. Wealthier tribal families gain the trust of others through giving. This accumulated trust (which is core to his thinking as it is to Putnam's, but in a different way) is then put to use when abundant labor is needed. In the absence of free labor, landholding families need voluntary help during harvest time, which they can acquire through appearing generous after each harvest (i.e. giving away excess agricultural produce).

Bourdieu points out that European societies have gradually replaced pure cash calculation for the ambiguous gift economy (through a stretched out "symbolic revolution"). However, the gift economy survives in the realms of religion, art, and family[10] (even if in more commercialized and rationalized form when compared to non-modern societies) (Bourdieu 2000, pp. 195–197). *In light of the growing salience of religion today, this observation gains added significance: an all-sweeping, global religious revival has the potential to subvert the modern ethical revolution through re-introducing "ambiguous" acts and "double-truths" to the center of social life.* Bourdieu fails to mention (let alone discuss) this most obvious logical consequence of his own theorization.

Even though Bourdieu has done little research on the topic, at the bottom of his theory of fields we find Weber's sociology of religion—and one essay where he translated Weber's insights into his own language (Bourdieu 1991). Bourdieu also returned to the topic in his late writings and lectures (since religion provided perfect evidence for his "double truth" approach to "disinterested" acts). Even though these texts are full of insights, they are also symptomatic in their ahistoricity. In a particularly strong lecture given in 1994, Bourdieu mentions that the more everything else is marketized in society, the more dramatized are the noneconomic logics of religion and the family. Despite this historicization-in-passing, the essay is marked by ahistorical statements on religion, such as (*Practical Reason* 1998, p. 114):

> The truth of the religious enterprise is that of having two truths: economic truth and religious truth, which denies the former. Thus, in order to describe each practice, as among the Kabyle, it would be necessary to use two words ... apostolate/marketing, faithful/clientele, sacred service/paid labor.

Here, the religious dynamics of the Catholic Church are equated with those of tribal Algeria. The sociologist handles the functioning of the Catholic Church itself as eternal and identified with religion as such (*Practical Reason* 1998, p. 116, emphases mine):

> Besides volunteer work, the free gift of labor and services, we also find here another central property of Catholic enterprise: it is *always* conceived of as a large family. There is a cleric, sometimes two, whose specific culture, tied to a whole collective and individual history, consists of knowing how to manage at the same time a vocabulary or a language and social relations, which must *always* be euphemized.

These timeless statements about religion cannot capture the processes I analyze in this book. For instance, in the course of neoliberalization, the line between religion's objective and subjective truths become blurred. Euphemization becomes less necessary. Bourdieu tells us that whenever bishops discuss religion as a "market," this is accompanied by ironic laughter. Yet, one can call the universe of religious organizations in the US a "market" without laughing about it. Bourdieu's approach would also be insufficient in accounting for redistributive religion, where entrenched religion's objective truth is *made explicit*, so that it can be attacked (even if the attack is still based on the subjective expectations religion has fostered).

Bourdieu's approach to the gift, along with other aspects of his theorization, have been criticized as "Marxian" (for an overview, see Silber 2009, p. 178). Bourdieu reduces, some scholars hold, all forms of human action to capital accumulation. This criticism is both valid and escapist. It is valid in that Bourdieu tends to be a reductionist; it is escapist to the degree that it morphs from a sound criticism of Bourdieu's overgeneralization to a neglect of the ever-increasing demands of capital accumulation. Even if we criticize Bourdieu's over-stretched projections of "capital" to non-capitalist history and societies, we need to realize the heavy transformation of giving into a capital-accumulating strategy in our era.

While sociologist Ilana Silber tries to resolve Bourdieu's inconsistencies by analyzing the gift as an intersubjectively constructed act, my approach cherishes the unresolved contradictions that his attempt to fuse objectivism and subjectivism generates. Through careful textual analysis, Silber (2009, pp. 182–187) demonstrates that the maneuvers in Bourdieu's late writings have resulted in an "inner tension and self-contradiction."[11] Bourdieu ultimately acknowledged that not all action is self-interested, but did not theorize how that insight could be integrated into his overall framework of "misrecognition." Rather than resolving this inconsistency through a return to the objectivist tendencies of his earlier work, or through dissolving the objective, critical level of analysis, I propose that we need to *stick to the late Bourdieu and make it more systematic*. We should use his late writings to build a truly post-objectivist and post-subjectivist research program that can deal with the unresolvable tensions of the "double truth."

In other words, *Caring for the Poor* takes *The Logic of Practice*'s criticism of objectivism and subjectivism seriously, while also realizing that *The Logic of Practice* itself heavily weighs on the side of objectivism. Bourdieu's final writings stand at a distance from his earlier objectivism, without discussing what this entails for the broad theoretical program specified in *The Logic of Practice*. A re-theorization of care and giving will lay the groundwork for a theoretical program that will integrate Bourdieu's critical insights with those of more intersubjective theorizations (which I borrow from the communitarians in sociology and political science, as well as the Maussians/anti-utilitarians in anthropology and continental sociology).

A quick look at recent anthropology reveals that there are many ways to experience and signify the gift. Generosity is not only a builder of community, but is frequently practiced and experienced as self-sacrifice. The "renunciation" account of the gift allows us to think beyond accumulation and community-making, even if (under the current circumstances) it is always circumscribed by capitalist dynamics. The Hindu *dan* (as a gift that allegedly expects no return) has been thoroughly studied in this regard (e.g. Parry 1986; Laidlaw 2000; Raheja 1988). Most recently, Bornstein (2012, pp. 26–28) has argued that the dan is starkly different from the Muslim *zakat* in that it does not entail any social obligations and the creation of a community; rather, it frees the donor from the material world. Such stark contrasts obfuscate that many people see zakat and *sadaqa* as tools to kill the love of wealth inside you: another kind of liberation from the material world. To drive her point home, Bornstein (2012, pp. 29–32) points out that the dan should be given without any expectation of return, including a good place in heaven. Yet, slippages in the argumentation (e.g. a quotation from a Hindu actor on page 29, which implies that when you donate, you guarantee rebirth, which is obviously a kind of return) suggest that the dan is also caught up in the ambiguities that late Bourdieu has underlined. Renunciation might be a strong tendency in some gift giving, but it is always contaminated by other tendencies.

Anthropologist Mittermaier (2014a, 2014b) develops an analysis of Egyptian giving that straddles the boundary between the renunciation and communitarian accounts. She argues that some Islamic giving in Egypt develops an "ethics of immediacy" that emphasizes the co-presence of human beings here-and-now, expressed in "simple act[s such as] serving food to whoever walks through the door (2014b, p. 55). Among Egyptian Sufis, "sharing food means becoming enmeshed in social relations and spiritual communities." (2014b, p. 64). Mittermaier insists that critical scholarship misses how charitable ethics "might be partially shaped by, but also exceed, the current historical moment" (2014b, p. 75). Such statements downplay the strength of capitalism: my ethnographic chapters will also demonstrate that there are vectors that exceed neoliberalism/capitalism in contemporary giving, but they cannot be developed to their full potential unless donors/volunteers *struggle to make them work as such* (as non-capitalist).

The power of generosity to produce new ethics will be further explored in the Conclusion, where I point out that this potential survives uneasily under capitalism; it can be developed to its full extent only in a post-capitalist society.[12] In short, rather than adopting an exclusively domination or communitarian (or "anti-utilitarian") perspective, I aim to focus on the variation within fields of benevolence: some organizations might emphasize solidaristic aspects of giving, while others focus on control over the poor, and yet others devise new ethics. The sociological task, then, is to study how each of these orientations blossom in certain environments but not others. However, in our present historical context, we should also note that "domination" accounts gain further credence, partially due to the organizational, political economic, and discursive developments summarized in the following section.

The World-Historical Institutionalization of Giving: The Rise of the Nebulous "Voluntary Sector"

The big questions on generosity come under a different light when we consider the novelty of late-modern forms of giving. The way actors practice and understand generosity today is thoroughly shaped by neoliberalism. This section will explore how three different angles on neoliberalization (new institutionalist, Foucaultian, political economic) inform us on different aspects of this refashioning.

Throughout the world, the scope of (and scholarly attention on) NGOization of charitable giving has considerably intensified. Key to this transformation is the post-1970s re-evaluation of the state's role in social welfare. The post-welfare state world has witnessed the global rise of a realm that is alternatively called the voluntary sector, nongovernmental world, the nonprofit field, third sector, and civil society—words with different connotations, but currently used to similar effect. Practitioners have refashioned charity and philanthropy as an integral part of this new reality. This does not mean this "third" realm didn't exist before the 1970s, but its place in the social imagination has definitively changed. The meaning and practice of charity have also metamorphosed as the latter became integrated into the third sector.

While little was published between the 1920s and 1960s on "voluntary" relief, the 1970s witnessed the rise of academic works on the subject (Kidd 2002, p. 329). The new discourse on poverty emphasized the degenerating aspects of state aid. It subsequently drew attention to the need to foster "active citizenship" (and undermine "entitled citizenship") through civil society. This language echoed not only Victorian England, but poverty debates that started at the end of the eighteenth century (Kidd 2002, pp. 329–330). Even the Left reproduced nineteenth-century liberal-conservative investments in civil society (Tocqueville 2000) as the bearer of nongovernmental mutual support (and therefore freedom). Both practitioners and scholars re-interpreted the rise of the welfare state in the mid-twentieth century as an unwelcome "compromise" of the voluntary sector (Finlayson 1994).

As historian Alan Kidd and political economist Jamie Peck have emphasized, think tanks were central to the rise of the voluntary sector. In the UK, the Institute of Economic Affairs published a series of books and reports that called for the revival of voluntary welfare. The institute further popularized Charles Murray's re-interpretation of the concept "culture of poverty" (which is core to poverty debates in Turkey too).

Moreover, during the same decades, civil society and the third sector economy also came to be deployed as remedies to the marketization of the economy and individualization of society (Brown et al. 2000, p. 32; Cohen and Arato 1992). De Tocqueville was now a prophet of community not only against central government but also market individualism. Especially in the US, communitarianism became a major intellectual trend (Brown et al. 2000, p. 34; Etzioni 1993; MacIntyre 1981).[13] Interest in civil society and the third sector exploded in the 1990s as a confluence of all of these trends (Brown et al. 2000).

Nevertheless, most communitarian and (Habermas- and Gramsci-inspired) New Left approaches in the Western world tended to overemphasize the critical edge of this explosion. Retrospectively, it is hard to miss how central neoliberalization has been to the rise of the voluntary sector. While NGOs were upheld as alternatives to bureaucratic and marketized ways of thinking, there is growing evidence that a thorough neoliberalization is undermining non-market practices and motives within the NGO world itself (Eikenberry and Kluver 2004). As voluntary associations compete with each other and even with businesses in the marketplace, they adapt business practices and discourses (Galaskiewicz and Bielefeld 1998, p. 237). This poses specific challenges when volunteers want to uphold solidaristic/altruistic principles and practices (Eikenberry and Kluver 2004).

As important is the explosion in the number of business, economic, and finance graduates and their colonization of the voluntary world. The extreme investment in these disciplines creates a vicious circle, where the social world is *made* to function with a market logic. A degree in these disciplines, it is now believed, can allow you to work in any kind organization (in a financial or administrative capacity). Consequently, organizations in the non-business world start to adopt a business management model. The boundaries between the profit world and the nonprofit world are actively, "performatively" undermined.

Western governments, rather than making the voluntary sector serve the public interest, also push the NGOs to become more businesslike. As voluntary associations compete for government recognition and funding, they open themselves up to pressures from bureaucrats (who have themselves come to adopt market-oriented understandings of professionalism and management) (Brown et al. 2000, pp. 53, 116). As a result of pressures and incentives from both governments and businesses, then, voluntary associations develop risk management and other businesslike practices (Brown et al. 2000; Warburton and McDonald 2009). Volunteers gradually become regulated (and paid) staff (Lie and Baines 2007). Though many volunteers still see themselves as altruists and amateurs (an attitude that invites communitarian and renunciation accounts of giving more readily), they are institutionally pushed to behave professionally and egotistically (Brown et al. 2000; Lie and Baines 2007). A focus on efficiency and professionalization of staff replaces traditional charitable concerns of reciprocity and solidarity (Brown et al. 2000, pp. 100–106).[14]

Following in the footsteps of the West, non-Western welfare languages too started to incorporate vocabulary from de Tocqueville and Putnam in the 1980s (Bano 2008). International NGOs and development agencies were the key actors in this process (Watkins et al. 2012). As earlier forms of Western provision (and state-driven development) had failed to produce the desired results, a new focus on "empowerment" and "sustainability" replaced direct provision (Escobar 1995; Watkins et al. 2012). The World Bank, a primary agenda-setter in this regard, helped institute a discourse of "ownership"—essentially a twenty-first century form of social engineering designed to re-create all human beings as entrepreneurs (Botchway 2001; Kühl 2009; Li 2007). Local communities, it was hoped, would be much more "efficient" in resolving problems if they "owned" them, as they (unlike states) would have the required local knowledge; and their participation would ensure sustainability (Bano 2008; Botchway 2001). In the name of empowering people, states started to dump their responsibilities on "communities," which, however, lacked the resources to tackle large-scale tasks (Botchway 2001). In this context, neoliberal assumptions in charity work came to weigh on even organizations built by local (and occasionally anti-Western) donors (Atia 2013; Roy 2010).

Moreover, "participation" was re-defined in a decidedly apolitical way (Botchway 2001; Watkins et al. 2012). Elite discourse discouraged, and the new institutions undercut, the political involvement of aid organizations (Bano 2008). It is ironic that participation was in the center of social movement demands for decades; but with the 1970s, it became a cornerstone of neoliberalism.[15] Empowerment, a term with feminist roots (but also very complex and contradictory political uses throughout the decades), suffered a similar fate.

The emphasis on sustainability also inhibited less ambitious, but more realizable, temporary relief efforts. Relief agencies have functioned better specifically because the World Bank and other agenda-setters do not expect them to produce sustainable results. Moreover, the projects that the international aid agencies contracted out created perverse incentives, as NGO administrators and employees started to prioritize fulfilling measurable (international) criteria to the detriment of building up membership and delivering actual aid (Bano 2008; Swidler and Watkins 2009). As aid becomes a career, it further undermines solidarity, despite the global prevalence of community-generating aid discourse.[16]

This global historical transformation lends further credence to the domination account of giving. Nevertheless, there are studies that document the persistence of (perceptibly) altruistic giving, though now in competition with *explicitly* self-interested giving. The latter obliterates the double truth Bourdieu speaks of and creates a disenchanted "generosity" shorn of illusions. In (what these studies call) altruistic giving, charitable volunteerism is based on "affective" ties; in the second, on instrumental reason. The first type of volunteer enters an organization for the benefit of others, while the latter type (self-consciously) wants to develop experience and networks for future employment (Brown et al. 2000, p. 107). Though such contrasts between older and newer types of charity might be too stark (and idealize certain types of organizations and volunteers), they shed light on some distinguishing (and threatened) orientations. However, the extant literature lacks the tools to historicize and theorize the root dynamics behind these transformations and threats.

New Institutionalism

The NGO literature draws attention to important transformations, but gets us so far in answering the question raised in this book: Why does the neoliberalization of giving systematically threaten other orientations? Even if there is no unifying theoretical perspective that runs through the NGO literature, new institutionalism[17] is the most common framework. A discussion of this approach can give us some insights into why the focus on NGOs provides only partial answers to the questions studied in this book. The new institutionalist perspective is able to specify the *mechanisms* that push organizations to adopt business practices (Eikenberry and Kluver 2004; Galaskiewicz and Bielefeld 1998; Warburton and McDonald 2009). Here is its usefulness. However, it underemphasizes the global *processes* at work (at both micro and macro levels): the rise of neoliberal discursive forms, the decline of the working class, and the business-intellectual-state assault on welfare rights. These come in to the picture at best as broad backgrounds, but do not thoroughly shape the analysis.[18] Certainly, new institutionalist scholars fall on a spectrum on this issue. Still, Galaskiewicz, a prominent scholar in this field, makes an unequivocal case for bracketing out historical change and political context (Galaskiewicz and Bielefeld 1998, p. ix):

> [T]he timeframe for [his] analysis, 1980 to 1994, span the Reagan revolution, privatization, the new federalism, two recessions ... [I]t would be foolish not to acknowledge that each of these events impacted the charitable sector in important ways ... Yet our analysis will ignore these contextual events ... [because] our goal was to build and test organizational theory.

By contrast, the analyses in the following chapters will emphasize how the study of interactions between institutions and individuals on the one hand and historical changes on the other can help us *reconstruct* theory rather than test it.

New institutionalism is limited not only in its analysis of the dynamics behind conformity, but of resistance and (non-neoliberal) alternatives as well. Due to its overall emphasis on the spread of institutional models through coercive, mimetic, and normative processes (DiMaggio and Powell 1983), it pays little attention to the development of unconventional models. Even when the birth of novel institutional models is under scrutiny (Moody 2008), the *overall neoliberal logic of the philanthropic field* is taken as a given: the global-political economic reasons behind this are not analyzed.[19] New institutionalism tends to take the legitimacy of business for granted due to decontextualized assumptions regarding American culture[20] (e.g. see Moody 2008, pp. 336–337).[21] It therefore neglects the political making of business legitimacy (which enables business-mimetic institutional moves in the first place). The new institutionalist approach thereby reproduces the circularity Bourdieu (1990) spotted in phenomenology (the meta-theoretical basis for new institutionalism): phenomenology provides an explanatory framework based on the explanatory framework of the practitioners in the field, but in a much more systematic way than they ever could.[22]

DiMaggio's solo-authored work gives an interesting twist to this literature. In his analysis of museums, the author pays special attention to the development of alternative organizational models (upper-class/middle-class audience, object-oriented art museums versus middle-class/worker audience, utilitarian art museums). Applying a field logic, he shows that these two models are in competition—a competition based on different kinds of capital. Based on this quasi-Bourdieusian analysis, DiMaggio (1991) criticizes institutionalist theory:

> [I]nstitutional theorists have focused upon the tendency for organizational forms to become more legitimate as they win wider acceptance. (p. 268) … [I]nstitutional theory has neglected the contradictory tendency of successful institutionalization projects to legitimize not just new organizational forms, but also new categories of authorized actors whose interests diverges from those of the groups controlling the organizations, and new resources such actors can use in their efforts to effect organizational change. (p. 272) … [S]tudies of institutional diffusion have emphasized that organizational forms become more legitimate as they spread, focusing on the form per se rather than on variation among organizations of a given form with respect to structure, programs, and missions. (p. 287)

Institutionalist scholarship has hardly heeded these calls in the decades following DiMaggio's article.[23] The classical new institutionalist articles (which pay exclusive attention to standardization and diffusion) are much more widely cited than DiMaggio's article on museums, which emphasizes variation, struggle, and novelty. My book, by contrast, takes each of the elements DiMaggio draws attention to quite seriously. I focus on the development of competing organizational forms; the making of actors befitting of these forms; and differentiation of structures, programs, and missions within organizational fields.

New institutionalism's main tendencies are reproduced in this paradigm's application to the global scene, namely Meyer's "World Society" approach. Meyer argues that (Western, and mostly American) organizational models "diffuse" throughout the world. Their adaptation also leads to the internalization of global values and an emergent world citizenship (Meyer 2000; Meyer et al. 1997). In the world of aid, the ("neo-Tocquevillian") American model that spreads to the rest of the world is "active" and "entrepreneurial" citizenship mobilized through communities (Vogel 2006). These arguments indeed capture some processes of interest. However, even the left-wing adaptations of Meyer's approach reproduce phenomenology's tendencies of decontextualization. For instance, while paying lip service to local variations, sociologist Ann Vogel fails to observe how the spread of American charitable ethics restructures *but not completely takes over* existing charitable fields. Vogel states: "The USA marks the global space of civil society with its own institutional design by extending its domestic operations into world society with the gift economy alongside" (Vogel 2006, p. 648). I ask: To what degree were charitable fields in two American satellites (Egypt and Turkey) indeed refashioned in the American way?[24]

In order to historicize the predominance of neoliberal charitable dispositions, I bring in two other literatures: analyses of neoliberal subjectivity and political economy. These literatures enlighten us on many dimensions of neoliberalization. Yet, especially the subjectivity literature falls short of accounting for the persistence of non-neoliberal forms of giving and the development of post-liberal forms.

Neoliberal Subjectivity

Organizational studies underemphasize the global and centuries-long making of the liberal ethical subject. The transformations I study in this book are not simply dictated by institutional pressures and organizational reform. They have deep roots in ethical history, best captured through Foucaultian lenses. Nevertheless, the blindfolds of new institutionalism and post-structuralism are quite similar.

The implications of subjectivity studies are not always clear-cut. According to one brand of the Foucault-inspired scholarship, neoliberalism re-creates the person as a self-governing (Brand 2007; Song 2010), autonomous (Fries 2008; McNay 2009), responsible, and self-esteeming (Matza 2009; Phoenix 2004) individual. It converts even caring into a pro-market activity (Atia 2013; Roy 2010). This strand of the literature depends on a strict definition of neoliberalism as the complete entrepreneurialization of all spheres of life (Brown 2003; Feher 2009, p. 30; Ong 2006a, p. 501; but see Ong 2006b). Wendy Brown, the clearest articulator of this strand, clarifies the "neo" in neoliberalism: Classical liberals did not attempt to collapse all spheres of life into the economic. Adam Smith, for one, had a complicated understanding of non-economic conduct (Brown 2015, pp. 92–98). The classical liberal subject was "split" into two halves: a caring one and a calculating one. Unlike liberalism, neoliberalism ultimately flattens the subject and jettisons all non-calculative aspects of personhood.[25]

Some Foucaultians, by contrast, argue that the rise of *communitarianism* (rather than simply individualism) reinforces the general trends of privatized control (Miller and Rose 2008, pp. 90–92, 104–105; Muehlebach 2012). Existing neoliberalism thrives by fostering non-market logic (including non-economized sentimentalities). While people of our era experience community and reciprocity through participation in benevolent work, this participation reinforces the broader philosophy of neoliberalism that prioritizes individual self-reliance over communities and reciprocity (Rose 1999, pp. 249–250, 265–266).

In other words, as Rose (1999) and Muehlebach (2012) have pointed out, the glorification of the "selfless gift giver" with "unconditional ties" to her community further reinforces neoliberalization, rather than disappearing under its weight (as in other Foucaultian arguments, see Feher 2009, p. 32). They therefore argue that neoliberalism has not flattened the subject; it reproduces, only more intensely, the split-ness of the liberal subject (into a selfishly calculating half, and a caring one). Influenced by these scholars, *Caring for the Poor* defines "neoliberal charitable ethics" as only a *more advanced* form of liberal giving (also see Chapter 3), which seeks to create an ever more aggressively independent individual through an ever more heightened sense of community.

Yet, Rose and Muehlebach do not seriously engage with the persistence of non-liberal forms of giving, nor do they probe into the emergence of new forms that might transcend both neoliberalism and communitarianism. Even if some forms of giving are not necessarily entrepreneurial to begin with, they necessarily reinforce neoliberalism (Muehlebach 2012, pp. 13–14, 24–25, 48–49, 65–70 and *passim*). This culminates in a story of inevitability, which reinforces depoliticization under neoliberalism by exaggerating the latter's omnipotence. *Caring for the Poor*, by contrast, explores the limits of neoliberalization as well as its invasiveness.

The restrictions of this scholarship can be traced back to the major pitfalls of post-structuralism. Foucault's earlier work emphasized the all-encompassing diffusion of disciplinary techniques (an emphasis that echoes new institutionalism). We can call this the first face of Foucault. His late work, however, revised this emphasis on omnipotent diffusion in three interrelated ways. The late Foucault pointed out that resistance is everywhere; biopolitics is always combined with sovereign and disciplinary power; and neoliberalism comes with internal contradictions (e.g. the state is summoned to implement marketization). This is the second face of Foucault.

Foucault did not turn these observations into a fully-fledged conceptualization. It was Deleuze and Guattari (1987) who filled in the gaps through their concept of "assemblage." Deleuzian takes on neoliberalism point out that the latter thrives by fostering non-market logics. But this move runs the risk of saving face through a permanent play on words: every contemporary articulation can be called a neoliberal assemblage through the deployment of phrases such as "exceptions to neoliberalism" and "neoliberalism as exception" (Ong 2006b). The looseness of these debates has prevented us from studying when, where, and why neoliberal techniques get entrenched; remain limited; and/or are overturned. Comparative-historical analysis, informed by political economy, helps us in this regard.

Changing Welfare Regimes

What is sorely lacking in organizational studies and the subjectivity literature is a focus on the way each NGO/charity field is situated within an international political economic context. The structural position of particular fields deeply shapes the possibilities for action and actor formation in each. The way the welfare state gets restructured is not an issue external to the charity fields, since the state intervenes in their making. The refashioning of charitable ethics is tightly interwoven with specific paths of macroeconomic reform. The following chapters will demonstrate the interactivity of these processes through comparative analysis.

Caring for the Poor heeds Brenner et al.'s (2010) and Wacquant's (2012) calls to study neoliberalization as a multifaceted, "variegated," partially state-driven process. Under neoliberalism, the state does not simply withdraw from the economy (as earlier studies suggested),[26] but seeks to re-shape it based on economistic principles. Moreover, the quite extreme focus on the withdrawal of the state (or neoliberal welfare programs such as micro-finance) has prevented scholars from noticing the recent spread of non-neoliberal practices within neoliberal regimes themselves (e.g. see Ferguson 2015 on direct, frequently unconditional, cash transfers). The state heavily intervenes in the process of neoliberalization (with at times contradictory logics).

However, in line with Peck's (2010) Gramscianism, I further underline how associations' *active and willing cooperation* with the state is a necessary ingredient in the making of neoliberalism. Moreover, top-down vectors of neoliberalization mostly work to the advantage of business and other dominant strata, but some middle and subordinate strata also partake in this process and seek to reap partial benefits. This subaltern embrace further expands the realm of civil society (variably in cooperation, in negotiation, and against the state). Charitable organizations are not simply and always the backyard of the dominant classes. *State-society blocs*—rather than Bourdieu's "bureaucratic field," which carries out a neoliberal "revolution from above" (Wacquant 2012, p. 72)—*are therefore the prime movers of neoliberalization.*

Hence, by combining Bourdieusian and Gramscian insights, we need to pay close attention to how state institutions and charitable fields are articulated.[27] Associations molecularly infuse the state with bottom-up energy; therefore, neoliberalization cannot be reduced to an "imposition from above." As charitable actors frequently emphasize (see ethnographic chapters), they give with a "heart," whereas the state gives with a cold face. This is a differentiation *made* on the ground by actors, rather than one that naturally emanates from an always-already existing state-society distinction. This heartfelt, wholesome giving (certainly supported by the state, but organized mostly by society) co-exists uneasily with the heartlessness spread by the state and frequently by these very organizations.

The "variegated" political economic focus on charity is in its infancy. Most of political economy focuses on how the restructuring of welfare states opens up space for religious charitable activity. "Welfare mixes" that bolster civic practice gradually replace Keynesian welfare (Göçmen 2010). A full understanding of these processes is necessary, but the issue I focus on is how the change in the welfare regimes transforms the nature of religious charity itself. This transformation does not simply expand the realm of civic charity, but restructures it in a neoliberal direction. Paradoxically, charitable giving becomes a terrain of struggle, where the state-supported associations push for a new understanding of generosity that puts individual responsibility (and market-oriented disciplinary mechanisms) in the center of benevolence. Other associations, and even actors *within* some of the neoliberal associations, frequently negotiate, and sometimes resist, this move (see Chapters 5 and 6).

Foucaultians, even when they look at variation within neoliberal subjectivities, neglect how the macro-context of policy influences subjectivities. Brenner et al.'s and Wacquant's calls to combine insights from both approaches (without getting lost in the ever-malleability of neoliberal techniques) is a welcome intervention. Yet, this insight should not turn into a call for analyses that demonstrate how each macro-liberalization context *dictates* a certain kind of subjectivity. We rather need to focus on how macro-reform shapes the fields and creates resources and motivations for certain kinds of subjectivities. Each macro-neoliberal context is *contingently* articulated to a field of charitable dispositions. As the two following, macro-historical chapters will show, this contingent articulation is driven by socio-political actors (more specifically, religio-political movements in each respective national context). New institutionalist, Foucaultian, and Bourdieusian accounts downplay such actors. State-movement blocs, we argue, are the core actors in these processes (de Leon et al. 2015).

Just like Brenner et al. talk about deepened neoliberalization in some macro contexts, I draw attention to a deepened neoliberal subjectivity in some of the organizations I study in the ethnographic chapters. Especially some organizations in Egypt approach a purer, textbook-like form of neoliberal subjectivity. Other Turkish and Egyptian organizations forge neoliberal and communitarian tendencies into what a Deleuzian would call "assemblages." Hail to the study of assemblages, but we should also notice how these are *unevenly structured* by global and national processes, and also how retaining the distinctiveness of an assemblage becomes more difficult in certain contexts. Studying the contemporary world's arguably most widespread assemblage just as religion + neoliberalism (Atia 2013; Rudnyckyj 2010) obscures how (and why) the specific weight of neoliberalism in the combination varies. In order to study micro-variegation in a structured way, *the Gramsci-inspired revision of Bourdieu recasts the study of neoliberal subjectivity as a comparative-historical study of contested fields.*

★★★

The next two chapters seek to situate fields of giving and their ethics in world-historical contexts. Here, political economy is the key to understanding variations in ethics of giving, but we get the full picture only when we pay close attention to the *institutional* contexts and *political* interventions, which are themselves shaped by religion. The ethical changes throughout the histories of Christianity and Islam are pretty enlightening in these regards.

Notes

1 My choice of wording for this perspective creates a possible confusion (as it is identical with one category of empirical actors and activities I am trying to account for). However, this overlap is not accidental. The "communitarian" perspective is thoroughly shaped by *what most charitable actors themselves believe to be the essence of their act*. The implications of phenomenology (of theoretical accounts based on actors' perceptions and feelings) for our cases will be discussed throughout the book.

2 These are not the self-designations of the scholars who adopt these approaches. Moreover, some of these scholars would not see themselves as having a perspective similar to those they are grouped with.
3 Some studies cast doubt on these arguments. For instance, Rosenthal et al. (1998) find no significant correlation between infant and childhood volunteering and adult volunteering.
4 The literature on the positive relationship between churchgoing and the likelihood of volunteering (and its criticism) is too extensive to cite here. See the literature reviews in Lim and MacGregor (2012), Ruiter and De Graaf (2006), and Wilson (2000).
5 I use the label "proto-Weberian" in a loose sense, in order to point out that these arguments put emphasis on the contents of belief—more specifically, on the textual injunctions of religions and their implications for ethical conduct. The label does not imply that these scholars follow Weber's line of thought regarding generosity and charity, which was rather underdeveloped and cynical (Silber 2010, pp. 542–544). Also note that this is only one face of Weber, and the other face is developed by Bourdieu.
6 The authors cited here do not necessarily refer to Durkheim, but make arguments parallel to the latter's overall framework.
7 There is an ongoing debate about such effects of religion. For instance, even though Lim and MacGregor (2012) have found that nonreligious people with religious friends are indeed more likely to volunteer; they show that in highly religious localities nonreligious people are isolated and their possibility of volunteering decreases sharply.
8 This is true for rational choice theory (Banks 1997; Wilson 2000), structuralist anthropology, and proto-Marxist accounts of giving.
9 Bourdieu's theorization resolves many criticisms directed against Mauss. Alain Testart (1998), Jonathan Parry (1986), and others insist that the lack of obligations to reciprocate characterize many practices of the gift, which is therefore completely distinct from exchange. Bourdieu's subtle conceptualization draws attention to how, at least in some instances, *the lack of a formal obligation* is a central part of the game of exchange (Bourdieu 1990, 2000).
10 The welfare state and philanthropy are also roundabout ways in which domination-through-caring is still central to late modern society (Bourdieu 1990, pp. 133–134). They are more complex articulations of the elementary forms of the gift Bourdieu had observed in tribal Algeria. As Bourdieu indicates in *Pascalian Meditations* (2000), however, *the welfare state* is under attack. Yet, unlike the *Logic of Practice*, *Pascalian Meditations* fails to discuss how *philanthropy* has played a similar role in late modernity. Why would late modern societies dismantle one complex form of gift-based enchantment, while sticking to another? This oversight also suggests that we need a much more comparative-historical understanding of how gift-giving varies, which Bourdieu's theorization of the transition from the gift economy to the cash economy (with its sweeping, Durkheimian approach to the evolution of giving from simple to differentiated society) does not allow.
11 Also see Fassin (2012) for Bourdieu's less-than-theorized turn to subjectivism in his final writings.
12 But what if the gift is the wrong place to start when looking for an alternative to the market? Most recently, James Ferguson (2015, pp. 51, 174–178) has argued that in analyses of distribution the paradigm should not be "the gift," but rather "the share." Distribution results not from generosity, but the acknowledgment of a rightful share and "the Commons" (p. 176). However, as Bonner shows (see Chapter 2), ideas of return, rights to shares, and common ownership go hand in hand in some versions of Islam (also see Tuğal 2016b for Christianity).
13 Also note that American scholars were more likely to hail the rise of the "third sector" as a positive turn, whereas many European academics interpreted it as the reproduction of a nineteenth-century conservative tendency (Seibel and Anheier 1990, p. 8).

14 The pinnacle of this neoliberalization was the emergence of "venture philanthropy" (in the late 1990s US), which explicitly transferred practices and values of venture capitalism to the philanthropy world (Moody 2008).
15 Appropriation of this term for inegalitarian purposes had certainly happened before (Cornwall and Brock 2005, p. 1046), but perhaps not in this thoroughly global and systematic way.
16 Lori Allen (2013, pp. 3–4, 17, 72 and *passim*) has analyzed quite similar outcomes of the increasing market-orientation, "professionalization" and depoliticization of human rights efforts, which have arguably resulted in a veritable "industry" and lucrative careers for activists in Palestine rather than improvement in the lives of Palestinians.
17 Here, I am referring to the new institutionalism in organizational studies as developed by DiMaggio, Powell, and Meyer rather than all new frameworks that take institutions seriously. The label is sometimes overstretched to include Bourdieusian and Foucaultian scholarship (e.g. Campbell and Pedersen 2001, p. 2).
18 The development of a charitable culture, new institutionalists argue, occurs through charitable professionals' interpretations of uncertain situations. While this is a valid point, it downplays how these professionals themselves are shaped by the global processes referred to above (Galaskiewicz 1985, pp. 640–641).
19 Resistance to venture philanthropy comes into the picture only as pre-1990s philanthropy's resistance to the most aggressive business practices transferred to the philanthropy world (Moody 2008, p. 336).
20 This is a blanket statement and there are new institutionalist scholars who study the historical making of neoliberalism. However, they do so through incorporating historical institutionalism and other non-phenomenological approaches (for an example, see Campbell 1998).
21 Moody states: "Venture philanthropy is part of a larger documented trend at this time in the nonprofit sector toward adopting and adapting business practices and concepts, a trend supported by the legitimacy of business in general ... Indeed ... the connection with pro-business values ... provides 'moral legitimacy' ... for certain new nonprofit practices. Entrepreneurialism is perhaps the most highly valued of these business-related notions in America."
22 Moody (2008, pp. 347–348) in fact recognizes that his explanations are based on the explanations of the practitioners.
23 For a comprehensive overview and criticism, see Fligstein 2008.
24 Vogel sets up an easy dichotomy between those who romanticize civil society as resistance and her own argument, which takes it as an extension of American-business culture. But as will be seen, much in civil society is both and neither ... many associations contain a bewildering mixture of many conflicting dispositions, as nurtured by (in our case, charitable) fields.
25 See Tuğal (2016c) for further discussion of this argument.
26 E.g. see Harvey (2005, pp. 76, 168, 177, 203 and *passim*; but see p. 183).
27 For an elaborate discussion of the concept "articulation," see de Leon et al. (2015).

2

THE GENEALOGY OF ISLAMIC AND CHRISTIAN ETHICS

From Renunciation and Redistribution to Interdependence

The following two chapters trace the genealogy of liberal charitable ethics. Christian transformations on the continent paved the way for a liberalized charity. But the major liberal innovations in charitable ethics and practice occurred in the Anglophone world towards the end of the nineteenth century. The rise of the welfare state sidelined these innovations for a century. The distinctiveness of our age lies not only in the revival of these ethics and practices, but in their increasing predominance in the Anglophone world and beyond. Nevertheless, the overall liberalization throughout the centuries did not follow a straight path; rather, competition between (and within) religious and nonreligious fields challenged and reconstructed it at every turn. Muslims and Christians drew on multiple and overlapping cultural frameworks to negotiate, embrace, or resist liberalization.

We will trace the contours of this story by focusing on the following questions: How did the ethics of charity shift within Christian history? In what ways is Anglo-American charitable ethics today an inheritor of that history? Does the current American charitable ethics (and organization) show the way to charity in the rest of the world? Is there a standardized neoliberal ethics of giving that can spread (to the non-Christian world too) through "isomorphic" processes? These two chapters will argue that there is indeed a model that can spread (even if that model is still contested in the US); yet, it does not do so through isomorphism but *selective adaptation*. Whereas new institutionalist theory assumes that Western culture (epitomized by American individualism) single-handedly diffuses throughout the world, struggles over the refashioning of the charitable subject show that both Christians and Muslims still actively *make* charity (but their impact is also shaped by field structures, which are themselves influenced by political struggles and uneven, global economic development).

Even though the changes through the centuries under scrutiny could be summarized with a single word (such as liberalization), these chapters will point out that elements of liberalization, rationalization, and secularization have to be differentiated from each other. My differentiation is guided by a couple of key questions: to what degree can these changes be captured as a progression from an ethics of interdependence to one of self-reliance? How has this transformation interacted with the overall rationalization of charity (and with secularization)? Is Anglo-American charity a unique trendsetter in these regards or is it simply swept up in the world's inevitable rationalization?

The aim of this comparative historical analysis is to demonstrate a unifying spirit of the age (self-reliance, "responsibilization"), its genealogy and causes,[1] while still drawing attention to some important differences between and within Christianity and Islam. These differences are neither residual nor exclusively due to cultural uniqueness and singularity. They are rather the results of field structures. The historicization in these two chapters has a double purpose. First, through showing how the still vibrant cultures of Christianity and Islam shape charitable ethics, it aims to cast a doubt on standardization accounts. Second, by integrating Islam and Christianity into *an uneven and combined world history of ethical reform* (and showing their shared contributions and resistances to liberalization), it rejects the exclusive attention to uniqueness. The genealogy provided here can only be suggestive (as a complete history of the global making of the liberal charitable subject would require not only deeper explorations of Islamic and Christian history, but also forays into Hindu, Confucian, Judaic, and Buddhist ethics). Nevertheless, the genealogy is essential to the understanding of the four ethnographic chapters, since the organizations in question are transfused by the traces of the Christian and Islamic (as well as secular) aspects of this global history. This double problematization requires us to walk through the historical junctures where Christian and Muslim ethics of interdependence and renunciation were produced, undone, and remade in response to changing social circumstances.

Chapter 2 starts us off on this task by focusing on pre-modern Christianity and Islam. It portrays the ruptures that led to the crystallization of an ethics of interdependence in both religions, despite their less similar beginning points (renunciative redistribution vs. bellicose redistribution). When it comes to generosity, there are apparently insurmountable theological differences between Christianity and Islam. For instance, in Christianity, giving to others is (apparently) not obligatory. Nor is it regulated by certain ratios. Some of my Muslim interviewees also brought up these issues to demonstrate the "superiority" of Islam to Christianity. But how did these differences develop? Historians show that the "orthodox" Christian position on giving was contested at every turn. We can appreciate this complexity by studying how the ethics of giving in early Christianity gradually metamorphosed into a charitable orthodoxy in the Middle Ages.

Early Christianity: the Ethic of Renunciation Dissipated

Jesus is reported to have encouraged rich members of the community to spend all of their wealth to help the poor, so that they could lead properly Christian lives. The precise nature of this injunction is open to interpretation, not least because versions differ on the exact quotation. According to Luke (18:22), a rich man approached Jesus and (after affirming his observance of the Ten Commandments) asked what more he should do to inherit eternal life; "When Jesus heard this, he said to him, 'You still lack one thing. Sell everything you have and give to the poor, and you will have treasure in heaven. Then come, follow me'." Matthew's version (19:21), however, is slightly different ("Jesus answered, 'If you want to be perfect, go, sell your possessions and give to the poor, and you will have treasure in heaven. Then come, follow me.'"). While the latter starts with a conditional ("if you want to perfect"), the former does not.

In the Acts of the Apostles, Christ's followers are pictured as living a commune life (2:45, 4:32), where all of the property is shared (though the historical accuracy of these depictions is challenged, see Kyrtatas 1987). The voluntary aspect of this giving does not imply that there were no sanctions at all. The sanctions were spiritual and communal rather than coercive (in the secular sense of the term): those who did not spend all of their wealth were threatened by divine punishment (on this earth and in the hereafter) (Laniado 2009). Moreover, as the story of the Young Rich Man demonstrates, those who did not follow the advice had to leave the community. The absence of legal force behind Christian giving seems to be partially due to Christians' lack of access to military force at that time.

Even though historical evidence is sparse, it suggests that these tendencies do not present strong parallels to modern redistributive giving (see Introduction and Chapter 7). The tendency to give away property was not inspired by a vision of a better society, but rather by a lack of interest in earthly well-being, which resulted from a conviction in the imminence of the end of time (Kyrtatas 1987, p. 40). Some early Christians, in other words, generously diminished not only their overall wealth (as can happen in communitarian ways of giving) but even their class distinction, not simply out of a concern for the poor, but out of disinterest in prosperity. Parallels to some Hindu and Sufi traditions of renunciation are telling: what drives generosity is a disinterest in the things of this earth, rather than a concern with fostering community or redistribution. This disposition to generosity can be labeled an "ethics of renunciation."

Such tendencies of renunciation, however, were feeble. As Christianity spread to the cities in its first century, they gave way to "allegorical" readings of Jesus's injunction to spend away one's property (Kyrtatas 1987, pp. 90, 177–179). By the fourth century, charitable expectations were further relaxed. Only "heretic" sects expected their members to give away all of their wealth (Laniado 2009). However, we call some of these sects heretical only in hindsight. Up until the fifth century, it was not yet crystal clear who truly represented the essence of Christian giving.

***

According to historian Peter Brown, the decisive battles over giving in Western Rome were fought between 350 and 550. By 350, Christian ethics of generosity were already fused with Roman traditions, despite vigorous attempts to differentiate them. Whereas Roman giving mostly consisted of gift exchange among the upper classes, Christians made a special point of reaching out to the poor (who were mostly anonymous receivers until then). This outreach (which was partially inspired by Christianity's Judaic roots but definitively solidified due to attempts at spiritual distinction from Roman society) required sacrifices upper-class Romans were not accustomed to. While this attempt at distinction unified the Christians, the exact meaning they attributed to wealth and giving divided them.

These divides ultimately laid the groundwork for medieval Christianity's departure from the early Christian understanding of giving. Despite many differences among early Christians, one assumption was more or less shared: The existence of the wealthy and the poor was an unavoidable "sin" we had to live with. It was not something to be cherished, since it was a reminder of humanity's big Fall (from a sinless condition where everything was shared). This common understanding was troublesome for the increasing number of rich converts to Christianity in the fourth century. What is more, the turn of the fifth century witnessed the further radicalization of this common understanding. This necessitated an intervention in order to keep the rich loyal to the Church.

St. Ambrose's teachings exemplify how the shared understanding turned into a criticism of wealth at the end of the fourth century. A grain and gold, boom and bust economy characterized that era. Landlords hoarded grain and converted it to gold. They further expanded their treasures through combining the power of office with the power of land (via semi-forced labor, tax collection, and other abuses). Ambrose and others were no longer content with calling the rich to denounce their *existing* wealth: they became active criticizers of the *accumulation of wealth itself*. Since wealth was based on expropriation, almsgiving became a duty. Ambrose forcefully stated (Brown 2012, p. 133):

> It is not anything of yours that you are bestowing on the poor; rather, you are giving back something of theirs. For you alone are usurping what was given in common for the use of all. The earth belongs to everyone, not to the rich.[2]

Ambrose was not simply responding to his times, but to the field of religious forces as well. Pagan priests faulted Christianity (which resulted in "the flight of the gods") for famine and other aspects of Roman decline. By locating the cause of decline in secular processes ("avarice" of the rich), Ambrose was waging a fight against Christianity's clerical enemies.

Ambrose's tone was a departure from more peaceful calls to the rich, but others further radicalized the criticism. Pelagian writings, especially *De diviitis* (*On Riches*,

AD 408–414), were mostly concerned with the sinfulness of *all* wealth (due to its criminal origins) and therefore the need to give it up. A key Pelagian text, *De vita Christiana*, even argued that it is better not to give alms if they come from sinful wealth (Brown 2012, pp. 310–318).

St. Augustine, arguably the initiator of the Middle Ages in the religious/charitable field, was confronted with these ideas after Rome was sacked in 410 and the Pelagian figures escaped to re-settle in North Africa. He was appalled by the Pelagians' redistributive tone, partially because his social justice concerns were based on a different interpretation of the social universe (than that in Rome). His North African world was not one of rich and poor, but of patrons and friends. He was not interested in redistribution, but upward mobility. He perceived the world as one of tightly knit patron-client communities, rather than as a big social unit divided into the haves and have-nots (Brown 2012, pp. 154–156).

Even when St. Augustine perceived any serious division between the rich and the others, it was between the "rich" officeholders and tax collectors versus the vulnerable "paupers." Both were distinct from the poor (in the sense of destitute people). The "paupers" were defined as those who could be "impoverished" by tax collectors and officeholders. Consequently, his criticism was not directed against the rich's wealth, but against the way they used it. Being extremely rich was not bad, if it was not paralleled by arrogance (a cornerstone of pre-modern ethics, both in Islam and Christianity, as much as its contemporary reproducers like Qaradawi, see Chapter 3). His *City of God* was defined by the unity of the rich and others. He wanted to get rid of pride, not inequality (Brown 2012, pp. 343–350).

St. Augustine's preaching transformed the understanding of giving. The two existing extremes until his times were total renunciation of wealth or ("Roman"-style) giving with an eye on one's glory. St. Augustine rather thought that people should give all the time, *but* in small amounts, since life was so full of sin that you had to fight its temptations through constant vigilance (aided by prayer and almsgiving). The rich embraced this new ideal as a way to both retain and purify their property. St. Augustine's interpretation came as a life vest for the rich against the preachings of Pelagius and his followers, who argued that the rich should give up all of their property in order to be able to enter paradise.[3]

The crystallization of St. Augustine's position as *the* Christian position demonstrates that charitable ethics develop not through simple diffusion (or domination, or singularity, or communitarianism), but through *differentiation*. The example here is the development of St. Augustine's position against the Pelagians. Yet, in order to get institutionalized as a social imaginary, such a distinction has to speak to broader social struggles. This is in line with Bourdieu's field analysis, but the link to broader social struggles is actively built, rather than automatically springing up from Bourdieusian "homology." Emperors and (after the breakup of Empire) the new nobility weighed in to functionalize and standardize St. Augustine's ethics. These political interventions pre-assumed a certain victory and crystallization within the religious field: without St. Augustine's position-taking, the power holders would not be able to instrumentalize charity for their (emergent) medieval purposes. To better understand St. Augustine's position, we should not handle it as the imaginative work of one great Christian, but rather as an imaginative position-taking in a field populated by competing Christians. St. Augustine's charitable ethics make sense only in their differentiation from St. Ambrose's less relentless critique of wealth; Christian-"heretic" revolts;[4] and Pelagians as the radicalizers of anti-wealth positions. It is with this clerical intervention in the religious/charitable field (and its "hegemonic" instrumentalization by the new upper-class) that the Middle Ages truly took off.[5]

★★★

In sum, voluntary poverty ceased to be the defining ethics of Christianity. The main turning point was the conversion of many rich people in the fourth century. This novelty created, for the first time in history, the possibility of a fully Christian society. But it also came as a challenge, due to the injunction to give to the poor (which the rich of ancient times were not used to, as their understanding of generosity was restricted by their own circles, and the beauty and honor of the city). Christians resolved this challenge between 370 and 430 (Brown 2012, p. 528). They came to accept wealth accumulation as an unavoidable sin, and—like all other sins in Catholic-Orthodox Christianity[6]—one which could be only mitigated rather than eradicated. (The borrowing of the Judaic notion that alms could cancel sins proved helpful here.) Already in the third century, the accommodationism of the church towards wealth and sin had resulted in expansive practices of charity, which also went hand in hand with this organization's expansionist impetus (Brown 1997, pp. 30–32); but only the momentous geopolitical economic changes of the fourth and fifth centuries[7] (as well as decisive changes within the religious field) enabled these charitable acts to become game changers. As the Roman aristocracy collapsed, the late fifth century witnessed the rise of the church as a wealthy and powerful institution (mostly thanks to practices of giving and to feelings of community). Christians (almost completely) abandoned radical critiques of wealth and started to emphasize how riches could be used to build strong communities (Brown 2012, pp. 529–530).

The ethics of renunciation was defeated, but did not disappear. Even though there were strong political and clerical attempts to confine charity to the church, brotherhoods and other lay organizations engaged in sustained and complex forms of generosity throughout the Middle Ages, many of them shaped by the legacy of voluntary poverty. By the thirteenth and fourteenth centuries, European political authorities accepted and regulated (rather than fought against) lay organizations of charity (Pullan 1994). The standardized medieval charitable ethics (which I will further analyze below) did not spell the end of internal tensions and gradual change.

Early Islam: Regulating the Bellicose-Redistributive Tendencies

Islam has arguably emerged as a religion of giving and receiving.[8] Trade and merchant capitalism had created immense wealth differences (but not an increase in absolute poverty) among Arabs in the century that preceded Muhammad. This resulted, not simply in immiseration, but in the lack of social protection and the undermining of connections between the impoverished and the better off.[9] Due to the harsh conditions of the Peninsula, the Arabs had always known absolute poverty, but the first historical record of the emergence of a distinct social category regarding deprivation ("the poor" as a class) shortly predates the emergence of Islam.

The Islamic response to merchant wealth did not develop in a religious void, but built on the Judeo-Christian heritage. The roots of the two key words for benevolence in Islam (*zakat* and *sadaqa*) are to be found in Semitic languages. Related words were used for purity/purifying oneself and almsgiving (in the case of zakat) and honesty (in the case of sadaqa) in this heritage (Bashear 1993; Singer 2008, p. 4).[10] However, the exact links between these usages and their appropriation by early Islam is a matter of controversy (Bonner 2003, p. 18), partially because there is scant reliable research on the *practice* of early Jewish "sedaka" itself (Singer 2002, pp. 22–23, 177). The most institutionalized form of sadaqa (the endowment, see below) also had precedents in Jewish, Byzantine, (pre-Islamic) Arabic, and Sassanid culture (Çizakça 2000; Weber 1978). Still, whatever the exact roots of these practices and meanings, Islam put a definitively new spin on them and developed original forms (Singer 2002, pp. 24–25), perhaps most significantly by rendering *some* giving obligatory and *strictly codifying* it.

Even though later Islamic law sharply differentiated between zakat (obligatory giving) and sadaqa (voluntary giving), in early law there was a slippage between the two: eighth and ninth century ulama (religious scholars) sometimes used them interchangeably (Lev 2007, p. 605). In classical or early Islam too, the differentiation was tenuous (Bonner 2003, p. 15). One Qur'anic passage (9:60) specifically calls the alms tax *sadaqat* (in the plural) and historians have noted many other ambiguous or contradictory passages (Bonner 2005, pp. 395–396).

Due to many such ambiguities, there is substantial disagreement in regards to how we should understand the basic Islamic sources on poverty. There are two major approaches. In the juristic equivalent of (the social scientific) communitarian accounts (see Chapter 1), property was seen as legitimate only to the degree that it met certain religious and communal conditions. In this sense, "private property," in the free market sense of the term, did not exist in early Islam (Kochuyt 2009, p. 100). Zakat aimed to "homogenize" the community. It also made sure that people would not be left to their own devices in matters of survival (Kochuyt 2009, p. 105). These points underline the non-liberal assumptions of this understanding of good works.

Thierry Kochuyt (2009) argues that the zakat relationship in Islam resembles Mauss's gift relationship: the rich have taken their wealth from God, and they are obligated to spend it to form the community of believers. Wealth is seen as neither the result of predestination (as in Calvin's thought), nor of hard work (as in later Calvinism and Puritanism): it is God's *gift*. Unlike in Mauss, though, the reciprocal relationship does not consist of a dyad, but a triad. God gives, and expects not only prayers, but affection for the poor and community formation in return. The wealthy give, and anticipate heaven and increased wealth. The poor receive, and pay back with gratitude. Even though this "communitarian" account is a plausible interpretation of how Islamic scholars perceived charity after the third century of Islam, it is dubious that this perception characterized the first century.

Both contemporary Islamists and outside observers have also come up with redistributive interpretations of the basic texts: Early Islam introduced a circular economy of paupers and warriors and was staunchly against the establishment of a rich class. The rich were supposed to impoverish themselves through constant giving and follow this up by amassing wealth through conquest. Whereas mainstream accounts emphasize the identity of the Prophet as a merchant, these accounts point out that he subordinated trade activities to war and redistribution. He was a rebel who fought against the merchant class from which he descended and threatened to demolish it *as a class*, but not the activity of trade itself.

Michael Bonner's more recent work has thoroughly developed this interpretation. Sadaqa is used in three basic senses in the Qur'an, Bonner holds: almsgiving and taxes; purification of property; circulation of property.[11] Sadaqa constitutes "good circulation" as distinct from bad circulation, *riba* (which did not have a strong commercial meaning back then, but was rather used in the sense of *gift exchange among the rich*). The Qur'an points out that good circulation will put a community on the right path and bad circulation will destine it for hellfire. Good circulation is based on the idea that in all surplus wealth (*fadl*) the poor have a right (*haqq*). If this right is not returned and the wealth not purified, all will suffer here and in the hereafter (Bonner 2005, pp. 397–398, 402–405).

Some of Bonner's work draws on these interpretations, but takes a more critical stance to argue that Islam restored the pre-market ethics of "good birth" and generosity. It appealed to the warriors (in their alliance with the downtrodden) whose status had been shaken. Seen from this angle, the redistributive aspects of charity look less like revolutionary interventions in a marketizing society than attempts to restore the aristocracy. According to the revolutionary interpretation, warrior charity was a self-marginalizing protest against corrupt wealth. In the critical perspective, warrior charity aimed at a restoration of "shawbuckling heroes" of the pre-Islamic era.[12]

The indeterminacy of the basic Qur'anic concepts for charity had much to do with this earlier *fluidity of practice*.[13] Charity's later institutionalization restored class balances, which had been shaken by the emergence of Islam. When, and how, sadaqa came to be differentiated as charity, and zakat as one of the pillars of Islam, is a matter of scholarly controversy. While Islamic scholars believe that Qur'an and Hadith are very clear on this issue, a long tradition within Orientalism contests the claim. Some post-Orientalist scholars also hold that zakat and sadaqa were not strictly separated from taxes and fines during the Prophet's lifetime. Consequently, there was resistance (especially among the Bedouins) when the caliphs after Muhammad attempted to collect zakat. Zakat and sadaqa, initially, tended to be fines paid for the purification of sins, not charity (Bashear 1993, pp. 93–99). Other Western scholars have questioned these criticisms and found support for the Islamic scholarly view. In any case, if there was serious controversy over the obligatory nature of the zakat, it was resolved by the second century of Islam (Bashear 1993, pp. 109–111).

After the death of Muhammad, it was not clear to whom Muslims should hand zakat and sadaqa. The caliphs Abu Bakr and 'Umar fought wars to collect them. Interestingly, 'Umar is reported to voice doubt, lending his voice to other opponents, when Muhammad first mentioned zakat as a condition of being a Muslim: how could people inherit anything under such conditions? What kind of property would they be allowed to possess? Two answers are attributed to the Prophet: people would be made to pay the zakat in order to purify the rest of their property (which lends more credibility to the domination accounts of giving, see Chapter 1); and that the best form of property is a tongue to admonish God, a heart to thank him, and a wife to support one in matters of religion (which lends support to communitarian accounts). 'Umar similarly opposed Abu Bakr when the latter fought the *ridda* wars, but was then convinced that, just as Bakr held, zakat could not be separated from (the Islamic prayer) *salat* (Bashear 1993, pp. 102–104).

The problems that tortured early Christians were thus reproduced in a new context. How could property be protected when the new ethics invited (or forced) the believer to renounce (or redistribute) it? How could the wealthy hold on to class privilege? It might be true (as Weber, Huntington, and many others have emphasized) that Islam was (at least *initially*) differentiated from Christianity from the beginning due to its emphasis on war. Still, this should not hide the fact that the renunciation-redistribution of property was central to both religions, which points to a common sensibility. We need to re-think the peacefulness or bellicosity of each in this context: whereas property redistributors were unarmed in one religion, they were armed in the other. Restoration took divergent paths due to this crucial difference, but in each case involved the taming of the initially more disruptive ethics.

The consolidation of the upper class went hand in hand with reclassifications of the subordinate strata. In the first two centuries of Islam, there was ample debate on who was eligible to receive charity. The differentiation between certain terms in the Qur'an (e.g. *fuqara* and *masakin*) was not clear, which led to disagreements among scholars (Mattson 2003, p. 32).

According to some scholars, the distinction between the deserving (*mustahiqqun*) and undeserving poor can be traced to the first centuries of Islam. There was even a control of the travelling poor through *tadhkira* (a visa that allowed only the deserving poor to enter cities). This practice was occasionally dropped and then revived throughout the centuries, up till late Ottoman times (Ener 2003, pp. 8–9). Women, widows, orphans, Sufis, and clerics were perceived as more deserving. Able-bodied men, men without kin or other connections, and people not able to find others to vouch for their morality came to be the undeserving poor.

However, other scholars have contested such accounts of sharp differentiation between the deserving and undeserving poor in early Islam. Bonner (1996) draws attention to two schools of legal thought, one that differentiated between the poor along these lines (and put a lot of value in patience), and the other that saw charity as an entitlement (independent of the *willingness* to work). These schools drew on different sets of *'ahadith* (plural of Hadith). Many 'ahadith pictured the Prophet as living the poor and modest life because he constantly gave away whatever he had; he also encouraged the rich to do so. These 'ahadith were averse to the production of goods: legitimate property came from outside the community (through war). The rich were supposed to impoverish themselves; the poor would thereby become rich, but then also impoverish themselves. In this "radical" juristic tradition, there was no differentiation between the active and passive poor, as there was in ancient Greek culture. The poor were classified in terms of whether they were convertible to Islam. Once they were in the community as Muslims and warriors, their property started circulating along with everybody else's (Bonner 1996, pp. 339–341).

According to the conservative juristic interpretation, by contrast, there was a solid poverty line, above which nobody should receive charity. The poor were defined based on what they owned, not their relation to Islam and war. The same Hadith tradition also specified that the poor should know their place: the deserving poor were those who did not beg. This juristic tradition also emphasized distribution of charity by the community itself (rather than the imam) (Bonner 1996, p. 342).[14]

Islam reached a consistent logic of giving only after the competing benevolent tendencies were brought under one orthodox roof. The next section explores medieval Christianity's institutionalization of charity (and of conceptions of poverty), which will further enable us to discuss the parallels to and differences from the Islamic institutionalization. In both cases, more dynamic fields in early religion gave way to standardized and monopolized fields during the process of institutionalization, though challenges persisted. Monopolization of charitable ethics, we will see, also went hand in hand with its class-driven instrumentalization.

Medieval Christianity: The Restricted Institutionalization of Communitarian Giving

As Bronislaw Geremek, the prominent historian of medieval charity, points out, modern people assume that poverty is "a bad thing." In the Middle Ages, however, it had a saintly face. This started to change in fourteenth-century Europe, and more so after the sixteenth (Geremek 1994, pp. 6–7). An analysis of the undoing of the poor's saintliness requires a sense of the overall, ambiguity- and tension-ridden features of the charitable framework that glorified poverty.

Before we reach any generalizations regarding medieval communitarian ethics (which reached its full maturity by the eleventh and twelfth centuries), let us take a quick look at the gradual changes from the early Middle Ages onwards. According to historians, the major contours set by the fifth and sixth centuries did not radically change, but gradually metamorphosed. The reason for this slow change was the scarcity of cash from the sixth to the eleventh centuries. Land was the primary, almost the only, source of wealth, which did not bode well for charity. In the Merovingian era (sixth to eighth centuries), the poor were simply crushed and barely survived. Moreover, infant death and widowhood were cross-class issues: they were not restricted to the poor. Mendicancy was widespread, as bands of the poor traveled from city to city, monastery to monastery (Mollat 1986, pp. 24–29). During the Carolingian era (ninth–eleventh centuries) too, survival was still an issue, although less so. Even the rich hardly made it through the winter. Yet, the kings became more aware of their responsibilities toward the poor in this period. But then, they had to delegate this responsibility to magnates, who were eventually to become the aristocrats (pp. 34–35).

Under these conditions of (power and wealth) fragmentation, clerical power—which was institutionalized in the fifth and sixth centuries—remained central to welfare provision. A fixed amount of all bishops' revenues (one fourth, but one third in the rural areas) were allocated for poverty relief, though extracting this wealth from the bishops was not always a smooth affair. Bishops' residences became equivalent to poorhouses. They were not required to give their personal wealth to the poor, but some did (to the extent of indebting themselves to do so). The bishops combined the (declining) Roman poor registration system with the dictates of the Gospels. This constituted not simply a theological, but an organizational change: during the seventh century, the poor list (a remainder of the Roman times) effectively merged with the bishop's poor house, and both came to be associated with rural monasteries (in contrast to urban-centered Roman poverty). During the eighth and ninth centuries, some of this wealth became lay property, which invited friction between clerics and the ex-churchwardens, who had severed their links to the monasteries and the poor (Mollat 1986, pp. 38–42).

Against this trend of secularization (which some Christians perceived as abuse), the most common reaction was the further protection of church monopoly of wealth and charity. Only a few among the clergy perceived the dangers of such clerical concentration. On the part of orthodoxy, the more common resolution was to envision a just king who would imitate the charity of the church in the secular realm. This consensual orientation led to the persistence of fifth and sixth century themes throughout the ninth and tenth centuries: poverty was created so that the rich could redeem their sins; the rich existed to protect the poor, and the poor to serve the rich (Mollat 1986, pp. 43–45).

In short, from the early to the mature Middle Ages, we see very few field-like qualities in charity provision. Gone were the colorful, imaginative controversies that bred figures such as Ambrose, Augustine, and Pelagius. This corrosion was due to several factors, including the scarcity of money and the predatory-rentier nature of secularization-marketization (rather than a rational and sustainable one). As a culmination of these trends, Christians took charity as a universal value; it was central to creating bonds in society. The ethics that guided the major charitable institutions were quite similar in Islam's middle period and medieval Christianity. Collective ownership and use by the religious community were at the origins of both church and institutionalized sadaqa (*waqf*, of which more below). Charity returned to the community what was God's right (and therefore, his flock's due) (Othman 1983). Even if occasionally collected (and disposed of) by individuals, the needs of the community determined (in theory) the right kind of use of charitable money.

Medieval Classifications

The cherished ("communitarian") interdependence between the rich and poor should not obscure medieval Christianity's occasionally quite harsh invectives against the poor. The harshness was based on a unique classification of the downtrodden (populated by partially overlapping categories such as the voluntary poor, the shamefaced poor, the honest and dishonest involuntary poor, and beggars). Voluntary poverty never became a value preached to the working masses. According to Christianity, their abandoning of work would be a sign of pride rather than humility. Life of the early Christian communities became the model for eremitic and monastic life. The voluntary poor sold all of their possessions. Such was the ethos of poverty from the second century to the eleventh and twelfth centuries, in spite of all attacks and dissipation.

When trade developed in the eleventh and twelfth centuries, voluntary poverty came to be perceived as "a rejection of the new social structures" (Geremek 1994, pp. 21–23). The church could no longer tolerate it. The creation of church-sanctioned mendicant orders was a way of taming such tendencies of social protest. Just like the ethos of poverty in the first millennium, the ethos among the *approved* mendicant orders sanctioned *and* controlled wealth, as well as its renunciation.

Medieval Christianity had a complex approach to the involuntary poor too. The churches distinguished people able to work from other involuntary poor (the Reformation's perception that church doctrines directly encouraged idleness is not correct). Christians grew highly jaded also due to the professionalization of begging (Geremek 1994, pp. 49–52). By the twelfth century, many had started to question whether beggars' prayers for the donors would count (Geremek 1994, pp. 47–48). Still, in spite of all misgivings, for centuries society could allow people to feed off charity (Geremek 1994, pp. 16–18). This did not become a problem for a long time.

The major brotherhoods, however, helped mostly the "shamefaced poor": those who were embarrassed of their poverty because of their noble origins. In other words, one kind of charity was actually an expression of upper-class solidarity. When other poor people were helped, even the honest ones were seen mostly as *objects* of charity. The emphasis was on the provider of charity in these cases (as distinct from charity intended for the shamefaced poor) (Geremek 1994, p. 24). Heartfelt communitarianism had a heartless underside.

The Late Middle Ages: The Threshold of Another World

From the twelfth to the fourteenth centuries, poverty came to be more directly associated with the lower classes. In the twelfth century, there were strong calls to provide aid to the honest, kin, old, and humble poor and carefully distinguish them from the dishonest, stranger, young, and arrogant poor. The *exaltation* of poverty had conflicted with its partial association with the lower class throughout the Middle Ages. But these transformations (and more precise classifications) sharpened the conflict (Geremek 1994, pp. 26–27).

The rise of mendicant orders, which marked the beginnings of the second millennium, became a core concern for the Church. This revivalist rise of voluntary poverty was in part a protest against the clergy's concentration of wealth. But the Church itself kept on sanctifying poverty, in part as a warning against the new wealthy (now concentrated in the towns). The Church did not intend to reject wealth, though, and only wanted to warn against sin—which, in the eyes of orthodoxy, frequently accompanied increasing wealth (Geremek 1994, pp. 32–35).

The twelfth century is a turning point in Mollat's account of medieval charity and poverty, as much as in Geremek's. A French expert of the era, Mollat points out that monastic practices of charity started to be clearly insufficient. Due to growing cities, famines, wars, and epidemics, the number of the poor exploded. As a result, there was a new charitable movement within the established clergy too (not just among mendicant orders). Pastors started to actively go out and seek the poor, rather than waiting for them to come to the monastery. Charity became an active part of life (Mollat 1986, pp. 87–90). Finally, merchants emerged as a third category of donors, rivaling the monasteries and the aristocracy (pp. 95–96).

The explosion of poverty and riches during the twelfth century made charity one of the highest concerns of theology. We therefore start to see the emergence of dynamic field structures of clerical (as well as lay religious) positions on charity. Just like in the marketizing fourth and fifth centuries, theologians were confronted with massive protests and movements of the poor. As a result, the rich were questioned, attacked, incited to charity intensely; and "sociological" sensibilities got much sharper. Theologians envisioned a new social order, in which everybody would fulfill a function and therefore merit respect.

Most notably, St. Francis (d. 1226) signaled a new kind of attention to the dignity of the pauper. This went beyond the traditional, merely spiritual dignity, which took the poor person as an embodiment of Christ, but failed to really explore his/her material situation. St. Francis and his contemporaries were in more intimate contact with the poor and strove to develop an empathetic ("secularized") understanding (Mollat 1986, pp. 156–157).

Despite this turn in theology, the poor were not treated much differently in practice; most persisted in their misery (Mollat 1986, pp. 102–113). Moreover, the basic hierarchical and contemptuous undertones of charity did not budge much. Poverty was still considered a necessary evil and an opportunity for the salvation of the rich. Even the teachings of St. Francis had a tone of pity. Mollat documents only one Dominican figure who goes beyond this hierarchical theology. The rest of the documents he studied from the era signaled an extremely hierarchical understanding, which shaped non-clerical sources as well. As reflected in one of the most read romances of the thirteenth century, the thinking of the era advocated almsgiving, but it assumed that the poor should work and die (in war) more than the rich and pay deference to them (Mollat 1986, pp. 189–190). Institutions reflected this too. The thirteenth and fourteenth centuries experienced a boom in charitable institutions, but the latter had little recognition that their clientele had changed: they neglected the special case of the working poor and treated all cases as the quintessential poor (who exist to serve almsgiving). Ultimately, in spite of Franciscan and other attempts to give communitarian charity a distributive bent, the rise of Thomas Aquinas (d. 1274) as the primary Christian theologian reproduced medieval charity's hierarchical underpinnings.

★★★

Throughout the centuries, then, the fallen and voluntary poor were always differentiated from the genuine, "involuntary" poor (those poor by birth). Nevertheless, the genuine poor were also occasionally honored due to their physical resemblances to the voluntary poor. Believers thought they saw a touch of Christ in their appearance (Geremek 1994, p. 36). Difficulties of classification filled the medievals with doubt regarding how much of the poor population was really a part of the community of Christians.

These ambiguities and internal tensions already attested to some rationalization and individualization within medieval ethics (as well as an undertone of renunciation, and even less so, redistributive bents to communitarianism). Therefore, the rise of commercial capitalism after the fourteenth century (and ultimately the Protestant Reformation) did not create the liberal charitable subject from scratch, but had some preliminary elements to work with. The Catholic/secular experiments of the mid-fourteenth through sixteenth centuries (poor shelters, control over vagabonds, forced labor for wanderers, Mollat 1986, pp. 290–292) paved the way for the Reformation. As Chapter 3 will show, further religious and political economic developments would ultimately marginalize communitarianism. Nevertheless, remnants of the medieval ethics of interdependence are still with us today and enter into "assemblages" with unexpected elements to mount resistances against liberalism.

Islam's Middle Period and Its (Variegated) Communitarian Ethics

There is no exact equivalent of medievalism in Islam (Varisco 2007). Some scholars have used another term ("the middle period") for Islamic history, frequently taking Turkic invasions as the end of early Islam. Here, based on strong *charitable* parallels between Islam and Christianity, I take the first moves towards the formation of communitarian charity as the beginning of Islam's middle period. Against established scholarly accounts that take Constantine's conversion as the definitive initiator of Europe's Christianization, Peter Brown argues that the real turning point was the mass conversion of the rich and the Augustinian institutionalization of their charitable contributions to the Church. We see as momentous a transformation in the accumulation and exchange of Islamic wealth when we look at the founding jurists' reformulation of charity, wealth, and poverty. Ibn Hanbal kicked off this era by fixing the conservative interpretation of charity and wealth as the mainstream scholarly interpretation.

The Religious Fields

Two juristic traditions had crystallized by the end of the eighth century (see above). One emphasized the rights of the poor and the circulation of poverty; the other a well-maintained balance between the rich and the poor. The goal of almsgiving in the conservative tradition was not reducing inequality, but fixing the balance between the rich and the poor. As conversion and economic decline resulted in a dramatic increase in the number of the poor, the conservative tradition gained momentum among the clergy and the upper strata. This resulted in a civil war and the siege of Baghdad (812–813), during which the urban poor fighters defended a redistributive (and quite expansionist) caliph against the merchant-backed forces. The merchant victory cleared the way for the ascending upper classes' and clergy's control of the urban poor, which culminated in broad popular support for ibn Hanbal's subsequent attack against rationalist Islam and his ultimate victory over it too in the 820s and 830s (Bonner 1996, pp. 343–344).

As in St. Augustine's intervention, ibn Hanbal and the other conservative clerics faced a flexible and dynamic religious field (rather than one single enemy condensed in a radical Hadith tradition). The conservatives had to win not only against the early/radical interpretation of Islam, as well as the ascetic ("heretic") sects at one end of the spectrum and rationalist Islam on the other, but also against many positions in between, such as clerics who toned down the radical criticism of wealth, but still argued against conservative glorifications of acquisition. A case in point is *Kitab al-Kasb*. Although this book has been traditionally interpreted as the manifesto of the rising merchant class (Gotein 1957), Bonner

(2001) shows that it rather expressed a coming to terms with expanding wealth, while at the same time remaining pro-poverty and suspicious of riches. *Kitab al-Kasb* seems to be composed of three clerics' writings. The first cleric reached a compromise between the idea of "circulation"/return and increasing merchant wealth. The second attacked Hanbalis through arguing that the poor have a right not only to surplus wealth, but even to the wealth that one uses to satisfy his family. He also argued that accumulating wealth (more than one's basic needs require) is a sign of evil. The third cleric inveighed against Islamic ascetics (who advocated not earning a living), but still took a mainly negative stance toward the accumulation of wealth beyond one's immediate needs. The main argument of *al-Kasb*, which cut across all three contributors, was that after satisfying basic needs, the believer should direct his attention to proximity to God. Almsgiving, *al-Kasb* authors held, was a major method of approaching God. In sum, an influential body of clerics developed positions on wealth and charity that only partially departed from the radical tradition; attacked the ascetic sects (which were also under conservative attack); and criticized ibn Hanbal and his associates too. As in the Christian case, these field-specific tensions were decisive in defining the limits of the possible, but the ultimate victory of one position over the others had as much to do with broader ("hegemonic") struggles, where the merchant class imposed its ideological line on the rest of society (and the religious field).

As a result of the conservative victory, Muslims developed a quite similar ethics of interdependence (to that of Christianity), though its story of (restricted) institutionalization and rationalization mirrored that of medieval Christianity only partially. The redistributive and renunciatory resistances against Islamic communitarianism were also of a partially different nature. The *waqf* system and the controversies surrounding it were at the heart of this partial uniqueness (see further below), but as important were the state's codification of taxes and charity (see next subsection) and juristic-scholarly positions on charity.

The juristic field evolved in quite particular ways. In early Islamic law, most of the scholarly attention focused on the sustenance of community and taking immediate care of the poor's needs. The founding jurists of the major schools of jurisprudence[15] emphasized two aspects of charity. First, charity decreased tensions among the believers by preventing social polarization. Second, if distributed within the community (rather than bureaucratically collected and distributed) it took care of the poor quite efficiently, since local residents had better, immediate, experienced-based knowledge of the poor and their needs (Mattson 2003, p. 40). Prestige accumulation on the part of the wealthy, the maintenance of order, and the obedience of the poor were at the heart of orthodox prescriptions for charity.[16]

The erosion of this communitarian ethics did not happen abruptly. Jurists of the eleventh and twelfth centuries slowly shifted the focus away from the narrowing of the gaps between the rich and poor. These self-proclaimed followers of the founding jurists put more emphasis on the sustenance of order, especially *the established status of members* of the Islamic community (see the Chapter 3 for

Qaradawi's liberalized reproduction of this logic). For example, they stipulated that a jewel trader needed more charity than a vegetable seller (Mattson 2003, pp. 42–44), echoing the medieval Christian concern for the "shamefaced poor." The early conservative jurists, by contrast, had no stipulations that would fix people in their positions. The founding jurists' vision was a relatively less hierarchical version of communitarianism; their followers were communitarians all right (as they still put vigorous limits on wealth accumulation), but in a much more hierarchical way.[17]

In sum, we need to pay attention to this centuries-long *war of position* among jurists. The interpretations of how to dispense with property were stakes in a struggle, not the simple outcomes of an ahistorical ("Islamic") logic. Imperial practice introduced further complications for the reproduction of communitarian ethics.

Imperial Appropriations of Communitarianism

One component of fluctuating middle-Islamic practice was the state's relation to zakat collection. In twelfth century Egypt, (Fatimid) rulers had started to treat zakat as a straightforward tax: the money collected from the rich went to the state treasury, as much as to the poor (Lev 2007, pp. 605–606). The state then used this to wage *jihad*, one of the legitimate uses of zakat as specified by the Qur'an. However, the later Egyptian dynasties (the Mamluk) strayed away from even this usage and treated zakat money as a simple tax to solidify the state, keeping the label zakat only for purposes of legitimacy (Rabie 1972). Under the relatively more pragmatic Ottomans, there was no official zakat office, but tax rates were usually based on zakat. Some key Ottoman clerics also blurred the boundaries between zakat and taxes (Singer 2008, p. 49).

Nevertheless, legitimacy concerns also tied the hands of sultans in certain ways. Mamluks, for instance, distributed food and freed slaves during major religious festivities, even in times of financial crisis (Lev 2007, p. 608). Sabra (2003) points out that the sultans could not be as pro-private property as the jurists, since they were under pressure from crowd riots. They frequently lowered market prices (especially of food) by threat or force. When this did not work, they organized the elite to distribute food.

Especially during the Ottoman Empire, food provision became one of the venues where scholarly concerns, the ethics of interdependence, and state-building intersected to reinforce inequalities. Amy Singer (2002) documents that soup kitchens distributed food to the deserving poor (those who had no family or household to support them) without attaching any stigma to receiving aid. However, the institutional setup also reinforced existing hierarchies, even those among the beneficiaries. Since the soup kitchens served traveling officials and religious scholars too, care was taken to distinguish the quality and quantity of their food, the vessels in which they were presented, and the circumstances of service (the table, the room, etc.) from those of the poor (Singer 2002, pp. 60–62). Food service unfolded in a *certain order* that further marked the hierarchies: First the notables were served, followed by the employees, then the learned poor, to be followed by the ordinary poor, and finally the female poor (pp. 63–64). Singer (2002, p. 170) states: "[Charity] did not aim to change the social order but rather to preserve it. Food distributions were not intended to help people free themselves from dependence on aid but only to succor and sustain them." Charity imposed *a just and inegalitarian world*. It aimed to foster interdependence among all ranks[18] (and the dependence of each on the Ottoman Empire). All of this attests to a very clear departure from early Islam, the warrior-charitable ethics of which disrupted rather than reinforced existing hierarchies.

Charity as (Communitarian) Development: Religious Fields and Islamic Endowments

Central to this institutionalization was the endowment system. The waqf presented the earliest signs of a "developmental" (though by no means liberal) cumulative charity in the land of Islam. Endowments enabled capital and prestige accumulation in the name of benevolence,[19] even if they did not open the door to what is today embraced as developmental philanthropy (making of entrepreneurial poor subjects and "individualization" of responsibility). This form of charity alerts us against the conflation between developmental aid and modern aid (and hence to the reduction of pre-liberal charity to non-developmental, haphazard aid), which is in high fashion in today's academy.

The word *waqf* has no Qur'anic origins, but is based on the examples set by the Prophet. It took several centuries for the practice to institutionalize and there is very little documentation on the early practice.[20] According to some sources, the first waqf was established either by the prophet Muhammad or right after him (Çizakça 2000, p. 7; Singer 2002, p. 16). *Awqaf* (pl. of waqf) seem to be widespread already after the Prophet's death, as a way of making concentrated inheritance and non-taxation possible under Islamic conditions.[21] This "double truth" of the endowment (as benevolence and wealth accumulation) again demonstrates the difficulties Muslims faced due to the disruptive ethics of redistribution and the euphemizations they had to endure in order to accumulate wealth (euphemizations that were necessitated by the emergence of a new redistributive ethics, rather than by a timeless logic of religion, as in Bourdieu).

The Ottoman controversies regarding family (or *ahli*) endowments[22] give us insights into the middle-Islamic religious field (and the ethics it fostered). Establishment of awqaf throughout Islamic history allowed rulers and elites to claim legitimacy, prevent their property from being divided or confiscated, and reinforce loyalty. However, even in the case of *awqaf ahli* (family endowments),[23] there were benefits to the poor (Ener 2003, pp. 4–5; Kuran 2001, p. 858; Singer 2002, pp. 31–32). In order to escape confiscation, the wealthy resorted to establishing endowments; yet in order to retain control of these endowments, they had to provide public goods (Kuran 2001, pp. 846–848).

The legal and scholarly controversies around the family endowment provide further demonstration that middle Islamic charitable ethics was not of one cloth: rather, the formation of this ethics attested to conflicts within the religious field. The status of legitimate property has always been one of the core points of divergence among even the top scholars (e.g. see Imam Abu Yusuf vs. Imam Hanifa). The controversy resurfaced in the Ottoman Empire again under Koçi (or Koçu) Bey (Çizakça 2000, p. 23). Koçi Bey launched an attack against family endowments by arguing that they did not serve the poor or the public. He insisted that they rather served to circumvent Islamic inheritance laws and distracted from the war making efforts of the state through withholding taxes (Singer 2002, p. 31).[24] In short, *capital accumulation through charity/benevolence has always been a tendency, but one actively fought against/for rather than passively accepted.* Just like we can talk of a "variegated" neoliberalization of charitable ethics in late modernity, we can talk of a "variegated" spread of communitarian charitable ethics in medieval and middle Islamic times. We can even construct a parallel here between pre-state communities that Pierre Clastres (1987) discusses and how they collectively kept the state at bay through active work. It seems that middle-Islamic scholars and notables were doing a similar active, collective work (but one against individualization and the market, not against the state), with the partial exception of some scholars in the Ottoman Empire.

The most market-oriented form of Islamic giving in these times was "cash endowments" (*awqaf al-nuqud*), which were most widespread in the Ottoman Empire. Unlike other endowments, these consisted of cash (rather than immovable)[25] supplies, to which even *fixed interest* (usually considered un-Islamic) was applied. Jurists deemed interest legitimate as long as it was used to pay mosque and Qur'anic teaching staff, but it frequently served the personal enrichment of administrators.

Other Islamic empires and states came to accept cash endowments by the twentieth century,[26] but they had become predominant among the Ottomans already at the end of the sixteenth century (Çizakça 2000, p. 43; Mandaville 1979). The Islamic justifications of this practice set a precedent for the theological vindication of current neoliberal practices. Leading Islamic scholars of the era legitimized this practice mostly through ignoring established opinion and resorting to intricate techniques of textual evasion (Mandaville 1979, pp. 293–297). Their main Islamic justification was based on the principles of *istihsan* (juridical preference) and *maslaha* (public interest): the scholars argued that cash endowments were good for the community. More complicated theo-legal justifications would come more than a hundred years after the practice started in the early fifteenth century (Mandaville 1979, pp. 298–299). Some Sufi lodges, the Sultan, and (a majority of) the educated elite were behind the practice. A minority of the ulama and subordinate strata fiercely resisted it as aberration from the classical texts, invitation to moral laxity and interest, injustice to orphans and the poor, and illegitimate wealth accumulation (pp. 301–306).

This important charitable practice constitutes one core proto-capitalist dynamic in pre-modern Islamic history. However, even the cash endowments did not lead to safe capital accumulation. Two questions arise: 1) To what extent could the endowments fulfill public needs and deliver on medieval Islam's communitarian promises? 2) Why didn't preliminary breaks with the ethics of interdependence lead to a more liberal or capitalistic path?

There is wide controversy about the contributions of awqaf to the poor and to the public. Timur Kuran (2001), one of the most prominent critics, argues that waqf was a highly corruptible system. It was also inflexible. The regents had to obey the initial wishes of the founder, long after his death. The system therefore failed to efficiently provide public goods. As it could not adapt to changing circumstances, it became outdated with the rise of modernity. Endowments, in sum, were poor performers in terms of both provision and capital accumulation.

Other scholars disagree with Kuran and underline the flexibility of the waqf (in terms of both provision and accumulation). Çizakça (2000 pp. 18–21) argues that especially under Hanafi law, pious endowments embodied a "certain dynamism" (p. 18) due to the condition of *istibdal* (the right to exchange an endowment for another property). Property was thus "responsive to market conditions" (p. 18). Still, the jurists stipulated conditions under which *istibdal* could be performed so as to prevent abuse (pp. 18–19). Amy Singer (2002, pp. 21–22) adds that as long as the innovations did not violate the spirit of the original founder's intent (which could be broadly re-interpreted), they were deemed Islamically acceptable.

Kuran (2001, pp. 871–872) seeks to refute these claims by pointing out that perpetuity of the founders' stipulations was the default and the managers only manipulated ambiguities. Such manipulation does not live up to Kuran's favored principle (profit maximization), which he assumes is a precondition of development. Even cash endowments do not live up to these modern standards, as the stipulations of their founders restricted future generations (in the form of ceilings to loan interests, restrictions of trade to certain localities, etc.). Moreover, cash endowments never became corporate bodies (Kuran 2001, pp. 872–875)—large entities that could exploit economies of scale: enterprise remained restricted to small businesses, built on cooperation between two to three people (Kuran 2004). While Kuran's criticisms stand on firm ground, they are all based on the fundamental assumption that there is only one way to development.

Singer's study of a prominent soup kitchen in Jerusalem sheds a different light on the issue. Singer emphasizes that waqf commodities were frequently exchanged on the market and were therefore *commodities* to an extent. However, the goal of these exchanges was the symbolic and religious aims stipulated by the founder (2002, p. 53) rather than profit maximization. The language of economic sociology allows us to re-think the subtle distinctions between the emphases of Kuran and Singer, and thereby helps resolve the debate: there was a flourishing market under high Ottoman rule, but *this market was symbolically and religiously embedded.* Since this was the case in the Christian West too (Polanyi 2001), Kuran's claims that Islam's (and the awqaf's) uniqueness lies at the root of failed development is dubious.

★★★

In sum, even though communitarian ethics and orientations predominate in academic constructions of Islam's middle period, Muslims developed strongly market-oriented ethics of charity as well. However, the institutions and morality of the times blocked the transition to a fully liberal understanding of benevolence.

The waqf, especially, became a condensation point where the pietistic, communitarian, political, and financial motivations intersected. It was core to the activities of conquering sultans who procured the blessings of the ulama. Conquest and waqf-building became irremediably linked after the tenth century, as Fatimids, Mamluks, Saljuks, Ottomans, and Safavids sought to build religious credentials against their Islamic competitors. In this imperial race, awqaf were central to creating loyal ulama (Singer 2002, pp. 26–28).

The question thus becomes why struggles over the waqf system did not culminate in a thorough liberalization comparable to the one the Christian world experienced. But to do that, we need an understanding of what the Reformation really entailed for charitable ethics. Rather than blanket statements regarding the rational and work-oriented results of the Reformation, we need to ask: did it really undermine the overall communitarian structure of medieval giving (in which case, the lack of a similar push in the Muslim world could be more readily attributed to a difference of religion)? Or did the Western world need an extra impetus from non-religious corners to decisively undermine medieval charitable ethics?

Notes

1 My approach combines Foucaultian genealogy and Bourdieusian sociogenesis, two apparently incompatible methodologies (the convergence of which I intend to discuss elsewhere).
2 Ambrose's understanding of wealth and giving exhibits strong parallels with the Islamic notion of "return" (see Michael Bonner later in this chapter).
3 This position was based on Pelagius's understanding of sin: unlike St. Augustine, he thought that after being baptized you could live a life free of sin (Brown 2012, pp. 361–365).
4 North Africa was frequently shaken by Christian poor men's revolts, which St. Augustine perceived to be heretical. Many of these revolts, such as the one in the late 340s, demanded the cancellation of debt. Many strong and poor men labored under unfavorable circumstances due to debt in the fourth century (Brown 2012, pp. 327–332).
5 The transition to the post-Empire Middle Ages did not introduce anything as revolutionary as St. Augustine's interventions, but extended and complicated them. For instance, see Brown's (2012) analysis of Salvian of the mid-fifth century; and the later monopolization of charity administration by the bishops, which had consequences that St. Augustine could not foresee.
6 The broad contours of charitable transformation in Eastern Rome were the same. Widespread "voluntary poverty" created theological and fiscal problems, such as perceived "immorality" and tax evasion (Laniado 2009, pp. 23–26). Byzantine Emperor Justinian settled these issues in the sixth century by institutionalizing "monastic poverty," which effectively banned laypeople from renouncing wealth. Less generous acts of charity became the norm. This also culminated in an imperial ethic that anticipated

Christ-like behavior from the rich and powerful, such as washing the feet of the poor and taking care of leprosy victims (Patlagean 1997).
7 For the impact of fifth-century economic changes in Eastern Rome on Eastern charity, see Patlagean 1997, pp. 18–21.
8 This interpretation dates back to Montgomery Watt (a historian of Islam who has especially emphasized the Prophet's commitment to social justice). Revisionist scholarship has attacked Watt's claims and assumptions about the importance of merchant wealth in seventh-century Arabia and the Islamic reaction to it.
9 Bonner (2003, pp. 20–25) argues that the rise of trade in late pre-Islamic times weakened war- and generosity-related values and replaced them with a glorification of wealth. The Islamic ethics of charity was a restoration of these values.
10 Classical "Orientalist" scholarship is rife with debates about how to trace these roots and where they lead (Bashear 1993). This seems to be guided by an investment in demonstrating that Islam was not "authentic." Other scholars trace the bulk of the charitable ethics of Islam to pre-Islamic Arabia itself (Bonner 2003).
11 Bonner points out one key Qur'anic verse to support his claim: "That which God has bestowed on His Messenger from the people of the towns is for God and His Messenger, and for him who is close [generally understood, to the Messenger], for the orphans, for the poor and for the traveler, lest it become something that circulates among the rich among you." (59:7).
12 Pre-Islamic Arab heroes, unlike some in the aristocracy who laid claim to a part of the war spoils, distributed all among the poor and their supporters. They thereby always remained in the ranks of the *sa'alik* (the wretched). Despite some continuity between this practice and the redistributive charity of early Islamic rebels, Islam definitively banned other aspects of pre-Muhammad potlatch, which wasted surplus wealth more via competitive feasting (*ta'aqur*), and less through "return," direct provision for the poor (Bonner 2003, pp. 24–25).
13 In other words, while conflicting strands in the scholarship have re-constructed early Islamic charity as either communitarian (Kochuyt 2009) or redistributive (Bonner), I attempt to integrate these strands: due to the fluidities, both tendencies were present in early Islam.
14 For a different interpretation, see Mattson (2003, pp. 37–39) who emphasizes juristic flexibility in definitions of neediness (rather than sharp oppositions between two traditions).
15 This characterization applies to the founders of the Maliki, Hanbali and Sha'afi schools of Sunni Islam, but not to the Hanafi. Also see Bonner 1996.
16 How did the founders of the four orthodox schools handle private property and the market? The founder of the Sha'afi school and his followers, were staunchly pro-private property and favored the market. The Maliki school and some Hanafis either had doubts about the virtues of trade or were outright against the free trade of some items (especially food). These two schools favored stricter regulations against the merchants' manipulation of prices. The Hanbalis too thought that the interests of the public were more important than those of private property holders (prices could therefore be regulated). However, according to Sabra (2003), none of them were as paternalistic as the nobles and masses of pre-liberal England as documented by E. P. Thompson (1966) (nor, for that matter, as the masses of Islam's middle period).
17 This vision would ultimately reinforce the "circle of justice" understanding of poverty and inequality, which had Persian and other local origins.
18 The soup kitchens also served as a tool of competition among the elite (Singer 2002, pp. 67–68).
19 Due to the scarcity of research, it is difficult to determine to what extent pious endowments enabled capital accumulation. Çizakça (2000, pp. 45–51) argues that even the most cash- and market-oriented endowments did not aid *productive* centralization in

the hands of entrepreneurs, but rather *distributed* capital among the well-to-do. Although endowments that granted fixed interest rates (rather than the Islamically more acceptable profit and loss sharing, *mudaraba* and *musharaka*) injected capital into the markets, this was to the benefit of the consumers (often endowment trustees) rather than the producers. This fine-grained study of awqaf seems to reinforce Weber's (1978, pp. 1095–1097) earlier generalization: the waqf—a rough equivalent of Western Christian churches, which appeared to Weber to be modeled after ancient Egyptian and Eastern Christian endowments—made large-scale accumulation impossible due to the inalienability of waqf property, its immobilization of wealth, and the subjective-arbitrary legal environment in which it was embedded.

20 The earliest legal document goes back to the late eighth or ninth centuries (Lev 2007, pp. 609–610; Singer 2002, p. 16)

21 Whereas pre-Islamic law was mostly based on primogeniture, Islam distributed inheritance among several heirs.

22 Singer (2002, pp. 31–33) among others, questions the validity of the distinction between family and charitable endowments.

23 Kuran (2001, pp. 854–857) finds the family endowments much more corruptible than the *waqf khayri* (charitable endowments). However, he also notes that both were venues of asset laundering. Exemptions and tax reductions were legion. Hence the thin boundaries between charity and capital accumulation in middle to modern Islam.

24 Çizakça (2000, pp. 24–25) still wants to argue that tendencies of personal/familial enrichment should not be exaggerated, since family endowments constituted a minority of endowments in many cases, even though there were exceptions such as Aleppo and early twentieth-century Cairo.

25 Other movables were already considered legitimate by a restricted number of earlier Hanafi scholars. The Ottoman innovation was adding cash to the list (Mandaville 1979).

26 Despite certain exceptions, the cash endowment did not become a widespread institution even in most of the Arab territories of the Ottoman Empire up till the twentieth century (Singer 2002, p. 18). Çizakça (2000, pp. 27–69) provides a detailed account of localities and jurists that have come to accept this form. Early twentieth-century Egypt, India, and Pakistan, sixteenth- and seventeenth-century Syria, and early and late twentieth-century Iran are some of the prominent cases.

3

THE WORLD HISTORICAL REVOLUTION IN ETHICS

The Dismantling of Interdependence and the Rise of the Liberal Subject

The medieval charitable ethics of interdependence—itself a contingent, ever-mutating, and contested cultural whole—was not unmade overnight. In fact, its traces are still with us today, and not simply in a passive way. It took centuries for the West to replace a new orientation to charity for this entrenched disposition. Even within the West, charitable actors still summon the ethics of interdependence to contest and restrict the new ethics. Nevertheless, the new charitable ethics of individual independence is well-established today, especially in the world leader of neoliberalization (the United States). Moreover, this ethics travels through and shapes the rest of the globe even where Westernization is apparently most resisted (the Muslim world). This chapter analyzes the long revolution through which the liberal understanding of generosity rose to prominence and weathered a few serious storms (such as the working-class challenge and the collectivist orientations of the welfare state). It discusses why it did not gain as much ground in two prominent Muslim loci (Turkey/the Ottoman Empire and Egypt) up until the last few decades. The chapter ultimately lays out the changing political economic frameworks that made the Islamization of liberal generosity possible. Nevertheless, as the following four chapters demonstrate, the story is far from over, as charitable actors still negotiate liberalization. They not only build upon historical reservoirs of communitarian ethics, but also develop novel communitarian and redistributive dispositions.

Even though this chapter handles American religious charity as the liberal revolution's ultimate culmination, I don't intend to imply that the US summarizes all neoliberal experience. As researchers have demonstrated, neoliberalization has taken very different shapes even within the West (Brenner et al. 2010; Fourcade and Babb 2002). Rather than *representing* "the Western" experience of neoliberalism, the US has been a *hegemonic trend-setter*. I therefore study and problematize the relative "purity" of American neoliberalism with a strategic purpose. In the eyes of many charity practitioners *and* academics, American charitable culture sends strong signals throughout the world, which others may then emulate or not. By dissecting the American model, I demonstrate that neoliberalization remains contested even within the world leader. In short, rather than providing a full explanatory account of contemporary Christian charity, this chapter analytically pulls apart the American charitable template, which many take as the paradigm of religious charity throughout the globe.

The Long Liberal Revolution

This section will trace how the rationalization of Western mercy passed through stages of "ambiguous humanitarianism" and "merciless rationalization" (from the Reformation to early Victorian times) to culminate in the welfare state.

Over the recent decades, historians have uncovered how pre-Reformation developments in theological classifications and practices prepared the ground for the Protestant attack against medieval charitable ethics. Rationalization of charity predates modernity and even the Reformation. As we have seen in Chapter 2, despite many significant differences among Catholics, a specific kind of communitarian ethos characterized medieval generosity. They perceived poverty as a part of the divine order of things: the poor depended on benevolence and the rich on their prayers. Giving was central to creating bonds in society through fostering this interdependence. Yet, as benevolent operations got larger and more systematic, many Catholics became concerned that some within the poor population had started to compete with the "real" victims of misfortune, (perceptibly) distorting the purpose of charity. Medieval classifications of the poor became quite complex to determine those that really needed help (as well as to ascertain the kinds of help that could be offered to less deserving poor people such as repentant prostitutes).[1]

However, pre-Reformation rationalization was non-standardized and *non-individualist*. The Reformation did not simply introduce more systematic rationalization into the world of religious giving, but pushed rationality in an individualist and exclusionary direction. (Yet, even then, neither the individualism nor the exclusiveness was conclusive yet.) Social legislation in many cities and states across Europe (and across the Protestant-Catholic divide) took Protestant criticisms of medieval generosity seriously and waged a fight against vagrants, beggars, and voluntary religious poor (Pullan 2005). What we are most concerned with for the purposes of this book is how an individualized ethics (which would ultimately culminate in "responsibilization") came to mark poverty alleviation.

Political economic and field dynamics interacted to move the Christian West in that direction. Even though my analysis cannot fully demonstrate the field dynamics in each of the significant turning points, it does hint that the individualization of charitable ethics was not straightforwardly dictated by economic changes (whether you call this the development of capitalism or the rise of complex, modern economies). Nor were the changes in charitable institutions simply pragmatic adaptations to changing conditions (which could be simply explained by a pragmatism-based institutionalist focus on "what works"). Rather, throughout the centuries, clerics, intellectuals, and experts struggled to consolidate their basis of authority (through arguments about what kind of charitable institution worked) in interaction with changing economic conditions, unfolding political interventions, and popular movements. The result was a context-dependent, but still globally predominant, ethics.

This complex, "variegated" history of the liberal revolution in charitable ethics will allow us to re-think discussions regarding the "diffusion" of modern charity throughout the world. The inconclusiveness of even the American case should prevent us from entertaining straightforward accounts of either global standardization *or* non-Western uniqueness(es). Since Islamic liberalization is part of a combined development of worldwide liberal ethics, we need conceptual-methodological tools beyond the sociologist's isomorphism and the anthropologist's thick description to appreciate its "distinct" contribution to this revolution.

From the Reformation to Political Economy

Martin Luther's attack against medieval charity is well-known, but shouldn't be credited for the entirety of the early modern shift. In the 1520s, the beginnings of an agrarian, commercial, and industrial cash economy (and the resulting downwards turn in wages) combined with bad harvests and epidemics to produce an uncontrollable situation. Vagrants and beggars flooded cities. Moreover, this was no simple population pressure, since some new claimants on charity (an emergent stratum of working poor) did not fit medieval classifications of the poor into the voluntary poor, the shamefaced poor, the honest beggars and vagrants, and the professionalized beggars (Geremek 1994, pp. 52–59, 64–71).

Neither the ethics nor the institutions of medieval Christianity expected such a huge magnitude of poverty. Urgent reform was necessary, which came in the shape of centralization and well-defined principles of charity regulation (Geremek 1994, pp. 120–124). This led to (a quite meandering and far from systematic) spread of earlier German municipal reform across Europe. Martin Luther wholeheartedly supported the banning of begging, but he also called for the provision of care for the poor not able to work. And he called for intensification of the fight against the mendicant orders. He further specified that aid to the poor should prevent starvation and dying from the cold: it would be unjust to give more, while others were working for it. Martin Luther was not simply a representative of the bourgeoisie (as in Engels's [1926, pp. 57–62] account), or an iconoclast (as in Weber's). He was partially a product of his times, more particularly the 1520s. In that decade, social realities (population boom, nascent capitalism, epidemics, famine, etc.) precipitated the condensation of the *clerical attack* on medieval charitable ethics that had been *unfolding for a couple of centuries* (Geremek 1994, pp. 180–183). *Martin Luther was a creative player in an already complex religious field*, which was shaped by (but also intervened in) the social transformations of the early sixteenth century.

Despite the apparently merciless (early) Protestant attack on medieval charity, *the sixteenth to early eighteenth centuries actually retained a sense of religious and communal duty toward the poor*. For instance, both the Austro-Hungarian Emperor Charles V and the religious reformer Luther, pushed to ban begging, spread forced labor, and crash mendicant orders, but they also laid the basis for generalized care for the sick and elderly (Geremek 1994, pp. 143–146). Along similar lines, if the Reformation-influenced Elizabethan poor laws (instituted around the turn of the seventeenth century) had a harsh face, they had a compassionate one too. Generally speaking, reforms punished (or imposed compulsory work on) the ablebodied vagrant, but made relief for the aged and disabled *compulsory* (Himmelfarb 1985, pp. 6–7, 25). Forced labor and decent living standards for the laborer were the two sides of the same coin (Polanyi 2001, pp. 83, 90–91).

Even Puritanism came in different shapes. One of its solid inheritors, Methodism, did not single-handedly put an end to traditional charity. If John Wesley emphasized thrift and hard-work, he also deeply suspected wealth and therefore encouraged his followers to give away the riches they had accumulated. (Incidentally, he was against interest-based gain, resonating with established Islamic economic ethics.) Wesley also rejected the insinuation that poverty resulted from idleness (Himmelfarb 1985, pp. 32–33, 40). Not only the Methodists, but many of the other evangelical preachers of the eighteenth and early nineteenth centuries eyed the emergent entrepreneurial ideology with suspicion: they were not ready to accept a world in which the upper classes had no responsibility with respect to the poor. Going with the dominant business mood of their era, they focused mostly on the immorality of the poor, but had a lot of harsh words reserved for socially irresponsible businessmen too. Their moral exhortations also made the business class weary: the latter resorted to Evangelicalism quite selectively (Bendix 1974, pp. 17, 68–72).

Neither the Elizabethan poor laws nor the Methodists thoroughly severed their links with old Christian understandings, which pictured *the poor as noble people and poverty as a blessing to be embraced* (Himmelfarb 1985, pp. 3–4). They guaranteed every Christian, in ideal conditions, a proper place in the community (Polanyi 2001, p. 91). Despite the apparent division of the poor into the "deserving" and the "undeserving" (as captured by practices such as sending some to alms houses and others to penitentiaries), the seventeenth and early eighteenth centuries still could not completely rationalize and standardize classifications such as these, since almost all of the laboring population depended on private charity or public relief. Employment was erratic. It was practically impossible to tell a "dependent" from an "independent" laborer. Inevitably, then, *Christians perceived poverty as a part of fate*—and therefore not necessarily demeaning or degrading (Bendix 1974, pp. 16, 40; Himmelfarb 1985, pp. 26–28, 41).[2]

The *decisive change came around the turn of the nineteenth century*: a new consensus replaced secular and complex classifications of (and prescriptions for) poverty for religious, private, and simple ones. In the ethos that characterized primarily England from circa 1750 to 1850, the poor were no longer noble and poverty no longer a blessing. The definition and moral evaluation, not just explanation, of poverty changed. The poor could pull themselves out of poverty through adapting the correct morals; neither the rich nor the government could help them (Bendix 1974, pp. 73–86; Himmelfarb 1985, pp. 12, 18; Polanyi 2001).[3] Especially the Malthusian and Ricardian versions of political economy aimed to introduce a harsh classification of the poor into deserving and undeserving camps; this new political economy attacked not only poor laws and subsidies, but (going against even Adam Smith) opposed high wages (Himmelfarb 1985, Chs 2, 4, pp. 134, 524–525).[4]

Malthusian political economy did not come out of the blue. It was a culmination of ideas and practices through which the English (educated) public grappled with labor shortages, poverty, rising costs, social disruption, threat of revolution, and moral change. The Speenhamland laws of 1795, the spirit of which Polanyi called "ambiguous humanitarianism" had destroyed the communities, status, and respectability of the laborers. Even though Polanyi labeled the old Elizabethan and Speenhamland laws paternalist, he found the latter much more destructive of community (Polanyi 2001 p. 103). Around the turn of the nineteenth century, then, almost all efforts to regulate the increasing pauper population (workhouses, old relief laws, the Speenhamland laws, etc.) had only further reinforced unwillingness to work among laborers, the decline in their social status, and the tendency to cut wages among employers (Bendix 1974, pp. 41–42; Polanyi 2001 pp. 82–85, 97–99, 101–103).

Malthusian political economy decisively intervened in this acute crisis. The idea that only experiencing hunger would force laborers to work was already established in the eighteenth century. Malthusians (and a couple of precursors such as Defoe, Townsend, and Burke) pushed this idea further by insisting that laborers unwilling to work should starve—a logical move which was unthinkable under the old, paternalistic Christianity (Bendix 1974, pp. 73–76, 79–80; Polanyi 2001, pp. 114, 118, 121).[5] If the New Poor Laws of 1834 did not adopt Malthusian political economy in all its harshness, they still imposed extremely undesirable workhouse conditions (but not starvation) on able-bodied yet "lazy" men and their families (Bendix 1974, pp. 96–98; Polanyi 2001, p. 106).[6] The rationalization of mercy had led to a merciless rationalization.[7]

Despite the ongoing influence of Puritanism and Evangelism, the worldviews and ethics of the entrepreneurial class gradually secularized. Even though initially helpful in the fight against medieval mores, rigorous Christianity was becoming a hobble. Secularization, individualization, and rationalization gradually merged (Bendix 1974, pp. 201–203). This certainly distinguishes our era (with its relatively more religious business-individualist ethics) from the mid-nineteenth century.

The apex of this merciless rationalization of poverty debates met not only an emergent socialist criticism (which focused on inequality and exploitation), but also a relatively more conservative one. The latter, communitarian critique, which some radicals also drew on, focused on the debilitating social consequences of the new political economy: the jeopardization of the paternalistic structure of society, of the social order's legitimacy, of the chain of connections that bound the rich and poor together, of mutual responsibility. It was here, then, that old radicalism, conservatism, and the cultural aspects of the new socialism overlapped: an uneasiness with the ways in which human relations were reduced to calculation and a cash nexus (Bendix 1974, Ch. 2; Himmelfarb 1985, pp. 526–528; Polanyi 2001).

Postwar sociology, as well as the social science of the recent years, has paid adequate attention to these nineteenth-century ethical transformations. Yet, a new, *liberal-conservative charitable ethics that developed at the end of the nineteenth century has taken a short shrift* (though documented in detail by *historians*). Sociology has focused more on the rise of the working class, the left, then fascism, and ultimately the welfare state as a response to the social disruptions of commodification. It is true that the "late-Victorian" charitable ethics (described below) did not have as long a shelf life when compared with these earth-shattering responses to liberalization. However, it is significant for an understanding of our age since *the late twentieth-century wave of intense commodification has not (yet) met working class, leftist, and fascist responses*. Rather, the buried experiments of *liberal charitable ethics*—which sounds like, but is not, a contradiction in terms—have been resuscitated. "Liberal charitable ethics" rejected the heartlessness of Malthus, yet urged donors to carefully rationalize their efforts to maximize the beneficiaries' individualization. The understanding of this ethics (and its re-articulations throughout the world) is indispensable for a full appreciation of the global, ethical revolution we are still experiencing today.

England experienced a golden age of charity in the 1870s and 1880s. The new charitable ethics, however, inherited the heart of political economy's attack against old Christian charity: the dependency of the poor had to be terminated (though the new charitable ethics also recognized a new kind of *necessary* "moral" dependency, see below). A personal and private, "volunteer"-based commitment to the moral transformation of the poor, rather than governmental planning and aid, was the solution. The spirit of the new compassion was decisively anti-socialist: it located the blame in the habits of the poor. Charity would do its proper work not through social justice, but by making sure that the recipients became frugal, hard-working, and punctual (Himmelfarb 1991, pp. 181–184, 206, 213). This late-Victorian charity strongly foreshadowed the global philanthropy of our era.

Another classificatory move brings late-Victorian charity closer to our age and takes it one step away from early Victorian times. The 1870s introduced an intermediate class between the deserving laborers and the undeserving paupers. The 1834 poor laws had declared the former independent and the latter dependent beyond salvation. The late Victorians declared an intermediate class (hard-working but somehow the prey of misfortune) to be the proper beneficiaries of charity: aid would save them from their temporary and accidental misery by further enhancing their work ethics. Again, foreshadowing *some* of the neoliberal philanthropists of our era, many late nineteenth-century philanthropists recognized the responsibility of the state in dealing with the chronically sick and the elderly (Himmelfarb 1991, p. 188–191). Late-Victorian liberalization, in other words, was "variegated" and state-summoning just like neoliberalization.

The late Victorians also paved the way for today's charity in terms of 1) gender ideology and 2) organization: they emphasized the family as the basic unit of political economy (rather than the lonely individual, as in earlier political economy); and they secularized and systematized the practice of "visiting" (which they had inherited from parish clergymen). The radical individualism of Ricardo was gone, as the mutual interdependence of the male breadwinner and his family was put in the center, and the dependence of both on social legislation (and charity) recognized. The late Victorians were also poignantly aware that friendly visits by charity workers would have to reproduce, day by day, the work ethic that would sustain an independent life. Visitors advised, cajoled, and rebuked the well-intentioned, deserving poor (Himmelfarb 1991, pp. 194–199, 213–214).

Gertrude Himmelfarb (1991, p. 203), a notable liberal-conservative historian, praises yet another aspect of late-Victorian charity which is quite parallel to today's charitable ethics and practice:

> The applicant was subjected to a moral test, and certified as having passed it when he received aid. In some respects this moral test contrasts favorably not only with the workhouse test imposed by the poor laws but with the means test that is the basis of [late 20th century relief]. A means test, judging only the need and not the character of the applicants, leaves open the suspicion that the need is a result of a failure of character; a moral test certifies that it is not.

Due to such learned criticisms of the welfare state and twentieth-century aid, many organizations throughout the world have refashioned their understanding and practice of giving. As will be seen throughout the book, especially the Turkish Islamic neoliberal charities have brought morality to the center of the aid application process.

If the influence of industrialization and political economy marked the poverty and charity debates in England, urbanization (and the breakdown of the rural moral order) defined the terrain in nineteenth-century America.[8] Puritan clergy and volunteers sought to establish "cohesive communities knit together by shared moral and social values" (Boyer 1978, p. viii). As the organized churches failed, it was primarily the evangelical voluntary organizations (Bible societies, tract societies, Sunday schools, and charitable organizations) that aimed to control the poor. At the root of the middle-class panic was not only increasing rates of poverty and crime, but also the Jacksonian threat of organized (and voting) masses, and later on, labor and antiwar protests (Boyer 1978, pp. 1, 7–9, 15, 145–146).

In other words, the evangelism of this era was almost a diametrical opposite of twentieth-century Islamism: it mobilized civil society and charity *against* the vote (Boyer 1978, p. 13), whereas most of Islamism strove to combine civil society *and* the vote against the secular elite.[9] Whatever the parallels between late-Victorian and neoliberal giving, then, the latter is quite novel in its more sustained mobilization of lower strata in favor of neoliberalization. Political economic and Foucaultian analyses alone cannot exhaust this novelty (and its variation from one country to the next): as the following sections will demonstrate, we have to take into account the political interventions in bloc-making.

Charitable efforts in America also peaked around the 1870s and 1880s. The intellectual and organizational developments in England were crucial in this American reformulation of charity (Boyer 1978, pp. 143–151). Central to these efforts were "friendly visitors"[10] who were instructed to hide their cataloging intentions from the poor. The assembled data were shared not only with charitable donors and organizations but also potential employers, landlords, and banks. In the meantime, visitors sought to establish interpersonal connections between the rich and the poor. However, these encounters failed to produce the intended results. The poor learned to act out middle-class selves when reformers were around and shifted back to their regular habits after they disappeared. Ironically, some of the reformers who did stick around adapted labor causes rather than converting the poor. Internal and external criticism and doubt increased after the 1890s, ultimately demoralizing and disorganizing the charitable movement during the turn of the century. These developments also undermined the public conviction that poverty results from individual failings (Boyer 1978, pp. 153–156). We lack any systematic (either large-N or comparative-historical) study of the practical impact of liberal charity on the ethics of the receivers, but this historical record gives us enough reason to suspect that even rationalized charity had the power to transform the poor.

One organization challenged these overall trends while replicating some of them. It merits special attention due to its stronger parallels with contemporary neoliberal charities. The Salvation Army (born in England but exported to the whole world, primarily the United States) chose the most destitute (and perceptibly the most undeserving) among the poor as its main target. It helped criminals, prostitutes, the habitually lazy, etc. rather than the hard-working but misfortunate poor (the deserving beneficiaries of the 1870s and 1880s). Unlike old Christian charity, however, it was adamant in transforming them into hard-working, honest, and chaste individuals. Moreover, in contrast to Boyer's middle-class American evangelicals and Himmelfarb's secular middle-class donors, the organization mostly mobilized people with roots in laboring and/or poor classes (Allahyari 2000; Davis and Robertson 2012; Himmelfarb 1991, pp. 223–225). The Salvation Army parallels today's charities in ambition and universalism, but differs from them with its more focused attention to the "lowest" tenth of humanity.

Due to its (back then) rather unconventional approach to poverty and the poor, the Salvation Army was frequently misunderstood as either a replica of old Christian charity or (more favorably, by some socialists including Engels) the expression of a semi-conscious class war against the bourgeoisie (Himmelfarb 1991, pp. 226; Tuğal 2016b). With not only hindsight, but also a proper comparison to the neoliberal Islamic charities of today, we can appreciate the Salvation Army for what it really was and is: a hegemonic, bottom-up, civil society-driven embrace of market ethics.

Nineteenth-Century Islam: Interrupted Institutionalization

Despite some claims to the contrary, we see growing rationalization in post-"middle period" Muslim welfare too. Nevertheless, the decisive centralization and rationalization occurred through state-making, which disrupted the precursory rationalization of civic charity. Initially, Islamic endowments, other charitable institutions, and municipalities became venues of population control and employment programs (just like charities during the Reformation). We see major pushes for centralization and rationalization in two key loci of the Muslim world: the imperial capital Istanbul and one of its ambitious colonies, Cairo. The awqaf here could turn into capital accumulation instruments, but governments confiscated or restricted them starting with the 1820s. In parallel fashion to the late nineteenth- to early twentieth-century Christian world (of which more below), state formation started to be intensely enmeshed with social provision in a way that undercut civic charitable potentials.

According to Çizakça (2000, pp. 79–86), an economic historian of the Ottoman Empire, several factors came together to reinforce centralization of awqaf. The endowments' corruption had been a concern throughout the centuries, but governments had not systematically used this excuse to undermine their autonomy (and rather dealt with issues as they arose, through the court system). Despite that, the awqaf's countervailing power was a historical concern, especially in that they restricted the state's war-making efforts. With increasing centralization, the modernizing sultans (Selim III, Hamid I, Mahmud II) made decisive moves to undercut the autonomy of the endowments. Colonial powers reinforced these trends after 1860. Two issues motivated European colonizers: the endowment system prevented them from confiscating land; Western states themselves had been moving towards liquidating or centralizing charitable networks ever since the seventeenth century and thus found decentralized systems of provision ideologically objectionable.

In both nineteenth-century Cairo and Istanbul, the instrumentalization of aid for state-making was the main trend. Nevertheless, population control did not always imply a straightforward and one-sided domination. As Mine Ener (2003, p. xvii) has shown, though the Egyptian government's motivation might have been control (e.g. clearing the streets of the poor), the results were not always in line with intentions. By 1850, many poor people actually *applied* in order to be sheltered. Many of these poor used these shelters only temporarily (p. 19). This Egyptian effort to confine the poor was exceptional in the nineteenth-century Middle East (Ener 2003, p. xix–xx): systematic confinement did not begin in Istanbul until the end of the nineteenth century.

The partial failure[11] of the state's intention to prevent begging (and clear the streets off completely) recalls to mind the United States, Western Europe, and Russia, which also had difficulties with implementing total control (even if the first two of these cases were relatively more successful). What differentiated Egypt was the impact of the colonial gaze. The reformers engaged in these activities to portray a more civilized Egypt to tourists and colonial administrators (Ener 2003, Ch. 1).

At the end of the nineteenth century, Egyptian associations tried to fill the gap in poor relief left by governments. They focused mostly on orphans. As different from the government, they also began employment programs. Finally, they served as a terrain for competition between the king and the elites, as well as among the elites (Ener 2003, pp. 22–25). Today's charities demonstrate remarkable continuities with these tendencies, as Chapter 4 and Chapter 5 will show. In Istanbul too similar factors with Egypt (the rise of an educated elite, the rise of the press, increasing poverty) led to competitions between the sultan and the elites in providing for the poor. In both contexts, governments responded to the competition by intense regulation.

Starting with the 1920s, the Egyptian government introduced new laws that restricted the activities of charitable associations. The government became more concerned in the 1930s with increasing communist and Muslim Brotherhood activity. The Ministry of Social Affairs was established in 1939 as an arm of both surveillance and provision (Ener 2003, pp. 22–25).

Christian charity had a peculiar impact on these developments, further attesting to the combined making of modern charity worldwide. Many scholars interpret the fact that the Muslim Brotherhood was founded at the end of the 1920s as evidence that Mustafa Kemal's secularization program initiated the birth of the modern Islamist movement (Hasan al-Banna referred to Kemal's abolition of the caliphate as one of the reasons he established the organization). Recent historiography, however, emphasizes pious Muslims' response to Christian missionary activity (which "hit [its] apex" in the same decade) as the main impetus (Baron 2014, pp. ix–xiii, 121–123, 129, 197–198 and *passim*). Due to worries regarding increasing conversion, Muslims learned from Christians how to merge charitable and missionary activities in a modern context—a combination they had been carrying out for centuries, but which they further rationalized in their competition with American, Swedish, and British organizations. Nevertheless, the Islamists were not the only ones charitable Christians spurred to action. The Egyptian state took its first formidable steps towards becoming a welfare state in response to both the Christian proselytization panic and the Islamist response to it (Baron 2014, pp. 187–190).

In parallel fashion to Egypt, Ottoman state-centralizing activities paved the road to confiscation. By the early nineteenth century, the *waqf* system tended to become the Ottoman economy *tout court*. Awqaf activities ranged from establishing and running soup kitchens, homeless shelters, and water facilities to shops and production facilities. Yediyildiz (1984) points out that at the end of the eighteenth century the combined income of the functioning 20,000 Ottoman endowments was equivalent to one-third of Ottoman state's total revenue.[12]

The first modern and systematic tendencies of confiscation started with the establishment of urban municipalities throughout the Middle East (following the 1820s and more consistently after the 1850s). Municipalities took over traditional foundation functions such as the production of water conducts (Kuran 2001, pp. 876–879). This brought them into clashes with the endowments. They also confiscated property whenever it prevented the building of roads (Özbek 2002, pp. 60–63). In 1826, the establishment of a ministry of foundations in Istanbul centralized the control over the endowments and curtailed the sway of the religious elite. Eventually, the ministry came to regulate the endowment resources to finance imperial parades, the construction of palaces and debt payment (Kuran 2001).

Throughout the nineteenth century, then, dynastic rulers (stretching from the Ottoman sultans to the Egyptian governors) moved to either confiscate the endowments or centralize their management. Even though similar moves were ever-present since the sixteenth century, now rulers could make them more systematic: the perception that foundations were abused for self-enrichment was now widespread, which made control legitimate (Çizakça 2000). The rulers also came to see confiscation and management as political checks against clerics. Abdülhamid II, the villain of Kemalist historiography and the hero of Islamist narratives, further centralized social assistance institutions through personally monopolizing control. While the establishment of endowments was the central way of providing welfare among previous sultans, nineteenth-century sultans founded very few endowments. Abdülhamid II (who reigned between 1876 and 1909) established only two (Özbek 2002, pp. 155–156). However, throughout his time this centralization did not lead to a smooth bureaucratization of welfare (Özbek 2002).

What is most important for our purposes here is that Islamic communitarianism did not simply collapse *or* get replaced (either by liberal charity or the modern-bureaucratic welfare state). Rather, the late Ottomans developed a modern form of paternalist communitarianism (much in parallel fashion to developments in other late industrializers of the nineteenth century). Abdülhamid II circumvented the waqf institution, but still built a personal giving regime, rather than a twentieth-century-type bureaucratic welfare regime. As Nadir Özbek (2002, pp. 25–26), a leading historian of Ottoman-Turkish welfare, emphasizes, the monarch and his state (rather than endowments) became the main welfare provider during his reign. But this was still modernist-monarchist welfare, rather than a simple replication of pre-modern Islamic logic or a definitive transition to modern bureaucratic welfare (the signs of which were also visible throughout the nineteenth century (e.g. see Özbek 2002, pp. 53–63). Abdülhamid II circumvented the bureaucracy and organized personalized charitable campaigns, a trend observable in Germany, Russia, Iran, and Japan at the end of the nineteenth century, with the significant difference that (unlike the German monarch) Abdülhamid II sought to eliminate most intermediary aid institutions (pp. 29–34).

Even though the Ottoman case partially converged with late modernizers, it clearly diverged from French, British, and other cases. Abdülhamid's regulation of the poor was more moderate when compared with much of post-Reformation Western European welfare reform. Most significantly, *the Ottoman elite* pushed for a total elimination of beggars from streets and public squares (for they not only distorted the European perceptions of the Ottomans and disturbed respectable citizens, but also encouraged loose working ethics). Nevertheless, *the sultan's* reforms never went this far and focused rather on saving the beggars from the streets in order to boost his image as a generous sultan (Özbek 2002, pp. 77–92). Paternalistic-communitarian concerns trumped a disciplinary reorganization of society along elite desires.

After the removal of the Sultan (as a result of the events of 1908–1909) and the rise of the Young Turks to power, the Ottoman welfare system moved toward bureaucratization. Paving the way for later republican reforms, the Young Turks more decisively mobilized (and thoroughly controlled) aid associations to legitimate their rule (Özbek 2002). As significantly, the Young Turk-controlled Ottoman Assembly passed laws much more in line with Western European modernity: the people's representatives heeded the call of the elites in the preceding decades and an all-out war on begging began. Özbek (2002) points out that even though a *modernizer* in many regards, Abdülhamid II had never become a *disciplinary* modernizer. Taking this role on, the Young Turks paved the way for the Republic and (much later) twenty-first-century Islamists.

Özbek's exposition of the conflicts between the conservative monarch and the secularist elite demonstrate what I will further detail in the concluding chapter of this book. Rather than a conflict between tradition and modernity, or for that matter between Western modernity and an alternative modernity, the two sides represented two faces of emergent modern welfare: communitarian-solidarism and liberalism. While solidarism became a more entrenched part of some Western mainstream welfare institutions later on, the Ottomans (like the other late industrializers, whether Western or not) made a personalized-paternalistic version of solidarism the heart of welfare already in the mid-to-late-nineteenth century.

Changes in Islamic thinking paralleled these institutional developments, but not with the same degree of intensity: the discursive making of new subjectivities did not supply as rigorous a basis for the refashioning of charitable ethics. Some Islamic reformers, such as al-Tahtawi, made philosophical and sociological moves to distinguish the deserving from the undeserving poor. He stipulated that the disabled, widows, seminary students, etc. were still worthy of governmental and private benevolence. However, people were lazy by nature, and they had to be pushed to work (Cole 2003, pp. 225–226). These were his liberal inclinations.

However, al-Tahtawi was also a strong defender of (non-revolutionary) redistribution. Under the influence of utopian socialists, as much as some Islamic thinking, he developed an interpretation of charity and property clearly at odds with conservative Islamic defenses of property rights. He reinterpreted some key reports from Muhammad to mean that landowners had to give 50 percent of their profit back to the laborers, who were the real source of wealth (not only through their manual work, but through their innovations). Still, unlike the utopian socialists, he did not believe that elites were useless and had to be discarded in an ideal society. To the contrary, they were the ultimate protectors of society and guarantors of the productiveness of laborers, an emphasis that attested to his paternalistic-communitarian inclinations. In sum, a major Islamic reformer of the nineteenth century preserved an overall paternalistic orientation, but incorporated strong liberal and redistributive inclinations.

Al-Tahtawi seems to have developed these thoughts not only under the influence of European and Islamic thought, but also as a response to the immense misery caused by Egyptian cotton capitalism in the 1860s, reinforcing the Polanyian insight regarding marketization and counter-movements. As the case of Al-Tahtawi (frequently taken as the major reformer of Islamic economics in this era) demonstrates, Islamic theology never became a liberal-revolutionary trendsetter in the nineteenth century. Many other influences muddled his liberalization. Other nineteenth-century Islamic reformers did not attack the communitarian foundations of Islamic charitable ethics either. This era, in short, did not produce the liberal counterparts of the founding jurists, who had paved the way for the institutionalization of communitarian charity in Islam's middle period.

The Rise and Decline of the Western Welfare State

When Western countries moved away from the harshness of nineteenth-century understandings of poverty (and towards notions of equality and universal rights), the welfare state started to shoulder most relief efforts. Pious civic organizations and churches recoiled in the late nineteenth century (if not always in terms of absolute amount of activity, then certainly in significance), leaving the front stage to the state and secular organizations.

This transformation was not simply a change of the leading actor. It was not just that the state replaced private donors. The entire understanding of poverty changed. If the first moves toward the welfare state still retained some notions of the deserving versus undeserving poor (and therefore some belief in the moral causes of poverty), as the welfare state got entrenched in Western democracies in the middle of the twentieth century, provision started to be universal because the perceived causes of poverty had changed. They were once moral and individual; now they were social (Himmelfarb 1991, pp. 383–384). Even though the causal significance of working-class unions and parties in the birth of the modern welfare state is still an unsettled scholarly issue (e.g. see Edwin Amenta 1998 and

Ann Orloff 1993 versus the Marxists), there is no question that the working-class challenge was one of the factors that transformed the understanding of poverty and the notion of deserved help. (By contrast, the Egyptian and Turkish cases were not marked by class challenges as serious as those in Germany, France, Britain, and even the US.)

However, this was much less true of the American welfare scene. This section will focus on the transformation of the American welfare state, not because the same transformation was repeated everywhere else in the West, but because it became the paradigmatic case of Western welfare restructuring in the late twentieth century. What resulted was not an identical welfare culture throughout the West, but shared *and* contested assumptions about how welfare should be changing. As Esping-Andersen (1990) notes, the US welfare system was always a liberal one (that is, more modest and *individual-targeted* than the continental varieties). Holding the poor responsible for their plight was relatively a more entrenched aspect of American welfare even before neoliberalization. Moreover, the secularization of welfare was less rigorous in the United States, as Protestants came to predominate in public welfare agencies and nominally secular organizations (which actually kept on propagating religious values). As a reaction, Jews and Catholics also strengthened their own religious-based welfare provision, frequently under secular guise (Schneider 2013, pp. 434–435).

Some of the expanding American pious charitable organizations in the welfare era of relative "civic invisibility" engaged in a liberalization (not just rationalization) of benevolence (Allahyari 2000; but see Davis and Robertson 2012). Early to mid-twentieth-century American charity, for instance, attempted to control the very psyche of poor people in order to turn them into thrifty, calculating and productive workers and consumers (Zelizer 1997, pp. 142, 168–169 and *passim*). These were the persisting signs of what this book focuses on: a positive relation between liberalization and religious-based charity (rather than a negative one, where many forms of charity would have to be suppressed in order to foster a sound political economy). These activities and spirit would come to occupy center stage with the transformations of the 1980s and 1990s. As this section will show, the already liberal American model became even more individual-focused through neoliberalization.

Now, the question becomes whether this American model spreads throughout the world today through isomorphic pressures, as new institutionalism would predict. Or is there rather intense "variegation" as Brenner et al. would hold? This book suggests that we get a fuller picture when we look at variations within and between fields (which are structured, but not completely determined, by "variegated" political economic processes). A field analysis would expose many overlaps and differences between Anglo-Saxon welfare transformations and their counterparts elsewhere in the West too. Nevertheless, I will restrict my exploration to the American and English welfare templates that have been imposed on the rest of the world (relatively more than other Western ones). We see a lot of influence, but no smooth import, of the American model in Turkey and Egypt.

Back to Charity as Ethical Transformation

After the 1970s, the socially based, universalistic assumptions of the welfare state turned out to be but a parenthesis in the long, liberal revolution in charitable ethics. The Western revolution kept on unfolding after that, with momentous consequences for Islamic charities (some of which explicitly modeled themselves after American, English, and Canadian charities). One dynamic behind the intensification of Anglo-Saxon charitable activity today can be traced back to the poverty debates of the 1960s. Scholars and policymakers back then located "pockets" and "cultures" of poverty in the United States and Britain. These were allegedly beyond the reach of the welfare state, according to some, and ultimately destined to be extinguished by the fine-tuning of the welfare state according to others.

However, these early debates paved the way for a more comprehensive defeat of socially based understandings of poverty and welfare. What were perceived to be "pockets" in the 1960s, came to be interpreted as the defining features of poverty in the 1970s. The perceived failures of the American and British welfare states were a core dynamic in the birth of neoconservatism. Intellectuals associated with the Democratic Party became convinced that exploding crime and illegitimate births were due to indiscriminate welfare provision. That is one reason the Victorian criticism of earlier Christian charity was unearthed (Himmelfarb 1991, p. 389):

> [W]e are now rediscovering one of the things that the late Victorians did not have to discover, only because they knew it almost instinctively. After making the most arduous attempt to ... divorce poverty from any moral assumptions and conditions, we are learning how inseparable the moral and material dimensions of that problem are.

Such intellectual interventions redefined the problem of poverty as one of morals as well as conditions. The welfare state would have to be scaled back to open up space for a "focus on the family" by charitable actors.

This was most certainly a transatlantic development involving both the US and the UK (just like late-Victorian charitable transformations). The British government cooperated with Christian charity organizations to carry out research on community development. Their research projects identified democratization with the expansion of the market economy and the inclusion of religious communities. In this new official construction of the world, religious people were seen as excluded from democracy (in the twentieth century). The task of the new millennium, then, was to mobilize them. In London, the moral reformers argued, faith-based organizations (FBOs) supported the development of the whole "community," but secular forces blocked funding for them due to their prejudices. This was detrimental for all of London, since religious communities produced high-degree, quality care and *trust* due to shared belief (Smith 2002, pp. 169–173). This government-funded research implied that secularism would need to be toned down and equal opportunity regulations relaxed.

In more scholarly circles, Robert Putnam's work on social capital (and later, religion) has deeply shaped the debate on charity and welfare (the UK-based research discussed above also used Putnam's work to frame the findings). Putnam and Campbell (2010, pp. 454–455) state that religious Americans are overall more prone to care for others when compared to nonreligious Americans. Moreover, they are more likely to belong to community organizations, contribute to community problem solving, take part in local civic life, and push for social or political reform. Though they are less tolerant of dissent, religious Americans of all stripes, these authors hold, are better contributors to American civic life than is generally believed. Though this is less true of fundamentalists, religious people also trust people more than secular people do (Putnam and Campbell 2010, p. 460), which also feeds giving for religious and nonreligious purposes. These British and American discursive moves (and the ensuing institutional innovations) travelled *unevenly* throughout the world at every critical turn, as I will suggest.

The political context further naturalized this ethical turn. The Reagan administration announced that religious organizations are more effective than state agencies and secular associations in the provision of welfare. But the importance attributed to religion and religious care cut across party lines. There was an overall change in ideological climate following the 1970s: government was no longer seen as the solution to poverty. Politicians now believed it rather perpetuated poverty through unconditional help, which reproduced vice. The ideologues Marvin Olasky and Lawrence Mead contrasted this presumed predicament with earlier America, where religious charitable giving was conditional on religious transformation. This approach actually valued the poor more, they argued, as religious donors cared for "the whole person," as opposed to the bureaucrat who just gives to the poor and exits the scene. Even the Democrats accepted the policy implications of this reasoning, if not all the arguments (Cnaan 2002, pp. 3–6).

Before the decisive national onslaught of the mid-1990s, there were some local attacks against the welfare system. These attacks are informative as they show how welfare reform involved not only the scaling back of governmental provision, but the mobilization of associations to induce ethical transformation. Mississippi Governor Kirk Fordice implemented a program called Faith and Families of Mississippi in 1994. Similar initiatives in Texas and Indiana followed. The program's goal was getting the poor off of welfare and making them "self-sufficient" with the help of congregations. Fordice enlisted 325 churches to develop discipline, responsibility, assertiveness, and parenting skills among the poor, with the ultimate goal of creating non-adulterous lives and abstinence from pre-marital sex, which would both allow the poor to find and keep gainful employment (Bartkowski and Regis 2003, pp. 61–63). Mississippi, however, eventually scaled back the program (some thought this was because of the unwillingness of fundamentalist churches to participate in *any* government program; others blamed the resistance of liberal Black clergy).

By the end of the 1990s, the welfare state had been radically restructured nationwide to mobilize faithful civic actors. FBOs (including congregations) became eligible to compete for welfare funding under President Bill Clinton. Section 104 of Clinton's Personal Responsibility and Work Opportunity Reconciliation Act of 1996 allowed fund-receiving congregations to religiously discriminate in their hiring policies, but not in their choice of recipients (or religious requirements for recipients). President George W. Bush further institutionalized this act by founding a White House Office of Faith-Based and Community Initiatives to regulate the FBO–state collaboration (Chaves and Wineburg 2010). In 2006, close to one fifth of all federal contracts went to FBOs, but state-level welfare did not replicate this surge (Sinha 2013, p. 564).

Despite the hopes invested in these policies, FBO's capacity to provide welfare services increased only slightly (Chaves and Wineburg 2010; Sinha 2013, p. 565). Many commentators came to point out that the expectations of the 1990s and early 2000s were overblown. Nevertheless, the bare numbers tell only a part of the story. As Robert Wuthnow (1995, p. 6) notes, the last decades have witnessed a radical spiritual change. A new civic involvement mentality now connects the federal government, churches, schools, the punitive system, and communities in groundbreaking ways:

> Community service requirements are being instituted in schools ... and the federal government has launched a modest but innovative national service program. With the jails overflowing, judges are turning increasingly to community service as a means of rehabilitating juvenile offenders. Churches and synagogues are recruiting teenagers to work in soup kitchens. In fact, nationally, two thirds of American teenagers now report having done some kind of volunteer work within the past twelve months.

Faith-based policies might not have restructured congregations and other faith organizations as intensely as first hoped, but the welfare state *is* being successfully revamped to mobilize the citizenry.

Most of the debate in sociology has focused on three issues: 1) how policy and institutional moves such as Charitable Choice (introduced under Bill Clinton) and Faith-Based Initiative (introduced under George W. Bush) have impacted the flow of governmental funds to conservative/evangelist (rather than liberal or mainstream) Protestant congregations and FBOs (Chaves 1999; Ebaugh et al. 2006);[13] 2) whether federal money would temper the religiosity and religious distinctiveness of civic associations and/or ultimately undermine the church-state separation (Bielefeld and Cleveland 2013; Sinha 2013); and 3) whether Charitable Choice and Faith-Based Initiative have indeed boosted the efficiency, capacity, and social service provision of FBOs (Bielefeld and Cleveland 2013; Chaves and Wineburg 2010). These are certainly important questions for the American political context, but the resulting research gets us nowhere near resolving the questions posed in this book: How does this restructuring of the American state influence the welfare *ethics* that associations spread on the ground? Anthropologists and (a couple of) sociologists have provided clues for answering this question, but the resulting data are not as rich as that compiled by sociologists on the issues mentioned above.[14] This neglect is all the more significant as Clinton's Personal Responsibility and Work Opportunity Reconciliation Act of 1996 introduced not only new flexibilities for religious organizations to use government money (the focus of most of the literature) but also work requirements for welfare recipients and other conditions for welfare provision (Pipes and Ebaugh 2002). The intellectual severing of the debate on Section 104 (on FBOs) from the rest of the discussion of the Act of 1996 is not a mere scholarly oversight, but a symptom of the over-specialization of academia.

In short, civic-religious charity is back in the picture. And it is back through conscious, intricate state planning. However, religious actors are quite divided regarding what to make of this state involvement. They selectively appropriate the privileges that come with "Charitable Choice" and similar initiatives. Some ethnographic work in sociology (Allahyari 2000) and anthropology (Elisha 2008) hint that conservative evangelicalism is refashioning itself to effectively make use of welfare state structuring. However, we still know little about whether welfare restructuring has pushed other faith traditions to spread neoliberal subjectivity.

The Remaking of the American Benevolence Field

One of our core concerns is the intensity with which the American model of benevolence spreads to the rest of the world. The previous subsection suggested that there is indeed an *official* American understanding of "caring for the poor." However, can we also say that there is an as singular *civic* American model of caring for the poor? When the labels neoliberal or developmental are used for certain charitable organizations in research done outside the Anglophone world, *scholars usually rely on a singular, united understanding of what this label entails in the US*; the same applies to scholars who want to argue that non-Western ways of giving are "unique." The American reality on the ground, however, is much more complex than these scholars grant.

Faith-based initiatives from President Clinton onwards aimed to awake the dormant energy in congregations (Chaves and Wineburg 2010). With the Obama administration, the goal became to mobilize the same kind of energy within communities, and neighborhoods too. But what kind of energy existed? In what ways did Americans help each other before the faith-based restructuring of the welfare state? What kind of an ethics of generosity guided their actions?

Formal organizations (and the governments) in the US (as much as in Turkey and Egypt) want people to channel money from unofficial, unstandardized, un-measurable and undisciplined ways of giving into more formalized associations. In other words, both communitarian and neoliberal organizations are operating in (and against) an *"ether" of communally embedded giving*.[15] In her study of a predominantly working-class neighborhood ("Colombo") in Boston in the 1990s, Susan Eckstein focused on local associations and churches, which organized most of generosity in this community. Eckstein emphasized that, in most cases, it was groups that organized and reinforced giving, rather than individuals (2001, pp. 833–834). Moreover, donors were also recipients: there was little unidirectional giving. Groups helped *each other*. Some associations in this network of generosity had neither office buildings nor official meeting times; even their registration as formal organizations had been imposed by the state (p. 835). The (Catholic) Church also inspired giving, but was not the primary organizer or motivator, though Eckstein also notes that the "secular" associations were deeply motivated by religion: the secular/religious divide was blurred. Yet, the giving had its limits: people did not help those who defied the norms of the community or those who did not participate in reciprocal giving activities (pp. 842–843). The contrast to neoliberal charity is obvious: help is withdrawn based on communal and moral expectations, rather than work ethics-related criteria.

In such contexts, community-sustenance takes precedence over the fostering of the liberal subject. Given that there are presumably innumerable communities like Eckstein's Colombo throughout the United States (e.g. see Stack 1974), we cannot say that a neoliberal ethics of giving has wiped away communitarian ethics. However, we *can* say that the latter is being eroded (as Eckstein and others recognize). Yet, this decline does not *necessarily* entail the transition from a ("traditional") communitarian ethics of giving to a ("modern") neoliberal ethics of giving. The modernization of giving can also develop along communitarian lines. In other words, the content of modernization depends on *hegemonic struggle*. This is where we need to bring political sociology into the picture. We have to closely study what kinds of organizations intervene to formalize giving and what kind of support they enjoy from political actors.

Unfortunately, we have little clue regarding what kind of a welfare ethics formal organizations spread. Most of the research focuses on which congregations and FBOs spend more on social services and mobilize more volunteers (Ammerman 2005; Wilson and Janoski 1995, pp. 148–150; Wuthnow 1991, p. 322; Chaves 2004). There is also abundant attention to correlations between faith traditions and economic conservatism, especially regarding attitudes toward welfare spending (Emerson and Smith 2000; McRoberts 2003; Hart 1992; Steensland 2002; Barker and Carman 2000; Pyle 1993).[16] Scholars have also explored denomination members' beliefs on the *right kind* (rather than simply the *amount*) of welfare spending (Will and Cochran 1995), which gets closer to the core of our issues.

While quite telling, this inconclusive research does not resolve the question of *what these actors do on the ground*. Do the FBOs based on these faith traditions also reproduce the same kinds of practices and ethics when it comes to *their own activities* rather than their *opinions about how the government should function*? Going back to questions of policy, does involvement with neoliberalizing government also impact the way these organizations go about doing their everyday work? Does means-testing start to replace less conditional charity when the government contracts welfare out to these associations? Another way to summarize all of these questions is: Is there really an American "institutional model" of faith-based charity that can diffuse to the rest of the world? How do particular organizations within the US adapt and contest this model?

Generosity, Solidarity, and Discipline

The handful of scholarly works that go beyond discussions of theological distinctions to focus on the *practical* differentiations among the competing actors are worth special focus. While the results above suggest a restricted acceptance of free-market logic among charity providers, a bottom-up look at the provision of charity reveals an embrace of free-market logic (at least in some circles) much deeper than in the Egyptian and Turkish cases (but see below). The American Evangelicals Lydia Bean interviewed at one Baptist and one Pentecostal church in Buffalo, New York helped the poor as an "expression of grace to people" (2014, p. 175), but they didn't find them deserving (because the recipients had cable and satellite TV). Bean (2014, p. 173) states: "definition of the 'deserving poor' was even more stringent than the institutionalized categories of the 1996 Welfare Reform, since *no* Americans seemed to qualify as worthy of help." Bean's observations demonstrate that levels of giving by themselves do not capture the whole story. Even when the American evangelists give, they do not really think that the people deserve it; they still do it out of a sense of duty.

Rebecca Allahyari's (2000, pp. 81–82, 89–91) study of the Salvation Army (henceforth SA) shows that this organization successfully enforces work requirements (in return for charity). The Black poor who were allowed to stay overnight at SA shelters (in Sacramento, CA) were expected to look for work in the morning (pp. 164–165). There were also curfew hours during the night. Those who abided by all the rules could stay at the shelter for an extra month (the usual limit was one month). Some of the beneficiaries eventually became shelter staff. The poor not only received aid, but they changed their "moral selves" (pp. 4–5, 9, 11–12): they became hard-working, sober, responsible individuals (in other words, neoliberal subjects).

There was a direct link between the expanding Black prison population and the SA's activities: most of the volunteers at the shelter were in-house residents or the court had ordered them to serve as volunteers. A minority of church-based volunteers did not get exposed to the same discipline. However, this "top-down" supervision was balanced by the incorporation of some of the poor into the staff, a recognition and privilege that Allahyari did not encounter in the redistributive charity (Loaves and Fishes) she studied (p. 91). The incorporated poor became role models for the beneficiaries (p. 164).[17]

The contrasts Allahyari found with the Catholic Worker-connected Loaves and Fishes Shelter are enlightening. The Catholic Worker's publications encouraged the middle-class providers and volunteers to change their moral selves, rather than the poor. They also addressed what the organization saw as the root causes of poverty: unemployment, housing policies, and questions of redistribution. The broader goal was to correct these wrongs. The shelter's environment was feminine and welcoming, and created an overall feeling of *entitlement* (in contrast to the masculine SA environment, which reminded the poor of their *conditional rights*).

Government involvement in the SA's quasi-voluntary disciplining is also striking. SA received more private donations than *any other charity in the whole nation* in 1993. The New York City SA, however, still reported that nearly half of its budget came from *government contracts* (Allahyari 2000, p. 216). Neoliberal organizations, then, seem to dominate the American charity field (even if the non-neoliberal organizations, such as the Catholic Worker, had more wiggle room than their Turkish counterparts). In the Turkish case, we will also see a homeless shelter that combined the SA's and the Catholic Worker's techniques: the Companion Association (see Chapter 7) fostered mutual, communal control *among* the in-house beneficiaries, while also mobilizing them to fight the structural causes of poverty.

Bartkowski and Regis's (2003) study of Mississippi's congregations show that (as differences of theology would predict) Black conservative churches are much less neoliberal in their dispositions, but they too have integrated some neoliberal practices. Some congregations go beyond just giving out money and food: their members aim to sit at the same tables with the poor, get involved in their lives, help them resolve psychological, familial, work difficulties, and also encourage sustainable work lives. They use rigorous measuring devices (visits, inspections, escorting the poor to the market) to discipline the poor (Bartkowski and Regis 2003, p. 75). But unlike the Salvation Army (which is also very involved in personal lives), these congregations do not blame the poor for their poverty: just like the Catholic Worker, they emphasize the root causes of poverty (classism and racism). They cultivate solidarity as much as discipline (e.g. see pp. 66–67).

It is telling how little research has been done on what American Christian activists *actually do regarding poverty*. In our era of religious-charitable revival, we have clues on money flows and denominational differences, but not much on actual *practices*. As social sciences and the humanities have shown (starting with Weber and stretching all the way to Geremek), the way Christians relate to poverty has been central to the unmaking of the medieval world and the making of modern society. We need to know: To what extent do organizations such as the Salvation Army, the Catholic Worker, the Mississippi congregations, and other less-studied ones remake actorhood and the modern association? Is there really a predominant organizational template in the American religious charitable field? The social sciences are full of statements on how American models of actorhood, NGOs, and religious templates spread to the whole world and standardize it (Strang and Meyer 1993; Meyer et al. 1997; Hwang and Powell 2009;

see the Conclusion for further discussion). Yet, we cannot even begin to test this claim outside of the United States, due to the dearth of research on how religious charitable actors *within the US* organize and behave. When it comes to gauging whether the "modern organization" is indeed diffusing through the globe, we are thus shooting in the dark as we move towards two other prominent cases of charitable revival.

The Dismantling of Egyptian and Turkish Corporatism and the Rise of Liberal Welfare

The Turkish and Egyptian republics initially instituted a solidarist understanding of poverty and welfare. However, ironically, they also did the groundwork for later Islamic liberalization of charity through undoing, marginalizing, or subordinating (communitarian) Islamic organizations of provision. Before we go into the details of how liberalized charity is exactly practiced in Turkey and Egypt, we have to develop a firm understanding of the republican-solidarist modernization of welfare, and of how its neoliberal dismantling drew on (and diverged from) American neoliberalization.

During the interwar years, the Turkish republican regime focused on re-creating the war decimated population and improving its health. Class struggle in Europe and the resulting Bolshevik revolution, as well as the nascent local working-class struggle that showed its first major signs in 1908, also incited the regime to take precautionary measures. The basic strategy was the prevention of working-class formation through solidaristic discourse and welfare practices (Özbek 2006). Even though this led to a ramshackle corporatism (especially through the development of welfare policies for governmental employees), the Turkish welfare system never moved in a completely corporatist direction, as did the Egyptian one. The much more intense corporatism in Egypt was based on state-run unions and workers' quotas in parliament and other elected bodies (Ayubi 1994). Even though a stateled, import-substituting industrial capitalism characterized both countries, the corporatist-solidarist welfare system in Turkey was more transfused with elements of democracy and the market when compared to the one in Egypt.

The early Turkish Republic (the statist one-party era) introduced social security programs only to meet the needs of formal employees. There was no systematic program of social provision for others (Buğra 2008). The regime rather dealt with these through clientelism. The ruling party also mobilized voluntary associations that focused on urban and infantile poverty (Özbek 2006, pp. 88–91); in that sense, it was not strictly statist. The party also mobilized semi-official/ semi-voluntary associations (the people's houses, the village institutes, Himaye-i Etfal) that carried out social provision and disseminated the regime's ideology (secular, solidarist nationalism).

After the mid-1940s, the interaction of a few factors (the increase in political competition; the globally fashionable solidaristic discourse on citizen rights; and the pro-welfare input of immigrant German and Austrian academics) ushered in the first systematic attempts to build a twentieth-century-style welfare state (Özbek 2006, pp. 159, 162). In this environment, the burden of welfare decisively shifted to the shoulders of the state, marginalizing the role of voluntary associations that had been central to the equation ever since the Young Turks (Özbek 2006, pp. 189–194).

Still, welfare policies disproportionately benefited formal employees in the public and private sectors (at the expense of informal workers and peddlers). The two major Social Security institutions (the Social Insurance Institution and the Retirement Chest) covered workers and civil servants. Two much smaller institutions (Bağ-Kur and the Social Assistance Institute) served the self-employed, the urban poor, the unemployed, kids, and teenagers. Much of this population also depended on patronage politics, as well as on religious orders and communities (Göçmen 2010, pp. 86–87).

In Egypt, before republican times, the private sector and charities provided education and health. The state contributed very little to social provision (Tadros 2006). Charities even dealt with major cholera and malaria epidemics. This all changed under "Arab socialism" in the 1950s and 1960s. One of the Nasserist state's priorities was universalizing healthcare, education, and the right to work.

This grand design, however, exceeded the Egyptian state's capacities. Welfare benefits remained restricted to formal (public and private) employees. Despite Nasser's initial hopes, full employment remained an impossible dream. Informal workers did not stand much to gain from this socialist-hued corporatism (Waterbury 1983, p. 223). Nevertheless, the more socially oriented Egyptian corporatism partially acknowledged this weakness by instituting subsidies of basic necessities; this direct provision, unlike corporatist elements of Egyptian welfarism, would cover the whole population. After Sadat, however, even the most essential subsidies (e.g. of bread) gradually became more erratic.

Intermittent liberalization in Turkey (from 1950 to 1980) did not upset the overall corporatist context, until the fateful September 12, 1980 junta. A new center-right platform (the Motherland Party or ANAP) further popularized the junta's struggles against the secular left and revolutionary Islam, getting ample support from secular and religious businessmen, tradesmen, and (private sector) professionals. This resulted in higher unemployment rates and lower average wages for unionized workers. American-trained personnel (primarily ANAP's founder Turgut Özal) implemented these policies, lending support to the diffusion account.

Özal's last couple of years witnessed mounting labor resistance. After his death, the center-right disintegrated once again, which rendered liberalization unmanageable. In response to a devastating financial meltdown in 2001, the Turkish economist Kemal Derviş, a top-level World Bank figure, reformatted Turkey's economy based on the post-Washington consensus model (see below). A core component of Derviş's program, unlike Özal's, was the implementation of liberal *welfare* policies.

Irregular waves of neoliberalization gripped Egypt from the 1970s to the 1990s. The balance sheet initially included sustained growth in the first half of the 1980s and fluctuating growth afterwards, declining real wages, and increasing unemployment and poverty throughout this period (Kienle 1998). Sadat was the first president to attempt thorough liberalization policies, known by the name of Open Door or Opening (*infitah*). These policies, initiated circa 1974, were much milder than what was to come decades later, but still imposed a new ethics and set of practices that constituted decisive breaks with the state-citizen "compact" formed during Nasser. The culmination of Sadat's liberalization was a stand-by agreement with the International Monetary Fund (IMF) in 1977, the epicenter of which was currency devaluation, budget cuts, and welfare-gutting. The IMF-stamped subsidy cuts of basic necessities resulted in riots and 77 deaths.

The riots led to new negotiations between the state and the IMF, as a result of which many subsidies were first restored, and then eliminated gradually (and without much public fanfare). Moreover, this dismantling of the welfare state unraveled in an overall political economic atmosphere of uncertainty, as Mubarak (president after 1981) initially engaged in more erratic liberalization. Egypt adapted another IMF agreement in 1986, but then abandoned it. Yet, an IMF agreement in 1993 had more lasting effects, such as thorough privatization and a decisive decrease in the budget deficit, even if Egypt never achieved the desired level of private-sector-led growth (Richards and Waterbury 2007; Suleiman 2005). This restructuring also involved the decrease of subsidized foods from 18 in 1980 to four in 1995 (Salevurakis and Abdel-Haleim 2008, p. 40). In the meantime, the government also abandoned universal healthcare and education without any constitutional acknowledgement (Tadros 2006, pp. 239–240). As a result of these policies, the last quarter of the century led to an overall deterioration in the poor's conditions and an increase in their numbers (Ibrahim, 2004, p. 482; Tadros 2006).

The deeper neoliberal turn in Turkey has resulted in more growth and more social disruption (for further details, numbers, and tables, see Tuğal 2012a and 2016a). But in response, Turkish liberalism has ultimately become more social. While dismantling the three major (corporatist) institutions of social provision (the Retirement Chest, the Social Insurance Institution and Bağ-Kur), the liberal-Islamic Justice and Development Party (henceforth Ak Party) also subjected all wage earners, the unemployed, and other vulnerable sectors to the same umbrella institution (Buğra and Keyder 2006). The Ak Party politically "normalized" Kemal Derviş's liberal, targeted, means-tested restructuring of the welfare state. This Turkish mass adoption of the post-Washington Consensus (the "social" turn of the Bretton Woods institutions to a restricted form of the liberal welfare state) attests to further diffusion of Western templates. Egypt has not experienced such a consistent turn to social neoliberalism so far.

However, local particularities "contaminated" this diffusion. The Ak Party further institutionalized arbitrary state generosity (especially direct provision to the poor closer to election times). As importantly, the popular perception of this generosity (as party leader Erdoğan's *personal* desire) revived paternalistic elements of communitarianism. In the meantime, rural to urban migration has partially undermined other types of provincial support networks (not only the extended family). Most central to these is both the decline and the refashioning of traditional religious orders, *tarikat* (Göçmen 2010). Religious communities throughout Turkey have responded to this decline by transforming religious support networks in urban and more modern contexts (Tuğal 2009). Even though research on this is inconclusive,[18] it has been suggested that traditional religious order support networks (as well as Ottoman style foundations) have inherited some of their resources and techniques to contemporary Islamic-inspired associations (Göçmen 2010). In sum, a new "welfare governance" (government-charity partnerships that mobilize poor people's entrepreneurial capacities, see Buğra and Candas 2011, p. 522) has replaced formal welfare in both cases.

Some scholars (e.g. Zeybek 2013, pp. 92–99) interpret this new governance as a return to the waqf institution and its gift-centeredness: Erdoğan has revived Abdülhamid II's spirit, as this is what the Turkish imaginary knows best. However, this diagnosis is only partially on target, as my ethnographic material (Chapters 4–8) further demonstrates: the new welfare regime rather undermines some aspects of the gift logic through the aggressive propagation of the market logic. Nevertheless, many elements of paternalist communitarianism do persist in Turkey. This persistence not only limits but even has the potential to undermine neoliberal diffusion. Through a partial revival of (Hamidian) communitarianism, the late Ak Party regime has gone beyond social neoliberalism and integrated rigorous elements of personalism, sectarianism, arbitrariness, and ample informal generosity into a neoliberalized welfare regime. Concomitantly, fractions among the poor have become committed to the regime not simply based on means-tested provision, but via moralized, personalized affect. Yet, these developments are better interpreted as results of field dynamics (rather than a straightforward return to Hamidianism).

Furthermore, scholars have noticed such contradictory developments in other neoliberal regimes as well. James Ferguson (2015) provides a detailed account of many (previously neoliberal) regimes' moves in redistributive directions (e.g. through cash transfers, which are conditional on school attendance on paper, but are distributed evenly in practice). These developments constitute a divergence from the American model. Increasing impurities of neoliberalism signal the global transition to a new era, I suggest, rather than Turkish-Islamic uniqueness.

Islamic Movements and the Charity Fields[19]

The histories of Islamic mobilization in Egypt and Turkey had a deep impact on good works. After the 1970s, benevolence came to be more central to Islamists' activities as a response to increasing impoverishment in both Egypt and Turkey: the restructuring of the welfare state and increasing pietistic activities coincided to give a boost to charity. In Egypt, some members and affiliates of Islamist organizations split from the main body in the 1990s to establish less religiously oriented aid organizations, leading to a *fragmented charity field*. These joined the largest complexes of aid-provision in the region, one of them boasting around 100,000 volunteers a year in the 2000s. In Turkey, despite the proliferation of competing aid organizations, the Sunni Islamic ones gradually converged on accepting the political leadership of the Ak Party in the 2000s. This created a still competitive, but ethically more *unified charity field*.

A field is composed of a competitive set of actors. Each actor (whether an individual, group, or organization) wields power based on its differences from the others (Bourdieu 1991, 1994, pp. 15–16). The actors distinguish themselves not only through certain resources (such as financial assets, distinct organizational forms and capacities, etc.), but also through contrasting dispositions as regards how the competition should be performed. The structure of religious fields vary cross-nationally (as well as on other scales) based on how unified or fragmented they are—i.e. whether one major organization can claim to speak in the name of religion (or one kind of religion, such as Sunni Islam) in the whole country. This can happen, for example, through absorbing the major religious (or Sunni) players into a mass party.

For the purposes of the current discussion, I restrict myself to Sunni Islamic (religious and charitable) fields and their monopolization and fragmentation. This focus is analytically meaningful, given that Sunni religious organizations compete over the monopolization of a certain kind of pious capital (i.e. the legitimate representation of orthodox Muslims). Similarly, Sunni charitable organizations compete over a specific kind of benevolent capital (that is, funding by pious Sunnis). Even though Christians, secular actors, and sizable non-Sunni Islamic communities (more specifically, the Turkish Alevis, see Massicard 2013 and Tambar 2014) also run benevolent organizations in both Turkey and Egypt, they are not a part of the competition (for the same pool of funding and resources) I study. The boundaries of fields are frequently porous (Massicard 2013), but this is less true of the boundaries between the Sunni charitable fields on the one hand and the Christian and secular ones on the other.

The relative unification of the Turkish charity field was based on the overall unification of the Sunni Islamic religious field. In Egypt, by contrast, the Muslim Brotherhood, official Islam (mainly represented by the vast, modernized seminary al-Azhar), and other (relatively more puritan) Islamist political organizations all sought to represent the true version of Islam. The latter two rejected the Brotherhood's spiritual and political leadership.

Such divisions remained central even as the Egyptian Sunni field as a whole gained vigor. Therefore, the point about fragmentation is not a point about overall weakness. During the last four decades, historical processes (especially the interaction between the states and the fields) produced fragmentation in Egypt and unification in Turkey. Starting with the 1970s, Islamists strengthened within the Egyptian student body. Sadat mobilized both Islamists and al-Azhar against the left (Zeghal 1999). The Muslim Brotherhood tried to help the regime prevent

Islamist students from taking part in demonstrations and strikes, but since it was not a political party, it could not control the students completely (Baker 1991). This provides an important contrast to the Turkish Islamic political party, which had considerable control over Islamist students even in the divisive 1980s. Such control helped build a unified field.

Furthermore, the Muslim Brotherhood poorly integrated urban middle class and peasant elements, which prevented a monopoly of this organization over the Islamic field, and reproduced influential violent Islamist organizations. Even though the latter mostly removed violence from their repertoire in the 2000s, Egypt remained divided among them and the Brotherhood. This provides a contrast to Turkey where Islamic associations, as well as party patronage, integrated the pious in the east and the west of the country. Even though the countryside and the fringes of the cities were home to poverty also in Turkey, the main Islamic political party's patronage networks connected the poor to official institutions (including welfare agencies).

The occasionally brutal repression of Islamists reproduced the Egyptian fragmentation, but did not single-handedly create it, as a comparison with the Turkish 1997 coup suggests:[20] This secularist military intervention bolstered the further unification of an already less fragmented Sunni field. The rise of the Ak Party brought under control the divisions that plagued the Islamic field ever since the rise of Islamism in the 1970s, since this post-coup party promised to fight effectively against anti-Islamist forces (and ultimately delivered on this promise). These processes resulted in popularized visions of what Islamic charity stands for in Turkey, whereas its meaning was more starkly contested in Egypt. This account draws attention to the centrality of effective state action (here, military repression) in aiding neoliberal diffusion,[21] while also demonstrating how field structures interact with state actions to produce the observed results.

There was also a contrast between the two nations' Islamists in terms of their official approach to neoliberalism. As early as 2002, the Ak Party incorporated neoliberal benevolent ethics to its official program. The party committed itself to investing in human capital, fostering self-reliance among society's members, and empowering the poor at the economic level (in individualized fashion) (Atasoy 2009, p. 111). By contrast, the Egyptian Muslim Brotherhood's commitment to neoliberalism, while growing ever since the 1970s, was always ridden with doubts, internal criticisms, and resistances, and many qualifications (Utvik 2006). In the post-2011 scene too, the instability of this commitment was reproduced due to pressures from the political left, workers' strikes, and less neoliberal Islamic circles (crucial players in a fragmented field) (Tuğal 2012a). In sum, field fragmentation led to foot-dragging with respect to neoliberalization in Egypt, whereas field unity in Turkey allowed the leading Islamic party to send unequivocally neoliberal messages to the whole nation.

Given that the Egyptian religious field as a whole was gaining momentum, its fragmentation did not necessarily imply weakness; but a major result was the reproduction of communitarian dispositions in the charity field. The tight linkage of political, charity, and *da'wa* (religious mission) activities *throughout a century* created a resilient inertia. What is more, this was not an unreflexive inertia: communitarians mobilized their resources in support of a comprehensive understanding of Islam (*fehm ed-din esh-shamil*,[22] a key phrase that came up in many interviews).[23] They controlled—through public and secretive, legal and illegal ways—civil society to a certain extent, preventing a complete shift in a neoliberal direction. Even though the religious field in Egypt was much more fragmented than the Turkish one, the melding of politics, charity, and religious mission was the shared and taken-for-granted assumption of one pole of the Egyptian field and the communitarian charitable associations under its sway. Actually, the fragmentation prevented any possible religious actor from intervening in either the religious or the charitable fields in a radically transformative way and shattering this assumption. As a result, communitarian tendencies were ingrained in both actors and organizations, rendering neoliberal diffusion quite difficult.

In Turkey, by contrast, neoliberal associations started to outpace communitarian charity by the early 2000s. Much like its communitarian counterparts in Egypt, the Turkish (communitarian-Islamist) Welfare Party also controlled charity activities in the 1980s and 1990s. Yet, the Turkish charitable field was not as united as it came to be in the 2000s; and this party's control of the overall field was consistent but feeble when compared to the Ak Party's neoliberal control in the 2000s. Welfare Party control did not have the same results for charity work as in Egypt (i.e. the entrenchment of communitarian ethics) for two more reasons.

First, mission-oriented Islamic mobilization in Turkey picked up pace only in the 1970s: it was of much shorter duration when compared to Egypt (where it was at least a century old). The reasons for this relatively late mobilization are complex, but a prominent one is the more solidly secularist legacy in Turkey and the concomitant submission of Islamic forces to the center-right, which seemed to be the only viable alternative to rigid secularism (and its unintended offspring, the militant left) up until the late 1960s. Rather than working to build an independent Islamist line as in Egypt, most Turkish Islamists spent their political energies to expand the power of the center-right against the secularist center and the left (which trained them to be expert politicians, but distracted them from mission and charity). This started to change only in the early 1970s (Çakır 1990). Rather than one movement being weaker or stronger, this resulted in the *uneven development of the movements' capacities*: till the 1970s, the Turkish Islamists were much more politically savvy, but much less committed to building mission (*da'wa/tebliğ*) and charity organizations when compared to their Egyptian counterparts. It is telling how this uneven development of Islamism was linked to the variegated diffusion of neoliberalism: the stronger investment of Egyptian Islamists in communitarian charity made it relatively more difficult for them to adjust to the new times once the globe shifted in a neoliberal direction following the 1970s. This was among the factors that prevented them from emerging as the victors of the new world, unlike their (politically flexible and effective) Turkish counterparts.

Second, a successful (interestingly non-fragmenting) split within the Islamist party as a response to the (secularist) 1997 military intervention led to the merger of the market-oriented wing of Islamism with the state. This split resulted in the formation of the Ak Party in 2001, but this wing's maneuvers against the communitarian Islamists and its strategic cooperation with the state go back to the mid-1990s. The neoliberal wing of the Turkish Islamic movement (formerly the less popular, if more resourceful, market-oriented flank of the communitarian Welfare Party) gained respect within the religious field, as well as among the benevolent actors. This rise to prominence was facilitated, among other things, by its unification of most of the competing Sunni factions (the relatively more puritanical Islamists, representatives of official Islam, non-Alevi Sufi communities, etc.) against the hardliner secularists. Thanks to this unification, the Ak Party became the governing party in 2002. Its leadership contained the distrustful antagonisms of the 1970s–1990s, whereas no such unifying actor emerged on the Egyptian scene. The Ak Party's rise spelled the end of consistent communitarian influence on the charity field (up until 2013).

The party's effectiveness against the non- and anti-Sunni forces made its aggressive neoliberalism easier to swallow among even potentially anti-neoliberal actors, such as some benevolent associations. The neoliberal Islamic party, the governing party of the Turkish regime from 2002 until the present, boosted the activities of the neoliberal benevolent associations (without facing any serious criticism from communitarian rivals, who came to be relatively weak, in stark contrast to Egypt). Consequently, one of the decisive developments in the 2000s was the explosive growth of two neoliberal aid organizations (*Deniz Feneri* and *Kimse Yok mu*) and the stagnation of a major communitarian aid organization, *Cansuyu* (Göçmen 2010). This latter organization remained loyal to the major (but now, relatively small and ineffective) communitarian Islamist party that was left behind after the Ak Party's split from the main body of the Islamic movement. This party, now called the Felicity Party, fell from (popular) grace in the 2000s and dragged down with itself the largest communitarian benevolent organization.

Hence, the unification of the religious field created a more unified benevolence field in Turkey. While non-neoliberal dispositions could survive with relative ease in the fragmented Egyptian benevolence field, the Turkish benevolence field (despite its diversity) was more receptive to neoliberal expectations and rhetoric (under the impact of a unified, neoliberal religious leadership). Another major consequence of these developments was that new, smaller entrants to the Turkish field unquestioningly took the neoliberal organizations as their model (as the communitarian ones were less influential and visible throughout the 2000s), while those in Egypt had communitarian *as well as* neoliberal organizations to model themselves on (as both could be construed as stories of success and survival).[24]

Despite these qualitative differences, the growing significance of religious giving in both cases is unmistakable. While Islamic NGOs, most of them involved in aid, comprised 16 percent of all Egyptian NGOs in the 1960s, in the

1970s this ratio increased to 30 percent, and then to 43 percent in the 1990s (Abdelrahman 2004, p. 138). Asef Bayat (2002) reports that Islamic aid organizations "accounted for one-third of all Egyptian private voluntary organizations in the late 1980s, and at least 50 percent of all welfare associations (or 6,327) in the late 1990s." The 4,000 registered *zakat* committees collected $10 million USD in 1992 and provided health services to 15 million people as opposed to 4.5 million in 1980 (Kandil 1998, pp. 145–146). These numbers, it should be added, do not take into account the informal (as well as illegal) Islamic aid activities.

The numbers are more difficult to track in the Turkish case, due to the relatively more secularist legal context: Islamic or religious organizations are not officially labeled as such (in most cases). Anecdotal evidence, however, hints that faith-based organizations have a huge impact in Turkey too. For instance, one study (Göçmen 2010, p. 144) has pointed out that only 13 Turkish faith-based organizations have a total budget of $66 million USD, a significant amount when compared to the budget of the biggest state aid agency, $395 million USD. Of the 80,000 officially registered associations, more than 15,000 have provided religious services of some sort, according to another study (Şen 2011). More than 20 percent of these define their main aim to be social assistance and charity.

The Theo-Organizational Underpinnings of Global Charity

The growth and structure of charity associations in Egypt and Turkey is an outcome of both the international explosion of voluntary associations and of the global Islamic revival. We cannot study them solely within the *national* context of the two countries. Even though the civic charity entrenchment in the two countries happened mostly following the 1990s, Saudi, Gulf, and other Islamic charitable efforts had laid the transnational groundwork in the 1970s. Hence, the explosion of oil prices in the 1970s was an integral part of the charitable story. Islamic Relief Organization of Saudi Arabia (founded in Jeddah, 1979) would later become an inspiration for many of the associations covered in this book. It mostly focused on Muslims in Africa. The Egyptian cleric Yusuf al-Qaradawi was pretty central to these efforts. His persistent calls for more charitable involvement led to the foundation of the International Islamic Charitable Organization in 1984 (Petersen 2012, p. 766). Qaradawi urged Muslims to help those in need in order also to prevent Christian missionary activity. Qaradawi's and others' efforts interwove the local (e.g. see Mahmood 2005) and global missionary (daʿwa) thrust of Muslims and their charitable activities.

While disaster and hunger in Africa (as well as Christian missionary activity) were the main impulses for action in the 1970s, military conflicts in Afghanistan and Bosnia became the main charitable mobilizing grounds in the 1980s and early 1990s (Petersen 2012, pp. 767–770). The United States was very much favorable to Islamic charitable organizations in the 1980s (due to the anti-Soviet resistance in Afghanistan), but it resorted to restrictive moves in the following decade

(Petersen 2012, p. 769). One of the main organizations in Turkey, the IHH, was established as a part of the pro-Bosnian charitable wave. Qaradawi remained an influential cleric for the organizations established in these years.[25]

In the late 1990s and 2000s, this global Islamic wave intersected with an all-encompassing global turn to religious aid. On one hand, especially after the 9/11 attacks, the so-called war on terror discouraged missionary (da'wa) activity, regarding which the West was already becoming suspicious during the 1990s. On the other hand, Western leaders invested ideologically and economically in religiously inspired (but *non-missionary*) "developmental" aid both in the West and outside (nevertheless, see previous sections for "variegation" on this theme even within the West). The increasingly global belief that religiously inspired moral commitment (built through bottom-up channels) would resolve poverty became an extra incentive for Muslim associations that sought to refashion themselves (along non-missionary lines) in the post-9/11, anti-terror atmosphere (Petersen 2012). Many of the largest aid associations in both Turkey and Egypt (Deniz Feneri, Kimse Yok mu Derneği, Resalah, etc.) were established in this atmosphere, attesting to strong tendencies of isomorphism.

Petersen (2012, pp. 773–775) notes that this has led to an "invisible" religiosity that de-emphasizes da'wa (mission), even among some of the most established, formerly mission-oriented organizations, such as Islamic Relief. These organizations "base their daily work on notions of poverty reduction, sustainable development and capacity building rather than on the Qur'an," she argues. Even though this is certainly a strong trend, this book demonstrates that there is a strong variation among *and* within organizations in this regard, as some organizations combine neoliberalization and missionary activity, *and* many members and volunteers of the non-missionary organizations occasionally operate in missionary and less-than-neoliberal ways. Such complexity requires a variegated analysis of charitable neoliberalization.

From Qutb to Qaradawi: the Reproduction of Communitarianism under Neoliberal Conditions

We should evaluate this apparently sharp turn to neoliberal charity in tandem with an assessment of changing theological understanding. Although the last decades have witnessed the rise of globally prominent theologians who call for liberal Islam in political, economic, and cultural affairs, no parallel development has marked Islamic jurisprudence as far as charity goes. As suggested above, Qaradawi (an anti-liberal figure in many regards) has had a big influence on the expansion of communitarian charity in the 1970s and 1980s. There is no similar, globally prominent cleric behind the expansion of neoliberal charity. Despite hopes that Fethullah Gülen would become the Calvin of Islam, he has remained a divisive (albeit somewhat influential) figure. He lacks the authority of Qaradawi, whom Islamists across the board respect. Unlike the prominent liberal intellectuals (Sourush, Jabiri, etc.), Qaradawi has extensively written on charity. His interventions in the Islamic understanding of poverty only make sense in their relation to others' alternative positions: the redistributive turn in Islamism that predates him and the neoliberal turn.

As scholars have noted, with Sayyid Qutb[26] and some of his contemporaries, zakat became one of the central venues of Islamic revival: not only a core tenet of Islam and its principle of social justice, but also a way to center an increasingly inegalitarian society's attention on piety (Singer 2008, pp. 202–205). Qutb's early work has arguably developed the most elaborate redistributive position on zakat and *sadaqa* and therefore deserves scrutiny. When compared to Qaradawi, Qutb (1975, p. 81) has a clear emphasis on the sharing of property; and political reinforcement of redistribution (though the author always talks of a double method, and voluntary redistribution is an essential part of the picture). The *mahrumin* (deprived) "have a right" in the property of the *qadirin* (powerful).

Property belongs to the community and charity is a way of returning it to where it belongs.[27] Even though redistributive and anti-capitalist, sadaqa's and zakat's goals are as much non-socialist: the community collects property (and *has the ultimate right to it*), but recirculates it among its *individual* members. Charity prevents wealth accumulation either in the hands of corporations/individuals or collectivistic organizations.

Qutb (1975, p. 237) relates a well-known story about charity (how during 'Umar's rule, his employees could not find poor people to give sadaqa to), but he innovatively ends it with an analysis of property accumulation:

> [P]overty and want are the fruit of inflated and excess [wealth]. And the poor at all times are the victims of the *mufahhishin* [excessive, obscene, impudent] rich. And the mufahhishin rich are mostly the outcome of stipends, land grants, favoritism, oppression, and exploitation!

Qutb transforms the moral of a common story by integrating social analysis in its midst (poverty *is a result of* riches). In the first editions of his book on social justice, Qutb was against riches without qualification, but then in the later editions he revised his stance: it is only in the latest edition of his book that Qutb added the qualifying adjective mufahhishin in the paragraph above (Shepard 1996, p. 259). Despite this change of heart, Qutb *always* took poverty as a result of corrupt wealth, even in his late writings (a clear contrast with Qaradawi).

Qutb (1975, p. 239) defines the goal of charity not only as the *elimination* of poverty, but also the *prevention of wealth accumulation* in certain hands, since Islam "hates" accumulation. There is no such anti-property sentiment in Qaradawi or Gülen: this specific position is both anti-communitarian and anti-liberal, even if Qutb's broader framework can be classified as communitarian with a strong redistributive bent. Qutb discusses the Prophet Muhammad's appropriation of wealth from the rich to redistribute it among the poor in the same paragraph, clearly indicating that he does not see charity and governmental redistribution as binary opposites, but two Islamic tools that complement each other. These tools fulfill two tasks: annulling "class differences that destroy general balance"[28] (this we could call Qutb's Marxist-Durkheimianism) and the prevention of what Bonner has called "the bad circulation." In short, my analysis establishes two points: Qutb has inherited "the early Islamic economy," but has put a Marxist-Durkheimian spin on it. He has made an Islamic contribution to the (combined and uneven) development of alternatives to liberalism.

Even if the tone and content of Islamists' take on charity change with Qaradawi, some themes remain the same. Among these is the firm emphasis on how Islamic economics is devised to serve the unity and cohesion of the community (1995, p. 11), once again drawing attention to the quasi-Durkheimian spirit in mainstream Islamic thought. The author also reproduces the anti-materialist language of earlier Islamic revival and emphasizes that, unlike in Western economics, pious Muslims engage in economic activity to approach God, not to pursue personal interest (1995, p. 28). Nevertheless, the practical implications of these emphases are much more modest than in redistributive thought. Qaradawi reduces Islam's contradiction with capitalism to the question of illegitimate interest and severely judges Islamic scholars who speak highly of governmental intervention in production (1995, p. 24, contrast with Qaradawi's earlier position, of which more below). Staying away from materialism, likewise, does not imply (as it did in Qutb) the avoidance of personal accumulation, but rather avoidance of criminal accumulation and illicit consumption (1995, pp. 30–31).

Qaradawi also further sharpens one liberal theme that Qutb had started to develop toward the end of his life. He argues that economic freedom (defined in extremely narrow fashion as the right to private property) is at the basis of political, ideational, and religious freedoms (1995, p. 327). Qaradawi moves much beyond Qutb when he links the Islamic experience of the Day of Judgment to private property. He points out that, on judgment day, people will account for their actions as individuals, rather than families, tribes, and peoples, which is a well-known theme of the Qur'an. But he further adds that in order to develop such individual responsibility, the Islamic order grants the individual rights of competition and inheritance. He recognizes the love of private property as such a fundamental component of human nature that it is only through the intensification of this love that people can prepare for the Day of Judgment.

Despite this extreme liberal position on the question of freedom, Qaradawi strays away from liberalism with his argument that Islamic economics prioritizes distribution (*tawzi'*) over production (1995, p. 319). Private property also comes with certain duties. The love of property, even though natural, cannot be left to its own devices; it should be balanced with justice (1995, pp. 350–353).[29] Based on this "social responsibility" argument, we could say that the author is taking communitarianism in a social-liberal direction.

Qaradawi's book on poverty reduction (1967; 1981)[30] further demonstrates his difference from both neoliberal Islam and redistributive Islam. For example,

Qaradawi points out that Islamic governments have the right to confiscate (*musadara*) half of the property of a non-zakat payer and/or physically punish him as necessitated by the public good ("*hasb al-maslaha*," 1967, p. 82).[31] Even though he quotes some of the same zakat- and sadaqa-related verses with Qutb (e.g. the poor having a right in the wealth of the rich), he does not draw the same redistributive results from them, nor does he incriminate wealth imbalances. As importantly, he strays away from Qutb's certainty regarding poverty-eradication by acknowledging that there are two legitimate schools in [Sunni] Islam (see Chapter 2, this volume), without heavily weighing on either side (Qaradawi 1967, p. 110): while the Sha'afis have argued that zakat should pull people out of poverty for the rest of their lives, Malikis and Hanbalis have argued that it should provide for the poor person only for a year (1967, p. 104–107).

Still, in a decidedly non-liberal way, he leaves it to *the Islamic state* (and not to propertied believers) to decide *which interpretation to follow*. Along the same lines, he allows zakat-spending authorities (in his account, the government) to build factories and other industries with zakat money in order to ensure that able-bodied believers will have a chance to work (1967, p. 110).

Unlike Qutb, Qaradawi spills a lot of ink on the deserving and undeserving poor. Like the early Hanbalis, he defines the deserving poor as those who are modest and chaste (*al-muta'affifun*) *and therefore do not beg*. They even avoid, he adds, being seen by the rich; so, the Muslim rich have to seek and find them. Still, beggars (even if less dignified than those who do not beg) deserve some zakat (1967, p. 98). The righteous have fallen in poverty because of disability (*qa'ada bihim al-'ajz*), fate ("times have hit them hard," *akhna 'alayhim al-zaman*), an increase in the number of dependents (*'ayalahum*), a decrease (*qil*) in their property, or the insufficiency of income to satisfy reasonable needs (1967, p. 99).

Since so much hinges on the definition of "reasonable needs," it is worth looking closely at Qaradawi's symbolic work in this regard. A very important twist Qaradawi puts on deserving-ness is a hierarchical, arguably communitarian desire to preserve social order and status. Even though able-bodied people who shun work do not deserve zakat, the latter can be given to the propertied (who have homes, horses, weapons, and even servants) whose expenditure exceeds their income (1967, pp. 100–101). Spending zakat for the sustenance of these privileged lifestyles would be unthinkable for redistributive Muslims (such as Qutb) and liberal Muslims (such as Gülen). What is remarkable here is not the ideas as such (which go as far back as the ninth century), but their reproduction in and adjustment to modern times. For instance, Qaradawi (1967, pp. 111–112) comments on the contemporary need to define healthcare and education as the rights of all citizens; in other words, his *organicist-hierarchical ordering* of the social is to be carried out and maintained *within an overall welfarist state*. Qaradawi, then, creatively combines classical Islamic jurisprudence and Central European welfarist corporatism.

Moreover, it is notable that Qaradawi focuses mostly on zakat and little on sadaqa and governmental distribution beyond the zakat (even if this comes into the picture more when compared to liberal Islamic interpretations): he has chosen to ignore Qutb's sociological insight that in "normal" times (where war booty is not abundant) Muslims would have to do much more than give zakat to deal with poverty.

With his persistent emphasis on personal as well as social responsibility, Qaradawi has taken communitarianism in a liberal direction. However, his points regarding property confiscation, the state's prerogative to fix theological interpretations of charity, and the preservation of the organic-hierarchical balance demonstrate that he is far from being the guru of neoliberal Islamic revival. This role falls to the much less influential Fethullah Gülen.

The Neoliberal Islamic Turn

Fethullah Gülen has written very little on charity when compared to Qutb and Qaradawi, but he has given eight long sermons on the subject (about 90 minutes each). In one of the articles he has written, he has drawn attention to how zakat multiplies the property of the giver.[32] What is original here is not the statement itself, but Gülen's dedication of about a half of the few charity-related pieces he has written to this pro-property point and its theological support.

Gülen's speeches, though including some communitarian themes, also decisively veer in this direction. The speeches reproduce the Islamic understanding that zakat prevents jealousy and rebellion on the part of the poor, and excessive greed on the part of the wealthy, thereby establishing social balance. However, they also point out to the work-ethic-inducing aspects of zakat.[33] While Qutb and Qaradawi (much like many other twentieth-century Islamists) also desire to develop the work ethic, they do not discuss zakat and sadaqa as strong paths to that end. In neoliberal Islam, even sharing one's property renders both the giver and the receiver more responsible liberal subjects.

As remarkable is how little emphasis on governmental duty we hear in Gülen's sermons (although he gave them in 1978, that is, before the heyday of neoliberalism). Even for the liberalized communitarian Qaradawi, it is incumbent on the Commander of the Faithful (and the governmental apparatus at his command) to make sure that the poor have access not only to livelihood, but also education and healthcare; when zakat and sadaqa are not sufficient to provide these, it is his duty to tax the rich. Qaradawi (1967, pp. 125–126) bases this assignment on what has been dubbed "the organic metaphor" in the social sciences (as well as an explicit criticism of Adam Smith):

> Islam has pictured [*sawwara*] society as one body [*al-jasad al-wahid*], so that every device/apparatus [*jihaz*] or organ [*'adu*] or cell [*khalia*] in this body is related to the others. ... The state ... "the imam" ... is the head of this body, he is the device that protects/guards [*yar'a*] the interconnection and solidarity [*tadamun*] of the individuals of a society.

Qaradawi brings up the organic metaphor on other occasions too (1967, p. 135). While this Durkheimian language permeates Qaradawi's writing, it is difficult to see organicist traces in Gülen, whose preaching is thoroughly individual-oriented.

In short, the most globally accessible and available body of Islamic scholarship on the topic of charity is communitarian. There is also some redistributive scholarship/theology available. Liberal scholarship and theology on charity is weak, but is growing at a quick pace. Fethullah Gülen, a most prominent neoliberal cleric, has said little on the topic. Moreover, his sermons on zakat are yet to be translated to other languages. Nevertheless, what liberal Muslims lack in theology, they make up for in practice and organization, as the following chapters will demonstrate. Still, the intensifying practice of liberal Islamic charity is not buoyed up by widely circulated and internalized texts. This does not mean that a thoroughly neoliberal charitable theology is not possible. The Egyptian preacher 'Amr Khaled has produced such a theology. But Khaled's writing and preaching, even though popular throughout the globe, have not become widespread currency among charity providers in Turkey and Egypt as much as the writings of Qutb and/or Qaradawi. Instead, Khaled and his followers have established their own charitable organizations, where his preaching is naturally well-known.[34] Khaled's and Gülen's preaching attests to an increasingly neoliberalizing Islam, but their charitable theology has by no means upset the predominance of the communitarian understanding among the clergy and lay Islamist thinkers, let alone charitable donors and volunteers.

The Logic of Fields

This chapter provided some indications regarding the dynamics of the charitable field (and the subjectivities it fosters) in the world leader of religious neoliberalization, the United States. It has also suggested how the making of the neoliberal donor/volunteer constitutes a *break* from everyday American giving, which still harbors strongly communitarian elements. However, we have also seen that Christian giving in America is not *exclusively* neoliberal. Other ethics still negotiate and challenge elements of the hegemonic understanding of charity. A more thorough study of the Egyptian and Turkish fields force us to go beyond the existing literature on Western charity, the focus of which on *fields* and *subjectivities* is rudimentary. The analysis of Egyptian and Turkish fields demonstrates that a story of overall convergence (as in new institutionalist models) is simply impossible (even though both universes *are* under Anglo-Saxon influence). A Gramscianized field analysis (in conjunction with a variegated political economy approach) helps decipher the dynamics of subjectivity in Islamic charitable worlds.

Notes

1 For more details regarding charitable rationalization and categorization during the thirteenth through fifteenth centuries, see Geremek (1994, pp. 38–44).

2 There were many other subtle shifts throughout these centuries. For example, eighteenth-century England broke away from seventeenth-century conceptions of poverty by emphasizing how the immorality of the poor was *one* of the core reasons of poverty. Even then, however, poverty was still taken to be a part of fate *and* the upper classes were held responsible for ameliorating it. Yet, the new upper class task came to be to educate the poor in Christian (work) ethics (Bendix 1974, pp. 60–68). This temporary move foreshadows some of the developments in charitable ethics studied throughout this book, even if not as strongly as late Victorian charitable ethics.

3 This semi-official, upper-class insistence on self-help had unintended consequences too: taking this idea of self-help seriously (though not in the individualist fashion it was intended), the lower classes of England ultimately organized themselves into a combatant working class (Bendix 1974, pp. 115–116; E. P. Thompson 1966). Polanyi ironically states: "whatever the future had in store for them, working-class and market economy, appeared in history together" (Polanyi 2001, p. 105).

4 Another core difference of Smith from Ricardo and Malthus was his ultimate subordination of wealth and individual interest to the common good of the national community (Polanyi 2001, p. 116). Also see Arrighi (2007) for more differences between Adam Smith and turn-of-the-nineteenth century political economy.

5 The new political economy (and incidentally, the new Evangelism) insisted that (except the very bottom rank of the poor) the laboring classes would be *able to develop virtue* if faced with unremitting misery (Bendix 1974, pp. 83–86). This was another core difference from much of the Puritan ethics of the eighteenth century (which, like Calvinism, perceived the majority of humanity to be naturally devoid of virtues such as thrift and hard work).

6 More recent statistics of the era reveal that not only the contemporaries but even the sociology and economic history of the 1950s–1970s exaggerated the level of impoverishment caused by the Elizabethan laws and the Speenhamland system, but the fact remains that the contemporaries experienced this period as one of impoverishment and most important of all moral degradation. See Block and Somers (2003) regarding how and why Polanyi was partially inaccurate.

7 I owe this phrasing to Ann Swidler.

8 Even if the anti-urban panic of the nineteenth century diminished after the 1920s with the discovery that urbanism led to a pacifying conformism rather than revolution (Boyer 1978, p. 289), anti-urban attitudes still predominate in American public life with an influence over even the social sciences (Wacquant 2002, p. 1522).

9 However, for the middle-class agenda of some Islamic charitable actors (and their disinterest in the poor's moral transformation), see Clark (2004).

10 Although eventually secularized (as well as rationalized), this idea and technique of "the visitor" had strong religious roots. American evangelicalism relied on *female volunteers* who introduced the Bible to the poor. In the words of the Baltimore Bible Society (1822, cited in Boyer 1978, p. 24): "men might be regarded as intruders, but what door would be rudely closed against female loveliness; what heart so hard, as to be insensible to the soft and imploring tones of her voice?" The parallels to today's Islamic mobilization are striking.

11 As different from England and other Western cases, the poor in the shelters were seldom put to work. But imprisonment and transportation of able-bodied men were common (Ener 2003, pp. 21–22).

12 By the time the Turkish Republic was founded, three-fourths of its arable land was waqf property (Kuran 2001, pp. 848–850).

13 Race has been an important factor in these debates, as Black churches were more willing participants (Makaye 2012). However, one scholar (Owens 2006, p. 70) raises the possibility that money flowing in the direction of moderate, liberal, and Black churches might actually produce counterintuitive results. It might *dissuade especially the*

Black churches from protest activity and decrease all three's suspicion of church-state separation. This hints that state-society cooperation in the neoliberal era might alter charitable ethics in subtle ways, e.g. through rendering Black churches less redistributive in their charitable orientations (rather than directly feeding into religious conservatism).

14 This is not surprising, since (as one top expert of the FBOs points out): "The impact of neoliberalism on social welfare provision has become a major focus in policy and academic debate although noticeably absent in mainstream U.S. professional schools of public administration and nonprofit management" (Schneider 2013, p. 433). If the impact of neoliberalization on nonprofits is understudied, much less analyzed is the causality in the reverse direction (the nonprofits' active furthering of neoliberalization).

15 This approach to the field of generosity is based on Bourdieu's Weber-inspired study of the religious field; the latter comes into existence when experts monopolize spirituality.

16 There is ongoing debate about which denominations are involved in charity the most (Mock 1992); which give most and least for their churches (Hoge and Yang 1994); whether intense religiosity impacts giving for non-denominational purposes in a negative way; how levels of religiosity correlate with volunteerism (Wilson and Musick 1997); and how all of these factors correlate with church attendance and individual prayer (Hoge and Yang 1994). As debates revolve around these measurable issues, the underlying theoretical premises have been exposed to less scrutiny.

17 Allahyari raises the question of whether these practices constitute "social control" (as most of the critical literature on the SA asserts) or sincere "redemption" and answers that it is both: "Perhaps the volunteers I observed did not experience the demands of The Salvation Army as social control, because their moral selving involved the acceptance of self-control … [T]he kitchen workers accepted a social ideal in which they welcomed strategies for disciplining the self." This is the beginning of a good answer, but the framing of the question and the conceptualization (it is both control and sincere redemption) do not go far enough. Rather than introducing control and sincere belief as alternatives, and then saying benevolent practices involve both, the concept of hegemony (as consent for domination) underlines that in modern times the tendency of the dominant classes has become to mobilize active participation (and sincere belief in the virtue of their control).

18 Unfortunately, research will remain far from satisfactory in the foreseeable future, due to the secretive ways in which religious orders operate, as well as legal sanctions against them.

19 This section is integrated from Tuğal (2017b) with minor modifications.

20 This and other contrasts throughout the book demonstrate that state-making also had an impact on charitable fields and practices, but did not structure them on its own. For more examples and theoretical discussion of the limits and strengths of state-based explanations, see Tuğal (2016a, 2017b).

21 Kandil (2012) and Sayigh (2012, pp. 21–23) have extensively analyzed the contentious and contested co-operation between the Egyptian regime and its military, with some focus on the implications for marketization, charity, and Islamization.

22 My transliterations from Arabic are based on the Egyptian colloquial whenever I quote from interviews and conversations, but I stick to the modern standard transliteration whenever I quote from texts (or when the interviewer emphatically uses classical or modern standard Arabic).

23 This emphasis can be seen also in the texts of an Egyptian sociologist revered by and connected to both the communitarian and the neoliberal associations: Ghaanim (2010, pp. 13–14, 70) argues that a meticulous study and knowledge of Islamic law (as well as morality based on the knowledge of that law) is *necessary* for effective benevolent activity.

24 The implications of massive religious and political disturbance after 2013 (in both countries) for the field structures analyzed here are too unpredictable at this point. For some suggestive analyses of these implications, see Tuğal (2016a; 2017b).

25 Qaradawi is still arguably the most influential cleric alive, though after 9/11 many in the West started to perceive him as having links with jihadi efforts. Similar perceptions of the Muslim Brotherhood, with which he has strong ties, have also led Saudi Arabia and Sisi's Egypt to further restrict his influence.
26 Petersen (2011) and Singer (2008, pp. 202–204) have noted that Qutb (along with Qaradawi) is one of the main inspirations behind the charitable revival among Muslims. Focusing on Qutb as representative of a major trend in Islamic charity might appear controversial, given that he is usually perceived as a theorist of violence, rather than provision. While Qutb is in some senses idiosyncratic, his reception among Islamists cannot be reduced to his role as a prophet of violence (though his impact in this regard is undeniable, see Tuğal 2017a). His current place in the Turkish public sphere is particularly interesting, given frequent endorsements of Qutb by *some of the regime's key intellectuals* against others who want to write him off. For example, see Hayrettin Karaman, "Seyyid Kutub'un düşünce, iman ve cihad hayatı," *Yeni Şafak*, October 2, 2016; Hakan Albayrak, "Vurun İslamcılara," *Karar*, July, 9 2016. Also see Tuğal (2009; 2016a) for further discussion of his influence and attempts to restrict it.
27 "huwa haq ta'hudhhu al-jamaʿa thumma taruddhu marra ukhra ila al-afrad muhaddidin. Fa takawwun wadhifa al-jamaʿa hina'idhn hiya naql al-mulkiyya al-fardiyya min … yad ila yad ukhra" (Qutb 1975, p. 119).
28 "bima yuʿid al-tawazun ila al-jamaʿa al-Islamiyya, wa bima yuhaqqiq al-raghba al-Islamiyya fi alla tuwjad fawariq bayna al-tabaqat takhal bi hadha al-tawazun al-ʿam."
29 Qaradawi (1995, pp. 365–370) stands with the equality of opportunity and against the equality of conditions, even though he defines equality of opportunity broadly (to include equality of access to health and education).
30 This text, written during the heyday of socialist influence among Arabs, has a clearly anti-socialist stance, and Qaradawi moved closer to capitalism later on. The English translation of Qaradawi's text on poverty is of additional relevance. The 1981 translation of the 1967 original has given it a more liberal flavor by altering some passages. This might have been done to render Qaradawi legible in Anglophone milieus, rather than with an explicit agenda of distortion. For instance, the words "deserving" and "undeserving" are repeated more in the English version; and they are integrated into subsection headings (though they are not there in the Arabic original). For instance, see Qaradawi (1967, p. 97 vs. 1981, p. 98).
31 Qaradawi (1967, pp. 90–95; 1981, pp. 89–96), like Qutb, insists that zakat-giving cannot be left to the goodwill of the rich: it has to be imposed by the state.
32 Fethullah Gülen, "Zekât ve Ramazan Ayı," September 12, 2007. http://tr.fgulen.com/content/view/14193/3/.
33 See "Fethullah Gülen: Zekât-1 (November 24, 1978)" and "Zekât Vaazı-2 (December 1, 1978)": www.youtube.com/watch?v=QcWF7nmb3Gs.
34 Since this neoliberal theology has been thoroughly analyzed by Mona Atia, I will not reproduce here what has already been said.

4

COMPREHENSIVE RELIGION

Communitarian Associations in Egypt

Egypt's biggest charitable associations had two prominent characteristics. They assumed that benevolent and religious activities are inseparable; and they desired to foster (wealth-wise) balanced communities through both. The interconnectedness of religious mission, charity, and the suspicion of wealth demonstrates how deep-rooted communitarian dispositions were.

Another striking characteristic of Egyptian communitarian actors was the double-embeddedness of charitable proclivities in one's family and one's organization. The biographies of benevolent actors and their families merged with organizational history. Actors did not stand outside of charity, simply manipulating it for their purposes. Benevolence constituted them. Certainly, there was rivalry among these actors. There were also signs of individual and familial gain based on charitable activity. Yet, even such self-serving processes were embedded within a collectivity. The textual thickness of religious motivation, the apportioning of blame for poverty, orientations towards one's benevolent activities (e.g. the non-technical understanding of success) and participants' perspectives on society and politics sharply differentiated them from neoliberal charity actors. Moreover, the differentiation was much clearer than in the Turkish case, where liberal orientations spilled more consistently into less neoliberal associations. Another distinguishing feature of these associations was their disinterest in criticizing other associations (while making derogatory remarks about others was a widespread practice in all Turkish, and neoliberal Egyptian, associations).

Some of these associations were highly organized. There were strong signs of rationalization too. Yet, neither intense organizational capacity, nor partial rationalization entailed strong liberalization. Let alone fostering "convergence," the restricted adaptation of "modern" templates only allowed communitarian practices to further implant roots. Moreover, the incorporation of certain neoliberal techniques did not simply lead to "assemblages;" rather, communitarian tendencies heavily subordinated these techniques and prevented a deep neoliberalization.

A scholarly classification of organizations as neoliberal or communitarian is certainly ridden with difficulties. The confounding factor was that actors across the board summoned religiosity and community. But neoliberal organizations did this in a distinct way: they instrumentalized religiosity and community for the cultivation of individual self-reliance. I classified an organization as neoliberal if its main goal was cultivating individual responsibility. I gauged whether this was the case from respondents' assumptions about poverty: neoliberal interviewees assumed that the fundamental cause of poverty was the individual characteristics of the poor, which needed to be changed for an effective resolution of suffering. The apportionment of funds also provided a window into these assumptions: neoliberal organizations aimed to channel relatively more funds to the market-oriented training of the beneficiaries.

I classified an organization as communitarian when its affiliates assumed and/or argued that the fundamental cause of poverty was the moral deficiency of society as a whole. Hence, for them, the main goal of charity was cultivating Islamically inspired modesty (rather than individual responsibility) among both the rich and the poor, which would purportedly result in a community with a balanced distribution of wealth. Consequently, communitarian organizations poured more of their funds to Islamic education and relatively little to career training. A final way to gauge whether an organization was neoliberal or communitarian was to look at its expectations from donors, managers, staff, and volunteers. While neoliberal organizations expected quantifiable career success from these categories of people, communitarian charities anticipated selfless dedication based on piety.

The following chapters also cover organizations that do not perfectly fit into these categorizations. As importantly, I demonstrate the frequent mismatch between beneficiaries and organizations. The chapters also document significant, though less frequent, misalignments between staff and volunteers on the one hand and management on the other. Rather than undermining the scholarly classification, the scrutiny of such complexity is one of the book's central empirical contributions. The analysis of this fluidity also reinforces the book's theoretical argument that the hegemonic and field structures impact alignments and mismatches among multiple actors and organizations.

Communitarian *Da'wa* Associations

These associations focused on da'wa and provision of necessities, while they also engaged in some developmental programs. At the end of the nineteenth century, Muslims reinterpreted da'wa (which refers in the Qur'an to the "invitation" to Islam) to mean the mission, incumbent upon each believer, of spreading the correct understanding and practice of Islam (Mahmood 2005, pp. 57–64). Through perpetual refashioning over the decades, the concept came to refer to a variety of activities ranging from the establishment of Qur'anic schools, mosques, and printing presses to the building of charity organizations. Benevolent activity is now one of the emblematic markers of being a Muslim in Egypt.

In related fashion, Islam was both the core motivation of communitarian da'wa actors and the main goal of their activities. Most of the religious vocabulary they used was textually-based. They carefully provided citations for their beliefs and arguments, even though they occasionally brought up magical stories too. They also thought that their activities would result in a socially just and happy society, not just a pious one.

The managers, staff, and volunteers of these associations distinguished themselves based on compassion and other pro-poor feelings, which (they held) were generally lacking in Egyptian society. They were also distinct in terms of the heavily Islamic-juristic vocabulary they used. The managers worked mostly on a volunteer basis. The staff too worked either as underpaid employees (sacrificing the higher salaries they would earn in for-profit organizations) or as volunteers. While the managers were mostly professionals or small merchants, the class background of the staff was more modest. They mostly came from working class families, though some had climbed up the ladder to become professionals.

These associations spread information and raised money through mosques on the one hand, and family and neighborhood networks on the other. Consequently, rich people contacted through mosque networks, small contributions from modest people, and family and neighborhood contacts constituted the bases of their funding structure (though, their detractors alleged, Saudi and Gulf support was crucial too). They took charitable activity in the current and historical Islamic states as their main models of emulation. Most of their members favored a mixed economy.

A sizable chunk of their volunteers, staff, and managers had been involved in the Islamist movement, or at least the da'wa movement and its mosque networks. Women had a separate but active role, though they were not as prominent as in the Turkish communitarian associations. There were some working-class and lower-middle-class staff and managers who had had personal experience with poverty, though personal suffering was not very prominent in their discourse. Even though these associations claimed an apolitical stance, they actively pressured the state to become more Islamic. Moreover, they were heavily infiltrated by communitarian political organizations (of which more below).

"Relieve the Anguish of All": Inspecting Islam's Forgotten Obligation

The Piety Association was one of the biggest representatives of communitarian charity. It was established (by a cleric) at the beginning of the twentieth century and hence predates the Muslim Brotherhood (established by a teacher in 1928). According to the documents of the association, it took care of more orphans than the government (close to 600,000).

The Piety Association allocated 50 percent of its funds to da'wa (establishing Qur'anic schools and mosques, organizing sermons, and shaping individual lives according to Qur'anic principles),[1] 20 percent to medical services, 10 percent to other necessities and orphanages, less than 10 percent to administrative costs, and 10 percent to development. In the body of its da'wa activities, the organization had dozens of Islamic institutes, close to 6,000 mosques (*masgid*), more than 1,000 Qur'anic schools (*kuttab*), as well as many weekly committees that traveled throughout Egypt to propagate the holy message.

The association provided ample and specialized medical services. In many of its clinics and hospitals, services were provided for free, regardless of socioeconomic background. Hassan, a doctor in his 40s who volunteered for a major clinic, emphasized: "Even if we see a patient driving a Mercedes, we don't ask for proof of poverty," echoing the (American) Catholic Worker's mode of operation (see Chapter 2). This would insult the patients, whereas they wanted to do everything "with dignity." Even though I kept on using the word service (*khidma*), both this doctor and a director at the clinic insisted that provision "is the beneficiaries' right [*haqq*], it is not a service." This non-conditional[2] provision, which did not differentiate between the deserving and undeserving needy, distinguished them from neoliberal associations, as the latter held that the behaviors of the undeserving poor were one of the root causes of poverty. This non-conditionality demonstrates the association's distance from neoliberalism, a distance the fragmentation of the charitable field enabled. The result is the obstructed diffusion of neoliberal criteria.

Despite their commonality with other communitarian associations in their evasion of attributing blame to the poor, the members of this organization differed from others in that they also avoided incriminating the rich and the government. Instead, they talked dryly about a multiplicity of factors. For instance, when accounting for the exploding numbers of premature children who needed to be put in incubators (one of the specialties of a Piety clinic), the members provided a laundry list of causes: mothers' chronic diseases, hypertension, smoking and narcotics, early or late marriage, and poverty. The interviewees could have combined any of these factors and built up accounts that assigned blame either to the socioeconomic system or to the poor themselves, frameworks which they avoided.

According to the association's director, there was a single idea that regulated all of their activities: the forgotten Islamic obligation that required the Islamic community to provide well-being to all of its members. This was the collective duty of the community as a whole and necessitated the total annihilation of neediness. It went beyond preventing hunger, which was doable simply through *zakat*:

> We can say with certainty that if the zakat funds were collected fairly and deposited in banks right way, there wouldn't be any hungry Muslims. ... Yet, there is another Islamic obligation than zakat, which is an individual worship. There is a communal worship called *fard kifaya* [communal

obligation]. This is a concept that has been lost, obscured, forgotten by the community [*hadha al mafhum ghayeb 'an al ummah*]. Let's say I have 10,000 ginih. I give him [God] 250. This is our Lord's due [*haqq*]. I keep 9,750 to myself. But our Lord has a right in our property other than zakat [*rabbina luh Haqqi fi mal gheir el zakat*]. ... Suffering frequently appears in front of us: Muslims need medicine, food, drink, or they suffer blockade (as in Gaza). The money that is left with me has the duty to relieve the anguish of all [*rafe' el karb kullina*].

The well-known, hunger-related Hadith ("Those who go to sleep with a full belly, while their neighbors are hungry, are not one of us") came up in many interviews both in Turkey and Egypt, among both neoliberal and communitarian actors. Yet no one other than Piety managers and volunteers stipulated hunger-alleviation as an Islamic obligation (*fard*). Moreover, Piety actors also emphasized that ensuring well-being in general (not just hunger alleviation) was an Islamic obligation. Still, the language they used clearly indicated that their responsibility was towards Muslims, even though managers and volunteers occasionally said they helped non-Muslims as well whenever they could, out of sheer humanity (*insaniyya*).[3]

The staff and managers of the association were motivated *and bound* by the Qur'an and Hadith (words of the Prophet Muhammad)—as one could tell from the description of the association's activities as *fard kifaya*. But divine inspiration also guided their activities. The director, a 60-year-old banker, told me that he had a special feeling inside him that let him know what to do and when. He gave an example:

> One day I was walking down an ordinary street. A voice inside me incited me to take care of 150 orphans. I saw an old man sitting on the pavement and told him what I wanted to do. His neighborhood had just suffered some hardship and he indeed knew of 150 orphans. I had no idea. I can't know what this voice was, but I believe it is coming from God.

Religion also played an organizational role as the donors and beneficiaries contacted the association through its mosques.[4]

Sayyid, a director of a major Piety clinic and a doctor in his 50s, had joined the association (upon the encouragement of his friends) so that he "could take with him something to afterlife." He emphasized, like the director quoted above, that he was performing a *fard kifaya*, which the Piety actors frequently used to characterize their duties ("every service is provided as *fard kifaya*," one said). *Fard kifaya* is a religious obligation incumbent upon the whole community and in this sense distinct from individual obligations. In other words, it was enough for *some* Muslims in each community to perform charitable services beyond the zakat. This association differed from neoliberal associations in that its members perceived *sadaqa* as a (communal) *obligation* and also used Islamic-juristic vocabulary to justify their position.

The managers also argued that their commitment to God was a guarantee of the quality of their services. Sayyid explained:

> When people encounter free services, they think: "These should be low quality." But we are doing this for God, so [what we offer] has to be better than the services provided anywhere else. People have to tell others that [the services provided for pleasing God] are better than services provided [with monetary motivations].

Religious motivation would create higher quality services when compared to cash-motivated medical services. Lacking medical expertise, I could not test this claim (even though the association's members took me on an informing tour of one of their clinics, which took a few hours). Still, what matters as much was the explanation of what produces better care. The managers and staff of neoliberal associations derided such beliefs and pointed out, like any orthodox economist would, that rational management, not a scientifically immeasurable commitment to God, would guarantee superior care. It is not that numbers and other claims to rationality were absent from the Piety Association's discourse; but these elements were subordinated to ultimately immeasurable qualities.

The director's comments regarding the forces behind their successful growth were along the same lines:

> God's accommodation is the secret behind success. We are not the smartest of people. There are a million, perhaps millions, smarter than us. We are not even the most pious of people. There are millions more pious than us. We are not the richest or the highest either. No, none of that. Charitable success comes only from God's preference. This is the message that has to be delivered, this is the truth that nobody knows.

God arbitrarily confers success, or better yet, grace. You cannot calculate, predict, or control it. What is interesting to note about this understanding of action was its extreme resemblance to Protestant theologian John Calvin's *original* position, which the Calvinists then "distorted." It was the latter, according to Weber (2011), which paved the way for capitalism. The Piety Association's anti-Calvinist proximity to Calvin ironically led to a less-than-capitalist ethical conduct.

The association's funds came from zakat and sadaqa. Its branches didn't organize any extensive fund-raising campaigns. Both the donors and the beneficiaries found them through their mosques, their main venue of organization. The critics of the association (ranging from a prominent Egyptian journalist to a politicized cab driver) argued that it was mostly funded by the Saudis. They also accused the association with not being accountable about the zakat money it collected in Egypt.

I attended a meeting the Piety Association held at a mosque, where the students of an Islamic school asked them why they did not engage in money-generating activities like other (neoliberal) associations. The director's answer was: "The local communities ask many questions. We don't want to run into issues of accountability." While neither the managers nor the staff explicitly attacked neoliberal associations, they implicitly and subtly differentiated themselves from associations that focused on profit-making.

Despite this difference from the neoliberal associations, the Piety Association got increasingly involved in developmental projects. The current director's experiences incited a turn to career training. In his travels, he noticed that many al-Azhar graduates (of sub-Saharan African origin) were unemployed and lived in poverty in their home countries. This impoverishment also prevented their da'wa activities. The association therefore started to provide job training to (sub-Saharan African) students. The field of training ranged from mobile phone maintenance to textile manufacture. Even though this technique could be interpreted as neoliberal, it was embedded within an overall missionary orientation. The association's other developmental projects (such as its bakeries) distributed their products for free (unlike neoliberal benevolence associations, which sold them on the market).

Both insiders and outsiders of the Piety Association emphasized that its members were paid very little. The top managers were volunteers rather than professional staff. But significantly, they used a distinct, religiously based word for top-level volunteers (*muhtasib*, rather than *mutatawwi'*, the standard word for volunteer). Muhtasib comes from the verb *ihtasaba*, "to anticipate a reward in the hereafter by adding a pious deed to one's account with God": muhtasibin were anticipators of heavenly reward, not just volunteers. The word also implied that volunteers had a religious duty to "inspect" society. In pre-modern Islamic societies, the word muhtasibin was used for public employees in charge of inspecting markets, crafts, urban infrastructure, welfare, and religious correctness of private lives with an explicit Qur'anic duty to "enjoin good and prohibit evil" (Foster 1970, pp. 140–142; Cook 2000). In short, the modus operandi of the managers was not neoliberalized. The Arabic word for volunteering was still used for regular volunteers, but for administrators the word *muhtasib*, "anticipator-inspector," was preferred. Highly differentiated patterns of socialization (through separate mosques and schools, as well as familial inheritance of associational belonging) enabled such distinct vocabulary. This differentiated socialization was a hallmark of the fragmented charitable field.

Self-sacrificing behavior was a part of being an "anticipator." The association's director told me that when he goes on a trip, he pays out of pocket:

> Since we are anticipator-inspectors on this project, there is no salary. I just went to Ethiopia for three days. I paid for the flight, my hotel stay, my food, and those of my brothers [the staff]. If I take 1,000 from you, 1,000 reaches Ethiopia. There are no administrative costs. The smallest relief committee on

earth spends 14 percent of the money on its own expenses. But we deliver 100 percent of the money [to the beneficiaries]. This is our particularity [*mayza*].

The managers of some organizations confirmed that self-sacrificing behavior was a pattern in associations such as Piety and indicative of their unprofessional approach and low quality (from their neoliberal standpoint). While communitarian actors did not openly denigrate their neoliberal rivals, one could sense, in between the lines, a deep suspicion regarding their administrative costs. Hence the implicit strategy of distinction with respect to unspecified rivals: the insistence that they were "anticipators," not volunteers.

The recruitment strategies of the Piety Association were quite distinct from the neoliberal associations. Many people joined it at a very early age. Their personalities were shaped through this involvement. The person, the organization, and the community of volunteers, managers, and staff were hardly separable. Whereas in most associations people emphasized the culture of giving they learned from their families (as in Wuthnow's account of American charity), in this association, giving (and its Islamic significance) was learned through organizational involvement beginning from childhood on. The director's story of joining the organization reflected this pattern.

The organization's mosque was very close to his first home ("by God's will") and as a young child he volunteered to clean the mosque, after a few years of following their Qur'an lessons. A more intellectual involvement (in the organization of Qur'anic lessons) followed the cleaning activities. As he matured, he took an active role in instructing others on how to read and memorize the Qur'an. Since he learned from his instructors that God wanted Muslims to take care of all the needs of children (especially orphans), he also aided their school work, showed affection to them, and supplied basic necessities when the need arose.

Hassan's story, though different from this director's on many accounts, also demonstrated the centrality of early recruitment. Hassan's father was the prayer leader at one of the organization's mosques. Therefore, he was born into a distinct way of practicing religion and helping community: "Ever since I was young, I wanted to help students. I gave them pencils. I found facilities where they could work. I also volunteered to teach students younger than myself." As soon as he finished school, he started to volunteer on a more regular basis. He eventually became one of the association's top figures as a result of his volunteering activities. This pattern of recruitment combined religious learning, volunteer activity, and familial-clerical surveillance. Such a tight integration of techniques of giving, charitable socialization, organizational history, and familial biography was a distinctive feature of the Egyptian communitarian scene: due to their shorter and more interrupted history (under a more secular and higher-capacity modern state), Turkish communitarian associations (let alone any of the Egyptian or Turkish neoliberal associations) did not have this level of comprehensiveness. The structures of a fragmented charity field allowed these patterns to persist.

All Piety Association members insisted that they were apolitical. Despite this insistence, the association was heavily involved in politics. It frequently mobilized people to demonstrate in favor of or against certain policies. It was very active during the constitutional referendum and elections between 2011 and 2013. This politicization and its denial were among the reproducers of the charity field's fragmentation.

"They Don't Hear the Pain and the Suffering:" Moralizing Society to Responsibilize the Rich

Kirama was a much smaller (and local) association that focused on orphans. It not only sheltered and fed them, but also taught the Qur'an. The main activities of the association included food, clothes, furniture distribution, and Islamic education, as well as direct cash provision. There were four Qur'anic schools connected to the association, with 20 to 25 students each. Aside from the director (who was also the founder), the organization had four permanent staff, but depended on a lot of volunteer work, mainly performed by the founder's extended family. Amalgamating aspects of the formal and the informal, the association strongly embedded itself in community.

The founder, Hazem, was a 58-year-old man, father of four, and a small merchant. He had been involved in organizing charity for ten years. Before that, he carried out benevolent work as an individual. He used to go to the homes of his neighborhood's orphans, study their situation, and offer any help he could. Over the years, Hazem slowly systematized these activities through cooperation with his brothers. He would get a certain amount of money on a regular basis from many extended kin. He then used the collected sum to buy secondhand furniture for the orphans.

Hazem explained to me that his rural region was economically and culturally poor. There had to be a connection, he reasoned, between these two kinds of impoverishment. Back when he performed charity only individually, he was also running a Qur'anic school. To combine the two activities, he declared he would enroll orphans in the school for free. As he came to have more orphans as students, he realized that their conditions were direr than he initially thought. For example, many of them came to school without shoes. This inspired him to find a solution. He began to regularly hand out bags with basic necessities (*shantat Ramadan*, which, as the name reveals, are distributed almost exclusively in the month of Ramadan). This provision quickly spread the school's fame. After a few years, he bought a piece of land, where he constructed a building to house both the school and a new charity organization. In short, from the very beginning, da'wa, family, and provision melded into each other. This story demonstrates that many quite active charity managers in Egypt are self-made and lack any grounding in professions related to NGO-management (whether through formal schooling or post-graduate training). This widespread condition in Egypt thoroughly restricted the "normative" pressures that Powell and DiMaggio have specified (which help spread certain organizational forms).

Another distinguishing feature of communitarian charities regarded the way they apportioned blame for social ills. In opposition to neoliberal charities, they did not see poverty as a result of individual characteristics, but of the oppressive and non-Islamic nature of Egyptian society and state. Hazem, who attributed the responsibility for blight directly to the better off and powerholders, exemplified this tendency:

> [The cause of poverty is] *zulm* [un-Islamic oppression]. The responsible persons severed their links with the poor. They don't hear the pain and the suffering. Poverty is increasing. ... Islam is the solution.[5] It is just rule: rule based on God's book (*Islam, huwa al-hal. Huwa hakim 'adil. Hukm bi kitab Allah*) ... And whoever does not judge by what Allah has revealed—then it is those who are the disbelievers.[6] ... Every leader has the responsibility to [take care of his group] and listen to citizens' complaints.

Finally, he got very concrete about how this should be done: "Every factory should build homes for their workers. The public sector should be as it was under Nasser." While the managers of neoliberal associations attributed corruption and inefficiency to state-owned enterprises, Hazem constructed them as strong and efficient, at least during Nasser's rule. He interestingly combined an allegiance to Muslim Brotherhood rhetoric with a yearning for "Arab socialism" (which the Brotherhood had subscribed to in the 1950s and early 1960s, and then repudiated after Nasser's repressive moves). The fragmented structure of the charity field resulted in the lack of clear messages coming from a monopolized center. This enabled smaller, new entrants to the field to draw on a multiplicity of discourses.

Hence, the burden was on the rich, but this did not mean there were no expectations from the beneficiaries. Appropriate responses from the poor needed to nurture the sense of giving among the rich. Hazem described the ideal rich person in conjunction with the kind of interaction that brought out the best in him/her. He had organized a birthday event for 22 orphans and ordered sweets from the region's most famous (and expensive) bakery:

> During the birthday party, we organized a contest for the orphans. We asked them the names of the daily prayers, details about the lives of prophets, and aspects of fasting. We then gave out awards and toys. The baker came and saw for himself the happiness on their faces. He was impressed. I offered to pay him 50 percent of the costs, but he rejected.

In other words, the provision was conditional on gratitude and proper knowledge of Islam (which Hazem assumed would bring good morality with it). However, still unlike in the case of the neoliberal charities, this conditionality was not up front and public. It was only implied. Hence, it was more open to divergent theoretical interpretations.

The association determined beneficiaries through visits to poor neighborhoods. It also announced its intentions to help the poor in public. It depended almost exclusively on informal networks of family and mosque. It did not use any standardized forms to assess poverty levels. There were no formalized recruitment techniques for staff. The fund-raising was also much unstructured and depended on the founder's free time and his family members. They visited bakeries and other stores, made calls to near and distant relatives for cash, and frequently, though unsystematically, asked for any volunteering the relatives could offer.

The association had no political affiliation, but Brotherhood members were active in it. It had no sustained links or cooperation with any ministries, even though it was a registered association. Attesting to the fluid boundaries in Egypt, this did not prevent the association from *receiving funds and administrative help from the major neoliberal associations*, which had tight connections with the state. These links perhaps rationalized the management structure in increments, but did not transform the association's overall communitarian orientation.

Hazem was in favor of a strong public sector. He expected public factories to produce the basic goods and services. However, given the current situation of the corrupt and weak public sector, he thought there was a big role for private charities to play, lest the poor of Egypt became "as numerous as the poor of Somalia." He ideologically identified with the Muslim Brotherhood, yet was not a formal member due to security reasons. His sons and daughters were full Brotherhood members. This shows that the Brotherhood had not rendered neoliberal orientations hegemonic (among its own base) at the time of this research, in 2010. Even though the official discourse of the Brotherhood was neoliberalizing, every day, practical charity did not reflect this transformation.

Ligan (plural of *lagna*)—officially regulated, but practically community-controlled, zakat committees—were another venue where I encountered communitarian dispositions. There were thousands of ligan in Egypt. I studied one under Salafi control. The association did not affiliate itself with any particular Salafi organization, but several Salafi individuals had major influence over it. Its activities included direct provision (of goods and cash). It also focused on arranging marriage for widows' offspring. Secondarily, it distributed clothes and Ramadan bags during religious holidays.

An accountant in his early 30s, married with one child, born and raised in Cairo, was one of the lagna's managers. A calm, composed, but nevertheless warm man, he started charity work when he was 18. At that point, only men in their 50s were active in this specific lagna. They needed young blood. They asked him if he would be willing to help and he agreed. He was already involved with the mosque as a student of the Qur'an. His first duties consisted of carrying boxes and collecting donations. He then started to serve as an accountant (*amin al-sanduq*), as he was being trained in that line of work in college. He did not cite any Qur'anic verses or Hadith spontaneously, but came up with many after probing. The verses and Hadith he brought up referred to da'wa as much as good works, signaling that he thought of pietistic activism and charitable works as inseparable.

Like almost all other communitarians, he did not blame the poor for their poverty. However, he did not bring up the rich of Egypt as the main culprits either. He rather focused on the government as the central villain:

> The reason why there is poverty is the government. It steals poor people's money. ... Education is free, but it is not good. There aren't enough good jobs. There is no good health system. ... There needs to be ... more chances in life. The government needs to stop stealing people's money.

Paralleling other communitarians, the accountant expected more and better *services* from the government. He also anticipated more and better *public jobs*, a desire more contested among communitarians (especially given that the Brotherhood, the biggest communitarian political force, had become increasingly more neoliberal). Yet, along with the global spirit of the times, he yearned for opportunity, not equality.

The committee employed no paid staff. All the managers and other regular contributors (a total of eight men) were volunteers. There was no training for volunteers of any level. All those in managerial positions, as well as plain volunteers, were recruited through informal networks, mostly those based on the mosque.

The monthly budget of the committee was around 40,000 Egyptian pounds. The basic source of funding was the donation boxes outside mosques. Another regular source was the monthly donations from a few wealthy individuals of the neighborhood. There was one major source of irregular funding in the summer: volunteers taught the neighborhood's children the Qur'an and the children's families donated a voluntary amount in return (again, they put the cash in anonymous boxes). The committee did not systematically raise funds.

The committee's methods of locating beneficiaries were more systematic than the Brotherhood's, but not to the degree of neoliberal associations. The neighborhood's poor people came to them. The lagna then sent representatives to their homes. These representatives also talked with the neighbors to determine the beneficiaries' level of need. The lagna only accepted widows as beneficiaries (it did not target specific income brackets). It regularly helped around 600 people. Even though there were at least as many widows in need in the neighborhood, the committee's budget was not enough to cover them. Many beneficiaries received monthly payments (ranging from 100 to 200 pounds) based on the number of their children. The committee also tried to keep a track record of how much help these families received from other organizations, although its members acknowledged that they had restricted means to double check.

The activities of the committee were legal and registered, and therefore closely monitored. It regularly reported its budget to *shu'un al-igtima'iyya* (and to Bank Nasser), the government's auditing agency. However, legality did not bring about safety. To the contrary, the police frequently harassed the volunteers due to the suspicion that they were disseminating "dangerous" Islamic ideology. One of the volunteers complained: "There is no freedom. The police officers always ask us why we are doing this and what we want from people."

In turn, the people at this mosque did not have high opinions about the government. They saw it as the root cause of poverty. When I visited the mosque in June 2012, one of them said "we made a revolution, but nothing happened yet," pointing out that the uprising had not resulted in any changes in socioeconomic policy. The police had stopped its harassment, as now it was forced to deal with the revolutionaries on the streets rather than tracking them down among charity providers. But, the volunteers said, they would go back to suffering the same system of harassment if Shafiq (the presidential candidate of the old regime) won in the coming elections at the end of that month (he eventually did not, winning them another year).

Conjuring "Discounts": Networks on a Magical Path to Formalization

Along with such formal associations, informal networks that paralleled the orientation of the Piety Association abounded. The managers of the neoliberal associations complained that such networks predominated in charity work and did more service than formal associations, but since these were unregistered activities, there was no way to test this claim. These networks operated in haphazard ways, though there were attempts at systematization and formalization. We need to ask: Do the charitable orientations of such actors thoroughly change as their activities become more systematic? Why or why not?

Fahmi was a 68-year-old man managing such activities. The owner of a small clothes store and a middle school graduate, he had devoted his life to his trade and to charity. He traveled around his town to find poor families. He took the donors with him to where the beneficiaries lived, so that they could "feel the pain" instead of just giving to anonymous beneficiaries. He mostly took used clothes from donors, as well as getting new clothes whenever he could. He also regularly donated some of the new clothes at his own store.

Fahmi got involved in charity activities through observing his family. However, his father, a government employee, and his mother, a housewife, were much less regular: they helped one person at a time. Unlike him, they did not actively search for the poor, but cared for them when the occasion arose.

As with the communitarians quoted above, Fahmi used a vibrant religious language. He brought up Hadith and Qur'anic verses spontaneously, without my probing. And like some of the above communitarians, his narration of charity frequently brought up magical stories:

> I decided to give 20 pounds to a poor woman I encountered, but I did not have the means. So I thought, I could give ten now, and ten later. But when

> I saw her next, I only had 20 [and no change]. So I gave her the 20 pound bill. At this time, the range of the daily sale at my shop was between 200 and 300 Egyptian pounds. But after she left, I earned 750 pounds in one afternoon! In the evening, I earned an additional 850! I link this number to my benevolent effort that day.

He told a few other stories to the same effect: whenever he decided to go out of his way to help the poor (to the dismay of his family), some unexpected shift in the market occurred to benefit his store; whenever he left his store to do good works, even during the busiest business days, he made more sales than he usually would have; under normal circumstances, he would have more problems with the factories and intermediary traders, but as he got more charitable, there were less and less headaches; etc. Among all of these stories, the most memorable for him was one that caused considerable friction with his family, but also made him more resolute about helping the poor for the rest of his life:

> I always used to buy sheep for the great holiday (*eid el-kebir, eid el-adha*). One year, I decided to buy a cow for the first time. My sons said "No, no." But I bought it anyway, in order to distribute more to the poor. The trader made a big discount without any explanation or any demand on my part. The cow came to the same price as the sheep I would buy.

After this point, he started to believe that he was automatically getting "discounts" (a more prosperous business day, better health, a happier day) whenever he performed good deeds. He believed these were messages from God. What is more, beneficiaries prayed that Fahmi not only had better health and happiness but more wealth. He was convinced that they prayed for him when he was not around. His increasing wealth was a result of these prayers. Fahmi used such stories to convince his sons that giving to the poor *in excess of* the 2.5 percent of one's wealth (as required by Sunni Islam) was not against their family interests.

Whenever his good works did not directly result in any tangible increase in profit, his sons cornered him and asked how benevolence helped him that day, implying that there is no magical link. "Where is the discount?" they asked, mockingly. He always retorted by pointing out that God kept them in good health, and that was the proof. That was the "discount" of that day. He also reminded them that the clothes store itself was God's gift in return for his charitable works; overall, he insisted, God always gave them more than they spent.

Magic has a persistent place in the contemporary world. Jean and John Comaroff (2001) have shown that, rather than "disenchanting" the world, neoliberal capitalism has reproduced magic. In our era, many (Western and non-Western) people conjure occult practices to accumulate wealth (pp. 19–22). Even though they explain this revival of the occult through neoliberal speculation's evasion of "effort" (p. 23), Egyptian communitarian charity demonstrates that effort can be central to accumulating wealth magically, while still not culminating in an *ascetically rational* effort. Such a combination between magic and accumulation could be misinterpreted as a "transitional" absurdity (that will finally disappear in a more modernized Egypt), but Chapter 5 will indicate that magic shapes even the most rationalized of charitable practices.

Fahmi's account indicates that some communitarians did not see wealth as a rational result of hard work, entrepreneurialism, and practical wisdom, or even the just operation of market forces, but as God's conditional bestowment in return for the correct practice of Islam (including charity). Unlike in Weber's rendering of the Calvinist ethic, wealth was not the result of an ascetic rational calculation motivated by the fear of God, but of abundant giving motivated by intense compassionate emotions (as well as by fear). Fahmi was proud that he had "no limits" in giving and did not turn any poor person who came to his store for help.

Such action provides us with material that can be interpreted within domination as well as communitarian theoretical frameworks. Certainly, Fahmi sanctified his wealth, implying that it was God-given. This was a clear legitimization of (unequal) private property. Yet at the same time, unlike in accounts that picture charity as unreturned gift, Fahmi had a very clear sense that the poor reciprocated (through their dialogue with God). More, the wealth (and inequality) was perceived to be conditional on sustained giving and God's will, not the hard work and superior smarts of Fahmi (nor the laziness or inferiority of the poor).

Fahmi's funding structure depended exclusively on informal networks. One of his main sources of funding was his brother who worked in the Gulf. He sent his zakat money to Fahmi, which was 2,000–3,000 Egyptian pounds annually. His funding structure resembled Hazem's initial years (see discussion above) and he had ambitions to move in a direction parallel to Hazem's trajectory.

In the beginning, Fahmi did not try out systematic methods. After years of charitable activity, he realized that there were more poor people in the countryside as compared to the city, where he had previously focused his attention. As a first step to deal with this incongruence between his acts and the poor's needs, he started to visit schools in less urban areas. The social worker in one of the schools put him in contact with many poor families. In time, these poor families introduced him to their relatives, friends, and neighbors.

Whatever Fahmi lacked in systematicity, he made up for it through feelings.[7] After mentioning the intensity of poverty (*shiddat al-fa'r*)[8] in some of the families he helped, Fahmi sobbed and shed tears, unable to speak for several seconds. Vigorous emotions did not come to the fore with the same disruptiveness in any other interview I conducted. Most managers, but especially those of neoliberal associations, avoided emotional remarks. Emotional remarks, but definitely not emotional displays, surfaced among the volunteers and lower-level staff of some neoliberal associations. Such remarks were more common among the volunteers and staff of the communitarian associations. One of Fahmi's relatives told me that "feelings" were the motor of Fahmi's charitable activities. It was after such intense encounters that Fahmi decided to announce to his relatives and friends the severity of the pain. He also began to distribute food as well as cash and clothes after emotional experiences.

In contrast to all of the associations I have studied, Fahmi did not electronically register the goods he distributed. He had a thick notebook in which he manually entered the information. Since his activities focused mostly on clothing, he had spent more time on classifying the garments in his store. He divided them by age, gender, and quality. He also took notes on every household he visited (mostly regarding population characteristics), so that he could, with the help of volunteers (mostly family members), determine what kind of clothes the family needed and make a suitable bag. In the initial years of his charitable work, Fahmi used to simply take the clothes with him and decide what to give to whom on the spot.

Recently, he had started to demand official papers from the beneficiaries attesting to their condition. For instance, he asked (widows) divorce papers or (orphans) proof of father's death. At the time of this interview, he felt confident enough with these techniques. For the last several months, he had been planning on establishing a legal association. In this process, he also wanted to save all the information he had collected on a computer and work electronically from then on. He also thought that he now needed paid staff as well as volunteer help, and certainly more cars. Paid, computerized, and motorized staff, he hoped, would enable him to develop a more systematic knowledge of the beneficiaries.

Fahmi not only thought highly of other communitarian associations, but had an active role in one of them, the Piety Association. He clarified that he was not a member, nor were there any formal cooperation between their charitable activities. However, as he appreciated what they did, he regularly went to their mosques and distributed candies and balloons to children to make them love prayer and the Piety Association mosque. (He also collected money for his charitable activities after these prayers, mostly from the children's parents.) Unlike the formal cooperation or competition among the neoliberal associations, the cooperation among the communitarian associations was much more informal and emotion-based rather than calculation-based. Presumably, countless networks and organizations in inner cities and the countryside interacted with the Piety Association, the Brotherhood, or other communitarian giants as they expanded and rationalized their activities. The availability of these models allowed rationalization to take non-liberal paths.

Communitarian Political Associations

The Brotherhood was by far the biggest communitarian political organization. While certainly not representative of all other communitarian political associations, the Brotherhood is central to my analysis due to its sheer size and comprehensiveness, which eclipses the benevolent activities of its rival organizations.[9] Insiders and outsiders estimate its number of volunteers to be in the hundreds of thousands (even millions). Its beneficiaries were said to be in the hundreds of thousands too. Though his was certainly an overblown estimate, the manager of the charity networks in Cairo argued that throughout the Republic they supported anywhere from 50 percent to 75 percent of the poor in each locality.

The blurry boundaries between informal and semi-formal benevolence networks, some formal welfare organizations, and the Brotherhood made it quite difficult to measure the impact of the organization (regarding the exact numbers of its members and volunteers, of those who cooperated with them, the size of its funds, the number of its beneficiaries, and the quality of provision). However, this blurriness further highlighted the significance of benevolence for the Brotherhood. All but one of the organizations and networks analyzed in the previous category (communitarian da'wa associations) had actively partnered with the Brotherhood during a substantial part of their history. A top director of Brotherhood charitable activity in Cairo was unable to provide even an estimate of how many Brotherhood members conducted charitable works regularly. This was partially due to a disinterest in a thorough numerical rationalization of the organization's activities. Nevertheless, it also reflected a vague notion of who actually *counted* as a member of the Brotherhood. He insisted: "Anybody who wants to reform (*islah*) society along the lines of comprehensive Islam is a Brotherhood member. Anybody who believes in our ideas is one of us. I can tell you that there are hundreds of thousands of people doing charitable work through belief in these ideas, but I can't give you an exact number." By this measure, all of the organizations covered in the previous section would count as Brotherhood organizations, and their volunteers as Brotherhood members. Such claims of incorporation created tensions with these organizations due to security concerns. Different degrees of emphasis on religious correctness added to the woes (as some da'wa organizations found the Brotherhood not consistent enough in its push for a purified understanding of Islam).

The political significance of Brotherhood charity lay in the (contested) link between provision of necessities and health on the one hand and political control on the other. The organization's members emphasized that many members of parliament got elected (in 2005) due to their charitable activities, such as being the directors of Brotherhood hospitals and healthcare centers or visible activists in *ligan* (local zakat committees). In other words, political control was a crucial factor in the Brotherhood's involvement in benevolence and, as we will see at the end of this section, the Brotherhood had complex ways of linking, infiltrating, and mobilizing civic benevolent activity and even official welfare.

The organization provided monthly salaries, food bags, clothes, writing materials, elderly care, conflict resolution, and education to the poor and orphans. Another central service the Brotherhood was widely known for was helping men and women (especially orphans) find marriage partners. Perhaps as important was the systematic provision of medical services. This organization had established innumerable small healthcare centers, as well as large hospitals in key localities.

The Brotherhood had only recently started to provide employment skills. One MP stated very bluntly, differentiating their organization of charity from the newer associations: "The priority for us is to feed [the poor]," not "developmental" and training activities. In other words, while the Brotherhood's understanding of charity was not restricted to distributing immediate necessities to the poor, it self-consciously avoided putting self-help, market-oriented activities in the center. Despite all, the Brotherhood *did* marginally provide poultry and farm animals in some rural regions to encourage the poor to feed themselves and occasionally, to use them for the market. This activity was pretty much the same with the central "responsibilizing" activity of one major neoliberal association I cover in Chapter 5. The Brotherhood also provided opportunities for urban families, mostly through encouraging women to invest the donations they received in sewing and then marketing their products. This was how Yusuf, a 50-year-old worker who currently serves as a Member of Parliament, explained their orientation and activities:

> We also support families with small projects so that they don't depend on us. We don't want them to expect support from us all the time. In this way, they can depend on themselves and be productive.

Although there was little such emphasis in the interviews and documents I collected, neoliberal language (based on the keywords of self-sufficiency and productivity) creeped into the overall communitarian picture I have been painting.

The organization also started to provide computer- and other skills-training to the poor youth after 2005 (when a huge chunk of Brotherhood candidates entered the Parliament). Such moves attest to a correlation between neoliberalization and positive links with the state—even if in this case, the positive link was restricted to a partial absorption into the state. In 2010, most of this training occurred in MP offices. These parliamentarians brought other bonuses too, such as the opportunity to employ the sons of Brotherhood-connected families in ministries or to find employment for them in the private sector. *However*, the prominence of such concerns also reproduced a patronage as much as a "responsibilizing" logic, attesting to how neoliberal turns were combined with the Brotherhood's already existing paternalist-communitarian dispositions (rather than undermining them). The post-2005 MP offices did not formally differentiate between career-training and patronage activities. *This further demonstrates how the global diffusion of templates does not necessarily result in the smooth consolidation of a world culture.*

The Brotherhood's so-far feeble shift to neoliberal aid displayed a parallel to the organization's more consistently market-oriented macro-policy position (for the latter, see Tuğal 2016a). The former shift could have become stronger if the organization had merged with the state (or at least co-operated with it). But after the completion of my Egyptian fieldwork (in 2012), such a development became even less likely.

"Some Brothers are Like Associations by Themselves": Setting Pious Models on Every Block

Benevolence was integral to the Brotherhood's overall mission. A major duty of every Brotherhood activist was memorizing the Qur'an and (some) Hadith. Accordingly, when I asked the organization's members why they got involved in charitable activities, they cited several Qur'anic verses and Hadith to explain their motivation (these came without probing). I did not encounter any members who invoked magical stories (a telling contrast with activists in other associations). This was in line with the "salafi" understanding of religion that the Brotherhood had been upholding for 80 years.[10]

Good works had transnational meanings. Activists emphasized the importance of *ligan*, the Brotherhood, and other communitarian organizations for the ongoing conflict in Gaza. Palestine was such a central point of concern that a crushing majority of the Brotherhood's transnational medical resources went to this country. For instance, the medical syndicate, which was under Brotherhood control, spent 90 percent of its resources on Palestine; doctors of all ranks, not all of them Brotherhood members, performed volunteer work, especially in the Gaza Strip. However, unlike in the Turkish case, the actors did not highlight Egyptian pride or bring up claims of Egyptian leadership of Muslims worldwide. (Turkish Islamists expected Turkish leadership to result from their benevolent activities.) Rather, the goal of transnational provision was upholding the global community of believers, the *ummah*.

Not all Brotherhood-linked charitable actors were engaged with religion in the same way. The syndicates under Brotherhood control, for instance, emphasized that they were not da'wa organizations. Nevertheless, religion played a critical role for them as well, beyond being just a motivation. Even though they did not make people more pious through preaching (as did communitarian da'wa associations), they invited them to pious lifestyles through setting examples. Abd al-Wahhab (in his 50s), the son of a government employee, went to public schools throughout his life and became an engineer. After some engineering experience (some of it in the US), he decided to become a professor. By the end of the 2000s, he became the director of a Brotherhood-controlled professors' syndicate. He had been active throughout his life in engineering and professors' syndicates. He portrayed the role of religion in the following way:

> We are not a preaching (*da'wa*) organization, but a social (*igtima'i*) one. Still, we employ an [Islamic] method (*namudhag*) of respecting (*ihtiram*) people, being just, and providing service (*khidma*) to them. There is no theft. This is a method of patience, justice and transparency.

The syndicate did not directly encourage (*shagga'*) people to become more pious, he pointed out, but instead embodied Islam's core values of patience, respect, justice, and service. The Egyptian people, who (according to this professor) already knew what was religiously permitted and forbidden but had lost *the method* of realizing these values, were spontaneously drawn to their syndicate when they saw what they had always yearned for, but did not know how to realize. In other words, *some* Brotherhood activity assumed already religiously constituted subjects and reinforced that subjectivity, rather than creating it from scratch (unlike the da'wa associations).

Brotherhood members perceived setting up these role models as a core part of poverty alleviation. As a response to the question about the root causes of poverty, they emphasized the weakness of the "correct" understanding of religion among potential donors (and the beneficiaries), attesting to the non-neoliberalization of their understanding of poverty. Hence, the Brotherhood did not differentiate its religious activities from its provision (a non-differentiation that also characterized communitarian da'wa associations). Hossam, a director of a Brotherhood-controlled professional syndicate, was a man in his 40s. A quite serious and cold man, he had degrees from the top colleges in Egypt and had also taken courses in London. Throughout the years, he had striven to make his own profession more Islamic. He had also taken courses and obtained certificates on relief work. He had worked on the managerial board of a few companies. Both his deep involvement in Islamic movements and politics and his strong career background put him on the forefront of not only this professional syndicate in Egypt, but also a couple of international professional associations. Hossam explained why we should not think of provision apart from making people more (and "correctly") religious:

> Charity culture in Egypt and in the Arab world is weak, in comparison with the USA and England. But Islam is the religion of good works. Charity culture is weak because people are far from the true understanding of religion (*fehm haqiqi ad-din*)! You can find in the mosques people who have memorized the Qur'an ... but they don't know charity. This will change through lectures, by talking about Islam, by talking about good works ... as well as building hospitals that provide cheap services.

He then gave examples of imprisoned Brotherhood members who had done this throughout their lives. The open target of these comments was unidentified and unspecified mosque-goers; Hossam did not criticize Muslim associations that did not combine benevolence with vibrant religion, at least openly.

Living up to his high demands of strong piety and religious knowledge from society, and certainly enabled by his cultured mastery of and comfort with classical language, Hossam backed up his claims about Egypt and benevolence with several Qur'anic verses and Hadith. He was one of the interviewees who cited these classical sources the most frequently. Such actors' cultured mastery of classical Arabic, which is possible only after years of immersion in religious training, enabled this speech pattern. Hossam's and many Brotherhood actors' use of language mirrored solidaristic organizations' tendency to invest vigorously in the religious formation of their affiliates, *a field-induced disposition that distracts from allocation of resources to career training* (and hence prevents neoliberal diffusion).

New institutionalist research has found close correlation between the predominance of professionals in an organization and its level of businesslike rationalization. Institutionalist scholars also hold that *the more these professionals are parts of professional associations*, the higher the degree of rationalization. Hossam's case, however, suggests that we also have to study how the professional associations are embedded in politics and religion. Both Hossam and Abd-al Wahhab (quoted further above) had been involved in professional associations throughout their lives. They, and many like them, had also gone through training in Anglophone world centers, *which should have further promoted the diffusion of business models*. Engagement in professional associations and training might breed neoliberalization in certain contexts. But when the infiltration of these associations is a core strategy of a communitarian religious movement, new institutionalist predictions fail.

The Brotherhood's funding sources were zakat and sadaqa, paralleling the communitarian da'wa associations. In addition, however, every member had to give 7–10 percent of his income to the Brotherhood. Moreover, the Brotherhood organized the shopkeepers (butchers, barbers, markets, etc.) and medical experts in each neighborhood to provide their goods and services to the poor for free—which members also perceived as a benevolence activity. The organization also built supermarkets that provided goods cheaper than market price. As in the case of the major communitarian da'wa associations, Brotherhood critics alleged that the Saudi and the Gulf states secretly funded it.

The information the Brotherhood could gather (about potential donors, volunteers, and beneficiaries), its level of organization throughout Egypt, and the moral connotations of this organization were tightly linked. An MP from the Brotherhood explained:

> There are many Brotherhood members who can be considered an association by himself [due to] the abundance of their links and their deep roots in society. They built these through trust, transparency. ... As a result, Brotherhood members are present on every street, in every neighborhood, and every house, thanks to which we can understand the problems as they emerge and resolve them.

The Brotherhood's penetration of society went hand in hand with its ability to provide benevolence. However, a befuddling counterpoint to this depth of societal penetration was a lack of rationalization in the organization's location of beneficiaries and resolution of problems. Unlike the newer associations, it had no standardized method to decide whom to help. Rather, the organization allowed the emergence of informal rules and patterns in every single locality, as it trusted its members (for it assumed that society trusted them). Consequently, the word trust came up frequently in most Brotherhood interviews and did not in the neoliberal association interviews. People in need found the Brotherhood's charity workers in mosques, in MP offices, as well as through people they knew. Thus, quite frequently, it was the beneficiaries who located the Brotherhood's charity personnel, rather than vice versa.

A distinctive characteristic of the Brotherhood was the identification of the actor with his benevolent activities (which, in turn, entailed seeing almost all aspects of life as subject to a benevolent logic). The only organization that matched the Brotherhood in this aspect was the Piety Association (where socializations into the family, into the association, and into benevolent dispositions were not distinguishable from each other). *Every* Brotherhood member was required to conduct *a'mal khayriyya* (good works, or charity in the broader sense). One of my interviewees focused on the education, sports activities, religiosity, and psychological development of children of ages 10–13—the age bracket the organization assigned to him. Likewise, the Brotherhood took care of other needs (clothing, food, medical treatment, etc.) through assigning its members as caretakers of specific families. Through these activities, the organization desired to foster (what it called) active and dynamic communities. Brotherhood members were critical of associations that had a more restricted notion of benevolence, which did not incorporate self-sacrificing, energy-intense, communally embedded good works (they implied, but did not mention, the neoliberal Islamic associations).

Scholars have interpreted this emphasis on "active communities" as neoliberal. Indeed, dynamic networks are central to communitarian-infused versions of neoliberalism (Muehlebach 2012; Rose 1999). However, the way the "active community" is embedded in a set of practices rules out this interpretation. As Ismail's case shows, the pious role model is meant to create an *interdependent society* based on standardized morality rather than an *archipelago of self-reliant communities*. As important is how Brotherhood members imagined their dynamism in opposition to that of neoliberal associations. Their managerial structures too were starkly different.

Ismail, the son of a mathematics teacher, one of five siblings, came to the Brotherhood with considerable civic experience. An architect in his late 20s, he had been a student representative in primary, secondary, and high school. His father sent him to learn the Qur'an in a neighborhood mosque. The instructors turned out to be Brotherhood activists. Neither he nor his father knew anything about the organization's teachings. The ideology the mosque instructors gradually introduced captivated Ismail, but he refrained from membership.

He then became a student leader in college. His activities brought him close to two key Brotherhood organizers with influential roles. He was not only more convinced by the Brotherhood's ideas, but started to think that the organization produced a model person who struck the perfect balance between material and spiritual life (*tawazun bayna al-haya maddiyya wa manawiyya*). He finally decided to become a full member during the 2005 elections, during which the old regime permitted some real Brotherhood participation. He felt that he could create change and joined the Brotherhood's campaign. The two candidates he rallied for (with whom he was now in close contact) became MPs.

So, what ideas actually charmed him? As a result of all his student activism, he came to believe that to make any positive change, a person needed to be a part of a community (*gama'a*). Moreover, within that community, he would have to follow the orders of the designated leaders. Finally, the whole community (the leaders and the followers) had to not only abide by Islamic law, but actively seek to implement it. He also called this the rule of God (*hukm Allah*).

It was, however, not only the ideology that was all-encompassing. Membership in the Brotherhood brought with it responsibilities that far exceeded what the new types of NGOs expected from their affiliates. The Brotherhood combined NGO activity in the narrow sense with not only political mission, but religious mission too. Ismail had to memorize at least one Hadith every week. He also had a duty to read at least one page from the Qur'an every day. However, the leaders could occasionally ask a member to intensify any required activity. For instance, Ismail was currently experiencing problems with his marriage and had a hard time handling these psychologically. His superior told him to read one chapter rather than one page every day in order to deal with his issues.

These individual aberrations aside, memorization of texts occurred in group settings where an elder supervised people of similar educational and generational backgrounds. Participation and memorization were compulsory. The organization also required each member to do research prior to the meeting on news items that they could then discuss under the light of Qur'anic verses and Hadith. Ideally, these meetings led to the memorization of the whole Qur'an, which was expected of every member (in the long run), for the organization saw the text as something that must saturate the life and heart of each. A key slogan encapsulated these beliefs: "God is our aim, the Qur'an is our constitution" (*Allah ghayatna, Qur'an dusturna*).

Benevolence came as a direct extension of these pious activities. Just like he learned piety from his supervisor in a group setting, Ismail gathered students and, while helping them with their studies and other needs, also nurtured their religiosity. When dealing with non-Brotherhood members, especially children and teenagers, the emphasis was not on direct indoctrination, but on discipline and morality (or on "ethical conduct," along the lines specified in the Introduction). These children had to memorize as much of the Qur'an as they could. But they also played soccer every week, which developed self-discipline (e.g. through avoiding curses while playing). They also went swimming together, not only in order to become better athletes, but, more importantly, to learn how to avoid looking at girls in bathing suits. Ultimately, the organization wanted to create a society where satellite TVs, sexually explicit media clips, and erotic movies might exist, but no one would watch them. Ismail had gone through a similar moral training and was now guiding teenagers through the same stages he had been through.

While the new organizations (covered in Chapter 5) did not standardize the link between religious motivation and benevolent deed, the Brotherhood systematized it vigorously. There was no escaping it. In the Brotherhood's inner circles, one could not think of benevolence apart from the memorization of the Qur'an. For the outer circles, there was still a tight connection in most cases, even when this was hidden from public view.

The organization did not systematically reward managers and foot soldiers of Brotherhood-related benevolent activity. If benevolent activities were carried out within Brotherhood networks, these were on a mostly unpaid basis. Benevolent actors received regular salaries only when they worked for Brotherhood-affiliated formal associations, or for the (official) welfare agencies the Brotherhood had infiltrated. Self-sacrifice, a disposition intensely induced by a specific field structure, is at the center of communitarian Islam.

Brotherhood members also emphasized that (unlike in newer organizations) their administrative costs were minimal, which minimized the risk of corruption. They were also proud of the more voluntary (rather than salary-based) participation of many managers, again attesting to the non-liberalized management structure. However, even when underlining these differences, Brotherhood members tried to be as discreet as possible: Unlike neoliberal actors, communitarian actors did not have a thorough critique of their rivals' overall vision.

Why did communitarian actors mostly avoid making derogatory comments about rivals? Unraveling the dynamics behind this silence gives us clues to the specificity of pious distinction in Egypt. Whenever Brotherhood members made disdainful remarks about neoliberal associations, they spoke quite abstractly, without implicating any of them. The harshest statements were grouped under two ideas: neoliberal charities were connected to the state, and hence dependent on the regime, and they were predisposed to be corrupt. "There are suspicions that their employees are not trustworthy (*al-a'milin fiha laysu ahl sika*)," one Brotherhood member told me, again referring to the informal code of trust that made the organization so self-confident. When I tried to push them to concretize the allegations, they usually switched gears and said they were actually talking about secular and Christian organizations (not the Islamic ones studied in Chapter 5). Only rarely did I hear sentences such as the following: "They are good, but we have no relations with them. Their staff and managers are usually good persons, but they also harbor shady people" (from an interview with a Brotherhood leader).[11]

Yusuf differentiated their work, which was "rooted in community and history," from the neoliberal organizations:

> These newer organizations started to spread after opening to the West (*infitah*), and the adaptation of a free [market] economy (*iqtisad al-hur*). They deal with a special slice of society; they don't deal with the very poor. They have restricted goals.

However, when asked to give specific examples, he avoided naming the neoliberal pious associations (the founders of which, as will be seen, had roots in the

Islamic movement). He named the Rotary Club instead, skipping over the obvious fact that his statements (regarding timing and content of associational activities) applied to neoliberal pious associations as well (for instance, the lack of concern in da'wa among these associations, as well as growing investment in capacity-building among middle-class youth). In this quotation, as elsewhere, the communitarian reaction to neoliberalization was explicit, but never systematic. In other words, communitarians avoided contention with fellow pious Muslims. Actually, communitarians were mostly proud of ex-Brotherhood presence among the ranks of such neoliberal associations: "*al-hamdu lillah* (all praise and thanks be to Allah), they are our students," they typically said of them.

Likewise, communitarians implicitly questioned the authenticity of neoliberal actors' motivations. Brotherhood members emphasized that "good works require a high, self-sacrificing morality." After discussing a couple of major natural disasters in the recent past, one argued that only a Brotherhood-controlled syndicate went to the calamity-struck places despite intense danger, while other relief organizations avoided them (since they lacked self-sacrificing morality). This understanding of benevolent work presented a sharp contrast to that of neoliberal associations, which held that the main problem of their rivals was the lack of scientific management, not self-sacrificing morality. The Brotherhood's criticism of rival organizations did not rely on the numerical measuring sticks of the newer associations.

"Symbiotic Wrestling" with the Neoliberal Polity

Up until now, I have discussed how Brotherhood members grappled with realities of marketization in their daily experiences. However, as the quotation from Yusuf indicates, the economy's opening to world markets was an issue that was frequently on the minds of Brotherhood members. Consequently, they had developed intricate understanding of marketization at the macroeconomic level as well. Due to this analytically informed folk wisdom, there was more diversity among Brotherhood members regarding policy preference than I initially expected. Not all Brotherhood members followed the official line. Some, for example, were strictly against privatization and favored redistribution. Ismail thought that Egypt needed a reformed and stronger public sector. He held Muslim businessmen in high regard, but did not think the government should sell factories to them. In fact, he thought all private monopolies should be broken, for wealth monopolization was against *fiqh*. While he favored redistribution, his plan for it was not clear, as he also favored lower taxes. He assumed that if the banks became Islamic and speculation was banned under an Islamic government, redistribution would occur through the just and efficient working of the public and private sectors. Yusuf, an MP, developed a different position and pointed out that there was no "Islamic economy" as distinct from existing and historical economic systems.[12] His organization would "welcome" any system as long as it did not favor *riba* (financial interest) and ensured *maslaha al-mugtama'* (achieve the main needs of society including security, food, medicine, and housing). Social benefit (rather than growth) was in the center of his thoughts, indicating how communitarianism might evolve into welfare capitalism if extended to the national level. The Brotherhood, said Yusuf, was against neither privatization (though it was against the way it was implemented [*tanfiz*]) nor the public sector.[13]

However, there were also those like Amr who, despite his origins in the working class, held the private sector in higher regard, especially in its relation to charity. He held that the governmental provision of aid was useless, as people did not "trust" the government and its agencies did not work in a "free" environment. Yet, Amr held that the government should either own or have a large share of big and heavy industries and infrastructure such as steel, much of manufacturing, electricity, water resources, and the Suez Canal. Still, even among some of those who favored a mixed economy, like Anwar (who thought that the government should have facilities for the poor), government provision was deemed problematic. Government money always came with strings attached and the care providers could not focus on the priorities of the needy (due to rigid bureaucratic expectations).

When it came to concrete projects, the Brotherhood vision did not differ to a great degree from current American piecemeal social reforms. A director of the medical syndicate said that their goal was creating a society where everybody had access to social necessities such as learning and health. When I asked him how this would be possible in his own sector, he proposed an Obamacare-like solution, after outlining the major players in the health field (Ministry hospitals, university hospitals, NGO clinics, private hospitals) and pointing out that none of them were enough on their own:

> Private health care is very expensive. But government hospitals have no money; they have no equipment. ... Health insurance is the hope for this country and other countries. [This] depends on the idea of getting small amounts of money from the whole population. [Everybody] shares in the expenses by paying a small percentage (2–3%) of their salaries. The government also makes some contribution. [Then] health care is provided to people regardless of the percentage they pay and regardless of their [socioeconomic level].

In their most concrete moments, then, Brotherhood members proposed social justice-oriented ideas, yet these did not challenge the economy's overall orientation. At this level, (Obama's version of) American scripts indeed traveled effectively, as a new institutionalist would predict.

Professional and class affiliation mattered more than organizational belonging in approaches to these macroeconomic questions. For instance, Brotherhood engineers advanced a national developmentalist line. Abd al-Wahhab emphasized "real development" (*tatawwur al-haqiqi*), by which he meant heavy industrialization, rather than what he thought characterized Egypt in the last decades (financial sector and light industrialization, for which he used the metaphor of "chewing gum factories"). Even though he accepted some privatization, he thought that the government should sell factories only to Egyptians. He was surprised that I even asked who should provide education, healthcare, and other services. He argued that this is the duty of the government "in the whole world;" and added that the government should leave no one malnourished. This strong belief in national developmentalism was simply absent among Brotherhood doctors, merchants, and businessmen (all discussed above), who held more sway over the organization.

Abd al-Wahhab also argued that they had no way to influence the government on these issues. As long as the Brotherhood was an officially banned organization, it could indeed have the face to claim that its hands were clean. Yet, this would not be an entirely valid claim, since the organization had infiltrated the state. If it did not systematically push the Mubarak state in a non-neoliberal direction, this was partially out of choice, not just necessity.

The Brotherhood had complex ways of linking its benevolence activities to politics, other civic organizations, and the state. It had immense experience in using multiple venues (occasionally for counterintuitive purposes). This could mean that whenever the organization goes through a major change of heart, it would have at its disposal multiple venues to generalize its new stance throughout society. However, in light of the far from standardized attitudes of its own members regarding macroeconomic policy, this political complexity could also suggest that the Brotherhood's will was so "dispersed" that (unlike the Turkish Islamist party) it would not be able to lead society in a single new direction, even if it wanted to.

The old regime attempted to register the Brotherhood as a charitable association, but it denied this offer. As the old regime suspected Islamic associations, association laws (such as those of 1964 and 2002) tightly regulated their provision (Abdelrahman 2004). Under these circumstances, remaining an illegal organization allowed the Brotherhood to be more flexible than some of the other major communitarian players.

However, we should not categorically oppose legality and illegality. The Brotherhood breathed within, and developed through, the channels in the body of the existing legal society (and in that sense, did not create an exclusive, "parallel society," as argue Wickham, Davis and Robertson, and other scholars). A less visible body of research documents how the Brotherhood benefited from (*and reproduced*) the regime's micro-structures.[14] In the old regime, the Brotherhood managed charity activities in four major ways:

1. Through partnership and merger with semi-independent charity organizations. Due to the illegal status of the Brotherhood, some of its partner organizations were unregistered. They had neither official buildings or headquarters, nor official bank accounts.
2. Through professional syndicates, such as the medical syndicate, which provided free medical services to the needy. The Brotherhood dominated most

syndicates starting with the mid-1980s. The syndicates were legal, but Brotherhood control over them was not always transparent. At the end of the 1980s, Brotherhood members started to win more syndicate elections. After 1992, the regime tightened syndicate laws and regulations to make clear election victories impossible. In the 2000s, the Brotherhood exerted influence on the syndicates through having its members elected to key offices.
3. Through the direct contact of the Brotherhood with neighborhoods, families, and individuals in need.
4. Through infiltrating legal aid organizations (ranging from the major da'wa organizations to the *ligan*). Brotherhood activists joined legal associations and worked as dedicated members. They occasionally occupied top ranks in their administrations (Ben Néfissa 2004, pp. 214, 224, 230). According to some allegations, when they distributed goods and services, activists told the beneficiaries that the source was the Brotherhood.

The person who coordinated the organization's charity activities in one major Egyptian town provided clues as to why the Brotherhood infiltrated these associations. Regarding the Piety Association, he said: "Their material conditions are better [than us]. They have material and organizational stability. There is no pressure on them (*Fiha istiqrar maddi ve muntazim. Mafish tadyik 'alayhim*). They have the freedom to work, more than us." However, he also specified that there was no longer any cooperation (*tansiq*) between them, but only complementarity and solidarity (*takamul*). The Piety Association mostly focused on orphans and people who required costly medical treatments; the Brotherhood cared for the poor in general, including but not restricted to orphans, with a special focus on people who were hungry or suffering from regular (*'adi*) sicknesses.

Hence, in order to develop an exact understanding of the Mubarak scene and the power of the Brotherhood within it, it is crucial to note that the organization did not build its influence and legitimacy only on networks itself created. A top Cairo leader expressed this bluntly when he said, "We have very good connections with society through our collaboration with these institutions," referring to non-Brotherhood benevolent associations.

These complex and complicated activities and links blurred the boundaries between the Brotherhood and the old regime. As much as the old regime tried to control Brotherhood presence in the syndicates, it also cooperated with them. For example, the Egyptian Red Crescent (along with many other governmental agencies and NGOs) cooperated with the (Brotherhood-controlled) medical syndicate in securing provisions for Palestine. While the Brotherhood was frequently pictured as an alternative to the extant society and state, such relations not only broadened the organization's influence over Egyptian everyday experience, but also made its impact indistinguishable (from the influences of communitarian associations, neoliberal associations, and the state).

★★★

When they emerged in the 1990s, neoliberal associations walked into this extremely charted benevolence territory. Perhaps they told themselves (and international interlocutors) that they were entirely different from the entrenched associations, but still, they had to compete with them for zakat and sadaqa money. The implications of this competition for the diffusion of neoliberal techniques were multifold, as Chapter 5 will show.

Notes

1 While in some theological scholarship da'wa is used in a comprehensive way to refer not only to these strictly religious activities, but also to welfare and politics; in the brochures, websites and spoken discourse of most aid organizations, the concept was used in the sense specified in this paragraph, along its late nineteenth to early twentieth century (pre-Muslim Brotherhood) re-interpretation (Mahmood 2005).
2 Non-conditional on paper: critics frequently pointed out that this association expected its beneficiaries to adapt more conservative forms of religiosity.
3 According to neoliberal charitable actors, the Piety Association did not help non-Muslims in any significant way.
4 Even though Egypt was a "secularist" dictatorship before 2011, the authorities allowed Islamic associations to operate in a way they could not, for instance, in the more democratic Turkey; this included allowing orthodox associations like Piety to have their own mosques.
5 This is the trademark slogan of the Muslim Brotherhood.
6 This sentence is a verse from the Qur'an (5:44), though the interviewee did not highlight it as such.
7 While I did not have the space to integrate the emotions literature in my analyses, especially Arlie Hochschild's work (as well as my discussions of it with Aynur Sadet and Ayşe Akalın) shaped my thinking throughout my research and writing.
8 Even though I have transliterated the Arabic letter qaf as "q," I elided qaf when speakers did.
9 However, since the major communitarian political rivals (such as Hizb al-Nur) developed starkly contrasting discourses about macroeconomic policy ever since the 2011 uprisings, it would be meaningful to look into their charitable activities as well, to see whether their macro differences are matched by differences at the associational level.
10 The Brotherhood's founders saw themselves as heirs of Muhammad Abduh's and Rashid Rida's salafism, which defended a return to the religion of the Prophet's generation. Yet, while this entailed a problematization of post-classical Islamic traditions, the founder Hasan al-Banna himself had Sufi (as well as orthodox) training. To this day, the organization has been ambivalent about Sufism. It is thereby differentiated from more consistently Salafi (with a capital S) groups in Egypt, which publicly attack Sufi beliefs, practices and shrines.
11 When communitarians criticized the neoliberal associations in general, the term they used for them was "the new associations," rather than "neoliberal," which is my analytical category. However, they did not use the term "new" in a chronological sense, since they did not direct such criticisms at recently established but communitarian and small organizations.
12 This position on the "differentiation" of the economy (and its recognition as a realm with its own, distinct, nonreligious mechanisms) has been gaining some ground in the

last decades (Tuğal 2009), which constitutes a departure from earlier Islamist positions (Tripp 2006).
13 Yusuf's exact words were: "iza kan haza nizam yitihaqqaq bi'l-qita' al-khas, ahlan biha; iza kan haza yitihaqqaq bi'l-itnayn, ahlan biha," which roughly translates as, "If the private sector realizes the [Islamic] order, we welcome it; if [a mixed economy] realizes this order, we welcome it."
14 For instance, on how the Brotherhood courted the regime's notables in poor localities, see Ben Néfissa (2004).

5

MOBILIZING VOLUNTEERS ON ROCKY TERRAIN

Neoliberal Benevolence in Egypt

Chapter 4 revealed the historically entrenched structures of communitarian charity in Egypt. We can now contextualize neoliberal interventions in the Egyptian field, which communitarianism so thoroughly shapes. The two distinct neoliberal interventions in the field faced mountains rather than sand dunes of communitarianism. As the following chapters will show, this was quite different from Turkey, where communitarian benevolence was strong within informal communities, but did not congeal into hard-to-move boulders.

Egyptian neoliberal Muslims developed two major ways of setting foot in this mountainous terrain. Some organizations aimed to mobilize armies of young volunteers to destabilize the sedimented ways of the old. The financially and organizationally more developed organizations, by contrast, counted on full rationalization and an unforgiving import of techniques from the business world. I will call these organizations "professionalized neoliberal associations." Most significantly, business rationale was much more marked in these organizations when compared to their counterparts in Turkey (though their area of influence was more restricted). In other words, the colossal, organized communitarianism I analyzed in the previous chapter had bred a purer (but less powerful) neoliberalism than in Turkey.

Neoliberal charities were smaller and relatively new. They started to be established in the 1990s. Some of them have been studied by other scholars, who have also used the label "Islamic" for them. Nevertheless, their Islamic-ness was a quite touchy subject back in 2009–2010 not only due to security, but also field-related issues. Many objected to this label, which would both jeopardize their operations in the post-9/11 world *and* make them look less than professional. Almost all of these organizations emphasized that they were not engaged in *da'wa*, even though their work was inspired by Islam and depended on *zakat* and *sadaqa*. However, there were shades of difference, as some associations indicated that they were happy to see beneficiaries become more pious as a result of aid. Also, some facilitated Qur'an recitation competitions and religious celebrations. What also qualified these associations as Islamic was their common stance against secular philanthropic organizations and (especially non-Muslim) international donors. Islamic actors across the board underlined that these rival organizations violated Islamic culture by attempting to change women's role in Egyptian society.

But most importantly, all of these organizations defined themselves as *gam'iyyat khayriyya* (which could be translated either as charitable or philanthropic associations).[1] They had a claim to the same religious word and thus to comparable sensibilities. They were thus competing for overlapping pools of zakat and sadaqa. Therefore, despite several actors' uneasiness with being classified as "Islamic," we can see them as a part of the same field.

When I asked about their motivations, volunteers, staff, and management talked about their "human side" (*ganb insani*) and empathy with the poor; desire to improve Egypt; and individual relation with God. For example, the director of the wealthiest organization (who comes from an established business family, but got even richer himself) said: "God was very generous to me and I want to pay back." Some did cite the Qur'an and Hadith, but (aside from one person) not without probing.

Volunteer-Based Neoliberal Associations

Though both clusters analyzed in this chapter were neoliberal, there were crucial differences between them. "Volunteer-based neoliberal associations," larger than the professionalized ones in terms of volunteers and activists, combined provision and developmental activities. In most volunteer-based associations, provision outweighed development. Yet, the Chinese proverb regarding the value of teaching people how to catch fish rather than giving them fish was still commonplace. In other words, *these associations were neoliberal in aspiration more than actual practice*. One of the biggest organizations emphasized "civilizing people" through development funds. What it meant by civilizing was training, teaching people how to "rely on themselves," and equipping them with the latest technological skills. The top management of these organizations was professionalized, but they still depended on a lot of volunteer work.

Nour Association, a prominent organization throughout Egypt, was founded by a professor and his students at the end of the 1990s. The students approached their engineering ethics professor and asked him what they could do to benefit society. He responded that he did not know! Their mutual discussions initiated a student club in 1999. In the beginning, their efforts were modest and included free computer classes to the poor, as well as visits to orphanages. A relative of one student was impressed by their activities and decided to donate a piece of land to the club in 2000. After that, their activities really took off. In the words of the professor, "this is the story of a course that initiated a movement." This association started without pre-given neoliberal ideas. Yet, in time, it imitated and internalized some of the globally predominant scripts and templates, in line with new institutionalist predictions that an organization built on a hypothetical, newly discovered island in our day would definitely adapt the basics of world culture. Nevertheless, given that Egypt is not a newly discovered island and many Egyptian associations still do not subscribe to these basics (and that even Nour adapted them with its own peculiar slant) we need to know why Nour developed its particular angle.

In about a decade, Nour was able to establish more than 50 branches. It mobilized around a 100,000 volunteers a year, mostly young people. It had 18 departments for different kinds of beneficiaries. Nour targeted not the richest, but average Egyptians as its source of funding. Though there were rich funders, the bulk of the cash came from the middle class. At least 250,000 donors contributed to this massive association. Funds were mostly spent on orphanages. The other activities included elderly care, cloth distribution, transportation, recycling, and training in literacy and communication skills. Even though the last two activities were on the margins, the organization was trying to broaden them. For example, volunteers taught poor youth how to write CVs and develop their job interview skills. Nour provided microloans too, though this was not one of its foci.

The director highlighted one central characteristic that differentiated them from others: the spirit of volunteerism. (This was, however, also emphasized by a board member of the second biggest volunteer-based association.) The director said, "If you want a hamburger go to McDonalds, if you want to volunteer go to Nour." In other words, the organization's mission was not technical-organizational superiority, but the mobilization of middle-class youth. It wanted to make charity as popular as fast food. In that regard, its spirit was differentiated from the dry rationalism of professionalized neoliberal organizations. However, the director also differentiated Nour from communitarian associations, specifically mentioning the Piety Association:

> People are used to charity in the normal sense: collecting money and helping poor people. ... Usually poor people wait in line in front of the charity organization to get help. We don't do this. We have volunteers to go and knock on doors. We have the energy of young people. ... This is different from the traditional way of Egyptian charity.

It was in part due to the gigantic networks of communitarian associations, with their resolute gerontocracies, that mobilizing young volunteers made sense. This was the kind of capital they didn't have; Nour challenged them on that front specifically. Even though the "Young, new vs. old, old" discursive oppositions also came up in the Turkish field, here they served a very specific purpose: destabilizing the communitarianism-dominated field. In other words, Egyptian neoliberals resorted to specific techniques not (only) because they imitated (or were "coerced" to adopt) certain models, as new institutionalists would predict;

they drew on the capital available in certain situations (e.g. a volunteer spirit, which partially resulted from the interactions between a professor and his students) *in response to an entrenched field of giving*. The director had learned a lot from charities in the US and Canada during his eight-year-long stay in the West. He therefore knew the Western templates and scripts by heart, yet mobilized them in ways distinct from others who also knew them (professionalized neoliberal actors).

Along the lines of this volunteerism, the classification of the poor was not imposed top-down, but emerged from below. Over the years, without any dictation from the director, young volunteers had developed questionnaires and then a classification of the poor into groups: A (handicapped and cannot work, receives regular funding from the association), group B (in between), and group C (only one-time help). Still, due to this association's field location, even its bottom-up classifications of the poor were in line with global practices. Work- and ability-based classifications materialized spontaneously.

Volunteer Spirituality against Comprehensive Religion

Another neoliberal intervention in the communitarianism-dominated field was the individualization of religion. Nour's objection to the communitarians' comprehensive religion went hand in hand with its eulogy of volunteerism. Seen from this angle, individualized religion is not the import of a world society script (nor simply the result of inevitable secularization), but a limited strategy in a specific field at a certain time. The director thus differentiated his Islamically inspired benevolence from Islamist benevolence based on a few principles (more restricted goals, non-political goals, and individualized motivation):

> We are trying to spread volunteerism. Our dream is that everybody helps everybody else. And anybody who tries to do anything will find a volunteer to do it. We hope that society will get there, even if [it takes] a hundred years. … We can't claim we are changing everything in society. This is different from the Islamic movement. They are thinking of building a new society. We do not dream that way. Our dream is just spreading volunteerism. And we think this is great in its own right. … If you need someone to help you with your studies, you find somebody to help you. If you are sick and you can't get food, someone will bring food to your place in an hour or so. This is our vision.

Despite this strong reaction to comprehensive religion, religiosity was still a part of the agenda. The director explained:

> Egypt is a very religious society. People consider volunteer activity as a way to come closer to God. Most of our volunteers are there because they think they are doing the [religiously] right thing. But this does not make them

Islamists. ... Our volunteers are religious in the sense that they love religion and God ... And [what they do] is a part of religion. ... But they do not [attempt to make] everyone else like us. This is one difference between us and the Islamist movement.

Religion was also a core impetus for beneficiaries. For instance, women beneficiaries in the literacy program stated that their primary aim was to be able to read the Qur'an. The beneficiaries, not only the administration, shaped and reproduced the association's religiosity.

The non-prescribed but still active reproduction of individual religiosity was embedded in the Nour's organizational structure. For instance, volunteers' interactions with beneficiaries and older volunteers increased piety. A volunteer, a woman in her early 20s, explained why she ended up at Nour after working for one of the professionalized neoliberal associations: "My previous organization was only about giving money and things to people. Here I can be like a member of their family. I can really take care of them." Her main life-transformative experience was being assigned to a girl when she was an infant (in the context of the "brother-sister program"). She was now six years old. Active caring, for this volunteer, involved a religious dimension. She herself went through a religious transformation as a result of this program. Nobody told her how to dress, but through observing her older sisters and their comportment, she came to understand that a caregiver needs to dress "modestly" (i.e. don the veil). Now she served as a role model for both other volunteers and the beneficiaries by combining the right kind of clothing with self-sacrificial volunteer work (a religious sense of being embedded, which brings her closer to communitarian actors, and distinguishes her from professionalized neoliberals).

There was, however, some internal disagreement at Nour about the influence of religion on the organization. One staff member (in charge of managing volunteers) consistently (and aggressively) denied that religious motivations played any part in her or in most volunteers' and staff's work.[2] This woman in her 20s, a 2008 graduate of a prestigious public university, insisted that it was incumbent on every human being to do volunteer work, regardless of religion:

> Nour Association has no relation to religion. We don't talk about religion. We do good works for the sake of good works [*ehna bna'mal khayr li agl al-khayr*]. This is a humanistic issue (*mawdu' insani*), not Islamic or Christian. ... The idea of service is not religious. ... Nour is a benevolent association, not an Islamic association. But I can't deny that spirituality is involved [*El-gam'iyya mish Islamiyya. El-gam'iyya khayriyya. Bas mish hanker inna fiha rawhaniyyat*].

This strong reaction from a mid-ranking staff signaled that the individualized-pious strategy (which the director specified and the Arabic-language brochures reinforced) brought with it many tensions.

Nour activists spelled out the word *khayr*, without any probing, as an essential motivation for giving. When I asked volunteers and staff to elucidate this word, some referred to religious texts, but most spoke in very broad terms, referring to positive feelings for human beings, love of education, and even the abundance of free time on their hands (as there weren't many work opportunities). But even among those who spoke of *khayr* in mostly non-religious terms, religious motivations came in, as with one woman beneficiary who said she wanted to better understand "the word of God." Similarly, a female volunteer (in her 20s) said that throughout her life she had spent a lot of time learning the Qur'an and now she wanted to pass it on.

The Nour's overall religious strategy, then, was *individualizing religion, but then also mobilizing it communally* through one-on-one interactions. This peculiar strategy was not a response only to the Egyptian charitable field, but also to the post-9/11 global environment. Reformers of welfare throughout the world are trapped in a double-bind they have themselves created: *the global power holders want to mobilize religion (in order to foster "active communities"), but don't want religion to shape society.*[3] The Nour empowered itself by developing a working solution to this dilemma. On the one hand, this appears to be a case of "normative isomorphism" in new institutionalist language. Yet, on the other, Egyptian actors creatively adjusted to these global pressures by building religiosity from the bottom up. Each volunteer and staff had to negotiate and re-produce the proper place of religiosity rather than blindly following a global script.

The Nour's re-signification of religion situated women in specific roles. Women were very active in this organization, not only as volunteers, but also mid-level managers. They also had much more fluctuating career paths than their male counterparts. They were on and off the job market (and volunteered in between). One of them, a business administration graduate in her 20s, volunteered for two years right after college. She then worked for a major food company. Subsequently, she got a position at her uncle's company and (due to her flexible hours) could become a regular volunteer at Nour, where she now directed one of the programs. More broadly speaking, volunteers and beneficiaries emphasized the important role of women in charity. Since women take care of children, interviewees stressed, they know how to help people. This validation allowed women to reconcile activism, their place in the (religiously justified) family structure and (partially gender-specific) flexible career paths under neoliberalism. The spread of female volunteerism thus rendered many aspects of contemporary life (such as career uncertainty) much more palatable by welding them to life-long engagement with attachments.

Incoherent Neoliberalization

The director held up the purest neoliberalism possible in macroeconomic affairs. He coded Nour as a part of the privatization endeavor. Likewise, he adamantly supported the business model for charity. He perceived good works as an extension of corporate social responsibility. He was also very critical of any public involvement in either the economy in general or in good works in particular: "The public sector is the root of all corruption. ... Everything should be privatized. The private sector is the best. This is the experience of humanity. ... What we are doing is privatizing welfare." He thought that only charity could resolve not only the poverty of the very poor, but general public problems such as housing and education. He overtly expressed astonishment at my suggestion that the public sector could have any positive role in the future of Egypt.

While the top management of Nour was unquestioningly in favor of privatization, I did not encounter the same level of commitment to the free market among the volunteers. Most beneficiaries and volunteers said they favored a mixed economy. They also thought associations could not shoulder the bulk of social provision and still saw government as the major responsible actor. Only one volunteer thought that the government should provide the basic infrastructure for charity (such as giving associations facilities and land), but not worry much about the rest. I also encountered mixed attitudes among the staff, though the latter veered more towards the management's position. For example, a female staff member said that the government should not do much beyond providing the legal framework for the buildings. Some volunteers and beneficiaries declined to respond to any question about ideal governmental action, possibly because they interpreted this issue as too political (answering it could jeopardize their security). This incoherence, as we will see, is in deep in contrast with the embrace of neoliberalism among many Turkish volunteers.

In light of this incoherence, it is difficult to see Nour staff and volunteers as a neoliberal army (as the subjectivity literature suggests) or an alternative to neoliberalism (as some scholars want to believe of Islamic charity). The partially informal *and* less government-regulated nature of their activities, among other factors, prevented a textbook case of neoliberalization. Nour had some connections with government programs. For instance, after they finished the literacy program at Nour, beneficiaries got a Ministry of Education certificate showing that they had completed an equivalent of primary education. However, such governmental sanctioning paled in comparison to the near-merger between state and civil society among professionalized neoliberal associations, which constitute the real neoliberal army (or, given their disinterest in mobilizing huge numbers, elite militia).

"Business to Business": Scripts and Complications

Another major association in this category was the Generosity Fund. The business tendencies in this association were stronger than in Nour, but the Generosity Fund did not go as far as professionalized neoliberal associations. Gamal, a board member, exemplified these tendencies. He came from a business family. Born in Cairo and a graduate of a commerce department, he was in his late 40s. His father was an army officer. "My father was a very proactive person. That is the way I was raised," he said. He started to be civically active right after graduation, especially focusing on businessman associations. He was central in the foundation of a prominent, nationwide business association.

In the following years, he joined the boards of many charity, philanthropic, realtors', health, and other NGOs. Many of these organizations featured not only the most prominent businessmen, but also ministers and other top officials as board members. As his engagement intensified, he decided to quit his position as chairman and CEO of several major companies. Even though he formally quit the business world, his mission became the thorough businessification of the NGO world.

Nevertheless, as far as this particular association was concerned, the transfer of business templates and scripts was only partial. Most important of all, the association focused solely on provision, not the re-creation of the poor subject in the image of an entrepreneur. Still, Gamal combined protective policies (and occasionally anti-market discourse, see further below) with market-oriented metaphors (such as calling care a "business"). This director contrasted "charity as business" to (what he perceived to be) traditional charity:

> The Generosity Fund focuses hundred percent on food. Our one goal is alleviating hunger. That is our mission. In order to do that, we have many programs.
> … We work B to B, that is, business-to-business, not business-to-consumer. We do not deal with poor people, at all. We only deal with NGOs located in certain places, because they are more capable of reaching poor, needy people. They have the accurate databases … [Through them] we reach the poorest villages. … We concentrate on orphans, widows, [the disabled and permanently sick], and elderly people—people who cannot work—so that we don't make people lazy. … We give them all they need in kind: food. So, we are not giving them 20 ginih like other organizations do. … We make a monthly contract with the NGOs to cover a specific number of families after studying each case properly.

Even though this association was not engaged in training, capacity-building, and income-generation (like professionalized neoliberal associations), its protective aid was definitively non-communitarian; and developed *in distinction* from "traditional" charities that sprinkled cash and (allegedly) could not control the consequences. (Gamal opposed their activities to those of communitarian charities without any probing on my part, but he used the word traditional rather than communitarian.) It resorted to quantification to ensure that each beneficiary got no more than what s/he needed for survival. People would have to *work* if they wanted more than that; and even basic survival was not granted to the able-bodied. This was good-natured neoliberalism in action. The founder who had lived in the United States and observed food-distributing charities there, Gamal emphasized, had conceived this model. Since (as Chapter 3 shows) many American charities operate with starkly different assumptions and techniques, we should underline that the founder has learned from *the predominant kind* of American charity.

Far from being "B"s, however, some NGOs they worked with were quite communitarian. One example of this was the Kirama Association (covered in Chapter 4), which had links to the Brotherhood and practiced communitarian charity. This specific link was not disclosed to me by Generosity Fund members. I learned about it fortuitously while spending time at the Kirama Association, which I had contacted through my Brotherhood networks (the Generosity Fund personnel were not happy to see me there, and I suffered a long lecture on the futility of my research). Neoliberal organizations couldn't control everything that happened on the ground. Their habit of perceiving non-liberal charities as businesses indicated either neglect or denial. They helped these charities, legitimized them, and thereby contributed to the reproduction of communitarianism. Such were the practical limits and ironies of Egyptian neoliberalism.

A second group of Generosity Fund activities involved working with hotels and other entertainment industries to collect the access food, through a cooperation with the Ministry of Tourism. In the beginning, the association paid the hotels and their personnel for the aluminum foil plates they used to store the access food and the extra time they put into the work. Gamal said that later on both management and workers refused to be compensated because they were "good people." The organization brought out the goodness in them, he reasoned.

In spite of all his connections to the bureaucracy, when asked in a general way whether any state agencies were helpful, the director gave the standard answer: the ministers were good people, but could not control their staff, so there was a lot of bureaucracy. "At the end of the day, we have to do things on our own." In response to my question about why there was such heavy bureaucracy concerning charitable affairs, he mockingly gave the answer:

> Why is there bureaucracy in *Egypt*? This is a 7,000-year-old civilization. It is 7,000 years of bureaucracy. Egypt is a very strong country, my friend! And bureaucracy here is very well-established. But then, there are many ways to deal with the bureaucracy.

He was surprised that this could even be posed as a question. Even though self-evident, Gamal's attitude revealed a multilayered complexity. The liberal hope that associations will weaken dependence on the state could pay off in an ideal situation where people do not have such attitudes about "bureaucracy;" but when people have an *internalized, taken-for-granted cynicism that both derides and accepts governmental bureaucracy*, associations can only strengthen the way things are. Liberal civil society, then, did not challenge the state (even though it abhorred the bureaucracy). Instead, civic actors developed networks with top-level state actors to take care of business. This mode of action can be reduced neither to Egypt's cultural singularity nor to the simple transfer of modern templates. We can make sense of it only in light of Egypt's specific (but structurally patterned) sociopolitical path. Gamal was not a passive placeholder who enacted "world culture." He wasn't an embodiment of 7,000 year of Egyptian culture either. He was rather an active position-taker who articulated the worlds of business, bureaucracy, and charity.

Individualized religion was at the center of this association's discourse too. Gamal punctuated: "The main thing is the goodness in people's hearts. We try to bring out this goodness. Some are motivated by Islam, some by Christianity; some secular people are good too." But interestingly, his construction of goodness did not squarely fit with his other neoliberal emphases. When I asked him whether any Hadith or Qur'anic verse had motivated him, he turned the answer into a critique of market logic (without any probing on my part):

> Benevolence is beyond any marketing philosophy or tools because the reward of being good is beyond what any product or service can promise you. It is the day-after, *gannah* [heaven], you cannot quantify it ... But despite that, we try not to use too much religion in our activities, because we do not want to be labeled as an Islamic organization. This is an Egyptian organization. There are Copts too working with us. ... [As opposed to communitarian organizations] we give to the people regardless of their religion. I personally believe this is the Islamic approach.

Gamal differentiated his organization from more neoliberal associations *and* communitarian associations. He criticized the former because they worked with an explicit market "philosophy" (in his own words), pressured their rivals to exit the market, and strove to quantify everything, even faith. He faulted the communitarians because, he thought, they tended to make people lazy.

He used more indicators to flaunt their differences from communitarian organizations (the Piety Association more specifically): *professionals* ran his own organization. They had systems and *procedures*, whereas the "old organizations" depended on mosques and *verbal* communication. Despite all of this, he thought that communitarian organizations played a pivotal role in Egypt; worked with the grassroots; were able to garner a lot of funds; were "very smart," so would be able to adapt some of these professional techniques in the longer run. "We cannot compete with them in many senses," he added.

Gamal's combination of communitarian and neoliberal discourses and practices was not necessarily the expression of a contradiction. Rather, some saw the differences of focus between volunteer-based associations and professionalized ones as a division of labor. The former would protect people who cannot work and the latter would push the others to labor. Consequently, some administrators of volunteer-based associations also worked for professionalized ones.

As importantly, some organizations not involved in training saw it as a part of their mission to support training-oriented organizations. For example, the Generosity Fund provided food for families who got microloans from professionalized associations, so that the very poor among them would not use the loans for basic necessities. This self-conscious cooperation between the more and less intensely market-oriented organizations contrasted with the relative lack of cooperation between neoliberal and communitarian organizations. Some neoliberal organizations made several moves to work with communitarian organizations in order to tap into the "grassroots," but all attempts failed (or unconsciously reproduced communitarianism, see Chapter 4). This was one reason why Egypt could not build neoliberal armies.

Professionalized Neoliberal Associations: Massive Funds, but no Masses

The organizations in this cluster were small in terms of staff, but they had extensive funds. The staff was composed of professionals. The salaries were competitive, attesting to the marketization of benevolent activities. These associations' managers were among the primary sources of funding for their organizations: whereas in communitarian associations many managers were also donors (as all better off Muslims are required to be), the class background of the managers in professionalized associations allowed a stronger overlap between the role of donor and aid manager.

The "developmental" tendencies among these organizations were stronger than those in volunteer-based neoliberal associations. A few of them told me that everybody already knows we should teach poor people how to fish rather than giving them fish, but their mission was teaching how to be clever fishermen, how to catch the fish with less cost, and even how to *make* a fishing net, underlining the deeper neoliberalization of both discourse and practice.

While discussing aid organizations, managers used an international vocabulary I did not encounter in other organizations.[4] They frequently employed words such as field, market, and industry when discussing aid. They also distanced themselves from the English word "charity" and said that even though most *khayr* organizations in Egypt focused on charity, they wanted to elevate khayr to the level of "sustained development" or "civil service."[5] They underlined that most Egyptian organizations (including not only communitarians, but many volunteer-based neoliberal ones too) belonged to a former era.

The language of these associations is significant also because it exposes the limits of Bourdieu's theorization. Bourdieu is adamant that religious actors can acknowledge the objective truth of their practices (that religion is a market, that the flock is a clientele) *only* in ironic moments and crisis situations. In an essay playfully titled "The Laughter of the Bishops," he observes that whenever bishops refer to religion as a market, they laugh (*Practical Reason* 1998, pp. 113–114). In business as usual, this objective truth has to be denied to make religion (and the volunteerism and charity that go with it) work. In other words, the objective and subjective truths of religion are completely at odds with each other. However, Egyptian actors in this cluster routinely and seriously used business language in their competition to monopolize zakat and sadaqa. Subjects unflinchingly recognized charity's objective truth. There was therefore nothing to laugh about.[6]

While communitarians referred to Islamic history as their model, managers of neoliberal associations put the US, Canada, and England on a pedestal, while also making some references to Islamic history. Professionalized associations were most ardent about this. The director of the largest professionalized association referred to the US as the "Makkah" of healthcare and Turkey as another model. Even though Turkey was a secular country, its *waqf* (endowment) activity was regulated by more liberal laws (according to his perception) and was therefore in continuity with Islamic history.

The largest organization in this category was the Patriots Association, which was established in the beginning of the 2000s. The founders were mostly businessmen. The organization operated more than 200 primary schools and served close to 6,000 students. It also supported (what it defined as) "productive families" through constant income, provision of livestock, and debt relief.

The organization invested sadaqa (but not zakat) in finance and industry, with the aim of then circulating this money back to charitable activities. Its managers wanted to create companies along these lines and build up "a circle of stakeholders." This heavy involvement in finance (another dimension of deeper neoliberalization) raised suspicion in some Islamic circles, but the Grand Mufti's engagement as a board member served as a shield against such doubts (or, alternatively, further reinforced some Islamists' indictment that these associations were merged with the Mubarak regime).[7]

Patriots Association managers were critical of volunteer activity (predominant in both communitarian and volunteer-based neoliberal associations), which they associated with lack of awareness and commitment. The top director told me that "civil service" should be "professionalized." He added: "civil service is an industry." The organization recruited multinational companies' employees in order to build a professional staff. Demonstrating the deep marketization of their actions and mentality, the managers underlined the "high returns" such highly qualified professionals would bring when compared to volunteers.

Oversight by the Minute

The Correct Path Association was among the largest organizations in Egypt. 80 percent of its funding went to development. Only around 3–4 percent was spent on urgent needs, for managers believed that people should get what they need through hard work. Self-reliance (*ta'tamid 'an nafsiha*) and civilizing people were the key words for this association. Managers emphasized that they not only gave goods but taught people how to work and make profit. The top director travelled all over the Arab world to collect more ideas to refine their "developmental projects" (*mashruʻat al-tanmawiyya*). The Correct Path Association also cooperated with organizations of the same mentality. Finally, it wanted to make Nour and other volunteer-based neoliberal associations adopt more developmental projects.

The organization mobilized around 5,000 volunteers (around 70 percent were students). But unlike Nour, organizational structure did not depend on volunteers. A manager explained:

> The association's projects are professional. It is necessary that the daily work is not interrupted. We have employees who put 24 hours into it. Our volunteers [work] at particular times. But the managerial structure is based on employees. Professionalism [is necessary] because we are engaged in tens of millions of projects throughout the republic. This requires oversight by the minute [*el-raqaba el-daqiqa*].

Managers put special emphasis on the word "professionalism," and the organizational structure placed volunteers in a highly specified niche. The difference from Nour was therefore both quantitative and qualitative: this funding-wise huge association not only mobilized as little as one-twentieth of Nour's volunteers, but explicitly devalued volunteer labor. Unlike managers at other professionalized associations, this manager did not attack volunteerism overtly, but implied that volunteers were not dependable laborers.

Religion's circumscribed, individualized role was further confined when compared to Nour. One of the top directors, an ex-general, explained that his current activity was a continuation of what he used to do as a soldier: working for the common good and managing people for this purpose. He also said as a Muslim and a human being, benevolence was something he carried deeply. But two staff members I talked to denied the role of Islam even as a motivating factor. A staff member, an art history graduate in his 20s, had never performed civic activities before he came to this association. His current involvement was based on two factors. On the one hand, he praised the organization because it *invested* in its employees and *trained* them in computer and telemarketing. It taught not only the beneficiaries but also the staff and volunteers how to be "civilized." This staff member frequently repeated words such as "*tamaddun*" and "*khadara*," as did all Correct Path-connected individuals. Thanks to his organization, he took courses on communication skills and administration. This was the more self-interested dimension of his involvement. On the other hand, as a person with special needs he had received help from other people in the past and he saw his activities here as a way of paying back. That is why he had switched from working in tourism (for seven months) to the charitable sector (where he had spent about seven years). He combined self-interested and altruistic dispositions in his orientation to charity, but did so in a way that subordinated reciprocity to neoliberal subject formation. He was also exemplary of many middle and lower level staff in newer Egyptian charities in that he had personal and interpersonal (rather than civic) experiences with benevolence prior to his current employment.

Another staff member, a lawyer in his 50s, also depicted pragmatic as well as humanistic motivations. Even though he got the staff position because he needed extra income, his reasons for sticking to it were more complex. He would get paid more at a non-charitable job. Also, he had a private office and could demand the market rate for his charitable services. The reason why he stayed at this association as a paid staff member was the willingness to help others, due to his human side (*ganb insani*). Just like the other staff member, he had not performed any other charitable or civic work beforehand. Moreover, just like him, he argued that religion was not one of the factors that motivated him to do charity. Finally, when compared to Nour, volunteers and staff at this association were rather low key, cool, unexcited people. They were much less emotionally invested in their activities. Rationality crowded out religion and emotions.

The Correct Path Association was heavily funded by businessmen. It was a non-political, non-partisan, non-religious organization (*"gamaʿ la-siyasiyya, la-hizbiyya, la-diniyya"*) with no government support (detractors disagreed). Just like they kept out of politics, Correct Path actors expected the government to keep out of their business: "The government should focus only on what it specializes in. Developmental projects are solely the responsibility of associations." Rich people, they said, were already fulfilling this duty. As Chapter 6 will show, Turkish neoliberals shied away from such pure free-market statements.

Blessed Careers

Some professionalized organizations, by contrast, deployed market-fused religious metaphors to elevate charitable motivations. A smaller organization is demonstrative of this tendency. The organization was established by a woman from a business family. In order to stabilize the disability her child was born with, the family visited the United States. There, they discovered not only the West's technological progress, but also its acceptance of the disabled. Touched by her experience, she decided to found an organization that not only helped disabled children, but worked on society's attitudes and facilities, to fully integrate the disabled of all classes.

The founder's disabled child benefited from a new technique ("biofeedback") that improved the mental and physical capacities of the disabled without medication. She thus decided to spread this to Egypt and made it one of the association's main programs. On top of making education more inclusive and spreading the biofeedback program, the organization also procured employment for the disabled. Disabled adults applied to the association and were interviewed. Afterwards, the association matched their skills with the appropriate jobs. Its experts trained both the applicant and the hiring company regarding interpersonal skills and inclusiveness. Around 2,000 ginih were dedicated to the training of each applicant. The organization had trained more than 80 applicants so far.

A staff member told me she had a "blessed career." The donors were also blessed. Her experiences exemplified the benefits of a blessed path:

> When I started to work in aid, I found it very blessing. You get paid to do something that benefits others. ... When I was working for an international company with a salary three times as high as my current salary, many bad things happened to me. Ultimately, I had a terrible car accident and my luxurious car was trashed. Now, I earn less, but I also lose less. With God's blessings, this is a more lucrative activity. ... This is *baraka* [God's blessed abundance].

She added that benevolence also taught her how to use her earnings more properly. Both English and Arabic allowed the association to blend religiosity with business. The words *blessing* and *baraka* saturated everyday life. The association cooperated with banks to put the phrase "shop and be blessed" on credit cards (in English). When consumers shopped with these cards, a certain percentage of their spending went directly to charity.

This creative blending of *baraka*, blessing, rationally guided careers, and shopping again brings to mind Jean and John Comaroff's (2001) point that magic and neoliberal capitalism are highly interwoven. Their argument, however, is marked by a slippage between emphasizing the complementarity between magic and "hyperrationalization" (p. 2) and an assumption that magic "def[ies] reason" (p. 23) and "transgresses ... the rational, the moral" (p. 26). The neoliberal women I observed in Egypt did not have a sense that there was something that defied rationality (let alone morality) in their belief that charity protected them from accidents. Magical belonging rather reinforced their integration into a rationalized organizational structure.

The staff (18 people) was composed of administrative, financial, and educational professionals. Some were recruited through regular and rationalized application procedures. But others came through personal and family connections. The association utilized volunteer labor only during certain events. The founder's friend and family networks were central to staffing this organization. Most managers were women. A staff member, for instance, came into charity through her friendship with the founder. This staff member accentuated that many people came to aid organizations due to personal connections and experiences, rather than religion:

> Some people come to this like a regular job, and others come through someone they know. But it is usually social: this is an NGO and employees have to believe in the cause. Most of them have been touched: they have a disabled cousin, a son, a sister. They see the cause.

In other words, even though individualized and marketized religion played a central role, the recruitment also depended on interpersonal and emotional links.

The funding initially depended on solicitations from donors who were connected to the founder through business or family. Later on, the founder's friends complained that they could no longer fund everything. She therefore hired a financial specialist with 17 years of experience in the banking sector. The specialist came to this organization after working for six years as a fundraiser for another benevolent organization, where she met the founder. She did extensive research, identified corporations more likely to give, and even discovered Egyptian businessmen and CEOs who had disabled relatives. She also designed a logo for companies willing to invest in the cause, which naturally served as good public relations. Acquiring the logo was conditional on holding periodic awareness raising sessions, complying with the association's code of accessibility, and participating in annual events along with other disabled-friendly companies.

The Ministry of Social Solidarity both closely monitored these processes and provided databases of disabled people and companies that might hire them. The Ministry of Education too cooperated with the association, and ultimately applied their model of education in more than 5,000 schools throughout Egypt. This relatively small organization shouldered a part of this burden by directly helping more than 130 schools implement an inclusive curriculum and architectural structure. The teachers also had to be thoroughly trained. A budget of 40,000 ginih was allocated to each school. Individual teachers were directly compensated with 2,000 pounds.

Managers and staff at this business ethics-fused organization pertinaciously favored the privatization of caring. The financial specialist said:

> The government should give all of this work to the civic world. [NGOs] have better knowledge of ... the problems. They get their work done in a shorter time and with sincerity and professionalism. ... The government should waive taxes for all donations to human causes. [Citizens] pay taxes to get better education, treatment and protection. If I am getting these from the associations [instead of] the government, then I should pay the same amount to associations.

Practitioners perceived disability services as market goods, which would have a just price only if the government got out of the way. One organization after another in this group provided intricate anti-government arguments even though they thoroughly benefited from not only networks with bureaucrats, but also cooperation with the government. Blessed careers would be unimaginable without government favors, but the link between the two was consistently denied.

Restoring Lost Loyalty to Build the Ownership Society

When compared to others in this category, the Loyalty Association was slightly more involved in da'wa activities. The television program that had initially inspired the organization (and led to its foundation) aimed to "explain religion [untinged by] any fanatical or extremist ideas." The founders perceived a direct continuity between the charity provided by the organization and the *'amal us-salih* (good works) of this television show. The organization defined one of its duties as promoting Qur'anic education. The founders believed that the holy book should be memorized (which was a communal obligation, *fard kifaya*). They organized contests among *kuttab* (Qur'anic school) students, of ages 5 to 15, then distributed awards and honors. The *hafiz* (Qur'an memorizer) contests drew around 1,500 competitors.

Nevertheless, the bulk of their activities centered on provision and training, and the latter gradually occupied more of their energies. In 2002, the Loyalty Association established a small kitchen to feed poor villagers and orphans in South Giza. The organization took soup to domiciles to avoid long queues (an activity that served other neoliberal organizations too as a distinction from communitarian charities). After many encounters with poor people, the founders realized other urgent needs, such as assistance with clothing, education, and health expenses. At that point, all activists involved in the organization, around 30 people, were volunteers. In time, the villagers trusted them regarding more private issues too: young men and women sought their help to find partners in marriage. The association gave additional aid packages to potential husbands and wives so that they could safely walk into the "holy relation," marriage.

In a few years, the organization expanded its coverage area to 16 villages. It now produced more than 3,000 meals every week. 7 percent of its budgets went to food; 15 percent to "social" activities (mostly marriage); 50 percent to medical aid; 20 percent to education and training; 5 percent to administration; and the rest to a subsidiary branch. Their budget was close to 10 million ginih. Though still dependent on volunteer energy, the organization built a staff of more than 30 people. Some, especially those in the steering committee, were recruited through friendship and business networks. A few were CEOs in multinational companies. The goal was further expanding this expert-based structure. The managers, however, did not sound as negative about volunteer activity as others in this cluster. Their mission was also "to promote the idea of the importance of volunteer work." Both in its relationship to volunteer activity and through its less individualized understanding of religious mission, this association straddled the boundary between the categories of professionalized and volunteer-based neoliberal benevolence.

At another level, however, the organization fit in neatly together with the professionalized associations and even claimed to be more aggressively business-oriented than them. The managers slowly but surely approached a purer business vision as they interacted more with the poor and discovered gaps in their own approach to poverty:

> We no longer wanted to just provide medical assistance. ... We wanted to change society. ... To give them the motive to change, first you need to

restore the loyalty that is lost. These people felt that they belonged to their street and family. But they did not feel belonging to the country. ... You have to build a sense of ownership.

But to do this, he added, the poor need to have access to basics such as food, clothes, and shelter. "You cannot request change from someone who has no running water." The organization aimed to take illiterate people, train them, and get them employment. The director argued that they ultimately developed an operational structure that distinguished them from other organizations: they first built loyalty then trained the beneficiaries and finally found employment for them and monitored their activities while employed:

> In our training center, we offer [the beneficiaries] professions, just like the Polytechnique. Carpentry, plumbing ... whatever profession is required. And we don't just train them and let them go into the market without any job opportunities. We talk to the factories. There are clothes and furniture factories around. We ask them if they need workers. And all of them do because they have a problem with consistency: people come, work for two months, factories invest in their training, and then they leave! We take the unemployed, train them, and factories hire them. ... [We tell the trainees:] If you don't work [for that factory], you are no longer in our database.

The "Big Four" benevolent organizations (as he called them) lacked such clear operational structure, according to the director. He further criticized the Big Four because they spent zakat on media and ads (a charge these organizations vehemently denied when I brought it up); they had poor administrative structures; spent as much as $8,000 USD on salaries; saved zakat money in banks; and the government did not properly audit them.

Despite being so heavily invested in the neoliberalization of benevolence, this manager also used anti-market metaphors and arguments reminiscent of those in the volunteer-based cluster (see quote from Gamal above):

> Khayr is not a profitable activity. ... We are working for the community and for God. We are doing this [so that] in heaven, insha'Allah, we find something good. Some reward in heaven, not on earth. If we all work for God's satisfaction [rida], there will be no competition. Nobody will say, "If you are not up to the competition, close down."

He was fed up with hearing (from larger professionalized associations) that they were more efficient than his organization. They were unwilling to cooperate, he complained. This rejection of market logic was, however, coupled with the use of market language throughout the interview: the director referred to beneficiaries as "clients" and benevolence as a "market."

To make sure that it stayed true to its mission, the organization tracked the activities of beneficiaries. For instance, when a young disabled person got help, he could not remain idle (or beg), but had to finish his studies in college or work in a factory:

> We get a lot of request for help with purchasing artificial arms and legs. But we only help when we know there will be a change. ... This is the change of status: From being dependent to independent, useful ... to have an added value.

The director then contrasted this method to the proverbial "Ramadan bag" approach: putting some necessities in a bag and then delivering it to people only during Ramadan. "This is not our goal, although it is a part of what we do." The director also criticized communitarian organizations because they helped the poor, but then sought their votes. One reason why they decided to make the transition from an informal to a formal mode of operation was *to distinguish their activities from such organizations* and gain further trust among both *the security forces and the beneficiaries*. Earlier, during their informal years, Brotherhood members had infiltrated their activities and this gave rise to frictions with the state. Luckily, his family had connections in the police, which helped the organization weather some obstacles regarding registration.

According to the director, one of the biggest obstacles in the path to the ownership society was the government's involvement in welfare. For instance, the association's water provision was efficient, whereas, the "bureaucratic" and "corrupt" water department could not provide properly. Most of the government's care money (especially in hospitals) was mismanaged. Also, a lot of people got privileges they did not deserve, and the government had no way of weeding them out. Furthermore, government employees were not well-trained and did not have the capacity to mend any of these problems.

The analysis of the Loyalty Association has theoretical implications. We cannot explain (even) convergence on a purer neoliberal organizational model solely based on diffusion through mimetic, normative, and coercive pressures. What mattered most in the evolution of this specific organization was a complex game of distinction (from both communitarian and professionalized associations) that allowed managers to delineate their unique neoliberalism, which subordinated serious religious missionary and volunteer activity to an overall professionalized vision. The globally available templates and scripts certainly mattered too, but only in their interactions with field dynamics.

Institutionalists occasionally recognize that imitation can unexpectedly lead to innovation (DiMaggio and Powell 1983, p. 151), yet this insight is undone through an emphasis on the overriding influences of homogenization. DiMaggio and Powell (1983, p. 152) paraphrase from John Meyer the following conference remarks: "it is easy to predict the organization of a newly emerging nation's administration without knowing anything about the nation itself." This chapter, by contrast, demonstrates the amazing (if structured and restricted) diversity even among neoliberal organizations within a field. There is no way we could be "predict" any of this without the empirical study of the Egyptian field. Moreover, even when they grant that innovation is possible, new institutionalists still shy away from theorizing the mechanisms that lead to it (which, I have argued, we can only do through a study of field dynamics properly contextualized in political and economic structures). We can appreciate Loyalty Association's uniqueness among other neoliberal organizations only by studying its differentiation from others (as Bourdieusians would expect), but the religious and political dynamics of Egypt highly structure its series of position-takings (which Bourdieusians would emphasize less). This organization's unique characteristics result from a field- and hegemony-structured institutional creativity.

Theological Monologues to Escalate the Competition

This section will finally cover an association that is somewhat of an exception in the Egyptian field in that it combines a vigorous missionary (da'wa) orientation with neoliberalism, as do some Turkish actors (see Chapter 6). This organization was founded at the end of the 1990s. Its initial goal was turning the mosque into an institution that speaks to more than the need to pray. The founders wanted to attract the youth, so they focused on things that young people sought outside the mosque, like fun and entertainment. They wanted young people to come to the mosque and find there Islamically acceptable versions of entertainment.

The overall mission was to make sure that young people were happy in the way God wants it (a manager called this "Islamic happiness"). The organization assumed that most Egyptian Muslims already knew how to pray and fast, so they were not worried about the formalities of rituals. Rather, they focused on four stages (*marhala*) of individual development: knowing God; knowing oneself; knowing others (family, friends, and organizations); knowing the universe. Beneficiaries (young boys) were trained and monitored from elementary to the end of high school. Every individual had to have a special and personalized relationship with God (*'alaqa khassa*) that went beyond the basic rituals and included personalized prayer (*du'a*), good intentions (*niyya*), trust in God (*tawakkul*), and monologues (*munajat*). In his relation to himself, every individual had to know his advantages and disadvantages. He then needed to systematically work to overcome his disadvantages through further training. More importantly, the individual had to discover his talents and work on them so that he could have an edge over others. In other words, the organization perceived *a competitive self* as a key to Islamic happiness. In their relations with others, it aimed to teach people how to deal with (*ta'amul*) friends, family, and all other human beings. The last stage, relations with the universe, aimed to prepare boys nearing high school graduation by instilling in them an overall sense of purpose, a meaning to life. It did this through focusing on their future goals. The organization had so far produced 30 graduates and currently trained 900 students. There were more than 40 trainers.

One of the top directors (an energetic and dedicated engineer in his late 20s) cited an *ayat* to clarify their goal: "*inna Allah la yuslihu 'amal al-mufsidin*" (God does not amend the work of corrupters, 10:81). There was a lot of corruption in Egypt, and this was not restricted to bribery and other scandalous acts. The real corruption was the lack of purpose, as well as the youth's obsession with flirtation, girlfriends, and other "superficial" things. Associations needed to build "character" and create "leaders" in order to overcome this purposelessness.

Despite high ambitions, managers and staff were not trained to do this kind of work (none had philanthropic, educational, or any other type of NGO certification). The organization did not have any elaborate hierarchy or recruitment mechanism either. There were no fixed posts; *friends* rotated within the hierarchy. Unlike other ambitious professionalized organizations, the managers and staff exhibited a spirit of volunteerism (they were not paid). However, they wanted to build up this professionalism in time and have a tighter managerial structure, as well as solid staff with certificates and diplomas related to this line of activity.

Even though I used the word "volunteering" for this type of activity, the young engineer was ambivalent about that word. "No, no, we are friends. We all share the same ideas." He wanted to differentiate their mode of behavior from that of volunteers mobilized by large organizations, who provided some help, but then disappeared without undergoing serious transformation (according to his account). His organization's trainers were, presumably unlike volunteers, all saturated with the same mission and structured all of their lives according to shared ideas. After a few minutes of reflection and uncertainty about what the alternative words would be, he decided on the word mission (*da'wa*, or perhaps, he said, *risalah*, Qur'anic message) as distinct from volunteerism (*tatawwu'*). Mittermaier (2014a, p. 520) argues that her "interlocutors point to a different meaning of tatawwu', the Arabic word usually translated as 'volunteering.' Tatawwu' is derived from ta' (to obey) and literally means 'being rendered obedient.' Volunteering here implies a relationship of obedience toward God." However, *tatawwu'* did not have this connotation for the more mission-oriented associations I studied. When I brought up the word, da'wa actors grimaced. As Chapter 4 shows, the largest da'wa associations even had an institutionalized word (*ihtisab*) to replace it. The young engineer pointed out one more difference between them and the volunteer-based associations (he specifically mentioned the Generosity Fund and Nour): "They produce service, we produce persons (*ashkhas*, plural of *shakhs*)."

This organization was also different in that it mostly catered to middle- and upper-middle-class kids. Attempts to integrate poor kids into this strict religious and economic discipline had failed: poor kids were not able to adjust to their curriculum. There was an unresolved debate about whether to more systematically reach out to the poor. But for now, the dominant tendency was to first work with the better off and then integrate the poor after full institutionalization. Moreover, unlike most neoliberal organizations, this one aspired to a global outreach (even though it did not have the capacity to do this yet) and was critical of other associations' focus on Egypt and Egyptians. Scholars have argued that new Egyptian charitable organizations combine Islamic and neoliberal subjectivity (Atia 2013). My research shows that this combination was mostly restricted to associations which worked on the middle classes. The poor were not fully exposed to this kind of double-subjectivation, unlike in Turkey.

Even though the organization's members appreciated and learned from the Muslim Brotherhood and the Piety Association, they kept them at a distance due to security reasons. In order to avoid any problems, they also integrated to their board an MP from Mubarak's party (prior to the 2011 uprising). In other words, even pro-Muslim Brotherhood organizations had networks with the previous regime, at least for pragmatic reasons.

★★★

The benevolence scene in Egypt consisted of four clusters, as Chapters 3 and 4 have shown. Though exhibiting many parallels, the dispositions; organizational structures; and backgrounds and perspectives of da'wa-oriented and politics-oriented communitarian actors and associations differed from one another to an extent. The same kind of contiguity characterized neoliberal benevolence as well.

Neoliberal and communitarian actors clearly diverged from each other in their orientation to Islam. The former strove to delimit the role of Islam in their activities to a motivational factor. Their religious vocabulary (to the extent they used it) emphasized the individual agent, rather than either dictums of religious texts or supernatural and inspirational stories (even though the latter came up now and then). Nevertheless, actors in volunteer-based neoliberal associations occasionally resorted to textual references, while the professionalized ones tended to exclude them. Communitarians disdained varieties of piety that remained restricted to individual and motivational roles. They wanted to Islamize Egypt and saw benevolence as one way of doing that. Their religious references were heavily textual, though communitarian da'wa actors deployed magical stories too. These religious strategies percolated not simply as a result of diffusion (of global templates and scripts), but in response to *a sociopolitical environment shaped by Islamist movements*, as well as to *the religious moves of other associations that competed to monopolize benevolent sensibilities and resources*.

These religious strategies were embedded in a larger set of differentiated practices. Even though the volunteer-based neoliberal associations desired to cultivate market-oriented sensibilities, they were also keen to engender the spread of volunteering. Defying any sharp separation between reciprocal and nonreciprocal giving, their activities were geared towards generating both. By contrast, professionalized actors ruthlessly pursued the cultivation of neoliberal subjectivities. They also admitted the self-serving aspects of benevolence more openly than any of the other actors. Desires to foster religious transformation and encourage mutual help occasionally surfaced, but were buried under the weight of a concern with producing individualistic self-help. This more textbook-like neoliberal approach was produced through *highly developed links with the state* and *incessant differentiation* from communitarian actors (that is, neither through random "assemblages" nor through direct "mimesis").

Communitarian da'wa actors underlined that Islamic benevolence would create not only a more religious, but also a socially just, moral, and happy society (though, in effect, the word "Islamic" captured all dimensions of this purposive universe). Among political communitarian actors, international Islamic solidarity (sustenance of the *ummah*) trumped other social goals: they paid less attention to social justice when compared to da'wa actors. These broad orientations structured the restricted diffusion of "Western" practices within these associations.

Volunteer-based neoliberal associations differentiated themselves based on their novelty and youth. They also vaunted their specific mixture of professionalism and volunteerism. Professionalized actors were much more aggressive in their distinction and showcased their professionalism, specialization, "civilization," and willingness to further sharpen these characteristics through training. Communitarian actors avoided such technical and scientific language and instead underscored their competitors' lack of compassion and Islamic erudition. While da'wa actors differentiated themselves via juristic mastery, political communitarian ones underlined the importance of allegiance to an (Islamic) authority. Table 5.1 summarizes the differentiation of the four worlds of Egyptian benevolence in terms of dispositions.

Organizational structure was another site of differentiation. Most importantly, the associations distinguished themselves based on the activities they focused on (which in turn emanated from their assumptions about the core reasons behind poverty). Volunteer-based neoliberal associations focused on direct provision, much along the lines of "traditional charity," but also on training the poor to make them self-reliant, assuming that individual shortcomings were at the basis of poverty. Professionalized associations, which took this assumption more seriously, minimized direct provision and maximized training. By contrast, since da'wa associations faulted all of society for its lack of piety, and especially the rich for their dearth of compassion, they concentrated transformative activities on the better off. Their relationships with the poor consisted mostly of direct provision. Finally, communitarian political associations coupled direct provision and da'wa with the exertion of political control, as they assumed that a change of political order was necessary to resolve poverty.

Since professionalized associations assumed that the most effective motivating mechanisms are financial and material, they sought to create career initiatives for their staff. Volunteer-based neoliberal associations integrated the spirit of volunteerism into their management structures too, whereas professionalized ones despised any mode of organization that did not rely on measurable (and cashable)

TABLE 5.1 Contrasting Dispositions of Egyptian Charitable Actors

	Volunteer-Based Neoliberal Associations	Professionalized Neoliberal Associations	Communitarian Da'wa Associations	Political Communitarian Associations
The Role of Islam	Motivation (along with humanistic and patriotic goals)	Motivation (along with humanistic and patriotic goals)	Goal and motivation	Goal and motivation
Religious Motivation/ References/ Vocabulary	Textual and individualistic	Individualistic	Textual (occasionally magical)	Textual
Overall Goals and Motivation	Cultivation of the market subject; the spread of volunteering and mutual help mentality	Cultivation of the market subject; pragmatic concerns	Socially just, moral, pious, happy society	A more religious society; ummah solidarity
Modes of Distinction (of Managers, Staff, and Volunteers)	Novelty and relative youth; specific mixture of professionalism and volunteerism	Specialization, expertise; the willingness to learn and be trained; civilization	Compassion and other pro-poor feelings; heavily Islamic-juristic vocabulary	Heavy reference to Islamic texts and authorities; moral purity and motivation (in contrast to cash motivation)

qualities. Communitarians, however, found such logic poisonous to benevolence. Charity could be effective only when done in a selfless way, they held. The staff at da'wa associations was underpaid; most of the management was not salaried. The remuneration of staff and management at communitarian political associations completely defied economic logic, as many of them had to contribute their time to charity only because they were members of the Muslim Brotherhood.

Funding structures varied sharply. Volunteer-based neoliberal associations counted on public visibility, which they built through advertisements and bank accounts. Professionalized associations were much less interested in public-ness and operated through informal networks of businessmen and friends. Da'wa associations tread another path by putting mosques in the center, on which they spawned family and neighborhood networks. Communitarian political associations had the most complex and least penetrable funding structures: they drew on sources as varied as member dues, political extortion, and networks forged via mosques, neighborhoods, and Member of Parliament offices. Conservative Arab monarchies generously supported all communitarian associations, detractors argued.

Despite their differences, the associations analyzed in these two chapters shared one tendency: except the Muslim Brotherhood, the political nature of which was obvious, they denied that they carried out any political activity. This denial notwithstanding, all had complicated ways of playing politics.[8] Professionalized associations were deeply engaged with the state. Regime opponents perceived them as extensions of the Mubarak government. Da'wa associations actively pressured the state to become more Islamic; they were also deeply infiltrated by Islamist political organizations. Communitarian political associations gained their significance through allegiance to the Muslim Brotherhood, which coordinated and managed their activities, and put them in conjunction with other associations and the state's welfare agencies. Parallels and differences between the organizational structures and logics of Egyptian benevolent associations are summarized in Table 5.2.

While professionals dominated the managing cadres of most associations, within neoliberal associations, business people and CEOs had exceptional weight. By contrast, small merchants and professionals occupied management positions at communitarian da'wa associations. Quite remarkably, workers also held managerial positions within Muslim Brotherhood-linked associations. In neoliberal associations of both kinds, the lower staff was mostly composed of professionals and white collar workers. Communitarian associations did not differ immensely in this regard, as they were staffed by professionals and workers.

Especially among lower-level staff and volunteers, neoliberal actors had been involved very little in civil society; their current associations were usually their first civic experience. Most of the *managers*, however, had experience with Islamic movements in their youth. Sediments of comprehensive religion in these actors' orientations is a sociologically complicating factor: if professionalization brings about rationalization, as new institutionalists argue (Hwang and Powell 2009), how do non-professional residues within one's habitus impact this causality? Actors had to negotiate, reject, and argue against past Islamist tendencies—this was a defining "cultural work" neoliberal managers performed. In glaring contrast, almost all communitarian managers, staff, and volunteers had a biography rich with associational involvement.

When it came to perspectives on macroeconomic policy and the international models that inspired them, neoliberals and communitarians were differentiated by a clear line. Neoliberals favored free-market policies and drew on philanthropic activity in the United States (and secondarily Canada and Britain), as well as charity in Islamic history. Communitarians were more likely to favor mixed economies (though within the Muslim Brotherhood especially, there was a wide spectrum). None of them mentioned Western philanthropy as an inspiration. They looked with admiration not only at the history of charity in Islam, but also at the charitable activity of living Muslims, some of which was modeled after Western philanthropy,[9] a fact they failed to acknowledge overtly. Table 5.3 summarizes the analysis of benevolent actors' backgrounds and perspectives.

TABLE 5.2 Egyptian Organizational Structures and Logics

	Volunteer-Based Neoliberal Associations	Professionalized Neoliberal Associations	Communitarian Da'wa Associations	Political Communitarian Associations
Main Activities	Provision of necessities and training	Training and income generating activities	Da'wa and provision of necessities	Provision of necessities and political control; da'wa
Managers' Status in Organization	Career professionals and volunteers	Career professionals	Volunteers	"Volunteers"[10]
Staff's Status in Organization	Career professionals and volunteers	Career professionals	Underpaid employees or volunteers	"Volunteers"
Funding Source	TV campaigns; widely known bank accounts	Heavily reliant on businessmen, and their family and business networks	Mosque networks; neighborhood notables; small contributions from people of diverse backgrounds; alleged Saudi/Gulf support	Members' dues; political extortion; alleged Saudi/Gulf support
Political Activity	Denial of political activity; elaborate links with the state	Denial of political activity; elaborate links with the state	Denial of political activity; Islamizing pressure on the state; infiltrated by political organizations	Highly politicized; infiltration of associations and state

In sum, benevolent orientations widely varied even within a country at a certain time. As associations and actors seek to situate themselves in fields of giving, they mix and match *seemingly incompatible* aspects of charity (see Chapter 1). A giver's class and religious background, specific path of charitable socialization, interactions with parents and authorities over decades, as well as an association's engagement with politics and the state (and competition with other associations) push some communitarian elements into the background, while bringing others to the front. Using the case of Mubarak's Egypt, these two chapters have shown that it is much more fruitful to study the field of giving in terms of competing clusters of benevolence, rather than basing our analyses exclusively on tropes either of domination or community. Chapters 6 and 7 will delve into another field of giving, which will reveal contextual differences in the making of benevolence clusters.

TABLE 5.3 Egyptian Benevolent Actors' Backgrounds and Perspectives

	Volunteer-Based Neoliberal Associations	*Professionalized Neoliberal Associations*	*Communitarian Da'wa Associations*	*Political Communitarian Associations*
Managers' Class	Professionals	Managers, business(wo)men, professionals	Professionals, small merchants	Professionals, workers
Staff's Class	Professionals, white collar workers	Professionals, white collar workers	Professionals, workers	Professionals, workers
International Models	The Anglophone world and Islamic history	The Anglophone world and Islamic history	Current and historical Islamic states and associations	Current and historical Islamic states and associations
Preferred Socioeconomic Policy	Free market	Free market	Mixed economy	Mixed economy
Volunteers', Staff's, Managers' Former or Current Involvement in Other Civic Activities/ Islamic Education	Islamist movement (at top management level); at lower levels, very low previous involvement in civil society	Among lower-level staff and volunteers, very low previous involvement in civil society	Islamist movement; da'wa movement; mosque networks	Islamist movement

Notes

1 While all of my interviews labeled their organizations as *khayri*, not all of them agreed with the standard translation of that word (charity). Some insisted that they were doing *khayr* (or good works), but in the mold of philanthropy, and distinguished their work from charity, which they perceived to be traditional and outmoded.
2 This denial contradicted the organization's Arabic brochures (though its English brochures did not emphasize religiosity). My status as a researcher from the US seems to have shaped the responses.
3 "Donors 'want to engage with the institutional forms of faith …, but remain suspicious about the spiritual dimensions of faith …'. … [R]eligion is regarded as a tool in the provision of … aid, but is not permitted to be part of aid, and religious organisations are acceptable in the aid field only when they agree to operate within a secular framework. Combining these discourses on faith-based organisations … with War on Terror discourses on … moderate and extremist Muslim NGOs, mainstream aid actors … perceive … invisible religiosity as a means of achieving 'good aid' and a sign of 'moderation'" (Petersen 2012, p. 773).
4 In contrast to all three groups, managers (and some staff) were fluent in English. More than half of the interviews with professionalized associations were conducted in English, whereas the interviews with individuals in the other categories were in Arabic, with the exception of one. Even though I mixed in Arabic to get information on local terms used in charity, one interviewee pointed out that they had not necessarily thought about the Arabic equivalents of these terms, since the managers also mixed English with Arabic when communicating among each other.

5 Even though the phrase "civic service" could have made more sense, I decided to stick to the respondents' authentic wording. The term "civil service" conveys the sense that aid associations execute a patriotic duty by both elevating Egypt's developmental level and relieving the government of its burdens (rather than manifesting an imperfect command of English, which most professionalized neoliberal association administrators spoke perfectly well).
6 It is not a coincidence either that the sociology of religion in the world leader of neoliberalization recognizes—without any laughter or criticism—that churches operate like companies.
7 The Grand Mufti is the highest *official* authority in charge of issuing *Islamic* legal opinions. A prominent Islamic law expert brought credibility to this association, but the fact that he was appointed by the (old) regime created a complication.
8 For the quite complex political motivations of a major communitarian organization's leaders (ranging from building counter-regime ideological influence to establishing patron-client networks within the regime's governing party), see Ben Néfissa (2004, pp. 227–235).
9 See Chapter 3 on Islamic Relief and similar Anglophone-inspired organizations.
10 Managers and staff of these organizations do not receive salaries; in that regard, they are volunteers (in the charitable field sense of the term). However, since being a member of the Brotherhood *requires* them to do *khayr*, they are not volunteers (in the dictionary sense). This partially applies to managers of daʿwa associations as well. That is one reason why these people were uneasy with the terms *tatawwuʿ/mutatawwiʿ*.

6

WALKING THE TIGHTROPE BETWEEN PROFESSIONALISM AND *TEBLİĞ*

Turkey's Neoliberal Associations

This chapter will cover Turkish neoliberal associations. Along with neoliberal pious associations (parallel to those in Egypt), Turkey housed a significant subfield of neoliberal *tebliğ* associations. This is an important difference from Egypt where the prominence of religious mission always went hand in hand with communitarianism. Smaller Turkish associations, by contrast, could combine a strong dedication to religious mission (tebliğ) with a commitment to neoliberal practices. Another striking feature of Turkish neoliberal associations was their surreptitious incorporation of communitarian discourses. This did not prevent the predominance of neoliberalism, but created a potentially unstable situation.

The major benevolent associations attested to a consolidation of liberal orientations in Turkish giving. The two, quite large, associations I cover in the first section demonstrate that managers, staff, and volunteers internalized neoliberal ethics in a (relatively) standardized way. Still, even among the more neoliberal Turkish associations, there were frictions, tensions, and exceptions. First of all, there were associations that sat, uncomfortably, between neoliberalism and communitarianism. Second, among the smaller associations, orientations varied quite a bit. Communitarian (even some redistributive) inclinations were widespread in the lower echelons of the hierarchy. Third, some of the smaller associations combined liberalizing and Islamizing missions. While this synthesis was more coherent among the top managers, the combination caused issues for lower-level managers, staff, and volunteers.

Pious Neoliberal Associations

These organizations focused on the provision of necessities and the training of people for the market. Islam had a central role as a motivator, but they did not seek to shape society along Islamic lines. In their recorded and non-recorded speech, the staff and managers made very little reference to classical Islamic texts.

The overall goals of these organizations revolved around the cultivation of the neoliberal subject (a productive and thrifty person with an investment mentality and a sense of private property). Building Turkish-Islamic influence abroad was also of utmost concern. Secondarily, pragmatic concerns (regarding charitable actors' individual success) also came to the fore.

Managers and staff emphasized their scientific distinctness. They used positivistic language to criticize traditional Turkish-Islamic culture. Managers, staff, and volunteers also distinguished themselves from others based on their thrift and rejection of rebellion (but as Chapter 7 will emphasize, the rejection of rebellion had a central place in *some* communitarian discourses too). Both managers and staff were paid well. The hierarchical structure was intricate. Elaborate staff recruitment techniques reinforced the functioning hierarchies.

These benevolent actors had strong clerical school and theology faculty backgrounds. This was an important difference from the Egyptian neoliberal associations. Some of them had also worked for the media of prominent religious communities. Some came from working poor backgrounds, but rejected the category of "poverty" when telling their stories. It is as if they were pre-destined to be the "giving" elites from the beginning; they were never of "the poor." Women were very active as staff, although few of them held managerial positions.

Pious neoliberal associations heavily relied on TV programs, as well as nationwide campaigns and seminars. Their international models included Western countries, and only secondarily historical Islamic states. They favored the free market, but expected some "responsibilizing" state participation in welfare. Due to their national prominence, television programs, and widely known bank accounts, small and medium sized contributions flowed massively to their treasuries. Still, pious businessman also contributed large amounts and had a say in management. Even though the members of these organizations denied political involvement, they actively put pressure on the state and universities in order to make them more "scientific" and deepen their "rational" (non-"sentimental") focus on Islam.

Piously Mobilizing Science to Fight the "Culture of Poverty"

The Hope Association was one of the largest benevolent associations in Turkey. It provided help to around 100,000 families per year. Its database contained 550,000 families (close to 3 million individuals), which it occasionally helped. The association was nationally visible due to an aid-focused television program. The program showed the staff traveling from one town to the next and handing over aid to beneficiaries. Its spectrum of activities stretched from courses on entrepreneurialism to first aid during natural disasters. The association had more than 70 full-time staff.

Talha, a former lecturer of Islamic history in his 40s, was a director of the Hope Association. After finishing a secular public high school, he graduated from a prominent theology department. Echoing Wuthnow's account of how biography is central to the making of charitable dispositions in America, he frequently referred to how certain people and events were crucial in motivating him. For instance, his grandmother had encouraged him to give to other people. The 1999 Izmit earthquake, when tens of thousands of people perished and the rest survived in the most wretched of conditions, also left a mark on him. However, Talha also emphasized that we should not get "too sentimental" about these issues at the expense of systematicity and efficiency, which he captured through words of English origin: "*Rantabıl*" and "*fızıbıl*." This discourse presents a sharp contrast to the neoliberal-communitarian "assemblage" analyzed by Muehlebach (in that it seeks to weed out feelings, which she argues is a key to the marriage of neoliberalism and communitarianism).

Along the same lines, Hope Association leaders downplayed the centrality of religious symbols. When I asked whether there is continuity in the Islamic tradition regarding charity, Talha said: "Aid ... is the same everywhere. ... We are not a religious institution. We do not use religious references." The driving actors in these organizations were pious people with solid religious formation; however, they did not explicitly structure *activities* around religious principles. Faith did not take a back seat: both secularists and Islamists perceived these organizations as belonging to Turkey's Islamic camp [*Islami cenah*]. The actors' denial that they were an Islamic organization rather meant that they saw the findings and methods of modern science as in line with Islam (and therefore, in their eyes, universal, "*evrensel*"). Hence, when one followed science, one in essence followed Islam.

Even though managers, staff, and volunteers thought that there were some structural reasons behind poverty (e.g. unemployment), they paid most attention to some inherent, some learned individual shortcomings. Referring to the Chinese saying (on the necessity to teach people how to catch fish), Talha said:

> When you give a fishing rod to a college graduate today, take him/her to the beach, even teach him/her how to use it, s/he still can't fish! ... Everybody's abilities are different. Not everybody is entrepreneurial [*girişimci*]. When you teach a person something, s/he doesn't immediately say, "I understand this, I can do this [*kotarırım*]." Not everybody can be a boss.[1] Some people have to be workers. ... Even if Turkey becomes the richest country on earth, there will still be poor people. We see this when we look at the world [implying the quite high American poverty levels].
>
> I don't believe poverty will ever end. It is not possible. Even in the richest countries, there are people who cannot manage their resources. They are perhaps not poor [*yoksul*], but needy [*muhtaç*]. ... I will give an example. My mother used to work in a factory. We were three siblings. In the house next to us, there was another family with three children, who had the same

income. They looked very poor. Their life standard was very low. The place was dirty and messy. The children were dirty and had shabby clothes. They didn't know how to manage their money! We call this the culture of poverty. [Some poor people] inherit this understanding from their families. We organized a symposium about this too. We need to struggle against this understanding, but this is the most difficult part of the struggle. You can give [this type of people] good employment and wages, but since they don't know how to manage money, they are always in need [*ihtiyaç sahibi*]. It is hard to distinguish these people from the poor, but they are different.

Talha's position was also remarkable for its implicit rejection of the concept of the working poor. He implied that if an employed family was still poor, it was not because of the income: entrepreneurial families could figure out what to do with restricted amounts.

Wuthnow emphasizes how people learn to care from their families. But they might learn how to blame the victim also from their family experiences (or at least, from the re-interpretation of biographic experience in the light of neoliberal discourse). Through such ideological and organizational moves, a history of generosity (and a lifelong engagement in giving) can turn into a weapon of domination.

These semantic struggles on what the very category of poverty meant constituted a conscious area of activity. Neoliberal associations rejected handling poverty as the lack of certain goods and services, or in reference to differences from wealthy groups; they focused on cultural traits that made people poor. Consequently, two families with the same level of income could be distinguished as "needy" vs. entrepreneurial, rather than lumped together as "working poor." This semantic turn exemplifies the global diffusion of conservative norms. (Chapter 7 shows that communitarian and redistributive associations defined poverty in a quite different way.)

Such re-definitions of poverty were also responses to the political climate. During the time of my fieldwork, anti-government newspapers and research reports were uncovering more and more stories regarding how poverty intensified in Turkey. They intended to prove that the Ak Party did not care about poverty, but also implied that voluntary organizations were highly inadequate in a marketizing world. By re-classifying some of the people included in these reports as "not poor," the Hope Association absolved both itself and the government.

The vision of the volunteers and staff did not differ from the managers. A high school graduate volunteer in her late 20s, who came from a working-class family, deployed the Chinese proverb on the need to learn how to catch fish and criticized overreliance on direct aid (*hazıra konma*). Another volunteer in her 20s, also a housewife from the working class, thought that luxurious consumption, lack of thankfulness, and rebelliousness caused poverty. The four volunteers and one staff member I talked to all emphasized the poor's lack of thrift, wastefulness, and insatiability (*doyumsuzluk*) as the reasons lying behind poverty. However, the volunteers differed from the male managers in their emphasis on faith. They wanted the association to pay more attention to religious education, as restricted religious knowledge (and the resulting immorality) was another core reason of poverty. In this instance, we see how *some* volunteers and staff pick *selectively* from the communitarian repertoire to bolster neoliberalization. This, however, cannot be seen as a thorough coupling of neoliberalism and communitarianism (as in Deleuzian accounts), since neoliberalism clearly has the upper hand.

Science provided the key in the fight against the culture of poverty. When asked "what differentiates you from other associations?" Talha responded:

> We focus on a topic no one has paid attention to: we take the scientific dimension of charity very seriously. Providing basic necessities to the needy is one dimension of our activities. But [we promote] job acquisition and career training too: we want people to earn their living. This is our second dimension. But third, in [developing] our and others' aid projects, we work with universities. In 2003, we organized a big symposium on poverty with 34 universities and 17 state agencies. After that, there was a jolt in scientific studies … and an increase in the number of books, conferences, and articles on poverty. We did this again in 2008 at the international level. This is our difference. We don't want to be stuck with sentimentality. We want to see [poverty] from a realistic angle in order to understand how people can be encouraged (*teşvik*) with good projects.

Hence, positivism united the state, civil society, and universities to show people the way out of poverty, through teaching them how to save themselves and "encouraging" them to work wisely.

The Hope Association differed from Egyptian neoliberal organizations in one important regard: it did not pursue income-generating activities. The managers had actually attempted such initiatives, but the donors had blocked their efforts. The donors, this experience shows, had major authority. In contrast to the donors of non-neoliberal organizations, some were considerably richer than the organization's managers. However, the Hope Association did have "enterprises" that helped to cover its costs.

Unlike in Egypt, there was a lot of emphasis on the state's duties even among the most neoliberal associations. The respondents insisted that the state should reduce unemployment and expand social policies. Still, they believed that the state should be aided by civic organizations, which would not only provide, but remind people more effectively of their duties (towards the poor, relatives, and neighbors). Their mission was cultural-social as well as dryly economic.

This civic acceptance of mild state intervention bolstered the consent of the poor (and the people in contact with them). It partially "socialized" neoliberalism in Turkey. Egyptian civil society, by contrast, was divided between a strong communitarianism and a relatively dogmatic neoliberalism, which was reflective of the harsher push for neoliberalization under late Mubarak.

Thrifty Generosity as Antidote to Sacralizing Poverty

The Ownership Association was one of the richest players in the field. With its annual budget of 50 million YTL, it helped 130,000 people. It boasted volunteer networks in many countries. In an interesting contrast to other associations that provided aid over the globe, it did not work with partner organizations. This attested to its organizational capacity: it didn't *need* partners, unlike the crushing majority of international associations. Its global outreach was much more direct. This was due to its exceptional background. The association was linked to one of Turkey's top clerics (according to some, *the* top cleric). This person had dedicated (some say, unquestioning) followers all around the world, although the nature of his links is still a matter of public controversy (and far from being transparent).

When I asked why they help, managers, staff, and volunteers emphasized religious motivations first and foremost (a telling contrast with Egyptian neoliberals). Ibrahim was a volunteer in his late 30s who graduated from a high school associated with the mentioned cleric-guru, but like many others, went on to study science- and engineering-related topics in secular universities. Coming from a family who owned a small crafts workshop, he set up his own small business (which focused on technology rather than industry). Still, he thought (based on the same cleric's teachings) that science and technology had to go hand in hand with religion. After saying there is a lot of "spiritual taste" (*manevi lezzet*) in giving, he added:

> The money does not belong to us anyway. That money is a deposit [*emanet*, entrusted by God]. The more we give, the more we receive [*ne kadar verirsek, misliyle bize gelecek*]. This is proven. If I have a hundred billion and I give 50 billion away, 100 billion or 200 billion comes my way. This is also what the Qur'an and Hadith say: "Give, so that your property will be multiplied by many" [*Verin ki, malınız fazlasıyla ziyadeleşsin*]. Therefore, we do not give only [the religiously required] 1/40 of our property, by going through meticulous calculations, but whatever we can.

A staff member in his 40s also brought in science to support an overall account that put spirituality in the center: "There is scientific proof that giving makes you happy." He told a story about an atheist who started to donate after he discovered this link. "This is a human thing. This responsibility to give is what differentiates us from animals." In accordance with the value the above-mentioned cleric put in science, his followers emphasized "proof." However, they did not use this word conventionally. "Proof" rather signified the mutual reinforcement between clerical teachings, personal experiences, and scientific reasoning.

Neoliberal actors occasionally resorted to tropes central to communitarian discourse, but deployed them for different purposes. Ibrahim (quoted above) referred to the belief that property belongs to God. As the Egyptian Piety Association managers pointed out, whatever we gave to the poor did not belong to us to begin with. Nevertheless, Ibrahim drew a divergent implication from this shared understanding. Based on classical Islamic texts as well as personal observations, he emphasized that generosity would bring the donor more property. Accumulation of wealth was at the center of his thoughts rather than the generation of community.

Firuze put more emphasis on the emotional aspects of giving, attesting to one important gender difference in this science-heavy association. She was a college dropout in her early 40s. After years of work in educational institutions (as data analyst and public relations expert), she became full-time staff at the Ownership Association. Her father was a military officer, but she had married a small shopkeeper, with whom she had two children. When in her 20s, she used to spend more time following private courses (*kurs*) for self-development. She changed in her 30s because of an emergent consciousness of the hereafter (*ahiret bilinci*). The more she thought about the other world, the more she desired to be beneficial. She also had encounters with the poor, which impacted her: "I look at those poor orphans and I think of my own children. Then I want to help. It's emotional. Perhaps, among women, this is more developed."

When compared to Egyptians in the equivalent category (non-mission, "pious neoliberal associations"), these actors used a much more religious vocabulary. This can be a real difference between the Turkish and Egyptian fields, but a methodological precaution is in order. The Egyptian interviewees might have submerged religious references because I was a foreigner.

Nationalist motivations also played a big part. Ibrahim talked at length about their "reading rooms" in southeastern Turkey, where young people got help with their coursework. After describing scenes of poverty in a Kurdish town, he complained that dangerous activists manipulated these conditions, if nobody else took them seriously:

> There is terror there. We went to Bingöl [a predominantly Kurdish town]. There are PKK flags everywhere. This shows serious sympathy for [the PKK]. If we don't pay attention to and care for them [*ilgi göstermezsek*], they will go up to the mountains [join the PKK]. The children there are in need of love. They go to whomever they can get this love from. ... [The PKK] has its reading rooms. Just like we take the best and send them to the universities, they also take the best and send them to the mountains.

Benevolent activity, then, aimed to integrate marginalized groups to the nation and "save" them from anti-state activity.

In their explanations of poverty, the association members put the poor's characteristics at the center. Transforming those characteristics was their top mission. When asked why there is poverty, Ibrahim responded: "Laziness is widespread. So is lack of satisfaction [*yetinememe*]. Some people have a television, but they want a better one." Such lack of satisfaction, rather than dire poverty, led the poor to contact charity organizations. "One needs to know how to be satisfied." Poor people did not know what they really needed. For example, their children walked with bare feet and they didn't understand they needed carpets. Their priorities were misplaced.

On top of these themes shared with other neoliberals, the Ownership Association's discourse had a distinct element: the emphasis on an ethics of property. Ibrahim described his frustration in southeastern Turkey, where he had spent a good amount of time teaching the poor how to make the best of their resources. One reason the Southeasterners flooded to the big cities in Western Turkey, he argued, was the lack of a property ethic:

> They expect everything from the state. ... A town needed rainwater drainage pipes. The municipality asked the residents for some contribution. They reacted and said, "Why should we do this, the state should do it." When a person does not labor for something, then s/he doesn't feel like s/he owns it. If they had worked, they could have stayed there. But perhaps this couldn't have been done alone. The state could have helped by giving goats and providing workers. Then, they wouldn't have come. Istanbul would be more comfortable and [Southeasterners] would be self-reliant.

While he rehearsed the belief in the tight link between labor and property that goes back to John Locke, Ibrahim also expressed resentment against the Kurds (not named as such in his speech) who now populated the city. Ever since the forced migrations of the 1990s, the Kurds had become a big presence in İstanbul, İzmir, Ankara, Mersin, and Adana. Mainstream (secular and religious) media held the Kurds responsible for the persistent problems of these metropolitan areas, paying little attention to the intentional destruction of their rural livelihood (to undercut the support for the guerilla). Even though much of social science pictures liberalism and authoritarianism, nationalism[2] and Islam, the state and religious NGOs as binary opposites, this particular association demonstrated how pious actors collated materials from all of these discourses and institutions to foster an ethics of property. In doing so, they articulated neoliberalism and authoritarianism (more than neoliberalism and communitarianism).

Neoliberal actors also questioned traditional religious understandings of poverty, a criticism that starkly differentiated them from communitarians. They believed that Turkish culture needed to change if an ethics of property and work was to develop. They were particularly disappointed that Turks found something sacred in poverty. The ways they portrayed Turks and Geremek pictured medieval Europeans were quite similar. While Firuze's emphasis on emotions distinguished her from the association's men, they were all on the same page regarding property, poverty and the appropriate religious orientation towards these:

FIRUZE: In Turkish culture, poverty is an acceptable [*makbul*] thing. People feel that if they are poor, they will win heaven. Perhaps this is the reason they don't work much. Or [at least] there is a psychological influence [in this direction]. But of course, there is also ignorance, immigration, the problem of unemployment, and the underdevelopment of social security. But the most basic [*en temel*] cause of poverty, according to me, is that we are a relaxed nation, and poverty is an acceptable and sacred [*ulvi*] thing. I know this from my own family. At home, we think: *azıcık aşım, rahat başım* [a rhyming Turkish saying to the effect of, "I have little food, but I have peace of mind"]. There is also the mentality: *fazla mal derttir* [another saying, "too much property is trouble"].

CT: But there is also the saying "*fazla mal göz çıkarmaz*" in Turkish culture. ["Too much property wouldn't poke your eye out."]

FIRUZE: (laughs) That is true. But people do not think systematically. They don't think like: "if I invest here, then wonderful things will happen." Instead, they spend as much as they earn. There is no thrift. There is a lot of frivolous spending [*israf*]. For example, some people are hungry, but they can afford luxurious clothing.

Firuze seemed to be right. When I was doing my dissertation research (between 2000 and 2002), I had taken social scientists from the University of Michigan to a field trip in İstanbul. Neat clothing was one reason why I could not convince them that my district of research, Sultanbeyli, was impoverished. Alford Young, an expert of American poverty, also commented that Sultanbeyli residents did not look depressed. There were even smiles on some faces. Both the clothing and the faces of the poor indeed look different in Turkey than in some Western countries, partially due to what Firuze calls Turkish culture. The goal of charitable activity thus became changing these habits so that people could cultivate the ambition to work and amass property (instead of looking and feeling good). Bad consumption ethics, the reasoning went, was a resultant of such a relation with property. Firuze continued:

> People spend water and electricity unconsciously. Since they haven't built [the infrastructure], they can't feel that they own them [*sahiplenemiyorlar*]. As a civil society institution, we [feed] the poor, but we also have to do consciousness-raising. We have to teach them how to spend responsibly. Perhaps the poor can make ends meet with the money they already earn, but they can't because they don't know how to spend. They are out of control. When they get the money from us, they go and buy a cigarette. When you help the poor, you also have to give a direction to their lives. That's the system we need.

Firuze was painting here an ideal society where people know not only how to work and own, but also how to spend. The ideal civic activity, therefore, would go beyond giving to the poor; it would control their habits of working, saving, and spending, as well their feelings of ownership. Yet, even in this institution with a huge community (and an internationally renowned cleric) behind it, there was no capacity to thoroughly implement this vision. Firuze admitted that the Ownership Association was able to control the poor only partially. Responsibilization was more of a desire than actual practice.

In line with its expectations from the poor, the association developed elaborate mechanisms to evaluate levels and types of poverty. Not only managers, but ordinary staff and volunteers could provide very detailed accounts of how they distinguished the deserving from the undeserving. I did not encounter such detailed and generalized mechanisms in Egypt; the selection criteria were extremely professionalized and bureaucratized in the Turkish case.[3]

The association had a systematic process of selecting and evaluating personnel. "Expertise" was a buzz word for the staff. The management evaluated not only CVs and reference letters, but also monitored the fresh employees during a standardized two-month probation period. It then decided whether to keep them based on their "efficiency."

The tight monitoring of the staff spilled over to their private lives as they self-monitored: Charitable activity involved not only control over the poor, but the disciplining of volunteers and staff as well. In their case, the gap between desires (regarding efficiency, thrift, and discipline) and practices was narrower when compared to the larger gap in the case of the beneficiaries. Firuze pointed out that her own life changed as a result of charitable involvement and the feelings that ensued from it: "I now calculate the smallest breadcrumb." There was a "revolution" at home: She used her experiences and the association's CDs to discipline her children. Responsibilization was a *domestic* reality. There was a strong gender dimension in this self-disciplining face of charity. Women were perceived to be at the center of the *liberal revolution at home* due both to their roles as mothers and their (naturalized) propensity to spend on luxurious items. This had to be curbed by charitable involvement, the women acknowledged.

Ownership Association members saw the United States as the model of a modern country on the correct path. They also defined their vision of poverty based on what America had achieved. Faruk, a marketing expert in a major pious company, had given some thought to American economy and society. After finishing a science-heavy high school (affiliated with the mentioned cleric), this son of teachers had recently graduated from a prominent economics department. He emphatically stated: "There is no country in the world that has resolved poverty. The United States is the superpower of the world, but there are homeless people there." Poverty was therefore perceived as fate (or, a part of creation) and the United States became the conscience of world capitalism: (their re-construction of) America demonstrated the limits of the possible—that is, the amount and type of good that they could (realistically) do under modern conditions.

This association actively cooperated with the state. The central government funded some of its projects. It also had common projects with the metropolitan governor (*vali*) and the local governors (*kaymakam*). Together, they decided who would be fit for career education. They found unemployed women whose husbands were deceased, imprisoned, or mentally institutionalized. While they trained these women for specific tasks, they also paid for their rents and nutritional costs (so that they would find the energy for career training).

The managers wanted this state-supported career training program to evolve into a profit-generating mechanism. Unlike Hope Association managers, they were sympathetic to the idea of income generation. The Ownership Association had recently founded an economic enterprise (*iktisadi işletme*). The intent was to sell the training program's beneficiary-produced goods through this enterprise.

The association also supported (through lobbying and public discourse) the regime's social provision policies. In line with its criticism of welfare in the Southeast (cited above), the association applauded the government's nascent responsibilizing projects. The state had started to give the peasants sheep and goats and take them back after a couple of years (by which time they would have lambs and kids). The association's managers and staff were enthusiastically behind this kind of social policy. In other words, they wanted to see the state as an inculcator of property ethics, rather than unconditional provider (they were sympathetic to the government's expanding health provision, as well as the new attention to disabled people, though ambivalent about the amounts spent on these issues). Direct provision was also necessary, on the side, to ensure that citizens were comfortable enough to focus on their productive capacities.

Faruk explained their overall position: "Citizens should not expect everything from the state [but] the state should certainly show the way." Another volunteer's account further clarified: civil society and state are not competitors, but "companions" (*refik*). The state had an important role in provision, both through model-setting (what a Gramscian would call "ideological leadership") and occasional support (in Mannian (Mann 1986) language, "infrastructural power"). The Ownership Association sought a combination of a Mannian and a Gramscian state: an interlinked set of offices that would mobilize civil society, but also create the material conditions for the realization of the latter's goals. Just like in the case of the Hope Association, the characteristic Turkish neoliberal position was a redefinition and restriction of the state's role as provider, rather than its rejection (as among the newer associations Egypt).

"I Cried for Days": Verging on Communitarianism

The minor players in this group, the less established and smaller organizations, did not have the capacity (or desire) to standardize their vision throughout their volunteer body. While all of the volunteers I talked to at the Hope Association had a neoliberal vision, the volunteers at one of the smaller organizations (the Disciples Association) fell on a spectrum: some exhibited "a tebliğ-neoliberal tendency," others combined a pious-neoliberal position with communitarianism. This association's *organizational* framework and activities were similar with the organizations covered above. However, its staff and volunteers nourished *dispositions* both in harmony and in stark conflict with this framework.

The Disciples Association was indicative of neoliberalization's limits. Many actors covered throughout this chapter were determined to push for liberalization. By contrast, Disciples Association affiliates strongly displayed non-liberal orientations, in spite of the fact that their association had organic ties to the most neoliberal regime Turkey has ever seen. On the one hand, this association's composite nature is a good warning against accounts of all sweeping neoliberalization; on the other, its marginal position in the field should be a check against the Deleuzian "assemblage" approach that exaggerates the significance of "exceptions to neoliberalism."

This association was the Turkish branch of an international organization, which had its headquarters in a Western country, and an additional branch in another Muslim country. Its activities were concentrated in sub-Saharan Africa (where it worked with partner organizations), though the association provided some education in Turkey. The Turkish branch was composed of four staff members and 40 donor-members (who provided most of the funding). It regularly mobilized around 1,000 volunteers annually, most of them medical personnel and students. It focused on direct health provision, but developmental activities (building hospitals, personnel education, etc.) were also part of the repertoire. The association also trained people in farming techniques, since many health problems emanated from malnutrition.

Among the staff members, personal experiences were at the forefront of motivating factors. They emphasized compassion and an internalized willingness to help. One of them, Hayrettin, an accountant in his late 20s, explicitly rejected any religious motivation. The son of a worker, he had attended educational institutions in a provincial town and Istanbul. When he was young, he used to help people as much as he could. He gave private lessons for free:

> Our families in Anatolia did not have many opportunities. No one showed them the way. [I wanted to] show the way to my neighbors' and relatives' elementary school-age children. They see actresses and soccer players on TV and they take them as models.

He demonstrated that there could be other role models. As a part of his upbringing, then, he liked helping people. Incidentally, after a series of unsatisfying jobs in the for-profit sector, he was looking for a new job. These two concerns intersected. As in the accounts of many staff members of neoliberal associations, his narrative (regarding how he ended up working at an NGO) blended pragmatic with altruistic factors. While we can spot pragmatic concerns among all kinds of charity practitioners, in neoliberal associations, actors are *transparent* about what they personally get from involvement in generosity. In other words, we should treat Bourdieu's double truth (or rather, its manifestations) as a variable.

The volunteers, by contrast, provided altruistic narratives devoid of pragmatic references. One of them said: "I saw most of this [charitable way of behavior] from my mother and father. [They gave] a part of their property to the poor. They showed love. My mother always said, 'Do not hurt anybody.' That is the morality we received [*Öyle bir ahlak aldık*]."

On property and poverty, the association's members did not share a single position. The staff was far from being neoliberal, yet the volunteers were quite so. There was friction regarding this issue among other associations as well (more in the Ownership Association when compared to the Hope Association), but the disunity within this association was at one end of the spectrum.

Hikmet, a staff member, was a graduate student in theology. He hailed from a well-educated family: even though his mother was a housewife (a common characteristic in my sample), his father was a mid-level bureaucrat and his siblings were also graduate students. He had a complex understanding of poverty. The reasons for poverty in Africa, he held, were threefold: "First, people can't stand on their own feet. [Second,] they cannot use their [natural and human] resources. And of course, there is ignorance." Regarding Turkey, his comments were much more political:

> When poverty does not result from personal reasons, it results from inequality of opportunity. Some people point out that Kurds can even become ministers, but I think these are exceptional cases. Especially in the case of Eastern and Southeastern Anatolia, inequality results from discrimination.

Hikmet's comments resembled those of redistributive actors, rather than either neoliberal or communitarian ones. In this sense, he exemplified the diversity within the governing state-society bloc. This diversity was to become a basis upon which the regime could later flex its muscles in non-neoliberal directions (see Chapter 7).

Hayrettin, the staff member quoted above, was also non-liberal (if less politicized):

> The reasons [behind poverty] are the same in Turkey and around the world. The primary one is income inequality. People don't want to share. They always think about themselves and they submit to their ambitions. The bosses think about how much more they can make rather than giving the workers their just share.

Civil society-state cooperation would resolve this problem. Hayrettin said it would start with one "giving" boss, who would set the example for others; then, the state and unions would step in with dialogue and provision of legal frameworks to reinforce that pattern.

Fatma, a retired nurse and a volunteer in her 40s, mixed neoliberal and redistributive concerns:

> [Income] distribution is out of balance. There is a lot of unemployment. The riches are extreme, and the people at the very bottom are really poor. But it also has to do with ignorance and illiteracy, especially in the East.

CT: How can these be resolved?

FATMA: We should not expect everything from the state. ... Everybody should work hard. It doesn't help to say, "There is no employment." You should sell water, if that is all you can do. The state should provide opportunities; but if it can't, it doesn't make sense to sit at home. Illiterate women can also do cleaning, make handicrafts, and cook.

Selling water on the streets and highways is indeed a common means of earning a few extra liras in Turkey. Fatma started off with providing *structural* reasons for the existence of poverty, but shifted to *individual* paths in her proposed solutions. Yet, her experiences had brought Fatma close to a redistributive understanding of poverty:

> When I saw the children and hospitals in Niger, I was very sad. I cried for days. I thought all of this was injustice [*haksızlık, adaletsizlik*] ... but of course, I absolve God from all shortcomings [*estağfirullah tabii de*]. I was deeply influenced. When I was on my way back, I was still crying.

She had come to the verge of formulating the problem of poverty as one of injustice, but shied away from it, due to her (implicit) belief that thinking so would be un-Islamic.

Even though she did not follow her redistributive inclinations to their logical conclusions, such misgivings prevented Fatma from developing a fuller neoliberal sensibility: "I regretted many things [*pişmanlıklar yaşadım*]. I regretted having so many things while they had none." She had no Calvinistic sense of entitlement to her property. A completely neoliberalized religion, in line with the "ethics of property" I outlined above, would give her such a sense. Ownership Association members could say she was still locked within "Turkish culture" and its suspicion of wealth, but Fatma's position emanated as much from her experiences in Africa. In other words, her specific combination of dispositions resulted from field-structured activities, not from Turkish-Islamic uniqueness.

There were also Disciples Association actors who echoed those in the Hope and Ownership associations. Abdullah was a quite dedicated volunteer who participated in the activities of many associations (among them, one "bifurcated" association, see Chapter 7). A shopkeeper in his 60s and a high school graduate, he was the son of a service sector worker. He said there was no poverty in Turkey, as sick children anywhere could find medicine:

> Poverty means the lack of service. There is service everywhere in Turkey. ... Some people think that everybody should have a place of residence and means of transportation [*herkesin atı, yatı, katı olsun*]. But such a condition doesn't exist anywhere in the world. ... Actually, Turkey is the best in the whole world in terms of human rights. Our police and people treat everybody equally. Until a few years ago, there was no purse-snatching [*kapkaç*] in Turkey. It is completely imported from Spain and Italy.
>
> In Greece, people burned down the cities . ... Now they are ready to burn down Spain. The same thing had happened in Argentina. It would never happen in Turkey. Why? Because the state and municipality help people. When that is not enough, we have almsgiving. When that is not enough, we have patience, belief, and faith. *Fitne* [disorder, disobedience] would never enter Turkey. ... Nobody should ever complain, for if they do, God will take away what they already have. ... This doesn't mean there isn't any suffering in Turkey. Of course there is. But everything exists with its opposite [*her şey zıddıyla kaimdir*]. We should have suffering so that we appreciate the worth of its opposite. And that's where the civic associations come in.

Abdullah not only provided a victim-blaming account with communitarian overtones, but also put the non-politicization of poverty in Turkey in comparative cultural context. He contrasted Turkey (where people are content with what they have and receive help from the wealthy and the state) with Spain, Greece, and Argentina (where people are presumably insatiable). Consequently, whatever vice existed in Turkey was due to foreign influence (i.e. poverty could not be the real reason of increasing crime).

Abdullah topped these off with nationalist motivations. He helped many people in the former Ottoman territories and saw his work as an effort to restore Turkey's influence in these (Christian and Muslim) lands. "The world is expecting something from us. They are saying, 'Where are the Ottomans?'" he exclaimed. He also added that civic associations are "the most beautiful doors to the conquest of hearts" (*gönüllerin fethinin en güzel kapısı*). In order to reinforce his point that "the conquest of hearts is more valuable than conquest through war," he quoted at length from a Hadith, where Prophet Muhammad tells 'Ali (the fourth Caliph) that the conquest of one person is more valuable than all the goods on earth. These imperial motivations for benevolence were completely absent from my Egyptian interviews, but this might partially be due to my status as a foreigner (as much as the remarkably more distinct presence of imperial desires in Turkish public discourse and history).

The disciplinary transformation of staff and volunteers was a central part of the narratives. Fatma talked at length about the ways she changed after her involvement, which was a very common story, especially in mothers' accounts. She started to be more frugal and spend less for her children. Whenever they demanded something luxurious, she told them about the children in Niger. Her daughter "rebelled" and pointed out that they lived in Turkey. Abdullah gave a dramatic account of self-discipline, but tied this back to his account of why poverty exists:

> I always pray that [charitable] activities also help control my own desires of the flesh [*nefs*]; that they become a means to correct the behavior of my children. For if we preach [*tebliğ*] what we do not practice, it does no good to anybody. ... I also see this as a process of education. We have to take our children to charitable activities. Our children should see those children [in the Balkans and the Middle East]. ... [I witnessed that] a family can produce four college graduates in the extreme poverty of the Lebanese camps.

Volunteers thus used charitable activities not only to tame themselves, but their families too. Acts of self-discipline, as well as *observing the success of disciplined families in dire circumstances*, also reminded them that poverty and ignorance resulted from the lack of self-discipline among the poor.

Regarding relations to the state, the Disciples Association again exhibited an amalgam of characteristics. The staff and volunteers shared the position that the state's involvement in provision should be restricted, bringing them in line with the position of other neoliberal actors. However, beyond this basic consensus, the political positions varied. Hikmet, for instance, insisted on civic-ness: "We try not to be engaged with the state," he said, even though they had links with one of the top ministers. He argued that the state (more specifically, TİKA) was able to guide other aid associations, but not them. This orientation to the state was in deep contrast to Abdullah's position, which almost reduced civic associations to arms of the imperial state.

Unlike many benevolent actors who were happy with the recent, semi-Islamic tendencies of the Turkish state, Hikmet (interviewed in 2012) wanted to avoid the state and politics:

> In this day and age, within this system, there can be no value-based politics. [The statesman] has to be a realist, a Machiavellian. I avoid the state because I might end up in a situation where I am unjust. ... In college, we went through an education which put liberties at the center. Now, I don't want to work in an environment where I would not be comfortable with this [Islamic] beard, these [Islamic] loose cloths; and where I would have to work under Mustafa Kemal's portrait. ... Sometimes we go to a seminar and the presenter cannot answer some questions because he is a state employee.

I pointed out that there were some changes within the Turkish state and asked whether the characteristics he enumerated could not change as well. "I don't think so," he said, with an ironic and semi-silent laugh. His issue was not only with the content of official ideology, but with the existence of official ideology as such. The organizational centrality of actors such as Hikmet partially account for why neoliberal orientations did not hold full sway in this association. The dispersed diffusion of a libertarian disposition prevented the generalization of *any* position.

Neoliberal Tebliğ Organizations

Some other organizations focused on religious mission, as well as provision and training in the liberal sense. Islam was both their goal and motivation. Their religious references were heavily textual. Their broader goals were the cultivation of the neoliberal subject; the furtherance of religion and nationalism; and sustenance (or rather, re-birth) of lived community. The members also displayed pragmatic concerns, but insisted that these were subordinate to their mission.

Members and affiliates distinguished themselves based on heavy reference to Islamic texts and a strong Muslim identity. They saw themselves as leaders of society and were proud of their thrift. They looked down on rebellious behavior. The managers were businessmen and small merchants, while the staff mostly consisted of professionals. They were recruited through personal, business, and religious networks; there were no elaborate techniques of recruitment.

Volunteers, staff, and managers had been involved in Islamist movements throughout their lives. Most of them were graduates of clerical schools (İHLs). Some of the staff and volunteers had a personal history of impoverishment. Women were informally involved in these organizations as mothers (though some of them employed women in their lower ranks).

These associations spread information mostly through family and business networks, but also secondarily through seminars and conferences. In spite of taking current and historical Islamic states as their international models, they favored a free market economy. They generated funding internally and marginally drew on non-member businessmen. These associations actively pressured the state to become more Islamic. They also hoped, like the associations in the first category, that the state would be more active in "responsibilizing" the poor, even though they didn't have a working agenda to push it in that direction.

The Sıckness and the Medicine: Worker Mentality vs. Data and Shame

The Candle Association regularly visited and took care of 300 to 600 households in adjacent neighborhoods. Through periodic visits, the association had developed a vast knowledge of its area. Its monthly revenue was approximately 30,000 dollars.

Religion and religious networks were central to recruitment and motivation. Ahmet had been active in Islamic organizations (dorms, foundations, and sport clubs) from his high school years onwards. He was a clerical school (İHL) graduate. He started school late, as a result of which others always perceived him as a big brother with a (religious) mission towards others. Therefore, service (*hizmet*) had been central to his life all along. He underlined that he and other association members carried all of their activities with religious purposes. They wanted to receive the prayers of the poor, which would help them in the hereafter; they were always eager to obtain God's consent (*Allah rızası*). He cited Qur'anic verses and Hadith to support his claim that donors and managers indeed obtained these returns. As different from many other associations, the Candle Association was explicit about its allegiance (*intisap*) to a religious order (*tarikat*). Ahmet argued that people could stay true to their religious motivations only if continuously disciplined: "If there is no spiritual authority, selfish desires will take over" (*Manevi otorite olmazsa, nefis devreye girer*).[4]

Religious networks were central to the establishment and staffing of this association in many other ways. The story of Şevki, a former carpenter and currently a Candle Association employee, is exemplary. A friend at Şevki's previous job invited him to a *sohbet* (gatherings where people pray, eat, read religious texts, and discuss their meaning). He eventually came to attend these religious conversations regularly. After a point, the *sohbet*s revolved around the idea that the attendees should establish an aid association. The Candle Association resulted from these conversations. Şevki ultimately accepted the founders' offer to work there as a staff member.

The recruitment of Yavuz (a previous worker and now a Candle Association employee) followed a similar pattern. After retirement, Yavuz started to work as a mosque *hizmetkar*: a "servant" in charge of citing the calls to prayer, cleaning, food distribution and conflict resolution. He gained a lot of charitable experience as he worked at this mosque. At the end of six years, the mosque's *imam* invited him to work full-time for the Candle Association. The (more educated) founders of the association taught him how to utilize a computer. He learned how to assign numbers to and write up Word files for aid applicants, a task he did manually at his previous mosque position. In other words, staff recruitment and training did not depend on rationalized mechanisms. Interpersonal trust was at the core. This attested to the blending of neoliberalization with communitarianism, but in a way that gave neoliberalism the upper hand (since, as we will see, the organization's practices were ultimately neoliberal).

Ahmet distinguished between his organization, which he said was based on "professionalism" and "data," and volunteer-driven organizations. Professionalism allowed them to easily differentiate between the deserving and undeserving poor. They indeed had an elaborate mechanism of eliminating people based on their possessions (such as HD televisions), truthfulness of proclamations (through fact checking with other associations and government agencies), but also observation of behavior:

> When we see people who talk too much, who cry too much, and who play with words, we immediately withdraw. These types knock on the door of every foundation they can find. They start to whine before they start to speak. It's a habit. They concentrate on crying. An innocent person does not immediately cry. If you ask her about her situation, she remains quiet, she persists [*sükut ediyor, dayanıyor, kendini sıkıyor, sıkıyor*]. When someone cries, we tell her to go out, wash her face and then come back. We primarily target people who cannot demand, who have a sense of shame. We feel that shame; we don't push them to talk and complain. When we see them swallowing their words [*tıkanıyor, kilitleniyor, düğümleniyor kelime*], we interrupt so that they won't be insulted.

Submissiveness and shame were the desirable, even *cultivated*, qualities of the recipient. The organization not only picked recipients based on the perceived existence of these qualities, it actively fostered them. Together with inducing submissiveness, shame, and piety (unlike the Hope Association), the Candle Association also strove to instill individual responsibility. In its quest to constitute the neoliberal subject, however, it ran into many difficulties. Ahmet specified:

> In the families we help, especially fathers have a very straightforward worker mentality (*düz işçi mantığı*). They don't think in terms of self-development and education. The municipality has free lessons for career development. If they were patient enough, they would have a career at the end of three months. ... This is the sickness of "learned helplessness" (*öğretilmiş çaresizlik*).

What Ahmet meant by "learned helplessness" was a propensity to prefer heavy jobs with daily payments to more stable, less demanding jobs with monthly salaries. The latter would require patience and a faculty of calculation. Not only the concept (psychologist Seligman's "learned helplessness"), but also Ahmet's explanation of it (e.g. the emphasis on calculation) draws attention to this heavily missionary association's discursive investment in science. Ahmet also gave examples of poor people (even religious ones, he lamented) who declined their job offers because they did not understand the benefits of stable jobs. This helplessness was so ingrained that nothing could be done once somebody got the "sickness." Hence, their priority was not those with the sickness, but their children. The long-term goal of generosity was to obliterate "worker mentalities" and transform the poor into career professionals. In this association's understanding of the world, everybody was a potential career professional (and only cultural factors prevented people from fulfilling this potential).

This vision was consistently shared. Şevki echoed the director:

> The poor have no professions [*meslek*]. Most have come directly from their villages. They have worked in the construction sector as *amele* [derogatory word for unskilled worker]. Also, they have conditioned themselves to receive

aid. Once you give them, they ask again. Also, their psychological structure is broken [*bozuk*].

Yavuz used religious vocabulary to explain how these issues could be resolved:

> First of all, we have to know that all of our gain [*rızık*] is given by God. We have to be thankful and content. But [among poor people] there is no contentment [*kanaat*] and there is little thankfulness [*şükür*]. Second, they are wasteful. God says he does not like wasteful people. And then, there is no effort. One woman said to us, "My spouse suffers from hernia." Naturally, he had lifted heavy loads and things like this happen. But he was still young. Instead of coming to us, he should have exercised and dealt with it.

The staff members converged on the idea that there should be more businessmen who offer work, but unfortunately poor people mostly did not *want* to work. Hence, the association's duty was to train them morally as well so that they would abandon aid dependence. Even disability did not always render one a deserving poor: Exercise, the magical medicine of late modernity, was upheld as the way out of debilitating conditions.

The disciplining mission had a gendered dimension. The association targeted women and children exclusively, for it saw the men as unsalvageable. The men were social "failures" and the association avoided putting "useless burden" on them (or perhaps, sought to evade their resistance). Instead, it convened the wives and children to provide "character education" (*karakter eğitimi*). In one sentence, charity aimed to save the poor children from the poor parents, as Ahmet underlined: "Fathers either consume alcohol or waste time in coffee houses. Mothers are desperate." Consequently, subject formation techniques were mostly geared towards the next generation, and least of all to adult men.

A different kind of gendered orientation enabled the managers and staff to distinguish charity providers from the rest of society. Here, they drew attention to the stable family lives they led. Ahmet iterated:

> The greatest benefit of those engaged in generosity is to themselves and to their families. If their wives are disobedient [*huysuz*], they calm down. If their children are disobedient, they become obedient [*itaatkar*]. These are the secrets ciphers of service [*hizmet*].

As much as charity aimed to discipline the poor, it strove to discipline the wives and children of the charity provider. The perpetuation of male-controlled families, in other words, depended on the sustenance of a giving hand. *Caring for the poor was at the same time caring for one's family (and one's authority over it)*. Liberalization of Islam went hand in hand with the re-assertion of patriarchy, a "template" that new institutionalists would not expect.

On top of its relation to a religious order, the association had systematic links with local municipalities, as well as governmental agencies. Its "character education" was not carried out in isolation, but with help from these institutions. The managers and staff held that cultivating the next generation's religious sense of responsibility was the joint duty of the state and associations.

In 2014, I visited this association again. My follow-up study revealed that the organization had deepened its project. It further mobilized volunteer labor; blurred the boundaries between beneficiaries and volunteers; and rendered the non-conditional portion of its benevolence partially conditional. On paper, the association did not demand anything in return for its first "six month-package," which was meant only to save people from starvation. However, the women receiving these packages were "invited" to volunteer for the association as often as they could. They cleaned the floors, prepared and served tea, arranged the clothes, and helped with the distribution. The arrangements were informal, so there was no solid, scientific calculation of how much each actually worked. Some came for three days, others only on Friday.

When I first visited the foundation some years ago, it had one director and two regular employees. Now there was an additional female employee. But the amount of food and clothing they distributed, as well as the number of beneficiaries they served, had increased. Even the additional employee could not make up for the difference. So they came to depend on the labor of the new volunteer-beneficiaries.

The director explained their evolving structure: "We work with BİM's logic. We make sure that everything is very cheap: we rented the cheapest place possible; we gather the cheapest possible clothing and food. And we gain from abundant and cheap supply." BİM is the name of a chain store that sells cheap goods in huge quantities. Even though the ultimate aim of the Candle Association was not profit, Ahmet explained their activities in reference to business mentality. "If we were like the other charities, we would have one room for a depot, one room for the employees, another for the director, etc. but instead, we have combined everything [to maximize gain]." Indeed, the only separate room was that of the director. Everything else was piled together. The cash register, employee desks, ranges of clothes, shelves of food, chairs for the beneficiaries, the common dining table were in one single, huge room. Ahmet drew this comparison with BİM in the context of explaining why they mobilized volunteer-beneficiaries, another profit-maximizing innovation.

How was all this received among beneficiaries? Most still stuck to an interpretation of poverty that relied on the traditional tropes of fate and *imtihan* (a "test" God puts you through to see whether you will behave righteously). They complained about employer dishonesty, "high society's" lack of the fear of God, and unjust practices in trade and the workplace. Most of them expected more help from the state rather than associations.

A more restricted number of beneficiaries were in complete disagreement with the ethics of the Candle Association, even if they did not highlight the divergence. They argued that the Turkish leaders and their lack of faith were *directly* responsible for poverty. One beneficiary specifically argued that Turkey's rulers contradicted the famous Hadith about one's neighbors' hunger ("He who sleeps on a full stomach while his neighbor is hungry is not one of us"). Another beneficiary went as far as giving an account of poverty that emphasized surplus exploitation, without using any leftist vocabulary.

Still, some specifically blamed their husbands' laziness for the family's poverty. Only a restricted number went further than that to engage in generalized victim-blaming. One said, "You can even gather herbs and make a living. ... But some people are lazy. ... They are used to receiving things. ... We shouldn't expect everything from the state." Beneficiary discourses, in short, were not standardized. Neoliberalization took hold among managers, staff, and occasionally volunteers, but not so much the beneficiaries (whom most Foucaultian scholars perceive as the primary target of "responsibilization").

Catching Them Red-Handed: Tebliğ-Based Charity as a Cure for Welfare-Induced Laziness

Wholesome Giving, another neoliberal tebliğ association, employed six staff members and regularly mobilized 150–200 volunteers. The association aimed to help 30,000 beneficiaries (and occasionally reached out to around 25,000 people), but regularly helped only 3,000. In order to avoid suspicions, it eschewed fundraising and generated funds internally. Many members were affiliated with religious orders (*tarikat*). Under the roof of this local association, they combined their charitable efforts and past experience (which they had accumulated within their respective religious orders). The association spent 40 percent of its funds on provision; 40 percent on education; and 20 percent on seminars and outreach. These activities blended neoliberal, religious, and nationalist purposes.

Süleyman, the association's director, referred to religion as his main impetus for generosity. A businessman in his 50s, Süleyman invoked God's injunction to help the oppressed and downtrodden [*mustazaf, düşkün*]. Among the many sources he cited was the Hadith: *Yarım hurmayla bile olsa kendinizi ateşten koruyun* [Protect yourself from hellfire, even if through [giving the poor] half a date [the fruit].

Religious references served multiple purposes. Beyond simply motivating people and justifying their acts, they provided a framework within which the benevolent act was practiced in a meaningful and correct way. An important criterion when helping a person, association members pointed out by referring to the Qur'an, is not to insult her. In order to live up to this expectation, they didn't put the word orphan in poster titles when they organized orphan-centered events. Instead, they wrote, "We are meeting our brothers and sisters." But then, in small letters, they added Hadith about helping orphans.

Staff expressed pragmatic reasons for involvement in charitable activity, as well as higher ideals. Adem, a former merchant in his 40s, now a full-time association employee, stated: "I am not here only for benevolence. I am here for a job, but it is in accordance with my culture. One has to be realistic. Most people do this because it is a job, not only because they want to do good. What is important is whether you can do the job with peace of mind." As in other neoliberal associations, employees mentioned monetary motivations explicitly.

Members frequently cited the Chinese proverb about teaching how to catch a fish. After uttering the proverb, Süleyman stated: "In order to prevent more people from being added to the 'army of the needy' [*ihtiyaçlılar ordusu*], we should raise a qualified, trained generation with a high capacity." They encountered many children who didn't have access to good education, so they aimed to contribute to the new generation through fostering "equality of opportunity." With this purpose, they provided lessons to the poor.

Fikri was a striking case, since he came from a Kurdish working-class background and not only thrived in this nationalist association, but internalized its victim-blaming discourse. Even though he worked in industrial workshops during his youth, he eventually finished a two-year higher education program (in business administration) and became a marketing expert. Highly involved in Islamist mobilization and benevolence from his youth onwards, he finally decided to use his business skills in charitable associations. A full-time staff member at the time of the interview, he aspired to become a manager of this association. After stating that his core motivation in joining this association was the "totality of Islam" (rather than specific verses or Hadith), he explained the basic reasons of poverty:

> As technology develops, people become lazier. I started to work when I was 12. But today's youth will not work even when they are 17. Some parents see their 20-year-old offspring as children. I lost my little finger when I was working at a lathe machine [*torna makinesi*] and I was 12! But today, people do not start to work early, so they can't develop the necessary skills. My older brother has a carpenter's workshop, and he can't find a lathe operator. People want high-salary office jobs. They want easy work with good benefits. Society is relaxed [*toplum rahat*]. ... There are jobs, but people don't want to work. We see the same thing in Europe: they have unemployment wages!

Fikri thus resorted to the theme of welfare-induced laziness. He clarified that their kind of provision would not create European-type dependency. Rather, their core aim was breaking people's habits of laziness. Part of the success of these associations rests in taking people from (sometimes pain-ridden) working-class backgrounds; providing them venues of upward mobility; and mobilizing them to cast work experience (including accidents and unemployment) in a light that disparages the ("undeserving") poor. Coming from workers, neoliberal discourse gains vigor and a "matter-of-fact" aura, rather than sounding like a harsh, elite indictment of victims.

What made tebliğ neoliberal associations so distinct was their emphasis on the necessary link between the fight against laziness and the struggle for correct pious practice. To start with, the education of the poor necessarily involved religious education, they held. Therefore, the composition of the lessons they provided differentiated them from the pious (non-tebliğ) neoliberal associations. Süleyman insisted: "It is not only physical sciences [*fenni ilimler*] that prepare children for life. Spiritual and religious sciences [*manevi ve dini ilimler*] are also necessary to equip children." The association also offered lessons to adult women, including Qur'an lessons and *ilmihal* (popular manuals regarding rituals). "These women are going to raise our children. So they have to be knowledgeable too." The maternal role of women was central to their social existence, again attesting to the mutual reinforcement of neoliberalization and patriarchy in tebliğ associations.

Wholesome Giving also offered seminars (to the whole public) with one theme per week. The themes included topics such as the human being, society, Islam, faith, the believer (*mü'min*), and the hypocrite (*münafik*). More focused seminars focused on how to do trade in a moral way; take the ablutions correctly; and pray properly. Süleyman summed up the motivation behind these lessons and seminars: "We want to hold our youth by the hand and prevent them from meeting the fire on the street. We want to protect them from Internet cafes. The fire is not only out on the streets and in cafes, but also at home. In order to render them strong against these fires, we inject spirituality. We make them encounter national and spiritual values."

Süleyman thought that these activities went a long way in fighting the causes of poverty. "If Islam were truly lived in Turkey [*İslami hassasiyetler gerçekten yaşansa*], if Islamic economics were applied; if [the rich] regulated profits out of fear of God; if people gave *zakat*, there would no poor. The main source of poverty is the departure from Islam." He also pointed out to the poor's consumption habits (which education would amend): fascination with technology; luxurious consumption; propensity for crime; and laziness. Their activities taught both the poor and the rich, the donors and the beneficiaries, how to be good Muslims.

The question for them was how to transform the poor without insulting them. They had developed certain techniques to avoid insult. Like in other associations, volunteers and staff compiled inventories of the income, property, and consumption patterns of the beneficiaries (through interviews, standardized forms, visits, and fact checking with neighbors and authorities). However, they banned volunteers from touching anything during visits (even if Süleyman jokingly admitted that he checked refrigerator contents whenever beneficiaries looked the other way). The best way was to catch them red-handed (as when a supposedly poor person inadvertently revealed her luxurious cell phone when taking a call). Such acts reinforced their conviction that religious education was necessary.

In short, the goal of orthodox religious training was to raise a generation that would not get involved in crime and instead contribute to productivity. Thereby, the association captured and merged the two core goals of conservative modernity: security-safety-stability that would go hand in hand with growth. The organization relegated women to responsible, "agentic," but patriarchal roles in this effort. This amounted to an active, subordinated female subjectivity.

Even though its members adamantly argued that they were "not political," the association was quite active. In the 2010 referendum, it publicly supported the amendments to the Constitution. Moreover, it regularly incited the public to call and write to RTÜK (Turkey's main censorship agency) regarding immoral TV shows, with the ultimate goal of banning them. It also strove to contribute to the making of a new constitution, through developing guidelines for an Islamic and "civil" legal framework. Süleyman explained the drive behind these actions: "We love every centimeter of this country. We aim to elevate the level of morality and spirituality in every part of the country through these activities." The association built solid links with the governing party as well.

Süleyman also underlined how they contributed to the founding of a politically stable society. "Civil society," he told me, prevented protests like those in Argentina.[5] He thereby echoed the Gramscian argument that civil society can become a barrier to revolution. In the long run, he added, civil society was a better aid-provider than the state, as donors and beneficiaries found the state "cold", whereas civil society was "warm."[6] He therefore demanded from the state that it hand over the welfare funds to associations; stop the regulation of charitable activities; and provide meeting and office space to charities. Despite this somewhat self-contradictory position against regulation, I fortuitously found out (thanks to a visit by an inspector during my research) that the association had applied for the status *kamu yararına dernek* ("publicly beneficial association," a highly coveted status in Turkey, with special benefits).

Yearning for a More Caring State: Communitarian Misgivings

Especially towards the bottom of this association's hierarchy, there was little consensus about the causes of poverty. Among those of the member-donors who were not a part of the management structure, there were intense communitarian dispositions. Tebliğ and neoliberalism, then, did not go very smoothly together. Perhaps this whole category of associations was trying to sustain an unsustainable assemblage. Even though it is vital to show how neoliberalism frequently merges with communitarian dispositions, it is as important to underline how some of these might dynamite neoliberalization in the long run. The "assemblage" literature has not explored such possibilities sufficiently.

One of my interviewees, Umran, started out with an explanation of poverty in line with the association's overall position:

> Poverty has to do, before everything else, with the person's level of education. Poor families do not give enough weight to education. This has to do with [incorrect] upbringing, a problem we have had throughout Republican history—and maybe in the last stages of the Ottoman Empire too, I don't know.

After this point, the interviewee started to meld neoliberal, structural, and communitarian explanations: "Since education requires a lot of money, many people are left without education. Then, they cannot develop goals ... and patience. If they had enough education and patience, God would give them *rızık*."

After a certain point, Umran completely slid to a communitarian-statist position. Providing education was the state's responsibility, he said, but since the state (which lacked religio-nationalist [*milli*] foundations) was unable to deliver, the nation was trying to make up for the gaps through associations. Yet, associations had limitations:

> We cannot claim to save anybody. Our strength would not be enough for that. We are only trying to share what we have. ... Associations like ours exist because religion has ordered us to help, to socialize [*kaynaşmak*] and to be aware of one another. We are trying to make up for what the state cannot do. ... First of all, we have to learn how to believe. We have abandoned belief [*inanç*]. I am not calling this faith [*iman*] on purpose. People have forgotten how to believe in their parents, their neighbors and their state. We always live in doubt. ... Of course, the most superior form of belief is belief in God. Our association tries to develop this further by working on belief and faith.

The goal of associations, then, was to help establish a more religious and caring state, and do their best to spread religion and care in the absence of such a state. Strikingly, this religious protest occurred during the reign of a religious regime. Umran's yearning presaged how subterranean protest would push the regime in a more religious (and less liberal) direction in the coming years.

Another interviewee was thoroughly communitarian. Adem (also see above) did not correlate poverty with laziness: Miners who worked underground for all their lives, as well as some professors who spent their lives for science, could be poor, but some "brainless" person who did no work at all could be the boss of a corporation. Some people also stole to get rich. When such is one's explanation of poverty, the community comes to the fore as the resolution:

> We have to share our bread. ... First of all, you have to think of your brother, your relatives and your neighbors. Up until the last years of the Ottomans, the villas on the Üsküdar coast had signs on them that said, "He who sleeps on a full stomach while his neighbor is hungry is not one of us. If you're hungry, or if have any other need, and do not knock on my door, it is not my responsibility. Knock!" ... There were no locks on doors. Now people are not content with locks, they install alarms.

This approach openly blamed the property-holders for creating an insecure society, not the poor's taste for crime. Adem went on to give an example of a man who lived in the old times and distributed bread to thousands of people while everybody was asleep. They could find out who he was only after he passed away (when bread distribution stopped). He contrasted this with today's associations, which widely publicized their help. "People have become very selfish," he said, and this was reflected even in benevolence. Most didn't give money to the poor and spent away wealth for their children's education, some of whom did not even attend their funerals! When there was a funeral in the old days, people would not work and watch TV for days. Now, brothers stopped drinking from the same cup and eating from the same pot ("*ekmeği bile bölerek yemiyorlar*"). Communitarian understandings of poverty hence came with a romanticization of the past and tightknit families. While Adem's understanding was in tension with the association's general mission, his emphasis on solidaristic families was shared across the board.

Samet's stance demonstrated that staff members were not alone in their communitarian misgivings. A 50-year-old middle school graduate and a key donor, Samet had held some managerial positions in the association's initial days. Though he had drifted from one small business initiative to the other over 30 years (in construction, clothing, electronics, food), he now concentrated on real estate. He had three stable employees, but occasionally employed more. After he defined his association's mission as the preservation of identity, sticking to the Qur'an and Hadith (including the Hadith about one's neighbor's hunger), and "overcoming the precipice between the rich and the poor," he summarized the reasons why poverty exists:

> First of all, ignorance. Second, discord, divisions and separatism [*tefrika, ayrılık, ayrılıkçılık*]. ... We need to understand: all property belongs to God. ... God has entrusted the property to the rich. Why? So that he creates livelihood [*rızık*] for the seven billion people on earth. And God has rendered some people needy [*ihtiyaç sahibi*]. This is where faith is needed. If the rich person does not understand this he will think that he has earned that property, whereas it is given to him. ... We do see some rich people who exploit and repress the poor and pay them low salaries. This results from ignorance. 90% of the rich are ignorant. ... If God wanted, he could have distributed property equally to everybody. But he hasn't. Because this is a test: he is testing whether the rich will give. A person without religion would not give. Why would he? He has stolen the property like a thief.

While the members of the Hope and Ownership associations explicitly embraced the Locke-ian belief in the earned nature of legitimate property, for Samet, even legitimate property was God-given rather than earned. He also pointed out that it was better to give one-tenth or even half of one's property away if one can, rather than the required 2.5 percent.

This kind of communitarianism clearly accepted and sanctified inequality. The parallels with and differences from neoliberal understandings of the economy, however, were striking: in neoliberal accounts too, the rich were praised because they created jobs. Samet shared that emphasis. However, he also believed that this did not apply to today's rich, but to the rich of an idealized past. Today's rich had to be reformed. So, it was not in the nature of the wealthy to be beneficial to society. Associations had to cultivate and regulate the rich.

The solution for Samet was therefore clear: The better-off had to model their behavior after the Prophet's and follow the dictates of the Qur'an closely; and the poor had to be content:

> The Prophet had his rich and poor times. God made him so, so that he would be a model of how to behave when poor and how to behave when rich. He was left without food for three days, but he did not lose his honor. The dirty poor man is the one who becomes an enemy of the rich. The Prophet never became an enemy of the rich.

Samet's communitarianism thus implied submission: He emphasized class compromise rather than class conflict. Differences of economic interpretation, then, correlated with divergent interpretations of the Prophet's life. In some liberal accounts, the Prophet was a merchant and everybody could become wealthy by following his example; there were no classes in society. Society consisted of people who just knew how to live (and trade) and those who didn't. In communitarian accounts, as in Samet's, different aspects of his life represented all of society (both the rich and the poor); classes existed and were inevitable.

Communitarian misgivings brought with them an explicit position regarding the regime's direction. Baha, a civil servant and a freelance journalist, was a volunteer in his late 40s. A silent yet passionate man, who became increasingly more willing to talk after the right kind of probes, he listed the causes of poverty as the governments' misuse of resources; laziness; the banking system, which benefited the "compradors" more than anybody else. He added:

> Most people have completely caved in to capitalism. ... Islam has an economic system, but applying it would not be possible in Turkey. The system is secular. Even demanding an Islamic economy would get you labeled as a reactionary. [The Islamic economy means] a just distribution of wealth; the most efficient use of resources; the belittling of laziness and glorification of work; the perception of the taking hand [charity beneficiaries] as inferior to the giving hand [donors]; and the illegalization of bank interest.

I shared with Baha (and some others) the Turkish translation of my book *Passive Revolution* and summarized the arguments. He conceded that the current Islamic government was far from implementing any of the structure he specified, but criticized my book because it implied that the whole movement was incorporated (although I pointed out that this was not exactly my argument). The movement was alive and well, he snapped; it didn't criticize the economic policies at the moment because it focused on tebliğ: it had not been able to practice tebliğ for decades and now was the moment. It would soon turn against extant economic policies. His association's goal was not only tebliğ, but also creating a consciousness of "we": "The whole system is trying to make us individualistic. Newspapers, televisions, advertisements… They teach us how to say 'I-me' all the time. Associations instill a consciousness of us-ness. They remind people of 'us-we'. If we say 'I' all the time, society's problems will not be resolved." Baha exhibited a more sustained communitarianism than his fellow travelers (while he still looked down on the poor) and was more vociferously critical of neoliberal orientations.

The limits of the Rose and Muehlebach accounts become clearer as we go through these discourses. Deleuzian-Foucaultians also document how neoliberal organizations absorb a lot of communitarian rhetoric. But they underemphasize how some actors within them have a clear intention to subvert the neoliberal policies of not just the organization, but of the whole country. "Assemblage" accounts do not appreciate the possibility of such a trajectory.

★★★

Was the lack of full standardization and rationalization a temporary condition for these associations? Would the ones caught in between communitarianism and neoliberalism move closer to the neoliberal side over time? Would tebliğ be dropped on the way as some of them grew or would the tebliğ-neoliberalization assemblage turn into a mainstay of the Turkish scene? This book cannot provide conclusive answers to these questions, but the discussion of communitarian and redistributive organizations in the next chapter gives us some ideas about what kind of associational venues are available to those who might become frustrated with the excessive neoliberalization of giving.

Notes

1 Talha was exceptional among neoliberal actors in that he rejected a core tenet of liberalism: the belief in human beings' natural (or at least nurture-able) potential to be entrepreneurial.
2 Certainly, this association is not alone in rehearsing liberalism to justify ethnic cleansing. For a striking parallel, see Locke's (1956) account of Native Americans, their lack of transformative labor, and hence the irrelevance of their claims to their lands.
3 Is it possible that Egyptian associations withheld information regarding their techniques of classification (and recruitment, another issue of contrast covered below)? Perhaps they feared international competition (if not necessarily espionage): I could smuggle their techniques to the Turks and render the latter's already wealthier institutions even more powerful. Although this possibility cannot be ruled out, it is unlikely that such a conspiratorial attitude would be shared so widely that not even one individual wouldn't let the relevant information slip out.
4 Petersen (2011, pp. 137, 191–193) has also observed similar dependence on religious authority despite all talk of professionalization and rationalization among some

transnational Muslim NGOs. She also notes, on the same pages, fluctuating commitment to religious mission even among actors who deny any such engagement (a pattern I have documented in Chapters 5, 6, and 7).
5 Many of my respondents referred to these protests that occurred in the early 2000s without any probing on my part.
6 This blending of communitarian emotionalism and market fundamentalism has been observed in non-Muslim contexts too (Muehlebach 2012).

7

PUNCHING ABOVE THEIR WEIGHT

Turkey's Communitarian and Redistributive Associations

Due to the quick spread of market-oriented associations in Turkey, non-neoliberal benevolent organizations occupied a much smaller part of the field when compared to Egypt. However, the development of a new form of Islamic benevolence (a redistributive one, of which only hints existed in Egypt) was striking. Moreover, one large organization, even though neoliberal in its outlook regarding Turkey, was strongly redistributive in its international charity. These complexities require a rethinking of global neoliberalization.

Turkish Communitarian Associations: "Balance" with an Edge

The main activities of these associations focused on *tebliğ* and provision. They were explicitly and heavily religious. Islam was not only a motivation for charity, but a framework that structured it. Their religious references were solidly textual.

As with Egyptian communitarian associations, the overarching goal was establishing a (virtuous) community without immense wealth differences. Turkish communitarians were more intensely suspicious of wealth accumulation. Still, the ultimate objective was thankfulness for whatever one possessed (and striking a balance between the rich and poor), rather than abolishing poverty, which they perceived as humanly impossible. However, beyond this basic starting point, there was ample diversity regarding the understanding of poverty and religion among even the managers. Disagreements intensified among the staff. Proclivities were not standardized as in some of the neoliberal pious associations covered earlier.

Turkish communitarians distinguished themselves from other charitable actors through heavy reference not only to Islamic texts, but also to Islamic authorities: they found guidance by a charismatic figure both legitimate and necessary (while pious neoliberal associations hid any such guidance from the public).

Nevertheless, just like the Turkish-Islamic neoliberals, they distinguished themselves from the rabble by a rejection of rebellion (which they more explicitly associated with the lack of religious traits such as thankfulness to God and *hamd*, praise for and glorification of God).

Volunteers, staff, and managers had a rich involvement in civic activities and religious education. Most of them had been active in Islamist movements. They tended to be clerical school graduates. A few of them were licensed clerics (*imam*). They employed a few women staff, but few or no female managers.

These associations raised funds through networks and campaigns. They secondarily utilized TV programs, though these were not as popular as the televised shows of pious neoliberal associations. Working- and middle-class families constituted the bulk of their funding source. They saw historical and current Islamic states as their role models of giving. Along the lines of this perspective, they favored heavy state intervention in the economy. Although they fervently rejected politics (which they saw as corrupt), they had direct political links to parties or sociopolitical movements.

In the Good Works Association, spirituality and spiritual leadership were of utmost importance. While pious neoliberal associations also harbored personality cults, they did not emphasize them in public. But a top manager of the Good Works Association could give the following answer as to why they established their organization:

> There is a target our *Hoca* [spiritual leader] has determined for us … This is the *Hoca*'s order [*talimat*] in realizing this target: "You can feed people's stomachs in many ways. Anybody can do this. But your mission is feeding their hearts and minds as well as their stomach." We are thus trying to strike a balance between the heart and wrist [*yürekle bilek arasında*]. We are trying to raise people's consciousness. We can thus distinguish ourselves from other associations. … We distribute bags of necessities, but we also put [religious] books in them.

Unlike Egyptian communitarians, the Good Works Association explicitly differentiated itself from liberal Islamic charities (because, unlike the established communitarian associations in Egypt, it needed to fight for a foothold in the field). There was also another distinction that its members "gave off" in the Goffmanian sense: The communal *hierarchy* was very clear. Charismatic spiritual authority was central to the working of the association.

Despite their now-explicit/now-implicit strategies of distinction, Good Works activists still *wanted* to perceive the field as solidaristic and *non-competitive*, much unlike Egyptian neoliberal organizations. This was how İhsan, a top manager, defined their mission: "Each association should specialize in an area. If we specialize in education, others should hone in on necessities, others on infrastructure. Unfortunately, everybody concentrates in the same areas." In other words, in an ideal world there would be no competition between organizations, but in the actual one, actors wanted to crowd each other out.

As can be seen in İhsan's formulation, the organization subordinated developmental activities to spirituality. When I asked about whether they aimed to provide career training (*kariyer edindirmek*), his rejection was vehement: "No, no, no career-development. Only morality and consciousness. We provide a consciousness about why humans were created and why we are in this world." This education was not restricted to giving the right books. Building and repairing schools constituted a big chunk of their activities. Interestingly, while Egyptian and Turkish neoliberal associations conceptualized their school building activities as a part of their training and development mission, communitarians packaged it as a religious mission.

In order to understand Turkish communitarianism's difference from a redistributive position, it is crucial to notice that the former did not aim to *abolish* poverty. İhsan explained why:

IHSAN: There is no way to abolish poverty. Actually, poverty needs to exist. This world is a place of examination [*imtihan*], we should never forget that. People are composed of tribes of different colors, languages and income levels. If we were all at the same level, that would go against the logics of creation and examination. But we also have a slogan: the real poverty and deprivation is lacking mercy [*merhamet*]. ... We have no intention of abolishing poverty and we would not be powerful enough to do that anyway.
CT: Is poverty a part of fate, then?
IHSAN: Rather than fate, it is creation: we are all different. ... [The real question is]: Do people revolt due to their hunger, or are they grateful and patient [*yoksulum diye isyan mı ediyor, sabır mı ediyor, şükür mü ediyor*]? May people have richness of heart! We see many poor people who say, "Praise be to God [*hamd olsun*], I have everything." ... But we see that he doesn't have anything. And we see many rich people who complain all the time despite their wealth. Therefore, we should question who is wealthy and who is poor.

The poor's rebelliousness was a concern common to Turkish associations across the neoliberal/communitarian divide. The logics behind their criticism, however, were different. While neoliberal associations desired to tame the poor so that they would be independent and hard-working, communitarians domesticated them so they would be dependent on the rich and thankful to God. Unlike both neoliberal and redistributive actors, communitarians assumed that poverty would persist forever.

The managers assigned a heavy role to the state in providing for the poor, and saw associations' role as mostly emotional and spiritual:

Our means are restricted, we cannot provide for many people. Nevertheless, civil society should not withdraw from this area. We are the spirit, we give spirit to welfare. When we go to people, we share their troubles [*dertleşmek*]. In contrast to the cold face of the state, we remove their stress; we warm up their hearts [*Onun gazını alma, gönlünü hoş tutma*]. We are more sincere. We reach people spiritually.

This rendering of benevolence was in line with Wuthnow's understanding of charity: kindness is expressed most effectively when it is not institutionalized, but is truly voluntary. The attribution of coldness to the state and warmth to civic organizations was among the communitarian instruments that many neoliberals also deployed freely. What distinguished Turkish communitarian organizations, however, was the insistence that *this warmth* was their real contribution: They could get nowhere near resolving poverty (while both Egyptian communitarians *and* Turkish neoliberals claimed they could).

Within the Good Works Association, some prominent actors moved in a redistributive direction. A manager, Şevket, for instance, differed from the organization's main line:

When God created this universe, he created enough underground and overground resources for everybody. The main cause of poverty (in our society or others) is the desire to accumulate more. [But he then shifted attention to global balances]. Those who have knowledge also have power. The powerful of this world monopolize the resources [*kaynakların üzerine oturuyorlar*]. The world's hegemonic powers do this through oppressing others. They also compete with each other. The result is wars, where many refugees fall into poverty. Throughout the world today, poverty is not an economic but a moral issue. When we resolve the moral issue, there will no longer be any poverty.

Here, we see hints of a redistributive approach, which we also occasionally encountered among some Egyptian communitarians. However, this interviewee jumped from one explanation to the other, without any transition between them; he combined communitarian and redistributive explanations in an *unsystematic* way. Still, not one of his explanations brought up "human creation" as the main cause of destitution, as did İhsan's explanations.

What motivated some communitarian activists was not just the conditions of the less fortunate, but systemic causes. Şevket was crystal clear: "What brought me here was the imbalanced distribution of income [*gelir dengesizliği*]." But even this "system-critic" interviewee denied Turks' power relation with Kurds. What social scientists would call structural explanations did not apply to Kurdish poverty:

Life in the Kurdish southeast was much more pleasant a century ago. People used to have gardens and fields and they sowed them [*ekip biçiyorlardı*]. ...

We lived together brotherly for thousands [sic] of years. In the last 100 years, or more specifically 30 years, the people there became like this [*böyle oldu*, vaguely referring to the Kurds' confrontational position]. An organization that said "I am going to bring you freedom".

Here, Şevket interrupted the sentence, and from a clause that had a subject, abruptly shifted to a clause without a subject:

all their villages were emptied and they came to the cities [*Ben size özgürlük getiricem diyen bir örgüt, ya da her neyse, tüm köyleri boşaldı ve şehirlere geldiler*]. They had fields there ... sheep, oxen. They came to the cities without skills, without literacy; they don't know how to do trade; and they are populous. What are they going to do?

He then talked very shortly about how the republic's authoritarian (*dayatmacı*) approach also created problems, but sealed this topic brusquely by saying "we shouldn't get stuck by discussing politics" (*siyasete takılmamak gerekiyor*). He insisted that the solution would come through associations and the culture of mutual help, based on his sociopolitical movement's[1] motto "*insanlıkta eş, dinde kardeş*" (roughly, "identical in humanity, brothers in religion").

This erasure of politics was emblematic of communitarian charity. Communitarians depicted a golden age (the Ottoman period), where there was plenty for everybody (neglecting the semi-feudal structure of Kurdistan, which has been historically more inegalitarian than Western Anatolia). Kurd's political organization was therefore the contaminating phenomenon in this framework, despite the fact that it was the Turkish state (not the Kurdish guerilla) that emptied the villages. Hence the necessity to switch to a subject-less clause: as Roland Barthes (1957) has demonstrated, the construction of subject-less sentences is usually indicative of an actor-hood that the speaker wants to conceal. This charity manager was actually quite knowledgeable about the political causes of poverty; his subtle avoidance *gave off* his political perceptiveness. However, his communitarianism *bracketed out* the political dimension of the issues to make them more manageable. Nevertheless, by avoiding politics, Şevket succumbed to the explanation of poverty he aimed to avoid: he accounted for Kurdish poverty partially based on the Kurdish poor's ignorance, incapacity, and bad habits (e.g. breeding too many children).

In sum, while communitarian dispositions predominated in the Good Works Association, its actors displayed redistributive and neoliberal orientations as well. These tendencies, however, were subordinated to communitarian ones. Nevertheless, the association's focus on the poor's education and morality could prepare a transition to a tebliğ-neoliberal mode of governing: managers and staff could re-coalesce around the understanding that the main cause of poverty is the poor's lack of a sound Islamic morality. It is noteworthy that the staff more directly involved with the *implementation* of projects and day-to-day contact with the poor were more neoliberal in orientation. Their direct experience with the poor could also push the managers to adapt a more consistent "blaming the victim" mentality in the future, especially if the role of the mentioned *Hoca* somehow decreases and the technical dimension of the association gains the upper hand.

Redistributive Organizations

The truly distinguishing characteristic of the Turkish field was the (contested and circumscribed) emergence of a redistributive Islam. The main activities of redistributive associations revolved around the provision of necessities, citizenship training, and protest activity. Religion tended to be a motivation rather than the goal. The overall goals of giving included the cultivation of self-reliant, self-confident, but also struggle-prone citizens. These associations also aspired to contribute to the establishment of a just economic system, whether at the national or international level, an emphasis which differentiated them from all the other organizations. They thoroughly politicized giving, but did this explicitly, unlike the others. Redistributive organizations attributed poverty to systemic causes and rejected victim-blaming. Like most other associations, they also wished to bring in "warmth" and "spirit" to welfare, thereby balancing the "cold" provision of the state. Indeed, benevolent actors of all kinds (with the exception of the most neoliberal organization in Egypt) emphasized this binary opposition (the cold state versus warm civic organizations).

Redistributive organizations claimed to reach people usually ignored by other charities, such as politically risky populations (e.g. Palestinians) or marginalized sectors within Turkey (e.g. prostitutes). They labeled obedience, rather than rebelliousness, as the unwanted (and stigmatizing) personal orientation. Members and affiliates distinguished themselves by using the language of political economy. While career professionals could be found among both managers and staff, most were volunteers. Managers came from professional and business backgrounds; the staff ranged from the poor and working class to professionals.

Most of the managers, staff, and volunteers had been active in the Islamist movement. A smaller subset also had experiences of suffering from poverty. Women were actively involved at every level, from managerial to volunteering positions. They participated in large numbers, undertook many tasks and activities, and held authority. However, their engagement was spatially and organizationally differentiated.

These organizations used the media heavily through sensational declarations. They also spread their message through demonstrations and other forms of protest. The members heavily drew on and referred to Islamic history as their model of giving, while some were also inspired by European social democracy. Most favored redistributive economics as an alternative to market capitalism. The main funding source was small contributions from people of diverse backgrounds.

"We Want Total Liberation": Redistributive Self-Reliance

The Companions Association, which exhibited redistributive tendencies most intensely, focused on homeless people. The Istanbul metropolitan municipality sheltered 5,000 homeless men during the winter months, but then let them go in March. In the temporary municipal shelter, the homeless lived in unfavorable conditions (e.g. they slept on floor beds). This association housed 20 of these men after March. There was no paid staff; everybody was a volunteer, even in the association's main office in Konya. The major donor of the organization, also its founder, was a rare, pious wealthy man who opposed market-friendly policies.

Although the most circulated narratives emphasized structural inequalities, redistributive actors did not ignore individual variation or psychological factors. Yet they understood individual variation and psychological factors as interacting with social factors (including mainstream responses to poverty, behaviors of governmental personnel and employers, and society's ignorance of its duties toward the poor). Since they did not disregard psychological factors, Companions Association members gave a lot of weight to the personal transformation of the poor. They even expected self-reliance, but did so in a markedly non-neoliberal way. This "alternative responsibilization" was neither individualizing nor depoliticizing, unlike in neoliberal discourse.[2] Here, we see how neoliberal norms (more specifically, the expectation of self-reliance from the poor) have indeed diffused (as new institutionalists would expect), but have been appropriated in collectivistic fashion.

The organization's mission undermined the dichotomy between the deserving and undeserving poor, a binary most other organizations internalized. Fevzi (an unemployed man in his mid-50s and a beneficiary-manager of the homeless shelter) walked me through a detailed account of how able-bodied men too could end up needing help. He had time and again encountered men who lost their jobs, then got marginalized and escaped their neighborhood. They thereby became homeless. Since they could not take a bath, people avoided them, and they avoided people, as their psychology was disturbed as a result of losing contact with others. Whenever they found suitable work, employers asked for an address of residence. Ultimately, these men had to consult aid agencies, even though they were healthy and relatively young.

Bahri (a beneficiary and former tourism worker) brought in the structure of work relations to draw attention to how even those who found employment could not easily escape reliance on aid:

> Most homeless people do not have skills. This doesn't mean they can't find jobs. They do. But they are abused [*Ama bulduğu işte de canını çıkartırlar*]. For example, they make him work from 8 a.m. till midnight. And they know he is desperate [*garipsin diye*], so if the minimum wage is 650 YTL, they give him 400.

As I will demonstrate further below, the organization's members had a complex understanding of why this was the case. Suffice it to say here that they thought a reorientation of society was necessary to change these relations.

A paramount dimension of redistributive organizations was the politicization of giving. The goal was not simply taking from the willing rich and giving to the needy. It was rather *making* the powerholders give the poor's due. These associations desired to enable the downtrodden to use their constitutional rights too. They endeavored to teach the poor how to wage this struggle, not only in order to have them fight for themselves, but so that they would teach it to other poor people. Recall that professionalized neoliberal actors in Egypt wanted to go beyond the Chinese proverb (by teaching people how to *make* fishing nets). Likewise, these Turkish actors ambitiously aimed to transform the poor into redistributors and educators.

Fevzi's first involvement as a "responsible" actor within this organization was carrying things (logs, etc.) around. But afterwards, he also started to take his fellow "beneficiaries" to official institutions and demand that they, for example, be healed. When he was at his first shelter in Konya, he took diabetes patients to hospitals and had them connected to dialysis machines. He took other, undocumented beneficiaries to social work offices; he fought directors so that they would be accepted into retirement homes. When his first attempts did not work, he called the press and complained that these offices were malfunctioning. Using such methods, he claimed to have placed 15 people in the relevant institutions. Fevzi's story indicates that charitable "responsibilization" can serve collectivistic and political purposes.

Companions Association members were strongly critical of mainstream religious communities and orders (*cemaat*[3] and *tarikat*). When these groups helped people, they claimed, they expected them to abide by their rituals (a charge the mentioned organizations vehemently denied, yet acknowledged in passing). But in their shelters, there were people of different religions; Muslims were not pushed to behave in a certain way either. However, this did not mean they had no behavioral code for beneficiaries.

The organization anticipated all residents would do certain chores (shopping, washing the dishes, throwing out the garbage). A schedule posted on the wall specified which tasks were assigned to whom. These assignments were not made in a participatory way: two of those who had stayed longer in the shelter decided. Bahri emphasized: "We try to do everything equally and in a just way." Still, there was an authority structure and hierarchy, even if it was one founded on friendly warnings rather than bureaucratized reward and punishment, which Bahri captured with the sentence: "We warn, but do not punish" (*ikaz var ceza yok*).

The unpaid staff members in charge were also beneficiaries of the same shelter. Consequently, unlike most of the organizations studied in this book, local management was in the hands of people who had personal experiences with, or rather a deep biographical story of, poverty. This involvement also led to a unique managerial structure, which defied diffusion accounts.

The managerial structure was not neoliberalized. There was no paid and professionalized staff at the Istanbul branch; everybody was a volunteer. Most midlevel managers came from within the ranks of the beneficiaries. These unpaid mid-level managers remained beneficiaries, since their home (and nutrition source) was still the association shelter. However, some of them also aspired to become higher-level managers once they found jobs and homes in the "outside world." These aspirations again attest to an innovative mixture under conditions of neoliberalization: the organization combined unpaid management (a communitarian practice) with a typical neoliberal inclination (a professed desire to climb up the managerial hierarchy).

How did the beneficiaries contact the association? What can the structures of contact tell us about redistributive subjectivity? Some discovered the organization after they read about it in the newspapers (hinting that a full development of redistributive subjectivity required a middle school level of education, which would allow frequent engagement with the press). Involvement in the organization instilled self-confidence and dispelled pessimism. Bahri and Fevzi consequently became a part of the new community and did not want to go back to their old environment. They even developed plans for the future, personal as well as organizational. In short, these poor men came to develop some of the virtues neoliberalism cherishes (self-confidence, responsibility, and future orientation), yet they nurtured this temperance not by relying just on themselves, but also on community and collective organization. Nevertheless, as I will demonstrate at the end of this subsection, there were structural barriers to the full adaptation of this redistributive subjectivity among all of the association's beneficiaries.

The Companions Association put emphasis on helping women who decided to quit prostitution, children who wanted to quit drugs, and men who had just been released from prison. The males could stay in this shelter as long as they did not cause trouble in the neighborhood. If they did, the organization still helped them, but in more specialized shelters. The association wanted to help outcasts, those whom other Islamic communities ignored.

Association members presented a sophisticated analysis of market capitalism and alternatives to it, ranging from populist romanticism to social democracy (without any probing prior to the interviews). They asked me about the regulations regarding homeless people in the United States, but before they got the answer they said capitalism is intense there, so they expected the worst. Fevzi exclaimed: "Isn't it capitalism that destroys us!?" [*zaten o kapitalizm değil mi bizi mahveden!?*]

CT: What is capitalism?
FEVZI: It is a monster. This doesn't mean I defend socialism or communism. Income distribution got worse after people like me lost agricultural land. Back then, we were self-sufficient [*kendimiz üretiyorduk, kendimiz tüketiyorduk*]. Even the poorest peasants could feed themselves and build their own furniture. This [self-sufficiency] was destroyed intentionally and systematically.

BAHRI: Let me correct that word. The problem is not capitalism, but distorted [çarpık] capitalism. You can check this on the Internet. Turkey is the most unequal country in the whole world together with Mexico and the United States.

Bahri was referring to a recent report on OECD countries (incidentally, not the whole world) that circulated in the media. Very low minimum wage; lack of insurance; overworked laborers characterized Turkish capitalism, he said. In the tourism industry, "The bosses win and the personnel [eleman] lose. Most of them are unemployed in the winter and don't know if they will get a job the following summer," Bahri said. He himself had worked as a plain laborer in tourism, which he ultimately quit without substantial savings.

Bahri also referred to scientific research on poverty and gave right-on-target numbers regarding Turkey's ranking in development and human development indices. Fevzi then argued that collective action was the only way out and remarked on his own participation in a sleep-in demonstration regarding homelessness:

> That was a message to the state. But it was also a wake-up call for sleeping people. ... There was no shelter in Istanbul at that time; there was only one in Konya. The foundations of the [Companions Association's] Istanbul shelter were laid at that demonstration. What we wanted to show to the state was that even a civil society organization could do something. We sent a fax to the mayor, to the minister. Can you believe this: not even one of them visited the sleep-in demonstration! They did not come to see our shelter either. Why? It is not because they do not have the capacity to. The system prevents them.

Bahri interrupted:

> When [our association's founder] participates in television programs, he does not say we are doing this and that, and the state should help us. Instead, he says "such and such is the duty of the state and it should take care of the poor." He also writes letters to [state agencies] with the same words, and uses documents to support his claims. ... What [our association's founder] wants is total liberation [toptan bir kurtuluş], he does not intend to save people with his individual attempts.

The organization's mission, then, was spreading a *social ethos* and *criticism of the individualizing tendencies of other aid associations*. Other associations also got a lot of airtime, but used it to demand either citizen or state support for *their* activities.

Most of this could be discussed in response to the Foucaultian question: What would an (effective) alternative subjectivity in the neoliberal context look like? In the Companions Association, we catch a glimpse of a still "disciplined," but also interactive understanding of responsibility "adequate to neoliberal times"

(Feher 2009). Feher (the renowned Foucaultian) uneasily swung between two terms when trying to name the leftist project of his dreams: "left-wing neoliberalism" and "a left adequate to neoliberalism." We see in the ethical conduct of the Companions Association that an organization that is *adequate to neoliberal times* (that thrives on the promises and contradictions of our era) does not have to be neoliberal.

Aside from these individual efforts under the roof of the shelter, the association itself pushed the state to care for the poor. For instance, it issued several press releases, petitions, and letters of complaint (against mayors, municipal managers and the police) to draw attention to the shortcomings of governmental relief. In these documents, it not only pointed out how the government did not live up to its promises (e.g. of constructing a homeless shelter in every major mayoralty throughout the country), but also showed concrete ways in which the government could do more.

As an Islamically inspired organization, the Companions Association strove to abolish sex work. It also sheltered sex workers and developed their capacities for non-sex-related work. However, the association also attempted to protect the honor of sex workers by challenging conservative Islamic codes. For example, it attacked the major Islamic labor union's use of the word B-girl [*konsomatris*] in a derogatory way (Islamic labor had just "insulted" Turkey's most established secular businessmen association, TÜSİAD, by calling it *konsomatris*). The press release was co-authored with a woman who had previously worked in this profession and then joined the association. While the mainstream press was busy complaining about Islamic labor's uncouth manners (they shouldn't have "cursed"), the Companions Association pointed out that the real problem was that *konsomatris* could be an insult.

Bahri also developed a pro-Western analysis. He emphasized that the labor and union laws that the EU required would never pass because of the resistances of those like Sabancı and Doğan (major secular business families). This was preceded by Fevzi's rather anti-imperialist analysis of the reasons of poverty (the American conspiracies against agriculture and military infrastructure, as well as the national governments' subservience to the American agenda). "I don't know how Turkey will be saved, and whether it will be saved," Fevzi said. Bahri interrupted again: "Well, Turkey will be saved, but citizens like us will not." Then he went on to his anti-bourgeois, rather than anti-imperialist, analysis: Turkey was in fact developing, but this was not reflected in the poor's lives; this could only change if there were a human-focused constitution, along EU lines. A redistributive organization with a different angle challenged this expectation of pro-poor civilizational support from the West (see the next section).

Before I analyze that organization, I will discuss my follow up visit to the Companions Association in 2014. There were some changes since I studied it in 2011–2012; the people staying there had started to receive psychiatric help. They were now also taking private training courses. (Again, this attested to an "alternative responsibilization," now bolstered through even further techniques. But this focus on the poor's psyche *could* slide into neoliberalization.) Bahri had become the director of the Istanbul homeless shelter. He had just moved in to the shelter when I first contacted the organization. As of 2014, he had been receiving psychiatric help, like everyone else in the shelter. He was also following an arts and crafts course. The walls of the shelter's uppermost floor were decorated with his beautiful art work.

A conversation with five men in 2014 hinted that the redistributive tendencies the organization cultivated were not completely shared. These men were now the most permanent inhabitants of the shelter. The youngest (28) had difficulty speaking. A man from Konya was the most silent. He was also the least educated and did not trust himself. He said again and again "all of our stories are the same." It was only after he was alone with me and the youngest man that he spoke in a more relaxed manner, attesting to some internalized organizational hierarchy. Another beneficiary, a college graduate in his late 30s, expressed his anger towards the whole world and was angry at my presence too. He was much more educated than the others and pointed this out without underlining it too much. Yet, whenever he spoke for more than a minute he could not follow the chain of his own thoughts. A couple of these beneficiaries were suffering from psychological, cultural, and physical difficulties (due to years of homelessness) and doing anything beyond taking care of their basic necessities seemed to be a tall order.

In our conversation, structural explanations of poverty surfaced again and again, but the beneficiaries pushed them to the background (especially in the absence of Fevzi and Bahri). They mixed and matched neoliberal, communitarian, and redistributive discourses. The older beneficiary-volunteers, most particularly the director, were trying to instill a collectivist ethic, but this seemed to penetrate the others' subjectivity only partially. As I concluded my revisit to the shelter, I had doubts about whether any of these recent beneficiaries would be as integrated into the Companions Association as Fevzi and Bahri. Yet, given that Fevzi and Bahri had suffered quite similar difficulties (and could ultimately become solid parts of the organization), the possibility could not be ruled out.

Charitable organizations had substantial difficulty in instilling their ethics among the beneficiaries (despite vigorous efforts in this direction). This was true not only of the neoliberal, but also of the redistributive organizations. The beneficiaries blended communitarian, neoliberal, and redistribute orientations to poverty in the most unsystematic of ways. We need much more research in order to ascertain how generalizable these conclusions are to broader populations of beneficiaries throughout Turkey, Egypt, and the United States.

Bifurcated Benevolence: International Collectivism Coupled with Local Neoliberalism

Unlike the Companions Association, the IHH was much more internationally focused, even though it also provided aid in Turkey. It was most active in crisis situations, including war, genocide, international blockades, and natural disasters. It was minimally involved in education and capacity development. In its mission statement, the organization mentioned social justice along with peace and human rights.

During my first visit (in 2011), the IHH was exceptional in its combination of a redistributive approach at the international level and a neoliberal one at the national level. As the case of the Candle Association shows (see Chapter 6 and further below), other organizations followed suit in 2014. These organizations did not necessarily have international branches like the IHH: They applied redistributive methods when dealing with refugees *within* Turkey, and neoliberal ones when dealing with citizens. In this sense, the IHH's "bifurcation" was a trendsetter, but smaller associations had to revise the model depending on their capacities.

The IHH has a distinctly political pedigree. University students were especially active in the organization's establishment in the early 1990s. Most were affiliated with the "National Outlook" movement, the religious community behind the Welfare Party of the 1990s (see Chapter 3). But they decided that the response to the humanitarian crisis in Bosnia had to involve a stance beyond parties and communities. It was very difficult to bring together Islamic politicians, or even Islamic communities. But the Bosnian War was so massive that all Muslims had to amass their strength to make a difference. Therefore, despite having strong feelings of belonging to the Welfare Party, they decided to be steadfast about non-commitment to parties and Islamic communities (*cemaat*).

"Realizing Oneself through the Deprivations of Others"

Regarding poverty outside of Turkey, the organization's members used redistributive arguments. According to Vehbi, an IHH manager in his 40s, the reasons behind misery were attributable to the powerful: social injustice; believing that they are God's privileged creatures; perceiving others as non-human. Even his definition was structural: in contrast to all neoliberal and communitarian respondents, Vehbi defined poverty as being below the living standards in any given location. He also provocatively argued that an annual investment of $139 billion USD for a consecutive five-year period would resolve all of the world's poverty. The world's military expenditure was much higher than this:

> As long as [the powerful] realize themselves through the deprivations of others [*diğer insanların yokluğundan kendini varetmeyi yöntem edinmiş bakış açısı değişmediği sürece* ...], there will be poverty. ... And how do people do that? Through arms [trade] and the fabrication of weaponry.

Therefore, the organization defined its method of humanitarian aid as a permanent struggle against the world's major states and companies (which allegedly promoted wars and armament).

IHH activists were therefore vociferous about the social justice component of aid. Vecdi stated point blank:

> There is a very unjust distribution of wealth throughout the world. The forces that have set up this system and who rule the world have a serious role in this. ... The world's resources would be more than enough for the whole world, but there are 1.5 billion hungry people today! One Swiss person's income is equivalent to 400 Ethiopians' income! . ... Correcting this is easy, but the systemic structures [*sistemik yapılar*] need to be willing [*iştiyaklı*]. ... The G8 countries are responsible for all of this. They sell weapons to the African countries at war with each other. 1.5 million people in the United States earn their living through the arms sector. What does this mean? If there are no wars in the world, these countries would come to the brink of collapse.

Just like communitarian actors, IHH members held that poverty resulted from the unjust distribution of wealth. But communitarian organizations (such as the Good Works Association) combined this account with a "fate" and "creation" [*fitrat*] explanation (unjust distribution was a part of creation, as in the medieval Christian conception of inequality). Here, "the system" rather than *fitrat* was the real cause. Moreover, unlike communitarians, most IHH actors believed that poverty was resolvable. The organization's online documents were also redistributive. Along the lines of pre-2000s Turkish Islamism (Tuğal 2009), the IHH promised a world without "exploitation,"[4] borrowing from leftist vocabulary.

But when it came to Turkey, IHH members' positions ranged from straightforward neoliberalism to social liberalism. Their concrete activities in poor neighborhoods also resembled Turkish neoliberal organizations' activities. They used the same procedures, background checks, and techniques for differentiating between the deserving and undeserving poor.

Some IHH members denied that there was real poverty in Turkey. They compared the levels of absolute poverty in Africa and Turkey to make their case (going against their own relative-structural definition at the global level). They pointed out that people's appetites were whetted by the media and they wanted too much (in that sense, even their definition of what constituted poverty was similar to those of neoliberal actors, as far as Turkey was concerned). Others conceded that there were some structural problems (such as unemployment), but they did not result from the wrong economic policies.

When I studied the IHH in 2011, this complete geographical partitioning of socioeconomic analysis was specific to this organization. The Ak Party government was flirting with the idea of discursively attacking national and global business, but the Prime Minister's vitriol had not become systematic yet. The IHH activists' systematic and entrenched bifurcation of not only charitable but overall economic orientation was to become *governmental ideology* in the following couple of years. In this sense, we can see the post-2013 "anti-imperialist" and "anti-capitalist" turn of the governing party not only as a manipulative, top-down, and insincere change. *Civil society had paved the way for this macro change in autonomous fashion.* Charity, once again in global history, was becoming a world-maker.

Global Travels of "God's Deputies": Tebliğ by Any Other Name

The organization's members had different approaches to the centrality of Islam for their project. Vecdi vehemently denied the label "Islamic organization," since they also helped Christians; he himself was sponsoring a Christian child in Ethiopia. But everybody at the IHH was a Muslim. Islam also played a motivational role, as Vecdi admitted: "In our works, our basic watchword [*düstur*] is 'Islamic rules' [*kaideler*]: being just, transparent, universal, truthful [*ihlaslı*], respectful both to the donor and the recipient." However, he emphasized that Qur'an and Hadith did not have a central place in their discourse (a claim some other interviewees rejected). These came up spontaneously in meetings, Vecdi said, but not very frequently. Organizational *documents*, however, mentioned religious responsibility as a driving motivation of volunteers[5]—even though in 2011 the emphasis on this responsibility was not as strong as that among tebliğ organizations. (It had started to increase by 2014.) Moreover, one of the aid activities the organization undertook was the restoration of mosques.

Contrasting with Vecdi's account, Hamdi, another top manager, emphasized the formative role of Islam (when interviewed in early 2015):

> The founders all come from the National Outlook. And their points of view have not changed. But of course, we could not control all the newcomers. They might or might not be from the National Outlook or Ak Party. Still, we make sure that they perform the daily prayers and are of good morals [*güzel ahlak sahibi*]. This is an organization that helps in the name of God. If an aid provider from our organization does not pray or becomes known by rompy [*haşarı*] behavior, then that would reflect badly on us. Some people will say that we need to separate private life and work: We should only pay attention to whether a provider accomplishes his tasks. But those who do the work of society [*toplumun işini yapanlar*] have no right to say that. We're not doing our own business. We're not doing trade. We are working with [God's] deposit [*emanet*]. We are working as [God's] deputies [*vekil*]. ... We have to factor that in when we are doing our work.

Whereas Vecdi mostly focused on attacking business *interests*, Hamdi was more interested in resisting the spread of business *ethics* within charitable work. Temporality mattered. My interviewees had rejected the label "Islamic organization" in 2011, but in 2014–2015 most underscored the IHH's Islamic roots and practices. This change was in line with Turkey's broader Islamic transformation (Tuğal 2016a).

Vehbi was exemplary of this new tendency, in that he perceived religiosity and charity as inseparable. When he was a child, his father's merchant friends gathered their money and opened a soup kitchen for students in their hometown. He maintained that his family was not an exception; civilian money always created miracles throughout Turkey. The reason for this was the deeply interwoven nature of humanitarian action, benevolence, and faith in the Islamic tradition, he held:

> You cannot separate benevolence from the rest of life. If you believe in Islam and you're trying to implement its requirements, then you have to do good works. You have to pray, you have to fast, but you also have to give *zakat* and *sadaqa*. If you are raised with this doctrine, you do not have a choice of staying away from benevolence. ... Having been raised in such a family, in my university life too I kept on doing the same things. I participated in youth movements. The Bosnian War erupted right around the time of my graduation. ... My college friends gathered and started to work on the crisis. ... You participate in this kind of activity only when you are already a part of a certain circle.

Vehbi's implicit denial of professional logic paralleled the anti-bureaucratic dispositions of communitarian actors. He underlined again and again that his actions did not result from what we would call rational-utilitarian action (benefit and cost calculation), but were rather imposed on him by his upbringing.

IHH's relationship to missionary (tebliğ) activity was quite nebulous. Some members completely denied that the organization carried out any tebliğ. But others, while denying that they were missionaries, described what we could characterize as *a kind of* missionary activity. Vehbi first counterposed their organization to Western organizations, which were explicitly missionary and helped people on the condition of conversion to Christianity. But he then affirmed that it was incumbent on *every* Muslim to spread his/her own religion:

> One of the things that a Muslim is required to do is to tell the truth ... because every Muslim knows that this world is temporary. We're here for a test [*imtihan*]. The real thing is our preparation for the other world. The Muslim cannot just help people to feed themselves and not tell them what they should do for the other world. ... We never put Qur'ans in our aid packages, but when the beneficiaries ask us, we tell them about Islam.

Christian missionaries allegedly made aid conditional on children's attendance to missionary schools; and gave out Bibles as a part of their packages. His organization, by contrast, presented good, practicing Muslim models to the public. "We don't have a separate tebliğ and *da'wa* [*davet*] department, but life is a totality. Everywhere we go, we are present with our identity." He also emphasized that this was neither an anti-Western nor an anti-Christian position, as they worked with churches to the extent that they were not missionaries. Vehbi also pointed out that it was not right to approach every Christian organization with this suspicion, since they knew by experience how such labeling could hurt benevolent activity (as Muslim organizations were frequently dubbed "terrorist" in the post-9/11 world).

"The Benevolence Race": The Recognition-Denial of Field Logic

As we have seen, Egyptian and Turkish neoliberal organizations were quite explicit about the field-like qualities of the charitable universe, while communitarians were more likely to deny it. IHH actors differed from both position-takings.

Vehbi was critical of some Muslim aid organizations because they claimed that associations could shoulder almost all of the burdens of welfare. However, his organization was very well aware that civic associations could only do certain things. Huge calamities, for example, required state response. Official aid agencies were (by nature) dependent, and therefore not able to carry out some of the necessary activist work that his organization could. But nevertheless, official agencies were *necessary* and *good*:

> [Some Muslim organizations] go to a country and build a good school. When you watch their [subsequent] videos, you would think they resolved the problem of education in that country! ... Giving hope is a good thing, but it is not right to create false impressions.

In other words, Vehbi differentiated between tasks and claimed that some could be performed only by the state and some only by civil society. In that way, he avoided market fundamentalism too.

Despite his criticisms, Vehbi believed that a mutual spirit of help shaped the relations between his organization and other Islamic associations. He denied that there was any competition, enmity, or rivalry involved. This rejection differentiated this particular organization from the other redistributive organizations in the Turkish field (in this sense, IHH resembled the Egyptian communitarian associations). Vehbi pointed out to a religious phrase which Islamic aid organizations frequently used: the benevolence race ["*Hayırda yarış etmek*"]. But he wanted to further clarify how this kind of competition was different from *market competition*. There was, indeed, a race, but it was completely different from competition between businesses and firms. The "benevolence race" did not entail, according to him, passing others in the amount of benevolence; rather, it had to do with maximizing one's own benevolence, but also being a means, a medium, a vehicle (*vesile*) for others' maximization of benevolence. He supported this interpretation with a Hadith:

> One who has been a means for benevolence gets the credit for that benevolence; it is as if s/he has done the benevolence ["*Bir hayra vesile olan, hayrı*

yapmış gibidir"]. Being a means for benevolence can involve telling somebody else about your idea of benevolence. When that person implements that idea, you will have become a means for benevolence. Or you can give your vehicle to a person. You might even give the whole project to that person, or just its name; or you might just begin the project and then hand it over. If you do any of this, you can expect God to give you credit for that benevolence, since our Prophet has promised so. This is how we interpret "race." It is very different from two merchants in competition, for those two have to block each other's paths instead of opening them, which is what we do.

But Vehbi also argued that they had a special edge in this race, since they combined what he called "advocacy" (in English original) and aid. Standard aid organizations were politically powerless when occupying militaries came around to destroy the good they had done (schools, hospitals, etc.). In a very different way, human rights organizations were also powerless, for even though they pointed out to the political misfortunes, they had no power and credibility on the ground. His organization, by contrast, was on the ground [*arazide*], knew the everyday problems, and had the trust of the locals behind it (due to its provision).

Vehbi also differentiated IHH from associations that depended on television programs and religious communities, but did so with a language much milder than the Companions Association. Just like the latter, he also underlined the need to warn politicians (though this was restricted to warnings regarding foreign policy). Since his organization did the most aid work in Syria, Egypt, and Palestine, it had "the duty" to convey their realities to Turkey's rulers. Such civic pressures indeed pushed the state to a more bellicose position in these countries (a process I have discussed in detail in a previous book, *The Fall of the Turkish Model*, 2016a). But unlike the Companions Association, this was not done with a spirit of opposition to the state. Rather, their duty was warning the rulers and exchanging recommendations. This, he accentuated, also differentiated the organization from those that took orders from leaders of religious communities. Such obedience to spiritual leaders, Vehbi said, opened the door to abuses (such as collecting benevolence money for a television program that promotes only community-connected aid organizations rather than collecting the money for the aid itself).

Activism Abroad, Explosion-Prevention at Home

Most of the IHH's middle-aged and older affiliates came from an Islamist past. Managers and staff were activists as much as NGO professionals. They spoke with a much more excited, agitated tone when compared with other charitable actors, though they did not skip technical information to solely display emotion: interviews with some were rich in technical, organizational, and statistical details regarding the IHH, as well as hunger and poverty throughout the world. They distinguished themselves from other organizations by their focus on Palestine, which they thought was an issue neglected in the field, even by organizations with an international orientation. They perceived charity as an extension of their past activism rather than a completely separate universe (a differentiated "field").

In terms of how poverty should be resolved, IHH activists again split their frameworks for global and national issues, just like they did in their explanation of why poverty exists. For aid work outside Turkey, the best method was combining provision with political mobilization; for Turkey, what they offered was responsibilization. Mehmet's story underscores the IHH's originality. Mehmet, now a top-level IHH administrator, was originally from a central Anatolian town. He held a PhD in the social sciences. His father and mother were workers. He had no one in his immediate family involved in benevolence (an exceptional quality in the aid world). He got involved in the organization first as a donor (at the end of the 1990s). He used to personally bring in his donations and those of his wife (a nurse), rather than mail them in. Mehmet worked as a reporter for a major Islamist newspaper throughout this period (the mid- to late 1990s); in the following few years, he published a local newspaper, geared towards local merchants. He then worked as a freelance translator. And in 2003, the organization invited him to take over its research and media projects. Mehmet pointed out that they operated in a different way when compared to the "standard Western aid organization":

> In the [West's] classical framework, the organization gives food, blanket, and *shelter* [he used the English original of the word]. ... But we add to this human rights activism. That is why we are criticized. The classical aid organization doesn't deliver aid when [a state] tells it not to. The IHH questions this: why shouldn't I? What is the legal justification preventing me from delivering aid to a particular location? The IHH's method of questioning this can be discussed. And it is being discussed. ... But in principle, we never separate humanitarian aid and human rights activism because this [separation] is the Western organizations' greatest handicap. They provide mechanically; they are never truly interested in why people suffer. They cannot offer sustainable political solutions. This is not the duty of aid organizations, it is said. They should just provide the medicine and then withdraw. But what is the reason of widespread sickness? Is it [weak] social policy? Is it military occupation? Is it something else? We ask these questions and then we write reports. And we criticize. ... Our third dimension is humanitarian diplomacy.

Mehmet appropriated the criterion of *sustainability* from neoliberal discourse, but redefined it as *political* sustainability: Charity would become a sustainable solution only when the root causes of misery were addressed.

Yet, the IHH developed a social-liberal framework for humanitarian work *within* Turkey. The organization used neoliberal techniques to differentiate the deserving from the undeserving poor. Only in Turkey, it deployed the whole gamut: the filling of forms and standardized checklists; the house visits; and fact checking with the neighbors and officials. Mehmet listed many structural reasons regarding the general causes behind poverty (such as wars, bad social policy, corruption, especially in Arab countries and pre-Ak Party Turkey), as well as conjunctural reasons (drought, floods). But when it came to (Ak Party-governed, Islamic) Turkey, he advanced a different explanation:

> There might be some chronic factors such as unemployment. But we need to separate two things: economic policy and social policy. The economic policies of a country might not be [egalitarian], but this can be balanced by social policy. Turkey is a good example of this. Around 10 million people are getting aid from the government. ... Unemployment is hovering around 13 percent at the moment, and that's because Turkey is still a developing country. ... Another reason is that Turkey is not rich in raw material. It needs to import [oil, natural gas, etc.] whenever it attempts big investments. ... No one has seen an economy develop overnight. As we see in the cases of America and Germany, this takes decades. As this happens, the economy is bound to create armies of the unemployed. And in the meantime, social policy will be the life vest. ... But at the societal level too [certain mechanisms alleviate poverty]. Families still take care of each other. People still give debt to each other. ... Even if the state slows down its aid, even if people start to live at the threshold of poverty, this will prevent social explosion in Turkey.

The IHH's more consistent use of monitoring techniques within Turkey made sense, given this geographically differentiated explanation of the reasons behind poverty.

IHH posed street mobilization as a central solution to international imbalances of wealth. Re-constituting experts, policymakers, and intellectuals was necessary but not sufficient. Vecdi, for example, got quite carried away as he started to speak about their protest activities:

> Yesterday, American senators sent a message to the Prime Ministry, asking Turkey to block [a Gaza-related protest activity that IHH was organizing]. ... States do not want to resolve these imbalances. ... It is not in the interests of states to change this [established, static] structure. This is where the peoples come into the picture. The Mavi Marmara incident [see below and Introduction] seriously upset the global balances. ... After the Cold War, the search for a new world order began. The peoples have no voice in this world order. *Mavi Marmara* changed [the game] by interrupting [*çomak soktu*] Israel's unilateral influence in the Middle East. ... After *Mavi Marmara* dynamited the world order, everybody started to think on their own accounts. This questioning initiated the Arab Spring: people decided that suffering what befell them [*başlarına gelene tahammül etmenin*] was not necessary. ... People started to believe that oppression is not fate.[6]

In his following sentences, Vecdi interpreted the Arab Spring not only as a rise against dictatorships, but against social injustice:

> Those dictatorships had to be overthrown. But the subsequent processes also need to be watched very carefully: [We need to] ensure that peoples of different belief in that region can coexist peacefully; and that the West does not re-establish the mechanisms of exploitation that existed during the old regimes.

Despite all of this protest against international inequality (and inequality within Arab countries), Vecdi denied that there was any serious inequality in Turkey. There seemed to be some in the Kurdish region, but the Kurdish organization PKK and the media exaggerated its extent. In fact, foreign intervention (and the foreigners' conspiratorial dealings with the PKK) caused Kurds' (apparently civilian) disruptive demonstrations. The IHH desired to politicize many issues throughout the world, but did not want to see the same politicization within Turkey.

After our interview was over, Vecdi expressed their support for the Prime Minister's position on the Egyptian and Tunisian uprisings, but discontent with his position on Syria. It was still early 2011 and Turkey had not thrown its full support behind the Syrian rebels. After the interview, almost the whole IHH staff departed to demonstrate in front of the Syrian Embassy in order to pressure the Turkish government. This pressure from below contributed to the change in Turkey's position in the long run, which again highlights *the world-making dimension of charity*: IHH was among the actors that led to the fall of Islamic liberalism (both in Turkey as a regime type, and in the larger Muslim world as a viable route, a model to follow).

Vecdi further emphasized that the only positive route for the Arab uprisings would be to model themselves after the current Turkish government: "We can show them the way. Davutoğlu has already had a role in nudging the demonstrations in the right direction. They call him Turkey's Kissinger." At this point, my liaison with the IHH (who had accompanied me to this interview) interrupted and said: "I wish you had not made that comparison." This student activist had a long involvement with Islamist mobilization despite his young age. His political circle was affiliated with the Companions Association, but he had also volunteered for the IHH many times. He was a trusted person in the neighborhood. Vecdi defended his comparison: "What I mean is the following: many administrations come and go, but Kissinger remains where he is. And he really defends America's interests and strengthens America." I kindly objected:

> The IHH has come here from a tradition of Islamic opposition. But it appears that now the Turkish state's interests are prioritized. Are these interests exactly in line with the international-balance-disturbing agenda you just

expressed? Would the Turkish state really benefit from a just redistribution of resources globally?

He responded swiftly, as if he expected this argument: "Some balances are well-established and it wouldn't be prudent to attack them immediately." I was quite suspicious of this answer (which implied that the IHH would get oppositional again), since there were many counter-signs, such as the rumor that the IHH's head director wanted to use his activism-based prestige to become a parliamentarian. My liaison, who also expressed (in private) his dismay at the association's decreasing autonomy from the regime, did not share my suspicion. "I trust Vecdi's good intentions despite the trends of the recent years," he told me after we left the building. The unfolding ramifications of the *Mavi Marmara* affair seemed to prove him right by the time of my re-visit in 2014–2015.

The Mavi Marmara *Incident*

The *Mavi Marmara* affair remains the IHH's most controversial action. The IHH purchased the ship *Mavi Marmara* in early 2010. In late May 2010, the ship participated in the eight ship-strong Freedom Flotilla, which attempted to break the Gaza blockade. Israeli soldiers attacked the flotilla in international waters. Nine activists were killed and several soldiers wounded. The exact circumstances of the clashes are still being investigated.

According to the Israeli side, the soldiers were attacked after they boarded the ship. According to the IHH's (2011) publication *Mavi Marmara: Gazze Özgürlük Filosu*, the soldiers started to fire as their helicopter descended, that is, before they boarded the ship. The IHH's eyewitnesses argued that at least one of the deceased was shot at close range after the soldiers made him lie on the ground.

The people on board had a broad mix of motivations. They also hailed from a wide range of backgrounds: Islamists fighting Zionism; social justice activists from many Western nations; human rights activists; Islamist politicians; leftist politicians from Europe; etc. (Kor 2011). Still, Turkish Islamists (more specifically, the IHH) constituted the leading force. There were a total of eight civilian ships in the flotilla; three of them belonged to the IHH (İHH 2011, p. 18). Out of this eight, the only passenger ship was the *Mavi Marmara*. There were close to 600 people on the ship, whereas the only other populous ship had 43 people on board. In that sense, *Mavi Marmara* was the center of the action.

Whatever the factual links between the Ak Party and this incident, the party and its leader made ample use of it. *Mavi Marmara*-focused IHH publications too reflect a quite positive attitude toward Erdoğan. In one compilation of interviews with Flotilla activists, several interviewees put the party leader in the center. Out of the only two politicians interviewed, the Palestinian Raid Salah thanked the Prime Minister for saving them from prison (his sentences of gratitude are singled out as one of the few highlighted aspects of the interview) (Kor 2011, pp. 26–27). In similar fashion, one sentence from a wounded activist constitutes the title of the interview with him ("We are proud of our Turkish brothers and of the Prime Minister of Turkey," Kor 2011, p. 223). The IHH did not publicly endorse all aspects of the Prime Minister's approach, but subtly painted him as the hero behind the scenes, up until 2014.

Mavi Marmara's Aftermath: The End of Islamic Liberalism

As I have explained elsewhere (Tuğal 2016a), a sea change washed away Islamic liberalism at the national scale following 2011. First gradually, then abruptly the Ak Party government stopped emphasizing individual liberties and increased its emphasis on conservative religion. It took major steps to Islamize education. The Prime Minister explained these changes as the fulfillment of popular will. The media started to use an anti-capitalist and anti-imperialist language to accuse critics of the government. The actors behind Turkey's most successful capitalist leap forward had rhetorically become anti-capitalists. In my other writings, I have traced these changes back to the contracting world markets, the overblown Turkish-Islamic imperial desires induced by the Arab uprisings, and the anti-government unrest at home (most prominently, the intensifying Kurdish civic insurgency). The IHH activists, however, offered another compelling account. Civil society and street politics (most centrally the IHH and the *Mavi Marmara* affair) had pushed the government in this direction.

Hulusi pinpointed the importance of the *Mavi Marmara* incident in terms of Turkey's foreign policy. As a result of the affair, Turkish-Israeli relations came to a standstill:

> These relations were established in the Cold War era under American control. They were never based on the will of the peoples [*halkların iradesi*]. ... Relations further developed in the 1990s after the [anti-Islamist military] coup. Turkish-Israeli relations reached their peak when Turkey's unhappy majority was under the highest duress. ... The Ak Party came to power by the votes of these dissatisfied people. These people were expecting certain things regarding Israel, Islamic covering, material needs, education, and civic rights. When Turkey was going through its most difficult financial times, the Israeli regime was reaping the benefits [*kaymağını yiyordu*] through special military deals. ... The Ak Party voters wanted these favors to stop. ... Turkey is offered to the region as a model and seen as the strongest candidate to implement Muslim democracy. And this "candidate" says yes to everything Israel wants! The Iraqis, Egyptians, Mauritanians, and Malaysians would wonder: "Turkey claims to be democratic, but it is not very democratic when it comes to America's and Israel's infringements on human rights." ... A country that claims to be a model for the Muslim world cannot be partners with Israel. So, Turkey made its choice; after the Gaza incident [Israel's

airstrikes in December 2008], its policy changed. Then came the Davos[7] and *Mavi Marmara* incidents. But the *Mavi Marmara* incident has nothing to do with state policy. We were planning the action before the Gaza attack. ... We were about to sign a contract to buy a ship the day before that attack. ... We had made the plan at a time when Turkish-Israeli relations were [quite good]. ... We had an anti-blockade land convoy in 2006. We factor in the state's preferences only as information. This shows that our humanitarian aid policy is independent of the state. We never decide policy based on the state's priorities. It is rather the reverse. The state follows us. We brought aid to Africa. We organized conferences on Africa. Then the state declared 2007 the year for Africa. ... So, when the *Mavi Marmara* incident occurred in 2010, the Ak Party had to claim it as its own, since its citizens were killed. Then this appeared like an Ak Party project, but this is far from the truth.[8]

This account, which puts the IHH at the center of Turkish history, might be overblown and not completely factual (for instance, there is still little public information regarding the exact role of governmental circles in organizing the Freedom Flotilla). But it expresses an (inter)subjective truth, which in turn shapes objective truth. The perception that the IHH and its fatal confrontation with Israel made the government change track was widely shared (if seriously contested). A good portion of the Turkish public clung to the IHH as their new hero. Up until 2010, the organization grew 10 to 15 percent annually. But after the flotilla incident, it started to grow 50–100 percent a year, due to a barrage of donations. Some key figures wanted to revert to a more manageable growth rate.[9] Regardless of this (as of yet unimplemented) management plan, the IHH's mind-boggling growth currently weighed on the government's foreign dealings in a precise way. The growth clearly signaled that the Islamic public supported an anti-liberal association, which put further pressure on the government to ratchet up Islamization to the detriment of liberalization.

The change was not unidirectional. The organization moved closer to the governing party (and away from autonomy). It is not crystal clear when the IHH switched from a pro-National Outlook to a pro-regime line. According to some eyewitness accounts, even during the farewell demonstration organized for the Freedom Flotilla, there were more Felicity Party[10] banners and flags than Ak Party symbols. However, some of my interviewees argued that people switched to a pro-regime position around 2006. According to Mehmet:

> If that change happened, it just reflects the overall change in society. The Felicity party gets less than 1 percent of the vote today. Then what happened to all the National Outlook people throughout Turkey? They're all in the Ak Party. The National Outlook did not evaporate. ... Things started to change when the Ak Party began to respond to people's material and social needs. ... The middle class expanded. ... Religious freedoms and the legal

framework of humanitarian aid were improved. We started to see the results of [Ak Party policies] after 2005/2006. During the first years, we didn't trust them, we thought everything was the same.

Hamdi echoed the account above (during an interview I conducted separately):

[IHH's shift from a pro-National Outlook to a pro-regime line] is the change of society itself. ... But we were never affiliated with either party. This is rather what our opponents argue. ... Why does it seem like we're affiliated? Because our policies might occasionally be parallel to those of the government. The Turkish state supports Syrian refugees, so should we avoid helping them just in order to save face? Why do the people who see these parallels ignore our occasionally negative relations with the government? ... We organized the *Mavi Marmara* despite all official opposition and still people can call it an Erdoğan project! This happens because society is extremely polarized and politicized. We don't like the tension being this high. ... They say the Ak Party organized the *Mavi Marmara*, but the party can't even internationally reinforce the court decisions regarding this incident. Why doesn't anybody mention this?

The rage against IHH critics was heartfelt, but skirted around many issues. Among some anti-government Islamists, the perception was that the IHH used to be an autonomous organization, but then became an appendage to the government. Interestingly enough, a few of these critics had been affiliated with the IHH in the past or at least worked as its volunteers. I insistently pointed out the situation to IHH activists until I could procure a more direct response. Hamdi's answer was the closest I could get:

We should still criticize [the government's mistakes]. But this should not be done through the media. When I see that a Muslim has made a mistake, first I have to tell him. If he doesn't correct it, then I do something. If counsel [*nasihat*] isn't enough, then I cut my trade relations with him. If even that does not work, I put an end to all relations.

Hamdi's response implicitly affirmed that they were in the same camp with the government (despite all of his lamentations about polarization) and would refrain from steps that would allow the other camp to hurt it. As the anti-liberal Islamist atmosphere in Turkey intensified, however, such caution was going to be cast aside.

The Redistributive Gaze Turns Inward

The increasing top-down Islamization in Turkey further emboldened the IHH. The association intensified its criticism of Israel, but also started to question the

Turkish government, even if only obliquely or semi-publicly. When Israeli security forces reportedly raided Al-Aqsa Mosque in November 2014, Turkish Islamists expected another heroic statement from Erdoğan. When that did not come, the IHH's head director Yıldırım seized the opportunity to attack the regime and its business class:

> They attacked your Qur'an. They attacked Al-Aqsa Mosque, which your Prophet has called the third sacred place. ... Are Israeli soldiers to blame? Muslims are the ones to blame. Those who live at their palaces; those who add money to their money; those who reside at villas and swim in their pools are to blame.[11]

Erdoğan, who had recently become the president, had built a huge presidential palace with more than 1,000 rooms. The secular press regularly criticized him for his lavishness, but the Islamist press defended the construction by pointing out that it projected Turkish strength. Vecdi's "Kissinger" comment above could lead one to think that the IHH would be at home with such a defense, but, apparently the honeymoon was over. Yıldırım did not stop at a criticism of the president either; by incriminating the actions more than the actor, his speech implied that wealth accumulation and luxurious lives diverted Muslims away from their real duties.

Despite recent signs of trouble, the IHH's criticisms were never this harsh.[12] Nevertheless, there were still limits to the IHH's criticism. In late 2014, Yıldırım gave a quite long interview to a publicly invisible, radical Islamist youth magazine,[13] where he attacked the government much more directly than in any of his former declarations. According to Yıldırım, the government was directly responsible for the derailing of the Arab Spring, civil war in Syria, and the coup in Egypt. The government had also allegedly spoiled all of the IHH's peaceful attempts in Syria[14] and elsewhere. Moreover, it had failed to exploit the legal possibilities regarding the massacre of IHH activists due to its cronies' trade relations with Israel. However, when *Zaman* (Gülen's newspaper) carried this interview to its front page,[15] Yıldırım made a U-turn and declared that he had been quoted out of context by the conspiratorial newspaper.[16] As Hamdi had pointed out to me in late 2014 (before *Zaman*'s journalistic "coup"), criticizing the government was okay, but criticism should never become public.

It is unpredictable whether this swerving will ultimately lead to a more consistent autonomous line. Even if it does, the implications for charity work are far from clear. For instance, the IHH members' positions regarding Kurdish poverty do not simply result from their problematic relationship with the regime. There is no reason to think that they will shed away "local neoliberalism" overnight as soon as they cut their links to the governing party (if they ever do). Yet, there is a (remote) possibility that their redistributive rebuke against the Islamic bourgeoisie will one day translate into more redistributive charitable practices.

Response to the Syrian Refugee Crisis: Bifurcation within a Neoliberal Organization

The analyses above handled the IHH's differentiation of its charitable orientations based on the analytical categories of "national," "international," "home," and "abroad." However, when I returned to the field in 2014, this categorization had become difficult to uphold. As a result of the civil war in Syria, millions of refugees had fled into Turkey.[17] Before 2013, Turkey had only a miniscule Arab population. Now, by contrast, Arab beneficiaries were no longer "abroad." Many Syrians were housed in shelters, but others lived on the streets and begged. The lines between these two populations were blurry, since the care in shelters was inadequate. Charitable associations walked into the picture to make up for the state's shortcomings.

One of the associations I covered in Chapter 6 followed the IHH model and bifurcated its charitable orientations. However, its bifurcation was not along the local versus international axis. Rather, it stuck to its neoliberal logic as far as Turkish and Kurdish citizens were concerned, but developed a communitarian logic for the Arab refugees. Bifurcation was now ethnicity- and (citizenship) status-based. In an unrecorded conversation, Ahmet, the Candle Association's director explained why (despite sticking to the neoliberal logic and activities I had observed a couple of years earlier) they had to nurture new orientations as regards the Syrians:

> As a foundation, we try to avoid helping people in a continuous manner. We don't want them to live off of us [*sırtımızdan yaşamalarını*]. ... But with the Syrians, it is different. We help them in a continuous way. We unconditionally give them everything, from sofas to carpets and beds. And our citizens are frequently ahead of us. For instance, we do the home visits, and determine what the refugees need. But once we're back with the necessary materials, we find out that our citizens have already helped them! ... When our citizens hear people who complain, they turn away and say, "This is a lazy person. She doesn't work and that is why she is poor." But when the same citizens see the Syrians, they completely change their direction [*180 derece dönüyor*].

Neoliberal help still shaped benevolence as long as it was a question of Turks and Kurds. However, orientations towards the Syrians were clearly communitarian.

But what was the logic behind the unconditional provision? Did it simply replicate, for example, the orientations of the Egyptian *muhtasibin*? That is, was Islamization expected in return for "unconditional" provision (see Chapter 4)? The director's further explication clarified that imperial concerns trumped da'wa concerns in this novel Turkish communitarianism:

> When they were back in their home country, these Syrians took lessons titled "Turkification in history." They have come to Turkey with many

prejudices. But here, they see that Turks are not preoccupied [with assimilation]. ... We organize *sohbets* in this neighborhood. We explain to them the compassion of the Ottomans. We tell them about the aid culture our ancestors have built. At the end, they say, "So what we have been taught is wrong."

As a response to these developments, Ahmet (who had a neoliberal discourse back in 2011) had developed a new language with anti-capitalist overtones and an explicit anti-Americanism. Along the lines of his neoliberal logic a couple of years ago, he still insisted that charity should make people hard-working. However, he asked me many questions about Christianity's understanding of poverty, and was eager to iterate that they were very different from Christian charities (not because, as the IHH members held, Christian good-doers were also missionaries, but because they were too harsh towards the poor). He criticized "Western capitalism" for allowing people to go hungry and thirsty (*insanları aç susuz bırakıyorlar*). "They are trying to eliminate beggars. They don't see them as human beings. This would never happen in Muslim societies." He asked me if this was due to Christianity. I explained that Protestantism (not Christianity as such) established some basis for this type of thinking, but did not go to the extreme of defending the biological elimination of the weakest. It was rather economic thinking that firmly established this perspective in the beginning of the nineteenth century, I wanted to argue. Ahmet repeated that such an (ideational) development would never occur in Muslim society; and *their* charity did not make people dependent anyway, so there was no need for such ("Protestant," he still insisted) extremes. In other words, their goal was to save people from (biological) "elimination." But once the poor were saved from the brink of the precipice, they and their relatives were responsible. Moreover, living on the streets was unacceptable in Muslim society. It was incumbent on society to prevent this. Even if millions of refugees came and such hospitality led to economic collapse, they could not be turned away.

Ahmet interpreted this generosity also as a preparation for the wars to come. The charitable activities (and the *sohbets* woven into them) were on their path to creating a new community, which would be strong enough to tackle the West:

Muslims are not able to wage war on America right now, due to military weakness. But there is a lot of accumulated anger. The Syrians here know that America is behind everything they suffered. America took weapons from Iraq and established ISIS. They did this together with China and Russia. The goal is encircling Turkey [*etrafını çevirmek*]. As we got stronger, they were disturbed. ... It is the first time since the Ottomans that we are truly national [*milli*]. ... The whole world saw our strength.

What was most surprising during my revisit of this association was its newfound belligerent anti-Americanism. The Candle Association was affiliated with an offshoot of the Naqshbandi order. Unlike another couple of such Naqshbandi offshoots, it did not become Islamist (and anti-American) well into the late 2000s. Its ideologues publicly wrote and spoke against Islamism in the 1990s. Their concern was quite conservative: the rise of Islamism disturbed social peace and pit believers against the state and the global order. This neo-Naqshbandi community (*cemaat*) occasionally supported center-right parties against Islamist ones due to these worries. The Ak Party's first success (in the early 2000s) was uniting this community, along with a few similar anti-Islamist "communities," under a single roof with the Islamists (see Chapter 3 and Tuğal 2016a). Many Islamists paid a price for this new coalition: they (temporarily) became center-rightists themselves. However, after the regime's Islamist turn in the 2010s, these previously anti-Islamist groups now became militants of a warmongering version of Islam (while one major actor who rejected to go down this path, the Gülen Community, got purged from the regime). In sum, the unintended result of a decade of neoliberalization turned out to be the instrumentalization of even charitable activities for a "war yet to come."[18]

The Candle Association's striking transformation suggests that more associations might follow (and revise) the IHH model in the coming years. These tendencies could intensify as the regime itself becomes much less liberal.

Different Field Logics

Tables 7.1, 7.2, and 7.3 summarize the findings of the two preceding chapters. Rather than re-iterate the information in each table, I will draw attention to how charitable fields in different political settings operate by mentally juxtaposing these tables with the three on Egypt (see Chapter 5).

First of all, these tables point out that the main axes of differentiation were different in the two countries. While solid neoliberalization ruled out religious mission in Egypt, the two could coexist and even thrive together in Turkey. It was thus necessary to include a new category of actors (neoliberal tebliğ associations) in the Turkish tables. Concomitantly, involvement in religious education, politics, and movements remained central to the formation of Turkish neoliberal actors (see Table 7.3, last row). Similarly, communitarianism was much more reflexive and anti-capitalist in the Turkish case (see Table 7.1). This reflexivity is reflected not only in the individual cells of the tables on Turkish associations, but also in the emergence of a new category of actors: redistributive associations.

Second, communitarian dispositions were more unevenly distributed within Turkey's organizations: many communitarian dispositions had seeped in through even the most neoliberal associations (see Table 7.1, row 3). This is a striking finding, given that these associations were strongly neoliberal in their overall approaches. Despite that, they had not excluded non-neoliberal techniques (as the Egyptian "professionalized neoliberal associations" did). The Turkish neoliberals

TABLE 7.1 Contrasting Dispositions of Turkish Charitable Actors

	Pious Neoliberal Associations	*Neoliberal Tebliğ Associations*	*Communitarian Associations*	*Redistributive Associations*
The Role of Islam	Motivation	Goal and motivation	Goal and motivation	Motivation
Religious Motivation/References/Vocabulary	Very little textual reference; individualistic	Textual	Textual	Textual and individualistic
Overall Goals and Motivation	Cultivation of the market subject; nationalist-imperial; secondarily: personal encounters with the poor; pragmatic (looking for a job)	Cultivation of the market subject; religious and nationalist; sustenance/ rebirth of lived community; pragmatic concerns present, but subordinated	Community without immense wealth differences; moral, virtuous community; balance; curbing the will to accumulate	Cultivation of self-reliant, self-confident, social struggle-prone citizens; overall just economic system; the politicization of giving
Modes of Distinction (of Managers, Staff, and Volunteers)	Reference to Islamic texts; "scientific"ness; criticisms of traditional Turkish culture; thrift; rejection of rebellion	Heavy reference to Islamic texts; being Muslims, leaders, and donors; thrift; rejection of rebellion	Heavy reference to Islamic texts and authorities; guidance by charismatic authority; rejection of rebellion	Focus on marginalized sectors; rejection of obedience; the language of political economy

were not necessarily less professionalized than their Egyptian counterparts; some of them were actually more rationalized (e.g. they used more elaborate recruitment techniques; and utilized science more systematically; see Table 7.2). Rather, they became more effective specifically through incorporating *some* elements of communitarianism.

Thanks to the incorporation of these elements, the neoliberal attack against communitarian charity had become more massive in Turkey. This clearly contrasted with the attack of Egyptian professionalized charitable actors, who had *massive funds, but no masses behind them*. This went hand-in-hand with the construction of a more hegemonic neoliberalism in the Turkish case (e.g. through restricted introduction of liberal welfare programs). Neoliberal Turks also recognized the beneficial aspects of such welfare (see Table 7.3, row 4), whereas neoliberal Egyptians tended to oppose any major state involvement.

The mental juxtaposition of these six tables demonstrates that a Gramscian-Bourdieusian field logic (rather than one of isomorphism) best captures the

TABLE 7.2 Turkish Organizational Structures and Logics

	Pious Neoliberal Associations	Neoliberal Tebliğ Associations	Communitarian Associations	Redistributive Associations
Main Activities	Provision of necessities and training	Tebliğ and provision of necessities and training	Tebliğ and provision of necessities	Provision of necessities; citizenship training; protest activity
Managers' Status in Organization	Career professionals	Professionals	Professionals	Volunteers; career professionals secondary
Staff's Status in Organization	Career professionals (elaborate recruitment techniques)	Employees	Employees	Volunteers; career professionals secondary
Funding Source	Businessmen; small contributions from people of diverse backgrounds (attracted through seminars; TV programs; campaigns)	Mostly internally generated; businessmen	Working and middle class families (attracted through networks; campaigns; secondarily, TV)	Small contributions from people of diverse backgrounds (through use of the media and demonstrations)
Political Activity	Denial of political activity; positivistic pressure on the state and universities	Islamizing pressure on the state	Denial of politics; but direct links to parties or sociopolitical movements	Highly politicized

uneven distribution of organizational techniques and ethics. The distribution of these techniques and ethics, as the preceding five chapters showed, depended on the structure of welfare states; the interactions of religio-political movements with states and charitable organizations; and the game of differentiation among charitable actors themselves. On the surface, the further strengthening of Turkish neoliberalism through an incorporation of communitarianism seems to lend support to Foucaultian-Deleuzian theses. However, Foucaultian approaches are ill-equipped to account for the emergence of a redistributive charity and the complications it introduces.

New institutionalist and Foucaultian arguments would be unable to grasp the emergent explosiveness of the situation and its structural bases. Neoliberal charity became more hegemonic in Turkey in the 2000s (than in Egypt at any point in time), but it owed this to the integration of heavier doses of communitarianism.

TABLE 7.3 Turkish Benevolent Actors' Backgrounds and Perspectives

	Pious Neoliberal Associations	*Neoliberal Tebliğ Associations*	*Communitarian Associations*	*Redistributive Associations*
Managers' Class	Professionals	Businessmen, small merchants	Professionals, small merchants	Businessmen; professionals
Staff's Class	Professionals	Professionals	Professionals	Poor, working class, and professionals
International Models	The United States; secondarily: historical Islamic states	Current and historical Islamic states	Current and historical Islamic states	Islamic history and European social democracy
Preferred Socio-economic Policy	Free market (with some "responsibilizing" state participation in welfare)	Free market	Heavy state role	Redistributive economy
Volunteers', Staff's, Managers' Former or Current Involvement in Other Civic Activities/Islamic Education	Heavy clerical education background; communities' radio stations and newspapers	Islamist movements and clerical education	Islamist movements; clerical education; imams	Islamist movement

Ultimately, however, the absorption of communitarianism not only disturbed the consistency of neoliberal charity, but precipitated the crisis of Islamic liberalism itself. This unexpected twist allows us to gauge the limits of new institutionalism and post-structuralism beyond the topic of charity.

Notes

1 Şevket's association was the aid branch of a wider sociopolitical organization under the spiritual leadership of their particular *Hoca*.
2 For a different kind of twist on responsibilization, see Ben Néfissa's (2004, pp. 240–241) discussion of an Egyptian communitarian organization, which attributes *individual* blame to the *charitable donor* who fails to help the poor.
3 Modernized offshoots of the traditional religious orders (*tarikat*) are called "community" (*cemaat*) in Turkish, even though this latter word has multiple and contested meanings.
4 See www.ihh.org.tr/calisma-ilkelerimiz.
5 See www.ihh.org.tr/13769/.
6 For a different reading of the *Mavi Marmara* affair, see Tuğal (2012b).
7 Hulusi is referring to Erdoğan's protest during a debate in Davos. See "Recep Erdoğan storms out of Davos after clash with Israeli president over Gaza," *The Guardian*, January 30, 2009.
8 When I brought up the Islamist criticism of Turkish policy (one of my communitarian interviewees had pointed out that Turkey still has massive trade with Israel), Hulusi

defended the government: Turkey had little diplomatic relations with Israel, and no financial links at the governmental level. The massive trade was completely private (he skipped the fact that most of the trading companies were connected to the government).

9. We could also see, in this context, how redistributive actors frequently switched to non-redistributive discourses. Hamdi said: "We are now growing because of social polarization. This is not something we want. We want to get everybody's support. We want to be mediators rather than polarizers." This was a quite interesting self-denial, given that the polarization they brought about had hastened the end of Islamic liberalism.

10. The Felicity Party is affiliated with the National Outlook.

11. www.internethaber.com/ihhden-hukumete-israil-elestirisi-737399h.htm?interstitial=true.

12. In December 2013, Yıldırım had presented *Mavi Marmara* as an exclusively National Outlook project, endorsed and perhaps even initiated by Erbakan, the National Outlook's deceased leader. Davutoğlu, by contrast, had allegedly attempted to prevent *Mavi Marmara* from sailing to Gaza. "İHH Genel Başkanı Bülent Yıldırım: İsrail özür diledi, hocaefendi de dilesin," December 28, 2013, http://t24.com.tr/haber/ihh-genel-baskani-bulent-yildirim-israil-ozur-diledi-hocaefendi-de-dilesin,247117.

13. "Bülent Yıldırım İle İslam Coğrafyasındaki Son Durumu Konuştuk," www.genconculer.com, December 22, 2014.

14. Secularist and leftist media have argued that the IHH was active in carrying weaponry to jihadi groups, which were fighting against the Syrian regime. These allegations might be baseless, or alternatively the IHH might be trying to wash its hands clean by implying that the government used the IHH as a cover in its pro-jihadi maneuvers.

15. "İHH Başkanı Bülent Yıldırım'dan çarpıcı tespitler; Türkiye, Suriye ve Mısır'da nasıl hata yaptı?" *Zaman.com.tr*, January 24, 2015.

16. "Bülent Yıldırım'dan Zaman'a sert cevap," *Sabah.com.tr*, January 25, 2015.

17. Turkey hosted more than 2.5 million Syrian refugees in 2016, but it was able to officially shelter only 200,000. "Pictures of life for Turkey's 2.5 million Syrian refugees," *The Independent*, April 5, 2016. www.independent.co.uk/news/world/europe/pictures-of-life-for-turkeys-25-million-syrian-refugees-crisis-migrant-a6969551.html.

18. The phrase belongs to Bou Akar (2012), who has analyzed Hezbollah's social activities along the same lines.

CONCLUSION

Combined and Uneven Liberalization

What do the preceding analyses tell us about the nature of modernity? This book has explored modernity through the lens of ethical liberalization. The four quite distinct clusters of benevolence in Turkey and Egypt, and the divergent logics of their differentiation in each country, problematize standardization accounts. Still, the preceding chapters also demonstrate that the main trend in the world of generosity was the further entrenchment of ethical liberalization. Even though we can document many instances of uniqueness throughout Egyptian and Turkish benevolent organizations, these develop partially in response to liberalization, rather than automatically reflecting historical legacies or agentic creativity on the spot. In that sense, the four worlds of giving in each country do not testify to completely distinct routes, but rather positions within integrated fields. With the neoliberalization of one last social realm (religious generosity) that had resisted individualization for centuries, the liberal revolution indeed becomes the unifying arc of human history. Analyses of modernity that draw attention to multiple paths, alternative routes, and unique experiences reach their limits. However, there are still acts, practices, ethical conducts, and organizations that not only limit liberalization, but can potentially pave the way for an entirely new ethical conduct. How can we make sense of this apparent convergence and its limits?

Modernity as Convergence: New Institutionalist Accounts

In sociology, new institutionalism provides the most coherent theoretical statement regarding modernity. New institutionalism is a phenomenologically-based synthesis of the major sociological classics (Weber, Durkheim, and de Tocqueville, though not Marx). Powell and DiMaggio (1991) provide a detailed account of the micro-sociological basis of contemporary sociology's re-evaluation of

Weber's meta-processes (bureaucratization, rationalization) and its flexible, post-Parsonsian re-marriage with the Durkheimian analysis of ritual, myth, and ceremony. The analyses in the preceding chapters engaged a similar theoretical terrain, as I tried to uncover how practical, "noncalculative" (or perhaps, semi-calculative) everyday activity (Powell and DiMaggio 1991, p. 24) resulted, over the decades, in a semblance of institutional order in fields of benevolence. While full of pathbreaking insights, which have resulted in a productive research agenda for nonprofit organizations, new institutionalism walks through similar fields without a "left foot" (as it has excluded Marx from its meta-theoretical synthesis), leading it to downplay some major tendencies and possibilities. Even though Powell and DiMaggio have called for a more thorough integration of analyses of power[1] and change into new institutionalism as early as 1991 (p. 27), some of the recent work cited throughout this book and in this chapter demonstrate that new institutionalism's basic assumptions have remained constants. Through a deeper engagement with Bourdieu (whom DiMaggio also frequently integrates), and an overall Gramscian and political economic framework, I have called for adding the missing left foot to the analysis of nonprofits. This Gramscian-Bourdieusian dialogue with new institutionalism also has profound implications for our theorization of modern society.

As early as the first foundational essays of new institutionalism, the goal has been to shift the emphasis of organizational studies from diversity and competition to homogenization (DiMaggio and Powell 1983, p. 148; Meyer and Rowan 1977, pp. 345–346 and *passim*). The core argument of new institutionalism is that organizations adopt certain structures not due to their proved efficiency, but in order to survive and be recognized; therefore, they adapt structures that are not necessarily the most efficient, but the most accepted (in order to prove their legitimacy). They thereby reproduce the primary "myths" in circulation (such as rationality and bureaucratic organization) (Meyer and Rowan 1977, p. 349). Even though this book shares the sociological assumption that myth trumps efficiency as a guide for action, it breaks with new institutionalism by exploring which myths become predominant and why (which we cannot understand without studying political struggles at national and global levels).[2]

In our study of Egypt and Turkey, we have seen that some of the more basic processes hypothesized by new institutionalism do not work as they are supposed to. DiMaggio and Powell (1983, pp. 155–156) have argued that ambiguous goals and technologies (both of a single organization and of the field as a whole) lead to isomorphism because, as a response to indeterminacy, organizations seek to legitimate themselves through imitating what they perceive to be legitimate. Entrants to such fields also seek to avoid liabilities (associated with their newness) through imitating successful models. Contrary to these predictions, the extreme ambiguity of the Egyptian benevolence field has led to little isomorphism. Ambiguities regarding relation to Islam were at the heart of this field (due to security, legal, and political reasons). Yet, the actors did not rush to legitimate themselves solely through mimesis (even though this was *one* of the strategies adopted by *some* of the actors).

More striking was how the Turkish IHH was able to break pressures of "coercive" isomorphism (and even re-craft these pressures) despite the Turkish Islamic-neoliberal regime's high degree of monopolization of resources. DiMaggio and Powell (1983, p. 155) assert that the higher degree of resource centralization in a field (which goes hand in hand with the central government's transactions with the field), the more organizations become dependent on the government (and thus obedient to the rules it sets down). We have seen how the IHH was able to turn the tables on Islamic neoliberalism. It acquired the power to do so from its deep roots in the Islamist movement, its creation of a dedicated cadre of Islamists, and its ongoing activism.

Such (mechanism-specific) limits of new institutionalism have already become clear after Chapter 1's theoretical discussion and the empirical demonstrations of the ethnographic chapters. What further interests us in this chapter is the broader understanding of society that results from these micro-foundations, which is most succinctly expressed by new institutionalism's inheritor, the world society approach. The world society approach expects modern (nation) states, (rationalized) associations, and (autonomous) individuals to become more similar over time (Strang and Meyer 1993, p. 501). New institutionalists occasionally recognize that contradictory ceremonies and myths are often available to organizations, which might adopt some of these in far from consistent fashion (Meyer and Rowan 1977, pp. 355–356). *However, they insist that organizations resolve such "inconsistencies" in ways that further produce isomorphisms.* While new institutionalist admit that organizations can "decouple" formal structure and activities—which would lead to *homogenization of formal structures but diversity in actual practices* (Meyer and Rowan 1977, p. 357)—this book has revealed how *even formal structures can be highly differentiated* (as demonstrated by the four worlds of giving in both the Egyptian and Turkish fields of benevolence).

New institutionalism's broad brushstrokes regarding modernity lead to a deficient understanding of human action too. Strang and Meyer (1993, p. 501) argue that societies are now organized as nations rather than primordial groups; and that individuals throughout the globe adopt notions of "moral worth" from "world centers." By posing "national" and "primordial" organization as binary opposites, the world society approach ignores that the degree to which a nation-state is (or is not) based on primordial belongings is a stake in the struggles. Similarly, struggles of how to define and measure moral worth are ongoing rather than finalized, not only at the national, but also at associational and individual/informal-interactional levels, as I have shown throughout the book. In other words, modernity evolves through selectively adapting traditions.

These struggles clearly put their stamp on charity. Rather than converging on a given (rational, individualist, etc.) model, the charitable field is still marked by struggle. Some techniques might be more likely to "diffuse" during certain eras, but not throughout the totality of modernity. Due to sidelining questions of political economy and social struggle, new institutionalist and world society approaches are unable to specify what distinguishes one such era from another. For example, even in the West, *liberal/neoliberal charity was/is much more likely to diffuse in the 1870s and then the 1980s–2000s, but much less so from the 1930s to the 1960s*. Broad generalizations regarding welfare and charity are doomed to fail, as they neglect economic, ideological, and political contexts.

If one theoretical basis for new institutionalism's sidelining of politics is phenomenology, the other is its particular Tocquevillianism. The Tocquevillian emphasis in new institutionalism leads to the exaggeration of the degree to which people associate "freely." Drawing parallels between de Tocqueville's America of the 1830s and today's globe, Meyer et al. (1997, p. 145) argue that "the *operation of world society through peculiarly cultural and associational processes* depends heavily on *its statelessness* [which diminishes] *the causal importance of the organized hierarchies of power and interests*" (emphases mine). The analysis of ethical conduct in the preceding chapters, by contrast, has demonstrated how politics shapes, channels, restricts, enables, and empowers "free association" (see Riley 2005 along similar lines).

There is a broad literature (based on a contrasting, pessimistic reading of Tocqueville) that expresses an institutionalist worry regarding the rationalization and bureaucratization of charity and nonprofit activity (Hwang and Powell 2009; Putnam 2000; Skocpol 1999). But this literature too fails to raise the basic Habermasian (1985) question: under what conditions does rationalization morph into reification? From the standpoint of ethical conduct, the question becomes: When does the rationalization of charity become "rationalization as neoliberalization"?

New institutionalists define rationalization in a broad way that does not distinguish between rationalization tout court and rationalization as expansion of the business logic. These two are considered the same (Hwang and Powell 2009, p. 272). The importation of strategic planning, financial audits, and quantitative program evaluations from the business world are indeed significant processes (and new institutionalism's contribution to scholarship is the fine, detailed description of this colonization). However, this importation does not result in rationalization pure and simple. New institutionalists deny the "causal importance of the organized hierarchies of power and interests," but in between the lines of their analyses, we find ample proof of the hierarchical organization of even knowledge, in a way that brings charitable actors in line with business interests (Hwang and Powell 2009, p. 275):

> There are two distinctive cognitive bases of professional expertise: one based on training in and command of a particular, substantive disciplinary area, and the other based on expertise in general management knowledge. The calling card of the latter is the view that organizations, in the abstract, are similar … Indeed, for decades the hallmark of the most visible center of management education, the Harvard Business School, has been its training of general

managers. ... The skills of managerial professionals are not tied to the rise and fall of particular substantive areas but to the broader pursuit of organizational rationality.

To paraphrase, this is how the logical steps in the argument unfold: The single way to become a good expert is through combining disciplinary training with general knowledge. The only valid general knowledge is the knowledge of business management, as taught by the Harvard Business School. What you learn through disciplinary training is volatile and could become useless at any moment. But management knowledge is eternal because it is rational.

This identification of business mentality with rationalization, as Hwang and Powell's sentences give away, assumes a hierarchical organization of universities and departments that puts the most business-oriented ones at the top.

On occasion, new institutionalist analysis comes to the border of recognizing business domination, but shies away from conceptualizing it (Hwang and Powell 2009, p. 291):

> As one [charity] director [in the San Francisco Bay Area] put it, "Why does everyone equate professionalism only with business practices?" ... [W]hen nonprofits are "constructed as organizations," with the incorporation of rationalized practices, the managerialization of substantive professionals may also ensue. Particularly in the current climate, in which everyone equates professionalism only with business practices, nonprofit leaders of all stripes may have to employ more managerial means.

This analysis provides a good beginning for further theorization: What is the "current climate"? Is the current climate the end point of modernity, or (as a Polanyian would predict) could counter-movements overturn it (thereby annulling the definition of rationalization the literature takes for granted)?

Modernity as a Combined, Contingent, and Contested Construct

I have argued against "convergence" models above; now it is time to question their nemesis, the "singularity" models. More widespread in the humanities than the social sciences, scholarship that draws attention to unique and alternative practices provides rich descriptions of diverse, generalization-challenging ethical conduct. Nevertheless, this attention to uniqueness frequently amounts to wishing away centuries of interconnected ethical development.

Capital has appropriated sharing, giving, and caring. It is not that people do not truly care in unique ways, but due to the intellectual and material domination by the business classes, their acts of caring are transformed into capital accumulation (either through the bifurcation of the working class, or through the creation of the right neoliberal subjects, or cultural consolidation of rising bourgeoisies). This has happened on a massive scale in nineteenth-century US and Britain; and is now happening (through what is known as the Islamic awakening) in another part of the world.

We should certainly recognize that community is not *essentially* opposed to capital. Everything from solidaristic forms of economy to the cases studied in this book would militate against such simplistic binaries. But the point is, ethics of caring gives us a *possible* way of thinking about how we could organize alternative ways of exchanging goods and services. The question, then, is: How to set the logic of caring and giving free from the logic of capital? Might the redistributive charities covered in this book show the way?

Although a communitarian form of gift-giving existed for centuries in the Muslim world, the smooth reproduction of this form is now impossible. Even the IHH's redistributive communitarianism can be converted into cash (or worse, imperial power). Yes, the IHH is not neoliberal in any straightforward way; but it can (and to an extent has) become an extension of capitalism. This oppositional organization provides a good demonstration of how Islamic giving can become an appendage to the rule of capital if it does not metamorphose into a thoroughly redistributive form of sharing. As the discussions at the end of Chapter 7 show, another possible non-liberal metamorphosis is in a thoroughly authoritarian-communitarian and imperialist direction. This might potentially put us on an even more disastrous path.

Rather than resulting in an Islamic exception or uniqueness, communitarian charity might undermine liberalism by producing a twenty-first-century version of interwar authoritarian-communitarianisms. Polanyi (2001, pp. 231–256) had pointed out that the nineteenth–twentieth century crises of liberalism produced Keynesianism ("embedded liberalism"), Stalinism, and right-wing authoritarianism. As a result of a world war, the first two triumphed, (temporarily) eradicating the last option. For complex reasons I cannot cover in this book, twenty-first-century versions of the first two options seem quite unlikely, whereas postmodern variants of right-wing authoritarianism are sprouting up everywhere from the United States and France to Muslim-majority societies. We are indeed witnessing Polanyi's "double movement" again, but this time the anti-market swing of his pendulum lacks centrist and left-wing components: Society's self-protection is challenging deep liberalization, as Polanyians have predicted, but the only strong counter-liberal voices emerge on the far right. Due to these broader balances, it is likely that as liberal charity runs up against serious limits, previously communitarian and neoliberal charitable actors will contribute to authoritarian resolutions to the intensifying crises. As Chapter 7 pointed out, the creative refashioning of a previously neoliberal charitable association (the Candle Association) suggests that this is a real possibility. In sum, the IHH and similar organizations (and their charitable practices) might become the primary makers of a post-liberal world. This would not be the first time that new charitable ethics ushered in a new era.

Building Unpredictable Equivalences

Uniqueness accounts are unable to face a simple reality: "postcolonial" (in our case, Islamic) challenges to the West closely resemble either liberalism or Western right-wing challenges to it. Postcolonial scholars (Chakrabarty 2000) argue that Marxists are in the "analytical" mode and they reduce every process to the development of capital; we should also have a "hermeneutics," they point out. In other words, we should focus on "incommensurable" meanings in each locality. The remodeling of pious charity (and what could be more culturally singular and exceptional?) after the image of capital raises the vexing question: what do we do now, when the self-understanding of Muslims (even their giving to others) is evolving in a liberal direction?

In his debate with Chibber (a Marxist sociologist),[3] the prominent historian Partha Chatterjee brings in his (and other postcolonial scholars') decades-long study of peasant consciousness to concede that peasants do have a notion of private property and "interest." At that level, they are not essentially different from people elsewhere. But whenever protest breaks out, whenever demands are politicized, this happens not along the lines of "interest," but religious and ethnic identities. Their political demands are not equivalent to those of Western laboring classes. We should therefore support struggles based on non-Eurocentric categories, especially given that most of the Global South still consists of peasants.

Chibber (2012) has attacked this argument by insisting that capital is universal. It divides and rules through ethnicity, so the lack of equivalence (which Chatterjee emphasizes) is compatible with capitalism (production for profit). Since capital is universal, effective struggles against it also develop based on universal categories: interests, basic needs, and "well-being" (pp. 202–206). Culture has an influence on these, but does not determine them completely.

The *combined and contested* development of charitable ethics in secular, Christian, and Islamic contexts shows that we can think much more strategically and world-historically than this dichotomy (between Marxist universalism and postcolonial particularism) would allow.[4] It is true that the richness of the struggles against capitalism cannot be reduced to basic needs, neither in the West nor in the Global South. We have to be more imaginative and comprehensive when thinking about alternatives to and struggles against capitalism.[5] The ethics of giving, as it has developed in Christian and Muslim contexts, is *potentially* one node of organizing the world in non-capitalist ways. While traditional Marxist lenses would miss that potential, post-colonial lenses would underemphasize the capitalist pressures on the ethics of giving.

The early agenda of post-colonial theory was more relevant to our questions: it not only realized, but emphasized that *non-modern anti-capitalisms would never be able to match the advantages of capitalism*. In his early work, Chatterjee (1993) himself had pointed out that only a new universality, which not denied but built itself on "particulars," could challenge capitalism. Indeed, *Caring for the Poor* builds on post-colonialists' fundamental insight that we cannot treat traces of other cultures in today's capitalism as remnants of "less developed" "stages" of human existence (Chakrabarty 2000, pp. 12, 31–32). However, the more heterogeneous new universality that the early Chatterjee called for can happen only if we actively and reflexively build *equivalences*, rather than suspect all attempts at equivalence (in orthodox Foucaultian fashion) as totalitarian and universalist dreams.

It is within a *combined and variegated history in the making*[6] that we should seek interstitial emergence of sustainable, programmatic alternatives to the rule of capital and liberal ethics. These alternatives can draw on non-Western, non-modern, non-utilitarian, etc. modes of action and thinking; but, as Chatterjee pointed out in his early work, cannot remain restricted to them if they are to avoid defeat, marginalization, or absorption.

In this book, I formulated the discussion not in terms of the history of capital, but that of liberal ethics, *which is highly entangled with (though not identical to) capitalist development*. Liberal ethics has similarly developed in combined and uneven fashion for several centuries. Muslims are ever more intensely participating in the making and contestation of these ethics. Both their adaptation of and struggle against liberal (charitable) ethics draws on unique (or better yet, "distinct") resources and legacies, but on Western ones as well. The communitarian ethics that they occasionally draw on is not a simple "remnant" of a backward "stage," but a complex formation that Muslims, Christians, and others have built over millennia. Some Islamic contestation remains local, but others become a part of world history, presaging that even the now-local adaptations and contestations might become world-historical makers and unmakers of liberalism. In this sense, some of the charitable ethics and organizations they develop are not alternatives *to* modernity, but *within* modernity.

The search for irreducible singularities has led some other scholars to the discovery/invention of "alternative" modernities, where there are none. A scholarship that especially flourished in the 1990s and 2000s invested overblown hopes in non-Western modes of modernity (Göle 2000; White 2002), neglecting that much of Islamic modernity was made in interwoven fashion, through heavy borrowing from conservative and other Western sources. Even though the scholarship on alternative modernity has already peaked and is now in decline, academics still evoke quite modern practices and organizations as "alternatives" (e.g. see Mittermaier 2014a). The development of Islamic charitable modernity is no exception to these overall trends. Özbek (2002) has criticized alternative and "multiple" modernities frameworks by pointing out that the nineteenth-century Ottoman organization of welfare shows too many parallels to Western, Russian, and Japanese welfare during the same century, even though the residues of past Islamic-Ottoman centuries are also visible in its practices and classifications.

Similarly, I have sought to demonstrate that Islamic generosity is a participant in the making of a variegated, contested modernity, rather than simply a passive victim of convergence or an alternative. Pre-modern Islamic practices and scripts have certainly shaped these transformations and some of them are still with us (such as the vestiges of the endowment system), but even Islamic challenges against liberal welfare are (unevenly) structured by Western anti-liberalism.

The struggles of the IHH and the Companions Association are good examples here. They build on many local sources, but also selectively use global (organizational, tactical, and discursive) "templates." These, however, do not simply come "from" the West. The IHH mobilizes the West for its Islamic struggle. The travel is not unidirectional: the IHH succesfully manipulates Western activists and politicians for its not-so-Western project. Its struggle can neither be reduced analytically to a human rights/basic needs agenda nor to a non-modern, essentially Islamic, or peasant-like ethical and religious struggle that avoids equivalance. The IHH builds equivalances in the most unexpected and unpredictable ways. Diffusion (convergence) and uniqueness accounts cloud the significance of what this organization is doing: the IHH neither simply diffuses modernity nor builds an Islamic alternative; it rather contributes to a global process of right-wing polarization (an emergent melding of imperialism, communitarianism, and capitalism) through creatively appropriating neoliberal and redistributive templates and scripts.

In sum, scholars suspicious of Western-based universalism have pointed out that many corners of the world have also experienced centralization of power, capital accumulation, and rationalization over the last two millennia (Salvatore 2016). Building my account on this scholarship, I point out that Islamic charity has been one of the makers of *all three processes*. Still, for the first time in history, these three processes congealed in the West to culminate in modernity as such (the centralized state, liberal ethics, capitalism, and predominantly instrumental rationality). The first coherent alternative to this formation developed also in the West: Socialism[7]—even if it shared much of its rival's premises, and proved unviable in its nineteenth-century and twentieth-century incarnations—has provided the (as of yet) most comprehensive challenge against modern society. In Islamic history, we witness not only proto-modern formations, but their internal criticisms too (Salvatore 2016), which justifies the claim that Islam "pre-announces" both modernity[8] and socialism. Nevertheless, it was only through engagement with the West that systematic forms of Islamic liberalism crystallized. So far, Islamic movements, frequently seen as one of the great challenges against modernity, have not gone much beyond reproducing (and further modernizing) liberal modernity and/or communitarian responses to it. Communitarianism too has roots in both Christian and Islamic traditions, and has culminated in modern solidarism in the twentieth century, rather than a non-modern or postmodern formation. While Muslims' further engagement with liberalism and communitarianism might indeed take us somewhere beyond both neoliberalism and the solidarisms it replaced, the concrete signs of such dynamics are weak for now.

Ethical-Moral Reform: Revisiting Gramsci in the Light of (Western) Welfare Debates

This study of Islamic charitable ethics has implications for the West as well. Neoconservatives got one thing right. Leaving welfare responsibilities solely on the shoulders of the state could corrupt the poor. From another angle, however, we can say that this is corruption not in the sense of becoming dependent on handouts, but rather of losing the capacity, spirit, and desire for self-organization.

What we need is in fact moral reform, as the neoconservatives emphasized. However, contemporary moral reform seeks to create liberal subjects. The only viable shield against this crusade is not the denial of the role of culture or morality in the reproduction of poverty (and its logical consequence, the resuscitation of the pre-neoliberal, morally blind welfare state); but the self-organization and the bottom-up ethical reform of the poor through a collectivistic spirit.

We can re-think Engels's apparently empty praise of the Salvation Army (discussed in Chapter 3 and Tuğal 2016b) through this perspective as well. Perhaps Engels was not entirely wrong in seeing a potential of class struggle in the practices of this organization. The kernel of his mistake was assuming that these ethical practices could spontaneously develop in that direction. In other words, Engels neglected bourgeois hegemony: how the bottom-up energies of the poor (and clergy and moral reformers who were not necessarily committed liberal capitalists) end up only reinforcing bourgeois domination (sometimes despite their best intentions). It is only through the activities of a leading sociopolitical organization that potentially anti-capitalist practices can become and/or remain anti-capitalist.

A new benevolent path, therefore, would seek to discover charitable ethics and practices that would enhance the self-organization of the poor (even if the original donors are rich and some of the volunteers are from the propertied classes). The next step would be linking these activities and ethics to broader social visions and projects, a bridging which only political work can sustain. Perhaps then, charity could cease to be the heart of a heartless world, and instead contribute to the making of affectionate social formations.

Notes

1 Even if not as centrally recognized as the works of DiMaggio, Powell, Meyer, Rowan, and Scott, there is some scholarship in the new institutionalist tradition that grants a central role to politics in the reconciliation of contradictory institutional practices and constructions (e.g. Friedland and Alford 1991).
2 For an example of how new institutionalism neglects world-historical context, see one of its foundational statements (Meyer and Rowan 1977, p. 350), which *assumes* the inevitability of Keynesian health regulation in workplaces. Such neglect renders new institutionalism's broad generalizations out of date as soon as those arrangements change.
3 The debate took place in New York in 2013. www.youtube.com/watch?v=xbM8HJrxSJ4.

4 For similar takes on NGOs, see Fassin's (2012, pp. xi–xii) call to study humanitarianism as a "global and yet uneven force" and Challand's (2009) "connection" approach.
5 For some initial steps in this direction, see Wright (2010) and Cihan Tuğal, "Those Who Want to Build, Those Who Want to Fight: The World Social Forum with a North African Twist," www.jadaliyya.com, April 4, 2015.
6 Even though Chakrabarty (2000, pp. 9–12) insists that all "uneven development" accounts are necessarily dismissive of the reality of God(s) and spirits, *Caring for the Poor* demonstrates that retaining *a structured, but non-historicist, unified understanding of world history* does not require us to treat engagement with religion, spirits, gods, magic etc. as anachronistic.
7 I take socialism not to denote state-led development, but a social formation based principally (though not exclusively) on collectivistic production and consumption, autonomous self-organization, and communicative rationality. That this formation, even in its most sophisticated practical and theoretical varieties, failed to develop an ethics/subjectivity that went beyond liberalism was one of the reasons for its unsustainability.
8 I would like to thank an anonymous Routledge reviewer for this wording.

REFERENCES

Abdelrahman, Maha. 2004. *Civil Society Exposed: The Politics of NGOs in Egypt.* Cairo: The American University in Cairo Press.
Allahyari, Rebecca A. 2000. *Visions of Charity: Volunteer Workers and Moral Community.* Berkeley: University of California Press.
Allen, Lori. 2013. *The Rise and Fall of Human Rights: Cynicism and Politics in Occupied Palestine.* Stanford, CA: Stanford University Press.
Amenta, Edwin. 1998. *Bold Relief: Institutional Politics and the Origins of Modern American Social Policy.* Princeton, NJ: Princeton University Press.
Ammerman, Nancy Tatom. 2005. *Pillars of Faith: American Congregations and Their Partners.* Berkeley: University of California Press.
Arrighi, Giovanni. 2007. *Adam Smith in Beijing: Lineages of the Twenty-First Century.* London: Verso.
Asad, Talal. 1993. *Genealogies of Religion: Discipline and Reasons of Power in Christianity and Islam.* Baltimore, MD: Johns Hopkins University Press.
Asad, Talal. 2003. *Formations of the Secular: Christianity, Islam, Modernity.* Stanford, CA: Stanford University Press.
Atasoy, Yıldız. 2009. *Islam's Marriage with Neoliberalism: State Transformation in Turkey.* New York: Palgrave Macmillan.
Atia, Mona. 2013. *Building a House in Heaven: Pious Neoliberalism and Islamic Charity in Egypt.* Minneapolis: University of Minnesota Press.
Ayubi, Nazih. 1994. *Overstating the Arab State: Politics and Society in the Middle East.* London and New York: I. B. Tauris.
Baker, Raymond W. 1991. "Afraid for Islam: Egypt's Muslim Centrists between Pharaohs and Fundamentalists." *Daedalus* 120/3: 41–68.
Banks, Erik. 1997. "The Social Capital of Self-Help Mutual Aid Groups." *Social Policy* 28/1: 30–39.
Bano, Masooda. 2008. "Dangerous Correlations: Aid's Impact on NGOs' Performance and Ability to Mobilize Members in Pakistan." *World Development* 36/11: 2297–2313.

Barker, David C. and Christopher Jan Carman. 2000. "The Spirit of Capitalism? Religious Doctrine, Values, and Economic Attitude Constructs." *Political Behavior* 22/1: 1–27.
Barnett, Michael and Janice Gross Stein (eds). 2012. *Sacred Aid: Faith and Humanitarianism*. Oxford: Oxford University Press.
Baron, Beth. 2014. *The Orphan Scandal: Christian Missionaries and the Rise of the Muslim Brotherhood*. Stanford, CA: Stanford University Press.
Barthes, Roland. 1957. *Mythologies*. Paris: Editions du Seuil.
Bartkowski, John and Helen Regis. 2003. *Faith, Hope, and Charitable Choice: Religion and Poverty Relief in the Rural South*. New York: New York University Press.
Bashear, Suliman. 1993. "On the Origins and Development of the Meaning of Zakat in Early Islam." *Arabica* XL: 84–113.
Bayat, Asef. 1997. *Street Politics: Poor People's Movements in Iran*. New York: Columbia University Press.
Bayat, Asef. 2002. "Activism and Social Development in the Middle East." *International Journal of Middle East Studies* 34/1: 1–28.
Baylouny, Anne Marie. 2010. *Privatizing Welfare in the Middle East: Kin Mutual Aid Associations in Jordan and Lebanon*. Bloomington: Indiana University Press.
Bean, Lydia. 2014. "Compassionate Conservatives? Evangelicals, Economic Conservatism, and National Identity." *Journal for the Scientific Study of Religion* 53/1: 164–186
Bellah, Robert N. 1991 [1970]. *Beyond Belief: Essays on Religion in a Post-Traditional World*. Berkeley: University of California Press.
Bellah, Robert N., Richard Madsen, William M. Sullivan, Ann Swidler, and Steven M. Tipton. 1985. *Habits of the Heart: Individualism and Commitment in American Life*. Berkeley: University of California Press.
Ben Néfissa, Sarah. 2004. "Citoyenneté Morale en Égypte: Une Association entre État et Frères Musulmans." In *ONG et Gouvernance Dans le Monde Arabe*, edited by Sarah Ben Néfissa. 213–270. Paris: Karthala.
Bendix, Reinhard. 1974 [1956]. *Work and Authority in Industry: Ideologies of Management in the Course of Industrialization*. Berkeley: University of California Press.
Bielefeld, Wolfgang and William Suhs Cleveland. 2013. "Faith-Based Organizations as Service Providers and Their Relationship to Government." *Nonprofit and Voluntary Sector Quarterly* 42/3: 468–494.
Block, Fred and Margaret Somers. 2003. "In the Shadow of Speenhamland: Social Policy and the Old Poor Law." *Politics & Society* 31/2: 283–323.
Bonner, Michael. 1996. "Definitions of Poverty and the Rise of the Muslim Urban Poor." *Journal of the Royal Asiatic Society, Third Series* 6/3: 335–344.
Bonner, Michael. 2001. "The Kitab al-kasb Attributed to al-Shaybani: Poverty, Surplus, and the Circulation of Wealth." *Journal of the American Oriental Society* 121/3: 410–427.
Bonner, Michael. 2003. "Poverty and Charity in the Rise of Islam." In *Poverty and Charity in Middle Eastern Contexts*, edited by Michael Bonner, Mine Ener, and Amy Singer. 13–30. Albany, NY: State University of New York Press.
Bonner, Michael. 2005. "Poverty and Economics in the Qur'an." *The Journal of Interdisciplinary History* 35/3: 391–406.
Bornstein, Erica. 2012. *Disquieting Gifts: Humanitarianism in New Delhi*. Stanford, CA: Stanford University Press.
Botchway, Karl. 2001. "Paradox of Empowerment: Reflections on a Case Study from Northern Ghana." *World Development* 29/1: 135–153
Bou Akar, Hiba. 2012. "Contesting Beirut's Frontiers." *City and Society* 24/2: 150–172.

Bourdieu, Pierre. 1990 [1980]. *The Logic of Practice*. Stanford, CA: Stanford University Press.
Bourdieu, Pierre. 1991 [1971]. "Genesis and Structure of the Religious Field." *Comparative Social Research* 13: 1–44.
Bourdieu, Pierre. 1994 [1991]. "Rethinking the State: Genesis and Structure of the Bureaucratic Field." *Sociological Theory* 12/1: 1–18.
Bourdieu, Pierre. 1998. *Practical Reason: On the Theory of Action*. Stanford, CA: Stanford University Press.
Bourdieu, Pierre. 2000 [1997]. *Pascalian Meditations*. Stanford, CA: Stanford University Press.
Bourdieu, Pierre. 2014 [2012]. *On the State: Lectures at the Collège de France, 1989–2012*. Cambridge: Polity.
Boyer, Paul S. 1978. *Urban Masses and Moral Order in America, 1820–1920*. Cambridge, MA: Harvard University Press.
Brand, Peter. 2007. "Green Subjection: The Politics of Neoliberal Urban Environmental Management." *International Journal of Urban and Regional Research* 31/3: 616–632.
Brenner, Neil, Jamie Peck, and Nik Theodore. 2010. "Variegated Neoliberalization: Geographies, Modalities, Pathways." *Global Networks* 10/2: 182–222.
Brown, Peter. 1997 [1996]. *The Rise of Western Christendom: Triumphant and Diversity, A.D. 200–1000*. Malden, MA: Blackwell Publishers.
Brown, Peter. 2012. *Through the Eye of a Needle: Wealth, the Fall of Rome, and the Making of Christianity in the West, 350–550 AD*. Princeton, NJ: Princeton University Press.
Brown, Kevin. M., Susan Kenny, Bryan S. Turner, and John K. Prince. 2000. *Rhetorics of Welfare, Uncertainty, Choice and Voluntary Associations*. Basingstoke: Macmillan.
Brown, Wendy. 2003. "Neo-Liberalism and the End of Liberal Democracy." *Theory and Event* 7/1.
Brown, Wendy. 2015. *Undoing the Demos. Neoliberalism's Stealth Revolution*. New York: Zone Books.
Buğra, Ayşe. 2008. *Kapitalizm, Yoksulluk ve Türkiye'de Sosyal Politika*. Istanbul: İletişim.
Buğra, Ayşe, and Aysen Candas. 2011. "Change and Continuity under an Eclectic Social Security Regime: The Case of Turkey." *Middle Eastern Studies* 47/3: 515–528.
Buğra, Ayşe and Çağlar Keyder. 2006. "The Turkish Welfare Regime in Transformation." *Journal of European Social Policy* 16/3: 211–228.
Çakır, Ruşen. 1990. *Ayet ve Slogan: Türkiye'de İslami Oluşumlar*. Istanbul: Metis.
Campbell, John L. 1998. "Institutional Analysis and the Role of Ideas in Political Economy." *Theory and Society* 27/3: 377–409.
Campbell, John L. and Ove Kaj Pedersen (eds). 2001. *The Rise of Neoliberalism and Institutional Analysis*. Princeton, NJ: Princeton University Press.
Carré, Olivier and Gérard Michaud. 1983. *Les Frères Musulmans: Égypte et Syrie (1928–1982)*. Paris: Gallimard.
Chakrabarty, Dipesh. 2000. *Provincializing Europe: Postcolonial Thought and Historical Difference*. Princeton, NJ: Princeton University Press.
Challand, Benoit. 2009. *Palestinian Civil Society: Foreign Donors and the Power to Promote and Exclude*. London: Routledge.
Chatterjee, Partha. 1993 [1986]. *Nationalist Thought and the Colonial World: A Derivative Discourse?* Minneapolis: University of Minnesota Press.
Chaves, Mark. 1999. "Religious Congregations and Welfare Reform: Who Will Take Advantage of 'Charitable Choice'?" *American Sociological Review* 64/6: 836–846.

Chaves, Mark. 2004. *Congregations in America*. Cambridge, MA: Harvard University Press.
Chaves, Mark and Bob Wineburg. 2010. "Did the Faith-Based Initiative Change Congregations?" *Nonprofit and Voluntary Sector Quarterly* 39/2: 343–355.
Chibber, Vivek. 2012. *Postcolonial Theory and the Specter of Capital*. London: Verso.
Çizakça, Murat. 1995. "Cash Waqfs of Bursa, 1555–1823." *Journal of the Social & Economic History of the Orient* 38/3: 313–354.
Çizakça, Murat. 2000. *A History of Philanthropic Foundations: The Islamic World from the Seventh Century to the Present*. Istanbul: Bogaziçi University Press.
Clark, Janine A. 2004. *Islam, Charity, and Activism: Middle-Class Networks and Social Welfare in Egypt, Jordan, and Yemen*. Bloomington: Indiana University Press.
Clastres, Pierre. 1987 [1974]. *Society Against the State: Essays in Political Anthropology*. New York: Zone Books.
Cnaan, Ram A. 2002. *The Invisible Caring Hand: American Congregations and the Provision of Welfare*. New York: New York University Press.
Cohen, Jean L., and Andrew Arato. 1992. *Civil Society and Political Theory*. Cambridge, MA: MIT Press.
Cole, Juan. 2003. "Al-Tahtawi on Poverty and Welfare." In *Poverty and Charity in Middle Eastern Contexts*, edited by Michael Bonner, Mine Ener, and Amy Singer. 223–238. Albany, NY: State University of New York Press.
Comaroff, Jean and John L. Comaroff. 2001. "Millenial Capitalism: First Thoughts on a Second Coming." In *Millennial Capitalism and the Culture of Neoliberalism*, edited by Jean Comaroff and John L. Comaroff. 1–56. Durham, NC: Duke University Press.
Cook, Michael. 2000. *Commanding Right and Forbidding Wrong in Islamic Thought*. Cambridge: Cambridge University Press.
Cornwall, Andrea and Karen Brock. 2005. "What Do Buzzwords Do for Development Policy? A Critical Look at 'Participation', 'Empowerment' and 'Poverty Reduction'." *Third World Quarterly* 26/7: 1043–1060.
Davis, Nancy J. and Robert V. Robertson. 1999. "Their Brothers' Keepers? Orthodox Religionists, Modernists and Economic Justice in Europe." *American Journal of Sociology* 104/6: 1631–1665.
Davis, Nancy J. and Robert V. Robertson. 2012. *Claiming Society for God: Religious Movements and Social Welfare in Egypt, Israel, Italy, and the United States*. Bloomington: Indiana University Press.
de Leon, Cedric, Manali Desai, and Cihan Tuğal. 2015. *Building Blocs: How Parties Organize Society*. Stanford, CA: Stanford University Press.
Deleuze, Gilles and Felix Guattari. 1987 [1980]. *A Thousand Plateaus: Capitalism and Schizophrenia*. Minneapolis: University of Minnesota Press.
Dezalay, Yves and Bryant G. Garth. 2002. *Internationalization of Palace Wars: Lawyers, Economists, and the Contest to Transform Latin American States*. Chicago, IL: University of Chicago Press.
DiMaggio, Paul J. 1991. "Constructing an Organizational Field as a Professional Project: US Art Museums, 1920–1940." In *The New Institutionalism in Organizational Analysis*, edited by Walter W. Powell and Paul J. DiMaggio. 267–292. Chicago, IL: University of Chicago Press.
DiMaggio, Paul J. and Walter W. Powell. 1983. "The Iron Cage Revisited: Institutional Isomorphism and Collective Rationality in Organizational Fields." *American Sociological Review* 48/2: 147–160.

Ebaugh, Helen Rose, Janet Saltzman Chafetz, and Paula F. Pipes. 2006. "The Influence of Evangelicalism on Government Funding of Faith-Based Social Service Organizations." *Review of Religious Research* 47/4: 380–392.

Eckstein, Susan. 2001. "Community as Gift-Giving: Collective Roots of Volunteerism." *American Sociological Review* 66/6: 829–851.

Eikenberry, A. M. and J. D. Kluver. 2004. "The Marketisation of the Nonprofit Sector: Civil Society at Risk?" *Public Administration Review* 64/2: 132–140.

Elisha, Omri. 2008. "Moral Ambitions of Grace: The Paradox of Compassion and Accountability in Evangelical Faith-Based Activism." *Cultural Anthropology* 23/1: 154–189.

Ellison. Christopher G. 1992. "Are Religious People Nice People? Evidence from the National Survey of Black Americans." *Social Forces* 71: 411–430.

Emerson, Michael O. and Christian Smith. 2000. *Divided by Faith: Evangelical Religion and the Problem of Race in America*. New York: Oxford University Press.

Ener, Mine. 2003. *Managing Egypt's Poor and the Politics of Benevolence, 1800–1952*. Princeton, NJ: Princeton University Press.

Engels, Friedrich. 1926 [1850]. *The Peasant War in Germany*. New York: International Publishers.

Escobar, Arturo. 1995. *Encountering Development: The Making and Unmaking of the Third World*. Princeton, NJ: Princeton University Press.

Esping-Andersen, Gøsta. 1990. *The Three Worlds of Welfare Capitalism*. Princeton, NJ: Princeton University Press.

Etzioni, Amitai. 1993. *The Spirit of Community: Rights, Responsibilities, and the Communitarian Agenda*. New York: Crown Publishers.

Fassin, Didier. 2012 [2010]. *Humanitarian Reason: A Moral History of the Present*. Berkeley: University of California Press.

Feher, Michel. 2009 [2007]. "Self-Appreciation; or, The Aspirations of Human Capital." *Public Culture* 21/1: 21–41.

Ferguson, James. 2015. *Give a Man a Fish: Reflections on the New Politics of Distribution*. Durham, NC: Duke University Press.

Finlayson, Geoffrey. 1994. *Citizen, State and Social Welfare in Britain 1830–1990*. Oxford: Oxford University Press.

Flanagan, Constance, Jennifer M. Bowes, Britta Jonsson, Beno Csapo, and Elena Sheblanova. 1998. "Ties that Bind: Correlates of Adolescents' Civic Commitments in Seven Countries." *Journal of Social Issues* 54/3: 457–475.

Fligstein, Neil. 2008. "Fields, Power, and Social Skill: A Critical Analysis of the New Institutionalisms." *International Public Management Review* 9/1: 227–253.

Fogelman, Eva. 1997. "What Motivates the Rescuers?" In *Resisters, Rescuers, and Refugees*, edited by John J. Michalczyk. 147–154. Kansas City, MO: Sheed & Ward.

Foster, Benjamin R. 1970. "Agoranomos and Muhtasib." *Journal of the Economic and Social History of the Orient* 13/2: 128–144.

Foucault, Michel. 1977 [1975]. *Discipline and Punish: the Birth of the Prison*. London: Penguin.

Foucault, Michel. 1990 [1984]. *The History of Sexuality Volume 3: The Care of the Self*. London: Penguin.

Foucault, Michel. 1992 [1984]. *The History of Sexuality Volume 2: The Use of Pleasure*. London: Penguin.

Foucault, Michel. 2008 [1978–1979]. *The Birth of Biopolitics: Lectures at the Collège de France, 1978–1979*. New York: Palgrave MacMillan.

Fourcade, Marion and Sarah Babb. 2002. "The Rebirth of the Liberal Creed: Paths to Neoliberalism in Four Countries." *American Journal of Sociology* 108/9: 533–579.

Friedland, Roger and Robert R. Alford. 1991. "Bringing Society Back in: Symbols, Practices, and Institutional Contradictions." In *The New Institutionalism in Organizational Analysis*, edited by Walter W. Powell and Paul J. DiMaggio. 232–263. Chicago, IL: University of Chicago Press.

Fries, Christopher J. 2008. "Governing the Health of the Hybrid Self: Integrative Medicine, Neoliberalism, and the Shifting Biopolitics of Subjectivity." *Health Sociology Review* 17/4: 353–367.

Galaskiewicz, Joseph. 1985. "Professional Networks and the Institutionalization of a Single Mind Set." *American Sociological Review* 50/5: 639–658.

Galaskiewicz, Joseph and Wolfgang Bielefeld. 1998. *Nonprofit Organisations in an Age of Uncertainty: A Study of Organizational Change*. New York: Aldine De Gruyter.

Geremek, Bronislaw. 1994. *Poverty: A History*. Oxford: Blackwell Publishers.

Ghaanim, Ibraahimal-Bayyuumi. 2010. *Maqasid al-'amal al-Khayri wa al-Usul al-Islamiyya lil-Musharaka al-Ijtima'iyya*. Cairo: Shorouk.

Göçmen, İpek. 2010. *The Politics of Religiously Motivated Welfare Provision*. PhD Thesis. Köln: IMPRS-SPCE.

Göle, Nilüfer. 2000. "Snapshots of Islamic Modernities." *Daedalus* 129/1: 91–117.

Gotein, Shelomo D. 1957. "The Rise of the Near-Eastern Bourgeoisie in Early Islamic Times." *Cahiers d'Histoire Mondiale* 3/3: 583–604.

Gregory, C. A. 1980. "Gifts to Men and Gifts to God: Gift Exchange and Capital Accumulation in Contemporary Papua." *Man* 15: 626–652.

Habermas, Jürgen. 1985 [1981]. *The Theory of Communicative Action, Vol. 2: Lifeworld and System: A Critique of Functionalist Reason*. Boston, MA: Beacon Press.

Haenni, Patrick. 2005. *L'islam de Marché: L'autre Révolution Conservatrice*. Paris: Seuil.

Hart, Stephen. 1992. *What Does the Lord Require? How American Christians Think about Economic Justice*. New York: Oxford University Press.

Harvey, David. 2005. *A Brief History of Neoliberalism*. Oxford: Oxford University Press.

Himmelfarb, Gertrude. 1985. *The Idea of Poverty: England in the Early Industrial Age*. London: Faber & Faber.

Himmelfarb, Gertrude. 1991. *Poverty and Compassion: The Moral Imagination of the Late Victorians*. New York: Knopf.

Hobsbawm, Eric. 1978. "The Forward March of Labour Halted?" *Marxism Today* 22/9: 279–286.

Hoge, Dean R. and Fenggang Yang. 1994. "Determinants of Religious Giving in American Denominations: Data from Two Nationwide Surveys." *Review of Religious Research* 36/2: 123–148.

Hwang, Hokyu and Walter W. Powell. 2009. "The Rationalization of Charity: The Influences of Professionalism in the Nonprofit Sector." *Administrative Science Quarterly* 54/2: 268–298.

Ibrahim, Barbara L. 2008. "Introduction: Arab Philanthropy in Transition." In *From Charity to Social Change*, edited by Barbara L. Ibrahim and Dina H. Sherif. 1–21. Cairo: American University in Cairo Press.

Ibrahim, Mohammed A. 2004. "The Political Economy of Poverty in Egypt (1975–2000): A Sociological Perspective." *Islam and Christian-Muslim Relations* 15/4: 469–495.

İHH Araştırma Yayınlar Birimi. 2011. *Mavi Marmara: Gazze Özgürlük Filosu*. Istanbul: İHH Kitap.

James, Wendy and N. J. Allen (eds). 1998. *Marcel Mauss, A Centenary Tribute*. New York and Oxford: Berghahn Books.

Kandil, Amani. 1998. "The Nonprofit Sector in Egypt." In *The Nonprofit Sector in the Developing World: A Comparative Analysis*, edited by Helmut K. Anheier and Lester M. Salamon. 122–157. Manchester: Manchester University Press.

Kandil, Hazem. 2012. *Soldiers, Spies, and Statesmen: Egypt's Road to Revolt*. London: Verso.

Kidd, Alan. 2002. "Civil Society or the State?: Recent Approaches to the History of Voluntary Welfare." *Journal of Historical Sociology* 15/3: 328–342.

Kienle, Eberhard. 1998. "More Than a Response to Islamism: The Political Deliberalization of Egypt in the 1990s." *Middle East Journal* 52/2: 219–235.

Kochuyt, Thierry. 2009. "God, Gifts and Poor People: On Charity in Islam." *Social Compass* 56/1: 98–116.

Kor, Zahide Tuba. 2011. *Witnesses of the Freedom Flotilla: Interviews with Passengers*. Istanbul: IHH Kitap.

Kühl, Stefan. 2009. "Capacity Development as the Model for Development Aid Organizations." *Development and Change* 40/3: 551–557.

Kuran, Timur. 2001. "The Provision of Public Goods under Islamic Law: Origins, Impact, and Limitations of the Waqf System." *Law and Society Review* 35/4: 841–897.

Kuran, Timur. 2004. *Islam and Mammon: The Economic Predicaments of Islamism*. Princeton, NJ: Princeton University Press.

Kuran, Timur. 2005. "The Absence of the Corporation in Islamic Law: Origins and Persistence." *The American Journal of Comparative Law* 53/4: 785–834.

Kyrtatas, Dimitris. 1987. *The Social Structure of the Early Christian Communities*. London: Verso.

Laidlaw, James. 2000. "A Free Gift Makes No Friends." *The Journal of the Royal Anthropological Institute* 6/4: 617–634.

Laniado, Avshalom. 2009. "The Early Byzantine State and the Christian Ideal of Voluntary Poverty." In *Charity and Giving in Monotheistic Religions*, edited by Miriam Frenkel and Yaacov Lev. 15–43. Berlin: Walter de Gruyter.

Lev, Yaacov. 2007. "The Ethics and Practice of Islamic Medieval Charity." *History Compass* 5/2: 603–618.

Lev, Yaacov. 2009. "Charity and Gift Giving in Medieval Islam." In *Charity and Giving in Monotheistic Religions*, edited by Miriam Frenkel and Yaacov Lev. 235–264. Berlin: Walter de Gruyter.

Li, Tanya M. 2007. *The Will to Improve: Governmentality, Development, and the Practice of Politics*. Durham, NC: Duke University Press.

Lie, M. and S. Baines. 2007. "Making Sense of Organisational Change: Voices of Older Volunteers." *Voluntas* 18/3: 225–240.

Lim, Chaeyoon and Carol A. MacGregor. 2012. "Religion and Volunteering in Context: Disentangling the Contextual Effects of Religion on Voluntary Behavior." *American Sociological Review* 77/5: 747–779.

Locke, John. 1956 [1689]. *The Second Treatise of Government*. Oxford: Blackwell.

MacIntyre, Alasdair C. 1981. *After Virtue: A Study in Moral Theory*. London: Duckworth.

McNay, Lois. 2009. "Self as Enterprise: Dilemmas of Control and Resistance in Foucault's The Birth of Biopolitics." *Theory, Culture & Society* 26/6: 55–77.

McRoberts, Omar M. 2003. *Streets of Glory: Church and Community in a Black Urban Neighborhood*. Chicago, IL: University of Chicago Press.

Mahmood, Saba. 2005. *Politics of Piety: The Islamic Revival and the Feminist Subject*. Princeton, NJ: Princeton University Press.

Makaye, Alicia Ann. 2012. *African-American Congregations and Charitable Choice: The Factors that Drive Willingness to Collaborate with the Federal Government.* Doctoral dissertation. Dallas: The University of Texas at Dallas.

Mandaville, Jon E. 1979. "Usurious Piety: The Cash Waqf Controversy in the Ottoman Empire." *International Journal of Middle East Studies* 10/3: 289–308.

Mann, Michael. 1986. *The Sources of Social Power.* New York: Cambridge University Press.

Marchetti, Sarin. 2011. "James, Nietzsche and Foucault on Ethics and the Self." *Foucault Studies* 11: 126–155.

Massicard, Elise. 2013. *The Alevis in Turkey and Europe: Identity and Managing Territorial Diversity.* London: Routledge.

Mattson, Ingrid. 2003. "Status-Based Definitions of Need in Early Islamic Zakat and Maintenance Laws." In *Poverty and Charity in Middle Eastern Contexts*, edited by Michael Bonner, Mine Ener, and Amy Singer. 31–51. Albany, NY: State University of New York Press.

Matza, Tomas. 2009. "Moscow's Echo: Technologies of the Self, Publics, and Politics on the Russian Talk Show." *Cultural Anthropology* 24/3: 489–522.

Mauss, Marcel. 1990 [1923–1924]. *The Gift: the Form and Reason for Exchange in Archaic Societies.* New York: W.W. Norton.

Meyer, John W. 2000. "Globalization: Sources and Effects on National States and Societies." *International Sociology* 15/2: 233–248.

Meyer, John W. and Brian Rowan. 1977. "Institutionalized Organizations: Formal Structure as Myth and Ceremony." *American Journal of Sociology* 83/2: 340–363.

Meyer, John W., John Boli, George M. Thomas, and Francisco O. Ramirez. 1997. "World Society and the Nation-State." *American Journal of Sociology* 103/1: 144–181.

Miller, Peter and Nikolas Rose. 2008. *Governing the Present: Administering Economic, Social and Personal Life.* Cambridge: Polity Press.

Mittermaier, Amira. 2014a. "Beyond Compassion: Islamic Voluntarism in Egypt." *American Ethnologist* 41/3: 518–531.

Mittermaier, Amira. 2014b. "Bread, Freedom, Social Justice: The Egyptian Uprising and a Sufi Khidma." *Cultural Anthropology* 29/1: 54–79.

Mock, Alan K. 1992. "Congregational Religious Styles and Orientations to Society: Exploring Our Linear Assumptions." *Review of Religious Research* 34/1: 20–33.

Mollat, Michel. 1986 [1978]. *The Poor in the Middle Ages: An Essay in Social History.* New Haven, CT: Yale University Press.

Moody, Michael. 2008. "'Building a Culture': The Construction and Evolution of Venture Philanthropy as a New Organizational Field." *Nonprofit and Voluntary Sector Quarterly* 37/2: 324–352.

Muehlebach, Andrea Karin. 2012. *The Moral Neoliberal: Welfare and Citizenship in Italy.* Chicago, IL: University of Chicago Press.

Murnighan, J. Keith, Jae WookKim, and A. Richard Metzger. 1993. "The Volunteer Dilemma." *Administrative Science Quarterly* 38/4: 515–539.

Ong, Aihwa. 2006a. "Mutations in Citizenship." *Theory, Culture and Society* 23/2–3: 499–505.

Ong, Aihwa. 2006b. *Neoliberalism as Exception: Mutations in Citizenship and Sovereignty.* Durham, NC: Duke University Press.

Orloff, Ann S. 1993. *The Politics of Pensions: A Comparative Analysis of Britain, Canada, and the United States, 1880–1940.* Madison: University of Wisconsin Press.

Othman, M. Z. H. 1983. "Origins of the Institution of Waqf." *Hamdard Islamicus* 6/2: 3–23.
Owens, Michael Leo. 2006. "Which Congregations Will Take Advantage of Charitable Choice? Explaining the Pursuit of Public Funding by Congregations." *Social Science* 87/1: 55–75.
Özbek, Nadir. 2002. *Osmanlı İmparatorluğu'nda Sosyal Devlet: Siyaset, İktidar ve Meşruiyet (1876–1914)*. Istanbul: İletişim.
Özbek, Nadir. 2006. *Cumhuriyet Türkiye'sinde Sosyal Güvenlik ve Sosyal Politikalar*. Istanbul: Tarih Vakfı.
Parry, Jonathan. 1986. "The Gift, the Indian Gift and the 'Indian Gift'." *Man* 21/3: 453–473.
Patlagean, Evelyn. 1997 [1992]. "The Poor." In *The Byzantines*, edited by Guglielmo Cavallo. 15–42. Chicago, IL: University of Chicago Press.
Peck, Jamie. 2010. *Constructions of Neoliberal Reason*. Oxford: Oxford University Press.
Petersen, Marie Juul. 2011. *For Humanity or for the Umma? Ideologies of Aid in Transnational Muslim NGOs*. PhD Thesis. Copenhagen: University of Copenhagen.
Petersen, Marie Juul. 2012. "Trajectories of Transnational Muslim NGOs." *Development in Practice* 22/5–6: 763–778.
Phoenix, Ann. 2004. "Neoliberalism and Masculinity: Racialization and the Contradictions of Schooling for 11-to 14-Year-Olds." *Youth & Society* 36/2: 227–244.
Pipes, Paula F. and Helen Rose Ebaugh. 2002. "Faith-Based Coalitions, Social Services and Government Funding." *Sociology of Religion* 63: 49–68.
Polanyi, Karl. 2001 [1944]. *The Great Transformation*. Boston, MA: Beacon Press.
Powell, Walter W. and Paul J. DiMaggio (eds). 1991. *The New Institutionalism in Organizational Analysis*. Chicago, IL: University of Chicago Press.
Pullan, Brian. 1994. *Poverty and Charity: Europe, Italy, Venice, 1400–1700*. Aldershot: Variorum.
Pullan, Brian. 2005. "Catholics, Protestants, and the Poor in Early Modern Europe." *Journal of Interdisciplinary History* 35/3: 441–456.
Putnam, Robert D. 2000. *Bowling Alone: The Collapse and Revival of American Community*. New York: Simon & Schuster.
Putnam, Robert D. and David E. Campbell. 2010. *American Grace: How Religion Divides and Unites Us*. New York: Simon & Schuster.
Pyle, R. 1993. "Faith and Commitment to the Poor: Theological Orientation and Support for Government Assistance Measures." *Sociology of Religion* 54/4: 385–401.
Qaradawi, Yusuf. 1967. *Mushkilat al-faqr wa-kayfa 'alajaha al-Islam*. Beirut: Dar al-'Arabiyya.
Qaradawi, Yusuf. 1981. *Economic Security in Islam*. Lahore: Kazi Publications.
Qaradawi, Yusuf. 1995. *Dawr al-qiyam wa-al-akhlaq fi al-iqtisad al-Islami*. Cairo: Maktabat Wahbah.
Qutb, Sayyid. 1975. *Al-'adala al-Ijtima'iyya fi al-Islam*. Beirut and Cairo: Dar al-Shurouk.
Rabie, Hassanein. 1972. *The Financial System of Egypt A.H. 564–741 A.D. 1169–1341*. London: Oxford University Press.
Raheja, Gloria Goodwin. 1988. *The Poison in the Gift: Ritual, Prestation, and the Dominant Caste in a North Indian Village*. Chicago, IL: University of Chicago Press.
Richards, Alan and John Waterbury. 2007. *A Political Economy of the Middle East*. Boulder, CO: Westview Press.
Riley, Dylan. 2005. "Civic Associations and Authoritarian Regimes in Interwar Europe: Italy and Spain in Comparative Perspective." *American Sociological Review* 70/2: 288–310.

Rose, Nikolas. 1999. *Powers of Freedom: Reframing Political Thought*. Cambridge: Cambridge University Press.

Rosenthal, Saul, Candice Feiring, and Michael Lewis. 1998. "Political Volunteering from Late Adolescence to Young Adulthood: Patterns and Predictions." *Journal of Social Issues* 54/3: 471–493.

Roy, Ananya. 2010. *Poverty Capital: Micro-Finance and the Making of Development*. New York: Routledge.

Rudnyckyj, Daromir. 2010. *Spiritual Economies: Islam, Globalization, and the Afterlife of Development*. Ithaca, NY: Cornell University Press.

Ruiter, Stijn and Nan Dirk De Graaf. 2006. "National Context, Religiosity, and Volunteering: Results from 53 Countries." *American Sociological Review* 71/2: 191–210.

Sabra, Adam. 2003. "'Prices are in God's Hands': The Theory and Practice of Price Control in the Medieval Islamic World." In *Poverty and Charity in Middle Eastern Contexts*, edited by Michael Bonner, Mine Ener, and Amy Singer. 73–91. Albany, NY: State University of New York Press.

Salevurakis, John William and Sahar Mohamed Abdel-Haleim. 2008. "Bread Subsidies in Egypt: Choosing Social Stability or Fiscal Responsibility." *Review of Radical Political Economics* 40/1: 35–49.

Salvatore, Armando. 2016. *The Sociology of Islam: Knowledge, Power and Civility*. Malden, MA: Wiley Blackwell.

Sayigh, Yezid. 2012. *Above the State: The Officers' Republic in Egypt*. Washington, DC: Carnegie Endowment for International Peace.

Schneider, Jo Anne. 2013. "Introduction to the Symposium: Faith-Based Organizations in Context." *Nonprofit and Voluntary Sector Quarterly* 42/3: 431–441.

Scott, James C. 1990. *Domination and the Arts of Resistance: Hidden Transcripts*. New Haven, CT: Yale University Press.

Seibel, Wolfgang and Helmut K. Anheier. 1990. "Sociological and Political Science Approaches to the Third Sector." In *The Third Sector: Comparative Studies of Nonprofit Organizations*, edited by Wolfgang Seibel and Helmut K. Anheier. 7–20. Berlin: Walter de Gruyter.

Şen, Mustafa. 2011. *Faith-Based Organisations and Social Exclusion in Turkey*. Leuven, Belgium: Uitgeverij Acco.

Shepard, William E. 1996. *Sayyid Qutb and Islamic Activism: A Translation and Critical Analysis of Social Justice in Islam*. Leiden and New York: E. J. Brill.

Silber, Ilana. 1998. "Modern Philanthropy: Re-Assessing the Viability of a Maussian Perspective." In *Marcel Mauss: A Centenary Tribute*, edited by Wendy James and N. J. Allen. 134–150. New York and Oxford: Berghahn Books.

Silber, Ilana. 2009. "Bourdieu's Gift to Gift Theory: An Unacknowledged Trajectory." *Sociological Theory* 27/2: 173–190.

Silber, Ilana. 2010. "Mauss, Weber et les Trajectoires Historiques du Don." *Revue du M.A.U.S.S.* 36: 539–561.

Singer, Amy. 2002. *Constructing Ottoman Beneficence: An Imperial Soup Kitchen in Jerusalem*. Albany, NY: State University of New York Press.

Singer, Amy. 2008. *Charity in Islamic Societies*. Cambridge: Cambridge University Press.

Sinha, Jill Witmer. 2013. "Unintended Consequence of the Faith-Based Initiative: Organizational Practices and Religious Identity within Faith-Based Human Service Organizations." *Nonprofit and Voluntary Sector Quarterly* 42/3: 563–583.

Skocpol, Theda. 1999. "Advocates without Members: The Recent Transformation of American Civic Life." In *Civic Engagement in American Democracy*, edited by Theda Skocpol and Morris P. Fiorina. 461–509. Washington, DC: Brookings Institution Press.
Smith, Greg. 2002. "Religion, and the Rise of Social Capitalism: The Faith Communities in Community Development and Urban Regeneration in England." *Community Development Journal* 37/2: 167–177.
Somers, Margaret. 2008. *Genealogies of Citizenship: Markets, Statelessness, and the Right to Have Rights*. New York: Cambridge University Press.
Song, Jesook. 2010. "'A Room of One's Own': The Meaning of Spatial Autonomy for Unmarried Women in Neoliberal South Korea." *Gender, Place and Culture* 17/2: 131–149.
Stack, Carol B. 1974. *All Our Kin: Strategies for Survival in a Black Community*. New York: Harper & Row.
Steensland, Brian. 2002. "The Hydra and the Swords: Social Welfare and Mainline Advocacy, 1964–2000." In *The Quiet Hand of God: Faith-Based Activism and the Public Role of Mainline Protestantism*, edited by Robert Wuthnow and John Hyde Evans. 213–236. Berkeley: University of California Press.
Stolle, Dietlind. 1998. "'Bowling Together, Bowling Alone: The Development of Generalized Trust in Voluntary Associations." *Political Psychology* 19/3: 497–525.
Strang, David and John W. Meyer. 1993. "Institutional Conditions for Diffusion." *Theory and Society* 22/4: 487–511.
Suleiman, S. 2005. *Al-Nizam al-qawi wa al-dawla al-da'ifa: Edaret al-azma al-maliya wa al-taghir al-siyasi fi 'ahd Mubarak*. Cairo: Dar Merit.
Sundeen, Richard A. and Sally A. Raskoff. 1994. "Volunteering Among Teenagers in the United States." *Nonprofit and Voluntary Sector Quarterly* 23/4: 383–403.
Swidler, Ann and Susan Watkins. 2009. "'Teach a Man to Fish': The Sustainability Doctrine and Its Social Consequences." *World Development* 37/7: 1182–1196.
Tadros, Mariz. 2006. "State Welfare in Egypt since Adjustment: Hegemonic Control with a Minimalist Role." *Review of African Political Economy* 33/108: 237–254.
Tambar, Kabir. 2014. *The Reckoning of Pluralism: Political Belonging and the Demands of History in Turkey*. Stanford, CA: Stanford University Press.
Testart, Alain. 1998. "Uncertainties of the 'Obligation to Reciprocate': A Critique of Mauss." In *Marcel Mauss: A Centenary Tribute*, edited by Wendy James and N. J. Allen. 97–110. New York and Oxford: Berghahn Books.
Therborn, G. 2012. "Class in the 21st Century." *New Left Review* 78: 5–29.
Thompson, E. P. 1966. *The Making of the English Working Class*. New York: Vintage.
Titmuss, Richard M. 1997 [1970]. *The Gift Relationship: From Human Blood to Social Policy*. New York: New Press.
Tocqueville, Alexis de. 2000 [1835, 1840]. *Democracy in America*. Chicago, IL: University of Chicago Press.
Tripp, Charles. 2006. *Islam and the Moral Economy: The Challenge of Capitalism*. Cambridge: Cambridge University Press.
Tuğal, Cihan. 2009. *Passive Revolution: Absorbing the Islamic Challenge to Capitalism*. Stanford, CA: Stanford University Press.
Tuğal, Cihan. 2012a. "Fight or Acquiesce? Religion and Political Process in Turkey's and Egypt's Neoliberalizations." *Development and Change* 43/1: 23–51.
Tuğal, Cihan. 2012b. "Democratic Janissaries? Turkey's Role in the Arab Spring." *New Left Review* 76: 5–24.

Tuğal, Cihan. 2013. "Contesting Benevolence: Market Orientations among Muslim Aid Providers in Egypt." *Qualitative Sociology* 36/12: 141–159.

Tuğal, Cihan. 2016a. *The Fall of the Turkish Model: How the Arab Uprisings Brought Down Islamic Liberalism*. London: Verso.

Tuğal, Cihan. 2016b. "Faiths with a Heart and Heartless Religions: Devout Alternatives to the Merciless Rationalization of Charity." *Rethinking Marxism* 28/3–4: 418–437.

Tuğal, Cihan. 2016c. "Neoliberal Populism as a Contradictory Articulation." *European Journal of Sociology* 57/3: 466–470.

Tuğal, Cihan. 2017a. "The Decline of the Legitimate Monopoly of Violence and the Return of Non-State Warriors." In *The Transformation of Citizenship, Volume 3: Struggle, Resistance and Violence*, edited by Juergen Mackert and Bryan S. Turner. 77–92. London and New York: Routledge.

Tuğal, Cihan. 2017b. "The Uneven Neoliberalization of Good Works: Islamic Charitable Fields and Their Impact on Diffusion." *American Journal of Sociology*.

Utvik, Bjørn Olav. 2006. *Islamist Economics in Egypt: The Pious Road to Development*. Boulder, CO: Lynne Rienner Publishers.

Van der Meer, Tom, Manfred Te Grotenhuis, and Ben Pelzer. 2010. "Influential Cases in Multilevel Modeling." *American Sociological Review* 75/1: 173–178.

Varisco, Daniel Martin. 2007. "Making "Medieval" Islam Meaningful." *Medieval Encounters* 13: 385–412.

Vogel, Ann. 2006. "Who's Making Global Civil Society: Philanthropy and US Empire in World Society." *British Journal of Sociology* 57/4: 635–655.

Wacquant, Loïc. 2002. "Scrutinizing the Street: Poverty, Morality, and the Pitfalls of Urban Ethnography." *American Journal of Sociology* 107: 1468–1532.

Wacquant, Loïc. 2012. "Three Steps to a Historical Anthropology of Actually Existing Neoliberalism." *Social Anthropology* 20/1: 66–79.

Warburton, Jeni and Catherine McDonald. 2009. "The Challenges of the New Institutional Environment: An Australian Case Study of Older Volunteers in the Contemporary Nonprofit Sector." *Ageing and Society* 29/5: 823–840.

Waterbury, John. 1983. *The Egypt of Nasser and Sadat: The Political Economy of Two Regimes*. Princeton, NJ: Princeton University Press.

Watkins, Susan Cotts, Ann Swidler, and Thomas Hannan. 2012. "Outsourcing Social Transformation: Development NGOs as Organizations." *Annual Review of Sociology* 38: 285–315.

Weber, Max. 1978. *Economy and Society*. Berkeley: University of California Press.

Weber, Max. 2011 [1904–1905]. *Protestant Ethic and Spirit of Capitalism*. New York: Oxford University Press.

White, Jenny. 2002. *Islamist Mobilization in Turkey: A Study in Vernacular Politics*. Seattle: University of Washington Press.

Will, Jeffry A. and John K. Cochran. 1995. "God Helps Those Who Help Themselves: Denomination, Religiosity and Perceptions of the Poor." *Sociology of Religion* 56/3: 327–338.

Wilson, John. 2000. "Volunteering." *Annual Review of Sociology* 26: 215–240.

Wilson, John and Thomas Janoski. 1995. "The Contribution of Religion to Volunteer Work." *Sociology of Religion* 56/2: 137–152.

Wilson, John and Marc A. Musick. 1997. "Who Cares? Toward an Integrated Theory of Volunteer Work." *American Sociological Review* 62/5: 694–713.

Wood, Richard L. 1997. "Social Capital and Political Culture: God Meets Politics in the Inner City." *American Behavioral Scientist* 40/5: 595–606.

Wright, Erik O. 2010. *Envisioning Real Utopias*. London: Verso.
Wuthnow, Robert. 1991. *Acts of Compassion: Caring for Others and Helping Ourselves*. Princeton, NJ: Princeton University Press.
Wuthnow, Robert. 1995. *Learning to Care: Elementary Kindness in an Age of Indifference*. New York: Oxford University Press.
Yediyildiz, Bahaeddin. 1984. "XVIII. Asır Türk Vakıflarının İktisadi Boyutu." *Vakıflar Dergisi* 18: 5–42.
Zeghal, Malika. 1999. "Religion and Politics in Egypt: The Ulema of Al-Azhar, Radical Islam, and the State (1952–1994)." *International Journal of Middle East Studies* 31/3: 371–399.
Zelizer, Viviana. 1997. *The Social Meaning of Money: Pin Money, Paychecks, Poor Relief, and Other Currencies*. Princeton, NJ: Princeton University Press.
Zeybek, Hilal Alkan. 2013. *Enchanted Welfare: Islamic Imaginary and Giving to Strangers in Turkey*. PhD Thesis. Open University.

INDEX

Page numbers in bold refer to tables.

Abdülhamid II 67–68
Abu Bakr 42
Ak Party: arbitrary state generosity 80–81; control by 84–85; political leadership of 82; poverty and 157
Al-Aqsa Mosque raid 209
Allahyari, Rebecca 76–77
allegiance (*intisap*) 171
alms notion 39
alternative ethics 6–8
alternative responsibilization 190
ambiguous humanitarianism 58
American charity models 5, 18–19, 74–78
Americanization of Islam 2–3
American welfare scene 70
Anglo-American charitable ethics 34–35
Anglo-Saxon charitable activity 71
anti-Americanism 211–212
anti-government Islamists 208
Arabic culture 40
Arab Spring 203–204
ascetically rational effort 110
authoritarian-communitarianisms 222
awqaf ahli (family endowments) 51

baraka (blessing) 139–141
Bayat, Asef 86
Bean, Lydia 76

Bellicose-Redistributive tendencies 40–43
benevolence: bifurcated benevolence 195–205; Christian charity 199–200; of communitarian associations in Egypt 114–120; informal benevolence networks 112; Islamic benevolence 148; religious activities and 96; semi-formal benevolence networks 112 *see also* charity; generosity; neoliberal giving in Egypt
Bey, Koçi 52
bifurcated benevolence 195–205
"blaming the victim" mentality 188
Bonner, Michael 41
Bosnian War 199
Bourdieu, Pierre 6–8, 14, 18–22, 25–27, 30–33, 38, 51, 54, 82, 94, 136, 145, 166, 213, 218
Brown, Peter 37–39, 48

Calvin, John 101
Candle Association 170–171, 174–175, 196, 210–212
capital accumulation 19–21
capitalism 7, 192–193, 222
career training (*kariyer edindirmek*) 186
caring for the poor: giving and world history 3–4; liberal revolution 8–9; methodology 9–12; political economic focus on 30; religiously-inspired kindness

6–8; Turkish charity 4–6; varieties of care 1–3
Carolingian era 44
cash endowments 53
Catholic Church 20–21, 39
charismatic spiritual authority 185–186
Charitable Choice 73
charity: American charity models 5, 18–19, 74–78; communitarianism 51–53; as ethical transformation 71–74; pragmatic concerns 166, 175–176; religiously-inspired kindness 6–8, 129–131; seemingly incompatible aspects of 151 *see also* benevolence; caring for the poor; Christian charity/giving; Islamic charity/giving
Chatterjee, Partha 223–224
Christian charity/giving: aid organizations 1, 119; American activists 77; benevolent activity 199–200; Elizabethan poor laws 60–61; impact of 66; introduction 3, 4, 34–35; Islamic giving *vs.* 4; Late Middle Ages 45–47; medieval Christianity 43–47; poverty and 8; property protection 42; renunciation ethic 36–39; secular aid and 7; summary 39
Christian West 58
church-based volunteers 76
Clastres, Pierre 52
Clinton, Bill 73, 74
Cold War 203, 206
collective independence 12
collective ownership 45
colonial gaze 66
communitarian associations in Egypt: benevolence of 114–120; *da'wa* movement 97–111; formal associations 108–111; goal of 184; introduction 96–97; moralizing society 104–108; neoliberal associations 155; neoliberal polity 120–124; political associations 112–123; significance of 150
communitarian associations in Turkey: bifurcated benevolence 195–205; comprehensiveness of 103; introduction 184; main activities of 184–189; poverty and 196–198; recognition-denial of field logic 200–201, 212–215, **213**, **214**, **215**; redistributive organizations 189–195; Syrian refugee crisis 210–212 *see also* Turkish neoliberal associations
communitarianism: authoritarian-communitarianisms 222; charity as 51–53; imperial appropriations of 50–51; misgivings over 178–182; neoliberal ethics 48–54, 75; neoliberal giving and 87–91; overview 28–29, 49; roots of 225; Turkish neoliberal associations 164–170 *see also* specific associations
community-generation in giving 2, 4, 15–22
Companions Association 77, 190–195, 204, 225
competition 145–147
Correct Path Association 137–139
culture of poverty 23, 155–158

da'wa (religious mission): in Egypt 97–111, 126; introduction 84, 97–98; Islamic benevolence 148
decontextualization 27
Democratic Party 71
Derviş, Kemal 79
differentiation ethics 38
disabled persons' charities 139–141
Disciples Association 165, 168–169
dishonest involuntary poor 45
domination, giving as 18–22

Eckstein, Susan 75
Egypt/Egyptian giving: colonial gaze 66; corporatism 78–81; dynasties 50; introduction 4–6, 9; Islamic mobilization history 81–86; real development 121–122; renunciation and communitarian accounts 22 *see also* communitarian associations in Egypt; neoliberal giving in Egypt
Egyptian *muhtasibin* 102, 210
Egyptian neoliberal associations 155
Egyptian Piety Association 159–160
Egyptian Red Crescent 123
Elizabethan poor laws 60–61
empowerment focus 24–25
endowment system 51–53
Ener, Mine 65–66
entitlement feelings 77
entrepreneurialization 28
ethical conduct 6–7
ethical liberalization: ethical-moral reform 226; institutionalist accounts 217–221; introduction 217; modernity construct 221–225; unpredictable equivalences 223–225
ethical-moral reform 226

ethics: alternative ethics 6–8; Anglo-American charitable ethics 34–35; capitalist ethical reform 7; differentiation ethics 38; liberal charitable ethics experiments 62; medieval charitable ethics 39; neoliberal ethics 48–54, 75; of property 161; renunciation ethic 36–39 *see also* global ethical formation
ethics revolution *see* global ethical formation
European social democracy 189
Evangelicalism 60

faith-based organizations (FBOs) 71, 73, 76, 86
familial-clerical surveillance 103
fard kifaya (communal obligation) 99–100
Felicity Party 85
field logic 200–201, 212–215, **213**, **214**, **215**
fluidity of practice 41
food-distributing charities 133–134
Fordice, Kirk (Mississippi Governor) 72
formal associations 108–111
Foucault, Michel 6–7, 11, 13, 18, 28–29; Foucaultian 23, 30–31, 54, 64, 175, 182, 193–194, 214, 224
free association 220
free-market policies 150

generosity: community-generation *vs.* domination 15–22; institutionalization of giving 23–31; introduction 15; neoliberal subjectivity 28–29; new institutionalism 25–28; thrifty generosity 159–164; welfare regime changes 29–31 *see also* benevolence
Generosity Fund 132–134
Geremek, Bronislaw 43–44
gift economy 20
giving: community-generation in 2, 4, 15–22; as domination 18–22; institutionalization of 23–31, 25–28; motivation in 16; obligatory giving 40, 42, 50, 99, 137; phenomenology of 19; politicization of 191; voluntary giving 40–42, 126, 137; world history and 3–4 *see also* Christian charity/giving; Islamic charity/giving; neoliberal giving
global ethical formation: charity as ethical transformation 71–74; communitarianism and neoliberal giving 87–91; interrupted institutionalization 65–69; introduction 2, 57–58; Islamic charity, mobilization history 81–86; liberal revolution and 8–9, 58–65; logic of fields 92; political economic dynamics 58–65; theo-organizational underpinnings 86–92; Western welfare state 69–70
global military expenditures 196
God's consent (*Allah rızası*) 171
Good Works Association 185, 186, 188
government contracts 77
Gülen, Fethullah 1–2, 87, 91–92

Hadith tradition 42, 100
health care 121
hegemonic struggle 7, 75
Himmelfarb, Gertrude 63
Hindu *dan* 22
honest involuntary poor 45
Hope Association 155–157, 164–165, 168, 180
human side (*ganb insani*) 127, 139

IHH Humanitarian Relief Foundation 1, 195–196, 195–199, 201–202, 201–209, 222–225
incoherent neoliberalization 131–132
individualization 61
individually-targeted welfare 70
informal benevolence networks 112
Institute of Economic Affairs 23
institutionalization of giving 23–31, 25–28
international collectivism 195–205
International Islamic Charitable Organization 86
International Monetary Fund (IMF) 80
interrupted institutionalization 65–69
involuntary poor 45
Islamic charity/giving: Bellicose-Redistributive tendencies 40–43; charity as communitarianism 51–53; Christian giving *vs.* 4; communitarian ethics 48–54; conclusion 54; imperial appropriations of communitarianism 50–51; introduction 34–35; liberalization of 78; mobilization history 81–86; poverty and 8; religious fields 48–50; religiously-inspired kindness 6–8; spirituality against comprehensive religion 129–131
Islamic inheritance laws 52
Islamic Relief Organization of Saudi Arabia 86

isomorphism 34
istihsan (juridical preference) 52
Izmit earthquake (1999) 156

Judaic roots of Christianity 37, 40

Khaled, Amr 92
Kidd, Alan 23
Kirama Association 134
Kitab al-Kasb book 48–49
Kochuyt, Thierry 40–41
Kuran, Timur 53
Kurdish poverty 187–188
Kurdistan Workers' Party (PKK) 216

Late Middle Ages 45–47
late-Victorian charity 62–63
learned helplessness 172
legal aid organizations 123
liberal charitable ethics experiments 62
liberal revolution 8–9, 58–65
liberal welfare 78–81
ligan committees 106, 114
literacy programs 130
Loaves and Fishes Shelter 77
local governors (*kaymakam*) 164
local neoliberalism 195–205, 209
Locke, John 161
Loyalty Association 141–142, 144
Luther, Martin 59–60

macroeconomic reform 29
macro-liberalization context 31
Malthusian political economy 61
market-oriented beneficiaries 4
Marxists 223
maslaha (public interest) 52
Mauss, Marcel 3, 4, 16, 18–19, 32, 40–41; Maussian 21
Mavi Marmara affair 1, 5, 203–208
Mead, Lawrence 72
medical syndicates 122
medieval charitable ethics 39
medieval Christianity 43–47
metropolitan governor (*vali*) 164
Meyer, John 27, 33, 77, 144, 218–219, 220, 226
microloans 128
military expenditures, global 196
modernity construct 221–225
moralizing society 104–108
motivation in giving 16
Murray, Charles 23

Muslim Brotherhood: impact of 111–113; neoliberal polity 120–124; overview 98, 105–106; political nature of 150; prevention of demonstrations/strikes 82–83
Muslim welfare 65

National Outlook 207
neoliberal aid organizations 85, 102
neoliberal ethics 48–54, 75
neoliberal giving: capitalism and 109–110; communitarianism and 87–91; introduction 4; local neoliberalism 195–205; pious neoliberal associations 154–170
neoliberal giving in Egypt: business-to-business 132–136; conclusion 147–151, **149**, **151**, **152**; disabled persons' charities 139–141; incoherent neoliberalization 131–132; introduction 126–127; oversight 137–139; ownership society 141–145; professionalized neoliberal associations 136–137; spirituality against comprehensive religion 129–131; theological monologues and competition 145–147; volunteer-based neoliberal associations 127–129, 135, 147
neoliberalizations 4–6, 24
neoliberal polity 120–124
neoliberal subjectivity 28–29
neoliberal tebliğ organizations 170–182
new institutionalism 25–29, 33, 70, 215, 217–221, 226
New Left approaches 24
non-governmental organizations (NGOs): amount of 85–86; businessification of 133; ethics of property 161; Muslim Brotherhood and 118; nature of 77, 134
non-market economy 3
non-religious organization 139
non-zakat payer 90
Nour Association 127–128, 130–132, 138

objectivism 21
obligatory giving 40, 42, 50, 99, 137
Olasky, Marvin 72
Open Door or Opening (*infitah*) 80
Orientalism 41–42
orthodox religious training 177–178
Ottoman Empire 50, 51–52, 65, 67–68
Ottoman-Turkish welfare 67
Ownership Association 159–164, 168, 180
ownership society 141–145

participation, defined 25
paternalist-communitarian dispositions 113
Patriots Association 137
Peck, Jamie 23
Personal Responsibility and Work Opportunity Reconciliation Act (1996) 73, 74
phenomenology of giving 19
Piety Association: communitarian associations 98–99, 102–104, 111, 128; introduction 1–2; Muslim Brotherhood and 117, 123
pious neoliberal associations 154–170
political associations 112–123
political economic dynamics 58–65
politicization of giving 191
positivism 158
post-colonial theory 223–224
post-9/11 global environment 131
post-structuralism 29
postwar sociology 62
poverty: cause of 105; charity and 8; communitarian associations in Turkey 196–198; culture of 23, 155–158; Egyptian neoliberal associations 155; explanation of 178–180; involuntary poor 45; Kurdish poverty 187–188; property and 166–167; sacralizing poverty 159–164; understanding reasons behind 11
pragmatism-based institutionalism 59
pre-Reformation rationalization 58
private health care 121
private monopolies 120
privatization 132, 141
professionalized neoliberal associations 136–137
professional syndicates 122–123
property and poverty 166–167
property protection 42
Puritanism 60
Putnam, Robert 17–18, 20, 24, 72, 220

qadirin (powerful) 87
al-Qaradawi, Yusuf 38, 50, 86–92, 95
Qur'an: aid packages and 199; literacy programs 97–111, 130; poverty dictates 181; recitation competitions 127, 142; three basic senses in 41
Qutb, Sayyid 6, 88–91, 95

"Ramadan bag" approach 144
Rational 5, 45, 54, 101, 110, 155; communicative rationality 227; rational action, defined 199; rationality 4, 58, 139–140, 218, 225, 227; rationalization 2, 5, 9, 20, 35, 47, 49, 58, 60–66, 70, 92–93, 96, 106, 111–112, 116, 126, 140, 150, 171, 182, 213, 218–221
Reagan, Ronald (administration) 72
real development 121–122
reciprocity concerns 24
recognition-denial of field logic 200–201, 212–215, **213**, **214**, **215**
redistributive organizations 189–195, 222
the Reformation 9, 45, 58
religious fields 48–50
religiously-inspired kindness 6–8, 129–131
religious order (tarikat) 171
renunciation 22
renunciation ethic 36–39
risk-management 24
Rotary Club 120

sacralizing poverty 159–164
sadaqa (voluntary giving) 40–42, 126, 137
St. Ambrose's teachings 37, 39, 54
St. Augustine's teachings 37–39, 48, 54
St. Francis 46–47
Salvation Army (SA) 76, 226
Sassanid culture 40
secular aid 7, 61
secularism 71, 75
selective adaptation 34
self-monitoring of staff 163
self-reliance 137, 190–195
self-sacrifice 22, 102–103, 130
semi-formal benevolence networks 112
semi-independent charity organizations 122
service (khidma) 1, 99
Service Movement 2
Silber, Ilana 21
Singer, Amy 40, 50–56, 95
snowballing technique 10
social benefit 121
socialism 225
society-state cooperation 167
sociology of religion 18, 20, 153
solidarity concerns 24
Speenhamland laws 61
spiritual authority 185–186
spirituality against comprehensive religion 129–131
state-driven process 29–30

subjectivism 21
submissiveness/shame qualities 170–182
success-oriented beneficiaries 4
Sufi-based recruitment 11
Sunni Islamic party 82, 90
sustainability focus 24–25
Syrian refugee crisis 210–212

tebliğ organizations 170–182
theological monologues and competition 145–147
thrifty generosity 159–164
Tocqueville 23–24, 217; Tocquevillianism 27, 220
training-oriented organizations 136
Turkish charity: corporatism 78–81; introduction 4–6, 10; Islamic mobilization history 81–86
Turkish Islamism 83, 85, 155, 197–200
Turkish neoliberal associations: communitarianism 164–170; communitarian misgivings 178–182; culture of poverty 155–158; introduction 154; neoliberal tebliğ organizations 170–182; pious neoliberal associations 154–170; sacralizing poverty 159–164; welfare-induced laziness 175–178; worker mentality 170–175 *see also* communitarian associations in Turkey

universalism 225
unpredictable equivalences 223–225

Vogel, Ann 27
voluntary giving 40–42, 126, 137
voluntary poor 45–47
voluntary relief 23–31
volunteer-based neoliberal associations 127–129, 135, 147
volunteerism (*tatawwu'*) 146

waqf, defined 51–53
Washington Post 1
wealth accumulation/concentration 19, 36–46, 49–52, 88–91, 109–110, 160, 184, 209, and *passim*
wealth, sources of 37–38, 40–41, 44, 69, 88, 109–110, 181
welfare-induced laziness 175–178
welfare regime changes 29–31, 78–81
welfare rights 26
Wesley, John 60
Western-based universalism 225
Western welfare state 69–70
worker mentality 170–175
working-class families 157, 176
work-oriented beneficiaries 4
World Bank 25, 79
"World Society" approach 5, 27, 129, 219–220
Wuthnow, Robert 16–18, 73, 75, 103, 15–157, 187

zakat (obligatory giving) 22, 40, 42, 50, 99, 137